D0083188

Strikes and Revolution in Russia, 1917

STRIKES AND REVOLUTION IN RUSSIA, 1917

Diane P. Koenker

William G. Rosenberg

PRINCETON UNIVERSITY PRESS

PRINCETON, NEW JERSEY

Published by Princeton University Press, 41 William Street,
Princeton, New Jersey 08540
In the United Kingdom: Princeton University Press, Guildford, Surrey

Library of Congress Cataloging-in-Publication Data

Koenker, Diane, 1947-
Strikes and revolution in Russia, 1917 / Diane P. Koenker, William G. Rosenberg.
p. cm.   Bibliography: p.   Includes index.
ISBN 0-691-05578-5
1. Strikes and lockouts—Soviet Union—History—20th century.
2. Soviet Union—History—Revolution, 1917-1921. I. Rosenberg, William G. II. Title.
HD5395.K64 1989   331.89′2947′09041—dc20   89-3891

This book has been composed in Linotron Sabon

Clothbound editions of Princeton University Press books
are printed on acid-free paper, and binding materials are
chosen for strength and durability. Paperbacks, although satisfactory for personal
collections, are not usually suitable for library rebinding

Printed in the United States of America by Princeton University Press,
Princeton, New Jersey

Designed by Laury A. Egan

To Virginia and Eugene Pomerance

and

Andy and Bob Adler

CONTENTS

. . . .

LIST OF ILLUSTRATIONS

. . . .

Since photography required some preparation in 1917, very few pictures were taken spontaneously. Many well-known photographs were actually taken by photographers who set up their apparatus in the hope that something interesting would occur, and then waited to see if they were right. Strikes and striking workers were neither predictable nor promising subjects, and the photo archives in Leningrad and Moscow consequently contain very few pictures that directly illustrate labor conflict. Those included here do, however, reveal a good deal about the social context of strike activity.

We are grateful to L. A. Protsai and A. A. Golovina of the Central State Archive of Cinema and Photographic Collections in Leningrad and to V. P. Tarasov of the Main Archival Administration in Moscow for helping us assemble the illustrations.

LIST OF FIGURES

. . . .

LIST OF TABLES

. . . .

PREFACE

. . . .

This book had a modest beginning. In the course of completing earlier work on the revolutionary period, each of us was struck by how little was actually known about worker activism in the Russian "workers' revolution," and by the fact that the strike phenomenon itself, one of the most important aspects of this activism, was virtually untouched in both Soviet and Western historical writing. The best Soviet analyses referred only to inadequate summary data compiled haphazardly in 1917 by the Factory Inspectorate or reviewed individual strikes as if they were representative of labor activism as a whole. In the West, partly because there was so little data, partly because of limitations in conceptualization and methodology, historians tended to do the same or left the subject aside altogether as they focused on other aspects of the revolution. We consequently decided to research the issue together as we each proceeded with other projects on late imperial and early Soviet history.

We soon realized that strikes were far more central to understanding the revolutionary process that we (and others) had thought. Although certainly not the only form of labor activism, strikes and the events around them constituted a primary point of conflict between labor and management, both within the enterprise and in the revolutionary milieu more broadly. Strikes articulated in varying ways the primary interests of these two major contending social groups and reflected the tactics, risks, and consequences each was willing to entertain in the course of economic and political struggle. What began as a modest attempt to systematize the available evidence on strikes soon developed into a major effort to record, to analyze, and most compellingly, to integrate strike phenomena into an understanding of the broader processes of Russia's revolutionary conjuncture.

As is so often the case, these tasks were more easily conceived than completed. A wide range of problems presented themselves: from data collection to thematic analysis, from determining appropriate statistical methodology to writing with confidence about matters of subjective experience and sentiment that were only dimly evident in the available sources. A project begun almost as an aside thus came to occupy more of our lives and energies than either of us cares to reckon, but with gratifying and we hope worthy results. Instead of our projected article or two, we have written a volume that, although focusing on Russian strikes, may have some interest for non-Russianists generally interested in the processes of social revolution as well as for our fellow specialists. We have learned a great deal about the complexities of social activism and about the analytic difficulties of discerning and interpreting social realities. And far from least, we have learned of the pleasures of joint research, a mode of scholarship rarely practiced even by historians who write with others. Working together day in and day out by means of linked personal computers has sharpened our analytical faculties, improved our ability to synthesize, and perhaps even bettered our writing. It has also, certainly, helped us to develop new levels of tolerance and to respond positively to constant scrutiny and self-criticism, some of which has been quite withering. *Strikes and Revolution* is a project neither of us could contemplate repeating, but from which each of us has drawn great rewards. Pain and pleasure *are* sometimes related.

The Center for Russian and East European Studies and the Horace Rackham School of Graduate Studies at the University of Michigan provided funding for our work in the form of research assistance, and we are grateful for the support and supportive environment they have provided throughout. Anne Bobroff, David Cohen, Irina Livezeanu, Dennis O'Hearn, Kira Stevens, Ann Peet, and Mary Chaffin helped us gather and record material in the early stages; Steve Coe, Elizabeth Dennison, Anne Gorsuch, Julia Rubin, and Dan Schafer contributed greatly toward the end. Luann Troxel was especially important to us. As some of our readers may know, statistical analysis does not always bring out the best in one's personality, and we want especially to thank Luann for mastering both the Michigan Terminal System and our crankiness as we checked, rechecked, and checked yet again our data.

At the earliest stages of our work we received research support from the Temple University faculty grant-in-aid program. As our project expanded, we were awarded a Research Grant from the National Endowment for the Humanities, which provided support for final research and writing at a critical stage of the book's development. We also gratefully acknowledge grants from the International Research and Exchange Board (IREX), provided with funds from the National Endowment for the Humanities and the United States Information Agency, and from the William and Flora Hewlitt Foundation. None of these organizations, of course, are responsible for the views we express.

Many colleagues and friends generously lent their time and critical faculties to read various drafts and parts of this work. We are especially grateful to James R. Barrett, Laura Engelstein, Moshe Lewin, Don Rowney, Lewis Siegelbaum, Charles Tilly and Reginald Zelnik for their meticulous readings and extensive written comments. Candor is an endangered species. Their critical and constructive observations have postponed its extinction and helped us greatly. Geoff Eley, Albert Feuerwerker, Daniel Field, Heather Hogan, Davis Mandel, Alexander Rabinowitch, William Sewell, S. A. Smith, and Ronald Grigor Suny have also read parts of our manuscript in its various forms and redactions, with varying degrees of scepticism about quantitative history in general and our own enterprise in particular. Each, however, has given us the benefit of great and varied expertise. We feel fortunate to have had such supportive colleagues in the midst of our scholarly struggles, although we hasten to absolve them from any responsibility for the finished product. Julie Marvin at Princeton University Press has done a superb job of editing.

We discovered early on in our work that we shared complementary interests with Leopold Haimson, whose work on prerevolutionary Russian strikes was not familiar to us when we initiated our project, but whose encouragement and support was soon a major stimulation. Seminars arranged by Leo at Columbia's Harriman Institute for Advanced Study of the Soviet Union provided a wonderfully congenial and supportive environment for us to present our findings and test our ideas. Other sessions organized by Leo and supported in part by the Maison des Sciences de l'Homme (Paris) and the Feltrinelli Foundation (Milan), as well as the Harriman Institute, gave us additional opportunities to explore some comparative dimensions of our work and to study labor activism in other historical contexts with colleagues from different countries. We hesitate to contemplate what our work might have looked like without these important opportunities. Leopold Haimson's contribution to scholarship and teaching on the late imperial period has been of singular importance, and each of us has benefitted greatly from his selfless investment of time, energy, and knowledge. It is a pleasure to acknowledge his role and express our deep appreciation.

Finally, the additional if awkward pleasures of thanking each other. For her part, Diane thanks Bill for his remarkable generosity and unfailing good spirits and for his lively communications over the computer mail system, which for several years now have nearly eliminated the necessity (and cost) of real-time exchange. Collaborative work in such an enterprise produces some frustration, as two individuals try to mesh different work styles and especially work schedules. In our case, we each wrote a draft of every chapter and then reworked them into common drafts, and this form of collaboration certainly lengthened the process somewhat. But these frustrations were more than compensated by the spirit of partnership that emerged from our work, by the intellectual challenge of forging a product that reflected a real synthesis both of our research results and of our individual approaches and interpretations. Diane will miss that interaction as she returns to the more normal solitary path to historical understanding.

Bill also feels very fortunate to have had the chance to work with Diane. Her extraordinary patience as we constructed and reconstructed this volume was matched only by her gifts of intelligence, wit, and understanding. Joint research has its pitfalls, but collaborative writing is a virtual minefield, especially when the original basis of collaboration, one that divided the work on the basis of methodological and interpretative emphasis, soon gave way to a full and genuine mutuality at all levels of research and writing. Bill thanks Diane for insisting on mutual statistical competence, for carefully explaining many of the techniques that underlie much of what follows, and for her patience as he tried to master them. The result was a remarkably enriching collaboration on all levels of analysis and exposition, one whose everyday stimulation will be sorely missed. Working alone may allow us historians to define our pace more easily, but also makes it harder to adopt new approaches, and it rarely provides a comparable level of intellectual excitement. Although happy to bring this project to a close, Bill regrets very much the end of these rewarding interactions.

Both of us also have debts to our families. Diane thanks Roger Koenker for his unflagging support, most importantly moral, but also for his attempts to raise the level of our statistical conceptualizations and for his expert advice on many specific matters. Hannah and Emma have contributed enormously by providing inestimable pleasure and by never using the strike threat too seriously. Bill thanks Roger as well, and returns the phone lines to the Koenker household with gratitude. Elie Rosenberg, too, has tolerated this project with grace and understanding, watching with some professional bemusement the emergence of contradictory passions about computers and modern technology, and reacting with familial compassion when the negative forces occasionally got the upper hand. Her sense of proportion about the relative importance and value of various matters large and small has eased many difficult transitions, including those involved in preparing this book. Peter and Sarah, alas, were never quite in awe over the work, but tolerated their father's enthusiasm with a supportive if sceptical detachment, and with admirable patience. To them, too, open phone lines once again, and once again his thanks.

LIST OF ABBREVIATIONS

. . . .

AMO	Moscow Automotive Works
MSFMO	Moscow Society of Factory and Mill Owners
PSFMO	Petrograd Society of Factory and Mill Owners
RTA	Russian Telegraph Agency
SR	Socialist Revolutionary
TSGAOR	Tsentral'nyi Gosudarstvennyi Arkhiv Oktiabr'skoi Revoliutsii SSSR
TSGIA	Tsentral'nyi Gosudarstvennyi Istoricheskii Arkhiv SSSR
TSSU	Tsentral'noe Statisticheskoe Upravlenie
VOSR. Khronika sobytii	*Velikaia oktiabr'skaia sotsialisticheskaia revoliutsiia. Khronika sobytii*
WIC	War Industries Committee

Strikes and Revolution in Russia, 1917

INTRODUCTION

. . . .

UNDERSTANDING STRIKES IN 1917

On Monday, May 1, 1917, by the old calendar, the Executive Committee of the Petrograd Soviet voted in emergency session to send official representatives to the Provisional Government. The margin in favor was 43 to 19.[1] Dual power, formerly shared uneasily between the Provisional Government and the Petrograd Soviet, now became institutionalized in a coalition government, and the attention of national and international political figures focused on Petrograd to see how the new coalition would handle the burden of revolutionary power. Not many noticed another event, in its own way as symbolic as the formation of the coalition. Also on May 1, several thousand Petrograd laundresses in over 100 small and large shops declared a strike against their employers. By the next day, three-quarters of all the city's washerwomen had left their jobs; soon, 5,500 women in nearly 200 firms had joined the strike.

The laundresses spoke through their trade union, which had been organized in the heady days after the February revolution. They demanded a package of reforms: an eight-hour workday, minimum daily wages of four to six rubles, the introduction of a pay book for accurate calculation of pay, required two-week notice for dismissals, recognition of the union, polite address on the part of employers, more and better quality food, improved sanitary conditions in the shops, two weeks' annual paid vacation, and one month's sick leave with jobs to be held for six additional months.[2]

Almost immediately after the May 1 walkout, employers began to resort to that "common Western European practice," as *Pravda* described it, the use of scab labor and the formation of an alternative, "yellow" trade union.[3] Tempers flared on both sides, and so did the use of force. When two union leaders failed to convince women in one shop to join the strike, they doused the stoves and hot irons with water, virtually forcing the recalcitrant laundresses to join the walkout. Management retaliated:

[1] *Rabochaia Gazeta*, May 2, 1917.
[2] *Pravda*, May 16, 20, 1917 (n.s.); *Delo Naroda*, May 10, 1917; *Edinstvo*, May 11, 1917.
[3] *Pravda*, May 25, 1917 (n.s.).

in this shop, the activists were chased away with hot flatirons. Elsewhere, shop owners poured boiling water on strikers, and reportedly went after the "damned vipers" and "unbelieving filth" with pokers and revolvers.[4]

In the face of this hostility, working-class Petrograd rallied around the laundresses. Contributions to the union strike fund poured in from district soviets and individual factories, amounting by May 21 to nearly 16,000 rubles. The laundresses held mass meetings around the city, where political activists like Alexandra Kollontai encouraged them in their solidarity. Within a week, owners of 40 small laundries had agreed to the strikers' demands; by May 16, 80 laundries were back to work, with more owners settling each day. On May 28, the strike ended triumphantly for the strikers with an agreement worked out in arbitration.[5]

The Petrograd laundry workers' strike was one of many in revolutionary Russia involving not muscular proletarians toiling at fiery furnaces but workers in nonindustrial and service occupations, often women previously unorganized and unheard from. In other features, as well, this strike typified the emerging themes of labor protest in the spring of 1917. It reflected the depth of workers' grievances and their conviction that the revolution would finally right past wrongs. It demonstrated the ways in which even unskilled and politically inactive groups of workers scattered throughout an entire city could mobilize, if they had to, in support of common goals. It also engendered strong expressions of moral and material solidarity from other workers in the metropolis, the experience in arbitration of the dignity of the workers' cause, and a sense of vindication as employers capitulated even to the demand for pay to be awarded for the time on strike. In its course and aftermath, moreover, the strike also undoubtedly raised consciousness about class position.

Also typical of the strike was the lack of response generated in the non-socialist press and in subsequent recollections of the events of 1917. The fact that most of the city's laundries had shut down was commented upon only once or twice in liberal or conservative newspapers, whereas socialist papers reported almost daily on the events surrounding the strike. Nikolai Sukhanov recalled this particular strike in his invaluable memoir of

[4] S. S. Goncharskaia, "Profsoiuz prachek v 1917 goda," in *V ogne revoliutsionnykh boev (Raiony Petrograda v dvukh revoliutsiiakh 1917 goda)* vol. 1, (Moscow, 1967), p. 48; *Edinstvo*, May 11, 1917; *Novaia Zhizn'*, May 12, 1917; *Pravda*, May 25, June 1, 1917 (n.s.); *Rabochaia Gazeta*, May 14, 18, 1917.

[5] *Pravda*, May 23, 27, 29, 30, June 1, 3, 8, 13, 1917 (n.s.); *Delo Naroda*, May 10, 28, 1917; *Zemlia i Volia*, May 10, 1917; *Izvestiia Petrogradskogo Soveta Rabochikh Deputatov* (hereafter *Izvestiia* (Petrograd)), May 9, 11, 16, 17, 19, 21, 30, 1917; *Novaia Zhizn'*, May 13, 17, 1917; *Rabochaia Gazeta*, May 14, 17, 18, 24, 26, 28, 1917; *Raionnye sovety Petrograda v 1917 godu*, 3 vols. (Moscow and Leningrad, 1964–66), vol. 2, p. 156.

the revolution published in 1922: "Notwithstanding the fact that the contingent of strikers was backward, unaccustomed to struggle and dispersed among masses of enterprises, the conflict was distinguished by the utmost persistence and it spun out over several weeks."[6] But aside from Sukhanov, this and other individual strikes were rarely mentioned by eyewitnesses, even though the press regularly demonstrated how much they had become part of the daily experience of the Russian revolution. Unruly street demonstrations and political strikes such as those of the February Days and the July Days alone seem to have stuck in the memories of participants in 1917. Of strikes, some memoirists recalled only the general phenomenon, "the excessive and increasing demands of the workers,"[7] or how at the same time as the Petrograd laundresses' strike, the Minister of Trade and Industry, A. I. Konovalov, "was faced with the threat of total stoppage of all Russian industry as a result of the steadily growing demands of the 'proletariat.' "[8] Alexander Kerensky denied the significance of strikes altogether; once work resumed after the fall of the tsar, "what problems remained were caused not so much by poor relations between workers and management as by the blockade."[9] In short, strikes and workplace unrest remained for outsiders part of the background hum of revolution, unremarkable in itself and unremarked upon in the historical record.

The indifference of contemporaries has subsequently shaped historical assessments of strikes. With little descriptive evidence on which to draw, both Western and Soviet historical schools have portrayed labor activism in broad generalities, mythologizing strikes without clarifying them as phenomena or analyzing their integration with other aspects of the revolutionary process. Historians have referred to the 570-odd strikes reported by the Factory Inspectorate from March to October 1917 as evidence, simply, of worker unrest and have offered various unsubstantiated interpretations.[10] To most of our Soviet colleagues, reality was close to

---

[6] N. Sukhanov, *Zapiski o revoliutsii* (Berlin, 1922–23), vol. 4, p. 143.

[7] V. D. Nabokov, *V. D. Nabokov and the Russian Provisional Government, 1917*, ed. Virgil D. Medlin and Steven L. Parsons (New Haven, Conn., 1976), pp. 97–98.

[8] Paul Miliukov, *Political Memoirs, 1905–1917*, ed. Arthur P. Mendel (Ann Arbor, Mich., 1967), p. 463.

[9] Alexander Kerensky, *Russia and History's Turning Point* (New York, 1965), p. 324.

[10] The aggregate reports of the Factory Inspectorate, collected in TSGAOR SSSR, f. 6935, op. 8, d. 349, were published by K. N. Iakovleva in 1920, and variously reprinted in Soviet document collections. See K. N. Iakovleva, "Zabastovochnoe dvizhenie v Rossii za 1895–1917 gody," in *Materialy po statistike truda*, vyp. 8 (Moscow, 1920), and the six volumes in the series *Velikaia oktiabr'skaia sotsialisticheskaia revoliutsiia. Dokumenty i materialy*, A. L. Sidorov et al, eds. (Moscow, 1957–1962). These are cited by their individual titles, *Revoliutsionnoe dvizhenie v Rossii. . . .*

the cinema images of Sergei Eisenstein's 1925 film, "Strike"—miserable workers, brutal managers, and repression by an unsympathetic, "bourgeois" regime. Trotsky describes a "wave of big strikes and other conflicts" in response to the industrialists' political offensive against the revolution.[11] The senior Soviet academician I. I. Mints describes strikes in equally heroic terms: "The strike struggle in May–June contributed to the class-based political education of the proletariat, to its consolidation around the Bolshevik party, to the strengthening of the unity of the working class, to the growth and authority of its vanguard—the proletariat of Piter, Moscow, Kharkov, the Donbass, and the Urals."[12] In the only historical monograph devoted to strikes in 1917, A. M. Lisetskii sees the strike process in terms of the Bolsheviks leading workers toward October.[13] Others, like the Soviet historian L. S. Gaponenko, regard strikes essentially as the "deepest manifestations" of ongoing class struggle in 1917, a "characteristic of all capitalist societies."[14]

Nor have Western accounts offered a substantive alternative, although the general interpretation is far from the Soviet view. Here strikes have signified essentially anarchic impulses among workers: a blind and insatiable lashing out for selfish gains or an irrepressible urge to settle old scores with no regard for consequences. A principal cause of Russia's shattered economy, strikes left economic and social devastation in their wake and paved the way for political extremism. These interpretations

[11] Leon Trotsky, *The History of the Russian Revolution*, trans. Max Eastman, 3 vols. (New York, 1980), vol. 2, p. 266.

[12] I. I. Mints, *Istoriia velikogo oktiabria*, 3 vols. (Moscow, 1967–72), vol. 2, p. 434.

[13] A. M. Lisetskii, *Bol'sheviki vo glave massovykh stachek (mart–oktiabr' 1917 goda)* (Kishinev, 1974). Lisetskii's study is qualitatively rich, however, and contains a wealth of interesting material, as do his principal articles: "K voprosu o statistike zabastovok v Rossii v period podgotovki velikoi oktiabr'skoi sotsialisticheskoi revoliutsii," *Trudy Kafedry Istorii KPSS, Khar'kovskogo Gosudarstvennogo Universiteta imeni Gor'kogo* 7 (1959), pp. 271–83; "O nekotorykh osobennostiakh zabastovochnoi taktiki bol'shevikov v period podgotovki velikoi oktiabr'skoi sotsialisticheskoi revoliutsii," *Uchenye Zapiski Khar'kovskogo Gosudarstvennogo Universiteta imeni Gor'kogo* 103 (1959), pp. 93–106; "O kharaktere stachechnoi bor'by proletariata Rossii v period podgotovki oktiabr'skoi revoliutsii (mart–oktiabr' 1917 goda)," in *Tezisy dokladov ob"edinennoi nauchnoi sessii instituta istorii AN MSSR* (Kishinev, 1961), pp. 7–13; "O nekotorykh voprosakh kolichestvennoi kharakteristiki zabastovochnogo dvizheniia v Rossii v period podgotovki oktiabria," *Uchenye Zapiski Kishinevskogo Gosudarstvennogo Universiteta* 65 (1963), pp. 3–15; "Ob otnoshenii bloka kontrrevoliutsionnykh sil k zabastovochnomu dvizheniiu proletariata Rossii (mart–oktiabr' 1917 goda)," *Uchenye Zapiski Kishinevskogo Gosudarstvennogo Universiteta* 95 (1968), pp. 3–23; "K voprosu o mezhdunarodnom znachenii opyta stachechnoi bor'by proletariata Rossii v period podgotovki velikoi oktiabr'skoi sotsialisticheskoi revoliutsii," *Uchenye Zapiski Kishinevskogo Gosudarstvennogo Universiteta* 104 (1968), pp. 299–309.

[14] L. S. Gaponenko, *Rabochii klass Rossii v 1917 godu* (Moscow, 1970), p. 376.

follow from the views of Russian émigrés and Western eyewitnesses like the Englishman R. H. Bruce Lockhart, who wrote, "Wage-earners made exorbitant demands upon their employers and frequently ceased work or interfered arbitrarily in the working of their factories. This behavior, together with the lack of fuel and raw materials, hastened the decline of industrial output."[15] As one historian puts it, "A rampage of strikes swept the country from March 1917. . . . The workers struck over any grievance without hesitation. No one—trade unions, Soviet leaders, or Bolsheviks—could control them."[16] Irrational strikers and irresponsible strikes were thus a principal cause of the Provisional Government's collapse and the onset of Bolshevik authoritarianism.[17]

The weaknesses of both Soviet and Western interpretations lie most of all in their failure to recognize the complexity of strikes as a form of collective action, one involving difficult objective tasks of organization and mobilization as well as subjective elements of attitude and consciousness. They also ignore significant differences in strike behavior among different industrial and service sector workers, as well as differences in the possible causes of strikes. They show little recognition of how interactions between workers and management might have affected the strike process or how strikes in turn affected the relations between labor and management and representatives of state or local governments, including the soviets. And they fail in their analysis of 1917 to appreciate either the vast array of strike goals and demands that emerged between March and October or their possible implications in terms of workers' relations to Russia's new order.

Thus, although the months between March and October were in large part a workers' revolution, the nature and import of strike activism in 1917 has largely escaped serious historical scrutiny. Strikes clearly shaped a whole range of attitudes toward the new state order on the part of workers themselves, for plant owners and managers, and for state and soviet officials struggling in various ways to build a democratic regime. They also played a central role in the mobilization of labor and in the ways in which shop owners and managerial associations organized them-

---

[15] R. H. Bruce Lockhart, *The Two Revolutions: An Eye-Witness Account of Russia, 1917* (Chester Springs, Pa., 1967), p. 83.

[16] Jay B. Sorenson, *The Life and Death of Soviet Trade Unions, 1917–1928* (New York, 1969), p. 36.

[17] See, e.g., William H. Chamberlin, *The Russian Revolution*, 2 vols. (New York, 1935), vol. 1, p. 275; W. S. Woytinsky, *Stormy Passage: A Personal History through Two Russian Revolutions to Democracy and Freedom, 1905–1960* (New York, 1961), p. 260; John M. Thompson, *Revolutionary Russia, 1917* (New York, 1981), pp. 73–74; John L. H. Keep, *The Russian Revolution: A Study in Mass Mobilization* (New York, 1976), pp. 73–75.

selves to resist change. They articulated workers' goals far more comprehensively and clearly than any other activist form, and are thus a way to explore the difficult and important question of workers' "consciousness," of what workers thought they wanted from the new revolutionary order. Strikes were therefore central to Russian politics and society in 1917, far more so than historians and others have appreciated. They constitute a critical point of entry into the complex historical relationships between social activism and political change.

SOME NOTES ABOUT THEORY: STRIKES AS INDICATORS

The image of enraged, anarchic strikers also fails to correspond to the general picture of strikes and strikers in Western Europe and the United States, which suggests that well-paid workers tend to strike more than the miserable and downtrodden; that strikes occur more often in times of economic prosperity than crisis (since workers understand the better opportunities for gain); and that few workers willingly risk their livelihood in conditions under which strikes might shut plants permanently or alternative employment is not readily available. Strikes are most often a consequence of rational calculus rather than blind impulse, a weapon and strategy adopted by workers in the expectation that their efforts will be rewarded and they will end up better off. And contrary to the arguments of most Soviet writers, strikes can sometimes serve the purposes of social stability rather than class conflict, particularly if they are a recognized, legal means of arguing labor grievances, and if there is an effective mediation mechanism available to both parties.[18]

[18] See, e.g., Michael P. Hanagan, *The Logic of Solidarity: Artisans and Industrial Workers in Three French Towns* (Urbana, Ill., 1980); Robert Gray, *The Aristocracy of Labour in Nineteenth-Century Britain, c. 1850–1914* (London, 1981); Michelle Perrot, *Les Ouvriers en grève: France, 1871–1890*, 2 vols. (Paris, 1974); Edward Shorter and Charles Tilly, *Strikes in France, 1830–1968* (Cambridge, 1974); Michael Shalev, "Trade Unionism and Economic Analysis: The Case of Industrial Conflict," *Journal of Labor Research* vol. 1, no. 1 (1980), pp. 133–73; Dick Geary, *European Labour Protest, 1848–1939* (London, 1981); Bryan D. Palmer, *A Culture in Conflict: Skilled Workers and Industrial Capitalism in Hamilton, Ontario, 1860–1914* (Montreal, 1979), P. K. Edwards, *Strikes in the United States, 1881–1974* (Oxford, 1981); and P. K. Edwards, *Conflict at Work: A Materialist Analysis of Workplace Relations* (Oxford, 1986), among others. See also Gerald Suhr, "Petersburg Workers in 1905: Strikes, Workplace Democracy, and the Revolution," Ph.D. dissertation, University of California, Berkeley, 1979; Laura Engelstein, *Moscow, 1905: Working-Class Organization and Political Conflict* (Stanford, Calif., 1982); Victoria E. Bonnell, *Roots of Rebellion: Workers' Politics and Organizations in St. Petersburg and Moscow, 1900–1914* (Berkeley, 1983); Heather Hogan, "Industrial Rationalization and the Roots of Labor Militance in the St. Petersburg Metalworking Industry, 1901–1914," *Russian Review* 42

There is, in fact, a long tradition of historical scholarship and a wide range of theory built around the study of strikes, testimony to their complexity.[19] A basic assumption of this tradition, often more implicit than explicit, is that strikes are best understood as an indicator of other, broader, forms of political and social change, a kind of proxy for larger social relationships. Hence, strikes are often studied in the past and present to test social theories on a broad level and to clarify policy alternatives.

One well-known view sees strikes as part of the broader processes of industrial modernization, an essentially transitional phenomenon reflecting the stresses of technological change and its accompanying social dislocation. Strikes here are regarded as a necessary, even functional, aspect of social development for industrializing societies, a way in which otherwise intolerable strains can work themselves out.[20] Another related theory concentrates on the social and technological structures of various work communities, identifying strikes with differences in the ways workers live or work together, the ease with which they can organize, and their relative degree of integration into broader social or political processes. In this analysis, isolation tends to encourage labor militance, provided workers are able to mobilize; integration weakens labor conflict because of various mediating and ameliorating influences, including alternative outlets for unrest.[21]

Still a third view focuses on the relationship between strikes and economic fluctuations, either in terms of the ways workers' wage (or other) demands reflect changing economic circumstances, or the influence broader economic factors might have on the readiness of contending parties to settle disputes in other ways. In one variant, strikes are mistakes, avoidable in most instances by informed and realistic bargaining.[22]

(1983), pp. 163–90; and especially Leopold H. Haimson and Ronald Petrusha, "Two Strike Waves in Imperial Russia (1905–07, 1912–14): A Quantitative Analysis," in *Strikes, Wars, and Revolutions in an International Perspective: Strike Waves in the Late Nineteen and Early Twentieth Centuries*, ed. Leopold H. Haimson and Charles Tilly (New York, 1989).

[19] A thorough listing of the literature can be compiled from the bibliographies in E. T. Hiller, *The Strike: A Study in Collective Action* (Chicago, 1928); Richard Hyman, *Strikes* (London, 1972); and Edwards, *Conflict at Work*.

[20] See, e.g., Arthur M. Ross and Paul T. Hartman, *Changing Patterns of Industrial Conflict* (New York, 1960); Clark Kerr et al., "The Labour Problem in Economic Development," *International Labour Review* 71 (1955), 232.

[21] See Clark Kerr and Abraham Siegel, "The Inter-Industry Propensity to Strike," in *Industrial Conflict*, ed. Arthur Kornhauser, Robert Dubin, and Arthur M. Ross (New York, 1954), pp. 189–212; David Lockwood, "Sources of Variation in Working-Class Images of Society," *Sociological Review* 14 (1966), pp. 249–67.

[22] See J. R. Hicks, *The Theory of Wages* (New York, 1948). See also the arguments of Orley Ashenfelter and George E. Johnson on the strike as an "equilibrating mechanism" in

Finally, there is the view that strikes are fundamentally political phenomena, occurring as workers mobilize to change the "balance of power" inside the workplace or out, or to express in some demonstrative way otherwise restrained or suppressed political grievances. As Edward Shorter and Charles Tilly put it, strikes are essentially "an instrument of working-class political action. Workers, when they strike, are merely extending into the streets their normal processes of political participation . . . not so much as real tests of economic strength as symbolic displays of political energy and resoluteness."[23]

James Cronin has very ably shown, however, that none of these theories fully explains the British experience, and each has its weaknesses when applied in other historical contexts as well, especially when used as a singular mode of explanation.[24] Modernization theory fails to explain fluctuations in the level of strike activity over time. It is also limited by a particular teleology, which begs analysis of social and psychological differences between different groups of workers or of the importance of interactions between them. It thus fails to explore the ways in which these differences may be related more to patterns of political control within the workplace itself (or the local community) than to broader socioeconomic formations.

The structuralist approach used by analysts like David Lockwood, Clark Kerr, and Abraham Siegel, however, which stresses the influence of work and community environments on the propensity of workers to strike, fails in its own right as both historical explanation and predictor. As Cronin indicates, one finds almost everywhere a significant variation in interindustry strike propensities over time, which cannot be fully explained by local circumstances. Also, too great an emphasis on local environmental factors precludes consideration of broader, national, or international phenenoma that might affect strike propensities, and carries with it the implicit assumption that coal miners or textile workers, isolated in their villages or towns, are essentially impervious to broader economic, political, or even organizational influences. Although structural influences clearly matter, they cannot fully explain strike behavior or serve usefully as a basis for a comprehensive analytical model.

"Bargaining Theory, Trade Unions and Industrial Strike Activity," *American Economic Review* 59 (1969), pp. 35–49. A recent survey of the economic theory of strikes appears in John Kennan, "The Economics of Strikes," in *Handbook of Labor Economics*, ed. Orley Ashenfelter and Richard Layard (Amsterdam, 1986), vol. 1, pp. 1091–134.

[23] Shorter and Tilly, *Strikes in France*, p. 343. See also Charles Tilly, *From Mobilization to Revolution* (Reading, Mass., 1978), esp. pp. 159–66; Perrot, *Les Ouvriers*.

[24] See James E. Cronin, "Theories of Strikes: Why Can't They Explain the British Experience?" *Journal of Social History* vol. 12, no. 2 (1978–79), pp. 194–218, from which the above categorization of strike theories was largely drawn.

Economic and political theories of strikes do have great value in calling attention to broader influences on strike behavior, and both emphasize important truths: that strikes are almost always related to disparities between workers' economic expectations and their real incomes, however great or small, and that all strikes are to some extent struggles for power within or outside the workplace, often reflecting broader efforts in this regard. But just as one needs to account for noneconomic factors such as the availability of resources and the ability to organize in explaining strikes, even over economic issues like wages, the question of power is itself multidimensional. Workers' perceptions of the likelihood of success in strike actions may be as important in determining their course of action as the availability of supporting resources, and this perception might derive as much from an evaluation of management's current state of mind as the workers' own goals and desires. Also, and in some ways more important, strikes can themselves alter the very political context in which they occur, creating new circumstances that subsequent groups of workers will probably take into account in making their own decisions to strike. To say that strikes *are* political events, or that they always reflect some degree of class conflict, is thus not so much explanation as description, useful as a way of conceptualizing important aspects of the strike process but less helpful as a means of understanding their motivation or determining their possible effect.

STRIKES AND REVOLUTION

These conceptual difficulties are especially relevant in attempting to make sense of strikes during moments of political upheaval. French government statisticians actually excluded massive one-day political strikes from their strike reports, on the grounds that these giant protests would overshadow smaller, "normal" strikes and turn strike statistics into an index of political demonstrations.[25] Yet our own concern is precisely that of understanding the role of strikes in revolution. How, then, can we frame our questions so as to gain some insight into the complex relationships between strike activity and Russian revolutionary development in 1917?

One obvious feature of the international context needs to be emphasized at the outset. The First World War had generated enormous pressures in every belligerent society and had rearranged many established institutional relationships. Inflation and full employment fostered by the war effort, as well as longer-term structural changes in industry and the consolidation of working-class communities, produced an explosion of

[25] Shorter and Tilly, *Strikes in France*, p. 353.

labor militancy in the years between 1914 and 1920.[26] Russian instability must first be seen in this broader context. In the United States, for example, major strikes reverberated throughout the country, often in sharp opposition to national trade union policy and even as the national unions participated in a state-sponsored mediation effort to quell labor militancy.[27] In Britain, the paradigmatic emphasis on moderation and reformism of the labor movement masked growing labor militancy and autonomous movements toward direct action; as in the United States, the national labor organizations entered into a partnership with the state for the purposes of the war economy. The unions tended to moderate their position as they gained power but in the process left rank-and-file militants without effective national organizations.[28]

A similar upheaval in the balance of power took place in Germany; in simplest terms, trade unions made a pact with the state in the name of defense, but at the local level workers engaged in direct action and militant politics that challenged this very order. In Saxony, for example, labor unrest continued even after 1918 to repeat the wartime pattern: food and not just wages sparked protests, and women and youths participated as well as male factory workers.[29] In Italy, the requirements of wartime production permitted for the first time the institutionalization of trade unions. The state here also erected structures to mediate working-class discontent. Within the parameters of this shift in power, Italian labor militancy escalated as well, culminating in the Biennio Rosso—Red Years—of 1919–1920, the occupation of the Turin factories, and the radical new settlement that followed.[30] In France, too, labor militancy reached un-

[26] See James E. Cronin, "Labor Insurgency and Class Formation: Comparative Perspectives on the Crisis of 1917–1920 in Europe," in *Work, Community, and Power: The Experience of Labor in Europe and America, 1900–1925*, ed. James E. Cronin and Carmen Sirianni (Philadelphia, 1983), pp. 20–48.

[27] David Montgomery, "New Tendencies in Union Struggles and Strategies in Europe and the United States, 1916–1922," and Melvyn Dubofsky, "Abortive Reform: The Wilson Administration and Organized Labor, 1913–1920," in Cronin and Sirianni, eds., *Work, Community, and Power*, pp. 88–116, 197–220.

[28] James E. Cronin, "Industry, Locality, and the State: Patterns of Mobilization in the Postwar Strike Wave in Britain," in *War, Strikes, and Revolution: The Impact of the War Experience on Italy, Germany, France, England, and Russia*, ed. Giulio Sapelli and Leopold H. Haimson (Milan, forthcoming); James Hinton, *The First Shop Stewards' Movement* (London, 1973); Robert Holton, *British Syndicalism, 1900–1914* (London, 1975).

[29] Gerald D. Feldman, "Labor Unrest and Strikes in Saxony, 1916–1923," in Sapelli and Haimson, eds., *War, Strikes, and Revolution*; and Gerald D. Feldman, *Army, Industry, and Labor in Germany, 1914–1918* (Princeton, 1966).

[30] See Luigi Tomassini, "Industrial Mobilization and State Intervention in Italy during World War I: Effects on Labor Unrest," in Sapelli and Haimson, eds., *War, Strikes, and*

precedented levels, largely outside the leadership of traditional labor organizations.[31]

Common to all of these societies was a political situation of great uncertainty and unpredictability, as well as rapidly changing social and economic conditions. In Russia, the collapse of the old regime intensified these uncertainties. For Russian workers in particular, revolution meant that the "ground rules" of strikes, which had remained more or less stable before the revolution, began in 1917 to dissolve. What is both exciting and analytically troublesome about investigating strikes in these circumstances is that the range of workers' assumptions about the rules rapidly expanded as events unfolded, changing the very nature of some strikes even as they were occurring. Strikes contributed simultaneously to defining *new* assumptions about the parameters of labor activism itself and about the possibilities of economic, political, and even social change. In other words, the strike process itself helped shape a new range of beliefs, attitudes, and values in 1917, for workers as well as their employers, affecting the limits of political and economic possibility.

More broadly, the dynamics of proletarian activism as a whole structured the contest for power and ultimately gave historical definition to the nature of Lenin's proletarian dictatorship. Thus the quantitative data and objective relationships described below must ultimately be integrated not only with aspects of a rapidly changing political, social, and economic milieu, but also with complex and analytically quite slippery subjective material, including most particularly the values and perspectives of those who exercised power, those who organized workers and others into contending social groups, and even those who had the more prosaic tasks of recording and reporting strikes themselves.

A study of strikes in revolution thus contrasts both with longitudinal analyses underlying most strike theory, which use a time-series approach to review strikes over substantial periods of time, and with episodic studies, which look in detail at, say, the American Pullman railway car strike in 1894 or the British general strike of 1926, and which form the basis of most descriptive analyses of strikes. By aggregating large amounts of data, longitudinal studies can display significant long-term patterns valuable both to understanding the history of labor protest generally and to theorizing relationships between "waves" of protest and other elements of social development. Episodic studies, while not, of course, based on large quantities of strike data, are especially valuable in displaying the

---

Revolution; and Paolo Spriano, *The Occupation of the Factories*, trans. Gwyn Williams (London, 1975).

[31] Jean-Louis Robert, "Les Grèves parisiennes (août 1914–juillet 1919)," in Sapelli and Haimson, eds., *War, Strikes, and Revolution.*

strike process as a rich and complex human experience, a vital element of good social history. In contrast, an analysis of strikes during a particular historical conjuncture must, on one hand, aggregate rather substantial amounts of data within a relatively short time span without particular concern for long-term historical patterns that they might in fact, contradict; and on the other, focus as clearly as possible on the particularities of context, without, however, overemphasizing the details of one or another strike episode. A study such as ours is, in effect, a cross-sectional analysis of what amounts to a single strike wave, but one that has as its primary focus not so much the strike wave itself as the interrelationships between this particular form of labor activism and the historical context in which it occurs.

We must therefore set two distinct but related objectives in exploring strikes in revolutionary Russia. One is to analyze the strike process as a social phenomenon in its own right in 1917, and to understand in this way its relationship to broader and common patterns of labor activism in other times and places. This will require us to explore such elements as the scope, intensity, and degree of organization of strikes in 1917, as well as their duration and outcome, and to explain them, at least in part, in terms of Russian and European labor history generally. The second must be to relate strikes as a specific element of labor activism to the political and socioeconomic evolution of the Russian revolution itself. Here our focus has to be on the ways that elements common to the strike process generally, in Russia before 1917 and elsewhere, both affected and were affected by the particular elements of Russia's revolutionary conjuncture and the fundamental sociopolitical relationships that defined it.

PROBLEMS OF IDENTITIES, PERCEPTIONS, AND INTERPRETATIONS

Defining these sociopolitical relationships is no easy task in the dynamic and fluid context of revolution, and one must recognize some of the conceptual problems involved in identifying the relevant attributes of labor activism in such a period. First among these is what Leopold Haimson has identified as the "problem of social identities": the ways in which an individual's sense of his or her place in Russian society corresponded to political outlook and the nature of collective action in general. As Haimson has argued, all social actors clearly brought multiple identities into the revolutionary period, and those actors most involved in the struggle for change in the years leading up to 1917 are identifiable not by any single characteristic of social position, but by combinations of indices related in each case to the inability of extant institutions and socioeconomic relations to accommodate their needs.[32] As we begin to analyze 1917, however, one central issue clearly relates to the difficult question of social group or class coherence: the degree to which the patterns and pressures of aggregate identities may have come to dominate tendencies toward social differentiation. The revolutionary process as a whole, in fact, may well be correlated in some important ways to the moments when aggregate identities like "worker" or "bourgeois," "gentry" or "peasant," began to overwhelm the more particularistic identities of trade or profession, geography, or traditional social status.

In terms of Russian labor, the question of how or why these unifying identities may have come to dominate particularistic ones cannot be separated from the changing nature and form of labor activism, especially strikes. In other words, the question of identities cannot be divorced from the actual experience of conflict. Strike activism in 1917 must thus be analyzed, at least in part, in terms of the ways in which it might have contributed to the complex process of class formation.

Second, one must also recognize the centrality here of social interactions themselves: those between labor and management that emerged in the course of specific conflicts, but also the triangular patterns of interaction between workers, employers, and both official and unofficial agencies of the regime (including, in some instances, the soviets). This dimension of the problem is very much complicated by variations among localities and industries, but everywhere in 1917, at the center or on the periphery, it was the nature of these interactions themselves rather than slogans or more elaborate forms of ideology that gave many workers (and others) a sense of who they were, or at least of who they were *not*, with equally significant consequences.

Finally, there are the closely related and extremely complex problems of representation and perception: the ways in which various social groups and political formations presented themselves to others and were perceived by them, and the ways, further, in which activist behavior actually signified values or other elements of sentiment and belief (consciousness) that may have underlaid political inclinations. These issues, too, are complex, but also central to our understanding of the revolutionary period both in the ways they affected expectations and judgments and in the manner they contributed to the formation of both class and political outlooks. To approach them, and to understand in particular their relation to strikes, we must consequently explore what might be called the language of strikes, expressed in both formal and informal demands, and

[32] Leopold H. Haimson, "The Problem of Social Identities in Early Twentieth Century Russia," *Slavic Review* 47, no. 1 (1988), pp. 1–20.

determine as well as we can the ways in which language may have reflected underlying commitments. And to evaluate the degree of complementarity in perceptions and outlooks between different social groups and political contenders, it is also essential to examine carefully the ways in which strikes were reported and represented in the press.

In this respect, the most fundamental labels concerning strikes must be carefully understood and even more carefully qualified. Strikes in Russia, whether before, during, or after 1917, are conventionally dichotomized as "economic" or "political." Before 1917 there was a clear distinction in law and practice between economic and political strikes in Russia. Economic strikes related directly to the workplace. Strictly speaking, they were legal, although "fomenting," "instigating" or "organizing" them was illegal.[33] Political strikes were always against the law, but took place frequently anyway. These were generally demonstrative strikes, occurring massively in the 1905 revolution and recurring on the anniversaries of important events like Bloody Sunday (the firing by troops outside the Winter Palace on demonstrating workers in January 1905) or the 1912 massacre of Lena gold field workers. Political strikes were thus a substitute for demonstrations and other forms of mass politics. They were carefully monitored by tsarist police, and during the war years in particular they were brutally repressed. In August 1915, for example, over 25,000 textile workers struck in Ivanovo-Voznesensk to protest the war. A crowd advancing on the city square was repeatedly fired upon by police, leaving 25 dead and more than 30 wounded.[34]

In recording strike statistics both before the revolution and after, factory inspectors always distinguished between the two categories. Strikes were recorded as either political or economic, depending on the overt object of protest. As we have already suggested, however, at one level all strikes were (and are) struggles over power, whether inside the factory or out. Hence in one sense, the distinction between political and economic has little meaning.

But the distinction nonetheless has descriptive merit. Despite the vital,

[33] Law of December 2, 1905, *Polnoe sobranie zakonov Rossiiskoi imperii*, sobranie 3, vol. 25, no. 1 (1905), pp. 850–52. N. N. Polianskii, *"Russkoe ugolovnoe zakonodatel'stvo o stachkakh" i drugiia stat'i po ugolovnomu pravu* (Moscow, 1912), pp. 1–130, and M. I. Tugan-Baranovsky, *The Russian Factory in the Nineteenth Century*, trans. Arthur and Claora S. Levin (Homewood, Ill., 1970), pp. 327–31, elaborate on this law and 1886 legislation on strikes. In practical terms, the distinction was impossible to enforce. Strike leaders were frequently arrested.

[34] M. G. Fleer, ed., *Rabochee dvizhenie v gody voiny* (Moscow, 1925), pp. 89, 214–15; K. F. Sidorov, "Rabochee dvizhenie v Rossii v gody imperialisticheskoi voiny," in *Ocherki po istorii oktiabr'skoi revoliutsii*, ed. M. N. Pokrovskii (Moscow and Leningrad, 1927), vol. 1, pp. 283–85.

dialectical relationship between strikes and the process of revolutionary change in 1917, one cannot assume there is always an overt link between any given strike and the broader political process. Strikers themselves often acted without reference to politics, and much of their behavior is only comprehensible in these terms. Life in the factory had its own momentum, its own timetable, its own issues and agendas, even in 1917. Despite appearances to the contrary, strikes occurring even in the midst of major political events like the April demonstrations or the July Days sometimes had nothing directly to do with these external occurrences.

Hence it is important to understand strikes over workplace issues in 1917 as fundamentally economic in character, continuing the Factory Inspectorate's distinction. Doing so will enable us to look as closely as possible at those structural elements of labor activism that might have had a direct and independent effect on strikes: who struck; what they believed they were striking for; how strikers mobilized in support of their goals; the strike process itself, from organizational meetings to demonstrations and walkouts; the particularities of labor-management negotiations; and the nature of settlements and their impact on subsequent labor unrest. It is here that we need to concentrate our effort to understand Russian strikes in 1917 as events in themselves.

In terms of interpretation, however, we must put these economic strikes back into the political context of 1917. No strike in Russia between March and October was merely economic. Overt political strikes occurred, of course, especially around the July Days and the Kornilov mutiny, and we must pay attention to these in due fashion, distinguishing them by their specific political content. But even ordinary economic strikes were themselves conditioned in some ways by the political context in which they occurred. Few workers leaving their shops or factories in the course of 1917 could fail to develop some awareness of how their actions might relate to broader political events around them. Regardless of goals, in other words, the act of striking was itself a part of the process of developing political consciousness in 1917, in ways it is essential to explore.

Economic strikes must also be considered carefully within the context of political relationships within enterprises themselves. Some workplace issues are quite central to issues of power and political relations. They touch directly the question of who (or which groups) will control whom, who will have what power to manage the processes of production. Here, of course, the Factory Inspectorate's bipolar schema of strikes breaks down. In order to realize our objective of understanding both the overt and subliminal political implications of strikes in revolutionary Russia, we therefore need to replace the economic-political dichotomy with new categories that distinguish strikes over wages or conditions from those that challenge managerial authority, and that distinguish both of these from political strikes whose target is the state rather than the enterprise.

By challenges to managerial authority we have in mind strikes that indicate a rejection of managerial prerogatives normally associated with a free-enterprise economy. Strikes over workers' rights to have a role in hiring and firing, for example, directly challenge managerial authority in the workplace in ways quite different from, say, strikes over higher wages, in which the right of management itself to *set* wages is not specifically in question. Similarly, strikes in which workers demand that plant owners share profits, guarantee a certain number of work days per month regardless of actual production, cancel cutbacks in production, or replace foreign directors also indicate a clear challenge to the power of management to control production, even if the challenge appears in less explicit fashion.

Strikes that test the good faith of management by demanding that past agreements be honored are also political challenges, since what is at stake is the viability of legal forms like contracts or court orders. These might be thought of as "secondary" strikes, since workers are demanding not that their primary demands be granted, but that promises to grant them be upheld. The outcome of such strikes might thus have a direct bearing on the ways in which workers think about political issues or the possibility of alternative political structures.

Some Notes about Methodology

These conceptual difficulties obviously create some methodological problems. How one thinks about a strike determines how it will be recorded and shapes the body of data from which analysis is drawn. The very definition of a strike in 1917 can vary considerably, depending on whether one pays attention to individual shops or factories, broader industrywide or citywide strikes, or the broadest forms of political demonstration like those sweeping Petrograd in February, April, and July of 1917, and accompanying the gathering of national leaders to the Moscow Conference in early August.

We define a strike according to the common practice in 1917 as a work stoppage with common goals. The unit on strike might range from a workshop within a factory to several enterprises striking at once for a single set of demands, or to an entire industry or several industries striking throughout a town or region. We think this is a sensible calculus. It reflects popular perceptions of strikes at the time, and it allows us to analyze important changes in the patterns of strikes over time (by contrasting, for example, the number of strikes in individual enterprises to strikes involving more than one enterprise). We therefore count as a single strike a work stoppage involving dozens of plants and tens of thousands of workers if it was initiated and implemented as a common action.

Our study is based on several sources. We began by collecting strike reports from a variety of materials but concentrating on contemporary newspapers and document collections. The result was a data set containing information on 930 strikes that began in Russia between March 3 and October 25 (inclusively). To these we were able to add data on some 458 of the 576 strikes recorded by the Factory Inspectorate, some 136 of which we had not recorded from our newspaper or documents sources. These data came from the Central State Historical Archive in Leningrad.[35] Our analysis is consequently built on information on 1,019 discrete strikes obtained primarily from contemporary public records, partly from Soviet archival material, and partly from subsequent documentary and other sources.

For each strike, we have recorded separately information we consider "objective," or relatively insensitive to bias, and "subjective" data more likely to be biased by the perceptions of the reporter. Objective data include such facts as factory location, industry and branch of industry, the date a strike began, and whether it was confined to a single enterprise or extended to more than one production unit. Subjective data include information on the number of strikers, whether white-collar employees (sluzhashchie) or other groups struck along with workers (or in some instances, against them), information on the participation of trade unions and factory committees, and the roles of specially formed strike committees. We also include here reports on whether violence occurred, the nature of mediation efforts, and strike outcomes. Most important is a listing of strikers' demands. We have been able to record up to 14 demands reported by any source about a particular strike, and have listed them both in 40 major categories and a drastically collapsed set of five categories: wages, hours and conditions, issues of control, issues touching workers' dignity, and politics.

In addition to this basic data set, we have also constructed a file of data organized by province. Here we have aggregated basic strike material for each of Russia's 1917 provincial units, calculating strike propensities (described below), the distribution of strikes over time and according to demands, length of strikes, outcome, and degree of organization. We have combined this with aggregate socioeconomic data for each province, extracted from tsarist statistical reports and early Soviet censuses. Included

---

[35] See appendix 1.

here is information on wages (nominal and real), productivity, age, gender ratios, literacy rates, and whether or not workers had ties to land. We include as well information about provincial level votes for the Constituent Assembly elections as a way of presenting general information about the relative mix of political affiliations in different regions. This aggregated data file is the source for the bivariate and multivariate statistical regressions that we use when we think such techniques are appropriate. Additional information on this can be found in appendix 1.

As with any body of historical evidence of this sort, there are several problems with our strike data set. It is obviously not complete, although we are confident it is more than sufficient to indicate major trends and relationships, our primary objective. Also, available strike records are surely biased against smaller strikes, especially among nonfactory workers, which factory inspectors ignored and which sometimes went unreported in other sources as well. On some important questions like the number of women strikers, we have relatively little information. Although women workers accounted for some 40 percent of the factory labor force in 1917, reports of strikes rarely distinguish the gender of strikers. For other questions, like the number of workers on strike, our data are necessarily imprecise, partly because of the turmoil of the time, and partly because such information is intrinsically difficult to come by. Factory employment statistics fall into this area, as do figures about wage levels, change in wages over time, and productivity.

The fact that we are dealing with a period of rapid change raises further problems about using constant figures across even a six- or seven-month span. Many provincial employment statistics, for example, are given as of January 1917, the base month for most Central Statistical Adminstration data. Obviously, changes had occurred in many places by August or September. This clearly leads to some distortion. When possible, we have taken steps to reduce probable error. In the case of probable strikers, we use consistent estimates based partly on what we know about the numbers of employed workers, and partly on the mean estimate of multiple reports. Hence we think that these and similar problems are surmountable, especially if we present our findings judiciously and with ample allowance for error.

This concern has largely dictated the nature of our statistical methodology. For the most part we use simple descriptive statistical tools; frequency distributions, rates, and measures of central tendencies (means and medians) furnish much of our quantitative insight. But in order to illuminate the powerful subjective aspects of strike protests that are so important for proper understanding, we rely also on case histories, and on what we think are sensible deductions from aggregate information on demands, outcomes, and particular components of the strike process itself, such as its mode of organization, tactics, or the degree of violence involved.

Our greatest concern has been to portray fairly trends and relationships by means of statistics but at the same time to avoid conveying through statistics a misleading aura of precision where none is warranted. We wish therefore to alert the reader to the conventions of our statistical presentation. It should be understood that "precise" numerical figures are always necessarily approximate, even though they are based on careful sifting of all available evidence. In those few cases for which the quantitative data are less reliable, we qualify our arguments directly in the text.

TOWARD AN UNDERSTANDING OF STRIKES IN REVOLUTION

The conceptual tension between economic and political strikes, between structure and events, is reflected in the organization of our book. We have chosen to structure our analysis chronologically, as a narrative of strikes in the course of the events of 1917. Yet such an approach risks obscuring a consideration of longer-term processes and nonchronological themes. We have therefore tried to weave thematic material, such as a consideration of the issue of strike demands, the role of management, and the questions of perceptions and leadership together with the broader narrative framework. The first chapter places labor unrest in 1917 in the broader picture of Russian strike activity before the revolution. Chapter 2 provides a quantitative and comparative overview of our data on strikes, linking the broad patterns of 1917 with strike patterns of the preceding years. Chapter 3 begins the story of strikes in 1917, which continues, with necessary thematic excursions, through to the conclusion of our study, on the eve of the October revolution itself. A certain amount of technical and explanatory information has been reserved for two appendices at the end of the book.

We thus proceed pragmatically, guided both by theoretical perspectives and by the empirical evidence that our methods supply. Our statistical methodology is straightforward. We can only plot what we believe are the most important lines of enquiry, charting the effects of organization, economic conditions, labor-management relations, political sympathies, and such elements as strike outcomes on the nature of strikes themselves in 1917, as well as on the course of Russian society at large from March to October. And while analyzing our data statistically, we need to stay especially alert to changes in attitudes about strikes as tactical weapons, to changing patterns in outcomes and their effects on workers' outlooks, to elements of violence, to changing images of strikes and strikers in the public record, and, also important, to a changing sense of the role non-revolutionary instruments of strike mediation might play in resolving grievances—in brief, to the whole panoply of essentially subjective phenomena that accompany strikes everywhere, but are not readily treated statistically, and have particular importance in an historical context in which the very nature of the strike itself, as a weapon of social protest, may be changing.

Our application of theory is equally cautious. The conceptual issues we raise cannot be neatly systematized into a model of social revolution. But they do constitute building blocks toward some future model that might better account for the explosive power of labor activism in 1917 than do explanations based primarily on ideology and politics. By examining strikes within this broader framework, we hope to bring our understanding of labor activism as a whole into sharper relief. Perhaps our conceptual approach will contribute as well to a better understanding of the special nature of strikes in revolutionary situations throughout the industrial world.

1

. . . .

THE ECOLOGY OF LABOR PROTEST
AT THE END OF THE OLD REGIME

The 1917 revolution began in a cascade of strikes. Early on the morning of February 23, International Women's Day, women from several textile mills in the crowded industrial Vyborg district of Petrograd left their looms and took to the streets. One of the largest of these plants, the Nevka thread works, was situated between two of the city's major metal-working plants, New Lessner and Erikson, where some 8,700 skilled and activist workers turned out machine tools and sophisticated electrical controls. As 3,000 Nevka strikers passed their gates chanting slogans and calling for support, New Lessner and Erikson metalists spilled out to join them, and so, within the hour, did hundreds more from the Sampsoniev-skaia Cotton Works, Russian Renault (Reno), the Parviainen and Bara-novskii machine plants, the Nobel works, and other nearby plants. By 10 A.M., Bolshoi Sampsonievskii Prospekt, the central thoroughfare in the Vyborg district, was overflowing with strikers. Some 50,000 workers had joined the protests by noon. By late afternoon, as strikers reached the center of the city by way of Liteinyi Prospekt, their numbers had doubled.[1]

Strikes spread quickly. On Friday, February 24, hundreds of metalists refused to report for the morning shift at the Langenzippen works, across the river from the Winter Palace. Their comrades at the Vulcan plant stayed away as well. By midmorning, electro-mechanical workers at the huge Siemens-Schuckert plant on Vasil'evskii Island had come out, joined by students from the nearby Petrograd University, and soon by hundreds from the Baltic shipyards. In the Narva district, some 24,000 or more Putilov workers prepared to join the swelling wave. Four days before, the Putilovists had been locked out of their plant in a dispute over the firing of militant workers, and many were eager to organize their own demon-

---

[1] I. P. Leiberov, *Na shturm samoderzhaviia. Petrogradskii proletariat v gody pervoi mirovoi voiny i fevral'skoi revoliutsii* (Moscow, 1978), pp. 123–31; Tsuyoshi Hasegawa, *The February Revolution: Petrograd, 1917* (Seattle, 1981), pp. 215–22

strations. Clashes with police took place at nearby Treugol'nik, the city's major rubber plant, which employed some 15,000 persons. For the first time, ominously for the regime, workers subject to military discipline at state plants like the Obukhov steel works stopped work as well.

Strikes continued to spread rapidly, turning into massive demonstrations. By Saturday, February 25, workers paralyzed the city. State Duma leaders conferred anxiously and communicated with army headquarters; workers and revolutionary activists began to organize their own revolutionary council, the Petrograd Soviet. Garrison soldiers at first fired on workers in several places but soon refused to do so. The city quieted briefly on Sunday, February 26, but then erupted again on Monday morning, with thousands of workers flooding every major artery, joined now in many places by sympathetic soldiers. The tsarist regime was losing all semblance of authority. In one wing of the Tauride palace, State Duma leaders formed a "Temporary Committee" and prepared to appoint their own ministers to a Provisional regime. Down the corridors in the same building, workers' representatives and socialist party leaders convened the Petrograd Soviet's first tumultuous session. By February 28, the tsar's ministers had resigned. In consultation with Soviet leaders, the Duma Committee drew up a new cabinet list, headed by the well-known liberal zemstvo figure, Prince G. E. Lvov.

Nicholas himself soon realized the hopelessness of his situation. On March 2, under great pressure, he abdicated in favor of his brother, who in turn refused to take the throne. Thousands of workers heard of these events, awed by the enormity of their accomplishment. Russia appeared to have moved from autocracy to democracy in a little more than a week, and overwhelmingly—at least in the first instance—because some 400,000 people in more than 900 enterprises, virtually the entire working population of the capital, had participated in some form of strike.[2]

THE FEBRUARY CONJUNCTURE AND LONGER-TERM PROCESSES OF CHANGE

The eight days between February 23 and March 2 constituted one of those rare periods in history when long-term processes of change come together under particular circumstances, and in a brief, intensive moment, fundamentally alter the basic structures of an entire social and political order. The eight months that followed reflected a similar, if broader, conjuncture, as attempts to fashion new social and political relations were themselves conditioned by elements of the moment as well

[2] Leiberov, *Na shturm*, p. 244.

as less apparent longer-term patterns. The distinction often drawn by historians between immediate and longer-term patterns of change is particularly important for understanding revolutionary Russia in general and strikes in particular. If the conjunctural elements we will examine in the following chapters were greatly affected by successive surges of strikes and strikers in 1917, these protests themselves took place in the context of a much longer historical experience. Processes of long duration, as they have been called, thus need attention at the start, particularly in terms of the ways they may have conditioned the historical memories of those who would play such an important role in events that followed the February upheaval. In statistical language, we need briefly to treat strikes in 1917 as one year in a longer time series, and before probing their particularities and their historical meaning, enquire in this and the following chapter how strikes between February and October related to broader historical patterns.

In fact, Vyborg metalists and others looking out across the river at the Winter Palace in February 1917 regarded the monarchy's collapse as the culmination of many years' struggle, not just eight days' effort. From 1905 until the very eve of the revolution, Russia had been awash in strikes. Despite narrow limits for legal strike activity and a pervasive police presence in industrial plants, nearly 10 million factory workers went on strike between 1895, when statistics began to be compiled, and 1916, averaging one-quarter of the factory labor force each year.[3] In the periods of peak strike activity before the war, 1905–1906 and 1912–1914, the average annual proportion of strikers approached three-quarters of the factory labor force. By contrast, only about one-third of the entire industrial work force, including workers in mines and metallurgical plants, went on strike in France in the entire period between 1890 and 1914, a time of militant revolutionary syndicalism.[4] Although there were years when the number of industrial strikers in Great Britain and Germany exceeded 50 percent of the workforce before the war, no other European country matched Russia's overall level of strike activism.[5]

Strikes were particularly intense on the eve of the war. In the first seven months of 1914 alone, more strikes occurred in Russia than in the entire period between 1908 and 1911, and more plants were shut down for political purposes than in 1912 and 1913 combined. If strikes had contin-

---

[3] K. N. Iakovleva, "Zabastovochnoe dvizhenie v Rossii za 1895–1917 gody," in *Materialy po statistike truda*, vyp. 8, (Moscow, 1920), pp. 5–6.

[4] Edward Shorter and Charles Tilly, *Strikes in France, 1830–1968* (Cambridge, 1974), p. 115.

[5] Arthur M. Ross and Paul T. Hartman, *Changing Patterns of Industrial Conflict* (New York, 1960), pp. 194–99.

ued throughout 1914 at the same intensity and frequency, the year would have seen more workers take to the streets than during Russia's first great revolutionary upheaval in 1905, nine years before. As Leopold Haimson's study of the period shows in exhaustive and convincing detail, 1912 and 1913 were years of an enormous resurgence in Russian labor protests, symptomatic to many people of a new revolutionary storm.[6]

The outbreak of war in July 1914 brought a brief period of quiescence to the labor front in Russia as it did throughout Europe. The lull, however, was short lived, much more so than in Western Europe. In France and Germany, it was not until 1917 that the number of industrial workers on strike surpassed 1912 levels; and in Britain, this did not occur until the war had ended.[7] The number of economic strikes in Russia increased in 1915 to levels approximating those in 1912. There was a resurgence as well of political strikes and strikers. As we will see, by 1916 the intensity of industrial strikes again approached the levels of the prewar period, and on the eve of revolution, in January and February 1917, more workers participated in strikes for political rather than enterprise-related goals than in 1913. For Vyborg workers as well as others, February was a final episode in the last of three great strike waves stretching from the first revolution in 1905 to the monarchy's collapse. And some in New Lessner, the Parviainen works, Siemens-Schuckert, and other enterprises in Petrograd had undoubtedly experienced all three.

INDUSTRIAL EXPANSION AND
THE WORKFORCE BEFORE 1917

We will look more closely at these strike figures below and in chapter 2, as we relate them to the data we have gathered for 1917. For now it is important to appreciate only how central the strike phenomenon itself was to Russia's workplace environment before February, and to recog-

---

[6] Leopold H. Haimson and Ronald Petrusha, "Two Strike Waves in Imperial Russia (1905–07, 1912–14): A Quantitative Analysis," in *Strikes, Wars, and Revolutions in an International Perspective: Strike Waves in the Late Nineteenth and Early Twentieth Centuries*, ed. Leopold H. Haimson and Charles Tilly (New York, 1989). By contrast, the number of British workers involved in industrial disputes in 1913 was less than half of what it had been in 1912, and two-thirds the figure for 1911; in Germany, 51 percent and 68 percent. The number of striking industrial workers in France was relatively constant, but industrial disputes as a whole fell from 1,502 in 1910 and 1,471 in 1911 to 1,073 in 1913. See Ross and Hartman, *Changing Patterns*, pp. 194–96.

[7] Ross and Hartman, *Changing Patterns*, pp. 194–96. For a discussion of strikes in Western Europe during the war, see especially *War, Strikes, and Revolution; The Impact of the War Experience on Italy, Germany, France, England, and Russia*, ed. Giulio Sapelli and Leopold H. Haimson, (Milan, forthcoming).

nize that the great feeling of protest reflected in strikes was related both to the stresses of an antiquated and repressive political structure and to the strains of very rapid industrial growth, particularly in the period between 1908 and 1913. This growth propelled Russia forward in the capitalist world, but not without bringing major changes to the workplace.

The aggregate statistics of industrial expansion in this period are well known: the output of cast iron increased some 64 percent between 1908 and 1913; coal, almost 40 percent; iron and steel, more than 50 percent; and the consumption of cotton, 22 percent, to cite just four examples. The value of imported goods rose from 912 million rubles in 1908 to 1,374 million in 1913, and that of exports from 998 to 1,520 million rubles.[8] From a level of around 1.5 percent between 1900 and 1906, Russia's annual rate of industrial growth soared to 6.25 percent between 1907 and 1913, and was even higher in the years immediately preceding the war.[9] Problems of capitalization, the quality and prices of imported goods, and relatively low levels of productivity led many Russian industrialists to insist that levels of profitability were not commensurate with these increases, and many looked to the state for help. In this respect as in others, the outbreak of war proved enormously beneficial—a "godsend," in the view of one recent historian.[10] By 1916, more than 30 percent of all industrial output went directly toward the war effort, and in the all-important metals and machine-construction sector, the figure was closer to two-thirds.[11]

Much of Russia's rapid industrial expansion was underwritten by foreign capital and administered by foreign managerial personnel.[12] Workers in St. Petersburg and elsewhere, particularly in South Russian metallur-

[8] P. A. Khromov, *Ekonomicheskoe razvitie Rossii v XIX–XX vekakh* (Moscow, 1950), pp. 454–55. See also the discussion in Peter I. Lyashchenko, *History of the National Economy of Russia to the 1917 Revolution* (New York, 1949), chap. 33.

[9] Alexander Gerschenkron, "The Rate of Growth of Industrial Production in Russia since 1885," *Journal of Economic History* 7, supplement (1947), p. 149.

[10] Peter Gatrell, *The Tsarist Economy, 1850–1917* (New York, 1986), p. 185.

[11] See the discussion in A. L. Sidorov, *Ekonomicheskoe polozhenie Rossii v gody pervoi mirovoi voiny* (Moscow, 1973), p. 333 and passim.

[12] According to the economic historian Khromov, more than eight billion rubles of foreign private capital and some seven billion rubles of foreign state capital were invested in Russia at the start of the war. The share of foreign capital in Russian industry generally in 1917 approximated 34 percent; in some industries like mining and metal processing, the figure by all accounts was much higher. Russia also imported as much as 60 percent of all capital equipment used in heavy industry, and almost as high a percentage of tools for manufacturing and commodity production. See Khromov, *Ekonomicheskoe razvitie*, pp. 380–93; A. L. Sidorov, *Ekonomicheskoe polozhenie*, p. 372; and especially John P. McKay, *Pioneers for Profit: Foreign Entrepreneurship and Russian Industrialization, 1885–1913* (Chicago, 1970), pp. 26–28.

gical plants, often found themselves bossed by foreign managers and engineers, whom they readily blamed for unsatisfactory wages or working conditions. Unrest at plants like Siemens-Schuckert, Russian Renault, Singer, or Moscow's Dinamo machine factory almost always involved some degree of xenophobia. Yet there was simply no escaping for Russia either this foreign presence or foreign economic dependency if industry was to continue to expand more rapidly than the supportive capacity of domestic resources. By 1913, in fact, imports of as basic a commodity as coal, which Russia itself possessed in enormous quantity, were increasing at twice the rate of domestic production, and despite higher costs, accounted for some 25 percent of all Russian requirements.[13]

To some extent the state itself attempted to mediate the labor conflicts arising in these years of rapid growth, even as direct state economic activity diminished between 1906 and the start of the war. Factory inspectors who served the Ministry of Trade and Industry enforced government labor legislation. They also assiduously recorded strikes and sometimes tried to resolve industrial conflicts. More commonly, the state lent its police powers to the industrialists, who often called on the militia and even the army to help suppress unrest.

All this was part of the life experience of older workers on the eve of revolution. At the same time, repressive factory conditions often shocked the tens of thousands of new workers brought into the workplace before and during the war. From January 1, 1901, to January 1, 1914, the number of workers under the purview of the Factory Inspectorate increased from 1,692,300 to almost 2,000,000. Within this group, the number of textile workers under Inspectorate jurisdiction increased almost 30 percent; workers in paper manufacturing and printing, some 37 percent; those in the manufacture of wood and wood products, almost 66 percent; chemical workers, 51 percent; and the all-important metals sector, which included metal fabricating, machine building, and the highly skilled workers of the electro-technical factories like Erikson and Siemens-Schuckert, almost 53 percent.[14] By 1917 these figures had changed only slightly.

These workers were, however, only part of the total industrial workforce. Employees in state enterprises, on the railroads, and in metallurgical plants remained outside the Factory Inspectorate's jurisdiction, and

[13] A. L. Sidorov, *Ekonomicheskoe polozhenie*, pp. 502–3.

[14] Tsentral'noe Statisticheskoe Upravlenie (hereafter TSSU), *Trudy*, vol. 7, vyp. 1, "Statisticheskii sbornik za 1913–1917 gody" (Moscow, 1921), pp. 4–39; A. G. Rashin, *Formirovanie rabochego klassa Rossii* (Moscow, 1958), pp. 42, 48, 71, 171; Rashin, citing Lyashchenko, gives a slightly higher figure for the number of workers under factory inspection in 1914.

do not figure either in prerevolutionary strike statistics or the common aggregates of industrial workers. According to best estimates, there were more than a million workers in these categories by 1917, and hence more than 3,300,000 workers in the industrial workforce as a whole by 1917, in almost 15,000 enterprises throughout the empire. Some 311,000 were employed in 74 state-owned plants, almost all related to defense production.[15] The major groupings can be found in table 1.1.

There were, of course, millions of additional workers in 1917 beyond those in the industrial workforce, in services, agricultural labor, retail trade establishments, and the like. Although no precise figures are available, the Soviet historian L. S. Gaponenko has made some very good estimates using archival material and other contemporary sources. By his account, there were nearly 15 million workers employed in some type of hired labor by October 1917 outside the formal industrial categories. His findings are summarized in table 1.2.

What do these figures tell us? It should be apparent, first, that Russia's industrial labor force was expanding much too rapidly to be staffed entirely by the offspring of factory workers, and that peasants, consequently, streamed into the factories in substantial numbers between 1900 and 1917. Moreover, subsistence agriculture and minimal educational opportunities in the countryside meant that these new workers possessed few industrial skills and little familiarity with modern industrial work habits. Skilled, self-disciplined workers were thus relatively scarce in industrializing Russia. At the same time, the rapid influx of new workers made it impossible for urban welfare systems to keep pace with social need. Urban living conditions were abysmal by any standard of the time, and recognized as such;[16] only the relatively more desperate agrarian conditions kept active the flow of peasant recruits into industry. In turn, these

[15] The figures are for June of 1917. The total strength of Russia's workforce at the time of the February revolution is simply unknown. Factory Inspectorate data was available for major branches of industry under private ownership; the Special Council for Defense had some data on state enterprises, railroads, and the large mines and metallurgy enterprises of the Urals and the Don basin. But these figures were not adequately adjusted for either the effects of the military draft or the role of supplementary labor provided in places by temporary workers or even prisoners of war. In 1917 itself, which saw the continued volatility of the level of production, there was no accurate count of month-by-month variations. The imprecision of this data, in fact, greatly frustrated many in the new Provisional Government who were involved with industry, trade, and labor, and prompted a thorough reorganization of statistical work under the Central Statistical Administration, which became so active as the Bolsheviks came to power. See the discussion in V. E. Varzar, *Ocherki osnov promyshlennoi statistiki* (Moscow, 1925), especially chap. 1.

[16] See the discussion in Robert W. Thurston, *Liberal City, Conservative State: Moscow and Russia's Urban Crisis, 1906–1914* (New York, 1987).

TABLE 1.1
Industrial Workforce, 1900–1917
(Estimated)

	1900	1908	1913	1917
FACTORIES AND PLANTS				
Under factory inspection[a]	—	1,768,200	1,960,860	2,093,862
State enterprises	—	—	—	311,467
Other	1,536,423	166,016	506,340	60,122
Total	1,536,423	1,934,216	2,467,200	2,465,451
MINES				
Coal mines	109,208	174,061	244,474	347,947
Oil fields	27,556	40,425	44,500	62,800
Other	228,350	182,087	207,829	171,026
Total	365,114	396,573	496,803	581,773
METALLURGICAL ENTERPRISES	141,368	197,138	150,942	291,356
Total	2,042,905	2,527,927	3,114,945	3,338,580

SOURCES:
1900: *Dinamika rossiiskoi i sovetskoi promyshlennosti* (Moscow, 1929–1930), vol. 1, pt. 1, pp. 96–97.
1908: Ibid., vol. 1, pt. 2, pp. 77–78, 106–8.
1913: Ibid., vol. 1, pt. 3, pp. 176–77.
1917: TSGIA SSSR, f. 23, op. 16, d. 318, 1. 7–32. Figures are for January 1. Workers under February Inspection: TSSU, Trudy, vol. 7, vyp. 1, p. 39; figures compiled by the Economic Council for workers under Factory Inspection on January 1, 1917, are slightly higher: 2,155,063. Figures cited elsewhere vary slightly. Cf. Lyashchenko, *History*, p. 761; Rashin, *Formirovanie*, pp. 61, 98, 120–21.
[a] Enterprises under factory inspection are mechanized enterprises or those employing more than 15 workers.

conditions meant that generations of Russian workers themselves never severed their relations with their rural villages of origin, producing what some observers regarded as a particular type of hybrid peasant-proletarian.[17]

In such circumstances, skill was obviously a scarce and valued attri-

[17] On the "peasant character" of urban workers, see especially Theodore Von Laue, "Russian Labor between Field and Factory, 1892–1903," *California Slavic Studies* 3 (1964), pp. 33–65; James H. Bater, *St. Petersburg: Industrialization and Change* (London, 1976); Joseph Bradley, *Muzhik and Muscovite: Urbanization in Late Imperial Russia*

TABLE 1.2
Nonfactory Hired Workers, October 1917

Workers in small urban and rural shops or working at home	3,000,000
Construction workers	1,250,000
Workers and white-collar employees in railroad transport	1,265,800
Workers and white-collar employees in water transport	500,000
Laborers and day workers	1,100,000
Agricultural laborers	4,500,000
Workers and white-collar employees in communications (post, telegraph, and telephone)	91,000
White-collar employees in industrial enterprises	250,000
Domestic servants and service personnel in enterprises and institutions	2,100,000
Workers and white-collar employees in commercial establishments and organizations	865,000

SOURCE: Gaponenko, *Rabochii klass*, p. 72. Cf. Rashin, *Formirovanie*, p. 171.

bute, particularly in machine building and the crucial electro-technical sector of metalworking. Because of their scarcity and centrality to industrial production, skilled workers trained in Russian industry enjoyed relatively high standards of living and significant autonomy on the job. At the same time, as new capital poured into Russian plants after 1905, the privileged position of metalworkers was also placed in jeopardy. To some degree, capital bought technology; particularly in the metals trades, tech-

(Berkeley, 1985); Robert Edelman, *Proletarian Peasants: The Revolution of 1905 in Russia's Southwest* (Ithaca, N.Y., 1987); and Robert Eugene Johnson, *Peasant and Proletarian: The Working Class of Moscow in the Late Nineteenth Century* (New Brunswick, N.J., 1979). The effect of Russia's accelerated economic development on its labor force has drawn attention from many scholars and continues to perplex and provoke historians. See especially Leopold H. Haimson, "The Problem of Social Stability in Urban Russia, 1905–1914," pts. 1, 2, *Slavic Review* 23, no. 4 (1964), pp. 619–42; 24, no. 1 (1965), pp. 1–22; Diane Koenker, *Moscow Workers and the 1917 Revolution* (Princeton, N.J., 1981), chap. 2; E. E. Kruze, *Polozhenie rabochego klassa Rossii v 1900–1914 godakh.* (Leningrad, 1976); and Iu. I. Kir'ianov, *Zhiznennyi uroven' rabochikh Rossii* (Moscow, 1979). On industrial and urban conditions generally, see M. I. Tugan-Baranovsky, *The Russian Factory in the Nineteenth Century*, trans. Arthur and Claora S. Levin (Homewood, Ill., 1970); L. M. Ivanov, ed., *Rabochii klass i rabochee dvizhenie v Rossii (1861–1917)*, (Moscow, 1966); Bater, *St.Petersburg*; and Thurston, *Liberal City*.

nology rendered some skills obsolete, although the extent and effect of "deskilling" and the degree to which skilled workers felt threatened in Russia is unclear.[18]

The distribution of industrial workers by branch can be seen in table 1.3. What is most impressive about these figures is not so much their relative magnitudes, but the changes between 1914 and 1917, to which we will return, and the fact that they show such a heavy concentration of workers in three quite different kinds of industry: metal processing and manufacturing, textiles, and food. Not only were the techniques and processes of production quite different in each of these branches, but so, too, were the degrees of social differentiation among the workers involved, and the physical contexts of work.

Metals and machine-tools production was concentrated in large urban

TABLE 1.3

Workers under Factory Inspection by Major Industry, 1914 and 1917

Industry	1914		1917	
	Number of Workers	Percent of Labor Force	Number of Workers	Percent of Labor Force
Minerals	174,438	8.9	101,638	4.9
Metals	346,989	17.8	546,117	26.1
Wood and wood products	106,273	5.5	87,780	4.2
Chemicals	76,767	3.9	92,679	4.4
Food products	322,043	16.5	338,591	16.2
Animal products (leather)	50,450	2.6	70,168	3.4
Textiles	736,809	37.8	724,059	34.6
Paper and printing	92,177	4.7	80,514	3.8
Other	44,380	2.2	52,316	2.5

SOURCE: TSSU, *Trudy*, vol. 7, vyp. 1, pp. 4–35, 39. See also the discussion in A. L. Sidorov, *Ekonomicheskoe polozhenie*, pp. 412–14.

NOTE: Enteprises under factory inspection are mechanical enterprises or those employing more than 15 workers.

[18] It is possible, for example, that the rapid expansion of industrial production decreased the skilled workers' share of the workforce in relative terms, and opened at least some opportunities for upward movement into supervisory and technical jobs, especially that of shop foreman.

plants often employing thousands of workers, especially in Petrograd. On the eve of the revolution, approximately one-third of the 60-odd machine construction enterprises in the capital employed more than 1,000 workers each. More than 19,000 worked at the massive Trubochnyi plant, some 8,000 at Petrograd Cartridge, 7,000 at Parviainen and New Lessner. Additional thousands were concentrated at Orudinskii, the Arsenal of Peter the Great, Langenzippen, Siemens-Schuckert, and Promet. Each of these giant complexes was, in effect, a conglomeration of smaller production shops specializing in pattern-making, smelting, rolling, and so forth, with quite different work forces and styles of work. Many here were common laborers (*chernorabochie*); others were skilled artisans who would not think of doing tasks they thought beneath them. Shop workers commonly ate and lived together and, in this way as in others, developed strong craft identifications. Their concentration in industrial neighborhoods like Petrograd's Vyborg district or the Zamoskvoreche region of Moscow also cultivated an intimate familiarity with the peculiarities of urban life and the pulse of the city in general. The other major geographical center of state plants and workers in the metals industry was the Central Industrial Region around Moscow, although important mixed-production plants existed in Nizhnii Novgorod (Felzer, Sormovo, Siemens and Halske), Kharkov (Helferick-Sade), Kazan (the Alafuzov complex), and elsewhere.

Large numbers of metalists worked in state plants not under factory inspection. By 1917, as much as 30 percent of the entire work force in Petrograd province labored in 31 state-owned defense plants. Obukhov and Orudinskii produced shell cases; the Trubochnyi works, which formerly produced steel piping and where 10 percent of the workforce was considered highly skilled, now manufactured artillery pieces and heavy shells.[19] The only other major complement of industrial workers employed directly by the state or by other public employers were chemical workers and leather workers. The former were again largely in Petrograd and Moscow; the latter were employed in large and small plants and workshops under the supervision of quasi-public organizations such as the zemstvos, War Industries Committees (WICs), and the Red Cross.

Textile workers were also concentrated in large cotton mills and other manufacturing plants, but with a few major exceptions like Kersten, Nevka Thread, Thornton Mills, Neva Cotton, and Pal' in Petrograd, and Prokhorov Trekhgornaia, Zindel, Girault (Zhiro), and Heubner in Moscow, these were largely located in industrial villages, especially outside of

[19] M. Bortnik, "Na Trubochnom zavode," in *Professional'noe dvizhenie v Petrograde v 1917 godu*, ed. A. Anskii (Leningrad, 1928), pp. 268–78.

Moscow in Vladimir and Kostroma provinces. Here craft differentiations were much less sharp. Large numbers of textile workers were women. Many could be characterized as semiskilled, operating looms or spindles after a few months of training. Textile workers in the main were far closer to peasant life and the political economy of the village than workers in any other industrial sector. Many (if not most) in 1917 still officially retained their peasant status, although as Robert Johnson suggests, this did not necessarily preclude their acting like their more urbanized colleagues.[20]

In the food sector, which included bakery workers, meat packers, and other food-processing workers as well as those in candy factories, cigarette and tobacco plants, tea-packing firms, distilleries, and sugar refineries, artisanal identities were highly developed, but skills themselves were not terribly difficult to acquire. Few in this sector required the literacy of a skilled pattern maker in the metal trades, for example, or even the craft techniques of a carriage or furniture maker. Most (but not all) food enterprises were small, and workers in them, even in cities like Moscow and Petrograd, often lived and ate in their shops and generally found themselves in much closer contact with their employers, who very much controlled their lives.

This broad diversity in Russia's industrial work force has long vexed historians interested in the complex processes of working-class formation and class consciousness. The relatively strong associational tendencies characteristic of skilled hereditary workers in the metal trades has generally been held as a major source of conscious political activism, especially by Soviet historians, while the attachments of textile workers and others to the countryside is associated with passivity and backwardness.[21] There are many problems with this conceptualization, as Robert Johnson and Laura Engelstein have shown so well, but the most important is that its formulation for the pre-1917 period as a whole rests overwhelmingly on impressionistic evidence.[22] The best one can say is that strong craft and shop attachments were clearly countered in most if not every industrial sector in Russia by a social environment of legally defined estates and by a growing antagonism between workers of all categories, industrialists, and the state. How these competitive impulses and identities themselves affected labor activism in the revolution of 1917 remains to be seen.

[20] Johnson, *Peasant and Proletarian*, chaps. 3, 7.

[21] See especially V. Ia. Laverychev, ed., *Rabochii klass Rossii, 1907–fevral' 1917 godov* (Moscow, 1982), chap. 6.

[22] Johnson, *Peasant and Proletarian*; Laura Engelstein, *Moscow, 1905: Working-Class Organization and Political Conflict* (Stanford, Calif., 1982).

EMPLOYER ASSOCIATIONS AND
RUSSIA'S DEVELOPING BOURGEOISIE

Russia's workforce was not the only social group undergoing significant changes in these years. An expanding industry meant the rapid growth as well of industrial managers, entrepreneurs, administrators, and merchants—in fact, the whole array of social groups that constituted Russia's developing bourgeoisie. Between 1907 and 1913 the number of joint-stock companies in Russia nearly tripled.[23] On the eve of the First World War, the Association of Industry and Trade (*Sovet S"ezdov Predstavitel'ei Promyshlennosti i Torgovli*)[24] counted almost 28,000 firms of all types throughout the empire, including Poland. The largest number, nearly 9,000, were in the food-processing sector; more than 3,000 were involved with textiles; and some 1,500 were listed in the important area of iron and steel fabrication or machine construction (excluding agricultural implements). The owners and major stock holders of many of these enterprises constituted the elite of Russia's business and commercial circles, particularly in textiles and metals, and especially in the 78 additional firms that were registered as electrical-instrument producers involved in the manufacturing of technologically sophisticated dynamos, electrical engines, and communication apparatus. These included Siemens-Schuckert, Siemens and Halske, Erikson, and the United Cable Factory in St. Petersburg, and Dinamo in Moscow, which, in addition to having some of Russia's most highly skilled metalists, also employed a number of the country's most able managers and best-trained electrical engineers.

It is an important characteristic of Imperial Russia's social development, however, that powerful and diverse cleavages kept these expanding industrial and commercial circles from developing a strong sense of social unity, as several historians have recently demonstrated.[25] Sharp divisions had long divided the old Moscow merchantry, with its Old Believer traditions of disdain for modern and Western ways, and the more recent industrialists and entrepreneurs who emerged in the course of Russia's industrial expansion in the last decades of the nineteenth century. Partly because of the state's role in industrial development, partly as a result of cultural traditions and the need for extensive economic contacts with Western Europe, this newer group of entrepreneurs tended to be concen-

---

[23] Laverychev, ed., *Rabochii klass*, pp. 24–25.

[24] Literally, "Council of Congresses of Representatives from Industry and Trade." Our simplified form follows Ruth A. Roosa, "Russian Industrialists and State Socialism," *Soviet Studies* 23, no. 3 (July 1972), pp. 395–417.

[25] See especially Alfred J. Rieber, *Merchants and Entrepreneurs in Imperial Russia* (Chapel Hill, N.C., 1982); Thomas C. Owen, *Capitalism and Politics in Russia: A Social History of the Moscow Merchants, 1855–1905* (Cambridge, 1981).

trated in St. Petersburg, where most of Russia's more modern plants and industries were constructed. Old Believer influence had faded considerably in Moscow before the revolution of 1905, but heirs to this tradition still dominated the Moscow Stock Exchange (Bourse) Committee, and many continued to reject modern approaches to factory management, investment, and labor relations. Men like the Exchange Committee's two chairmen during the last three decades of tsarist rule, the banker V. A. Naidenov and G. A. Krestovnikov, who owned a large candle factory in Moscow, were also persuaded that foreign influence in Russian industrial development was generally harmful in any case, and regarded many entrepreneurial activities with suspicion. The South Russian metallurgical trusts were seen as a particularly unwholesome aspect of foreign intrusion. So too, for some, were the railroads, which likewise relied heavily on foreign capital and employed many foreign managers and technicians.

For these various industrial and commercial groups as well as other sectors of Russian society, the 1905 revolution thrust the issue of social identity and the related question of class interests to the fore. Representative politics, even in limited form, required some programmatic definition of group welfare, and hence sharper and more carefully delimited notions of class than those associated with the traditional Russian estate categories. Yet scions of the Moscow Exchange Committee and bearers of the Old Believer traditions continued to resist these aspects of economic modernization. They looked with suspicion at employer groups like the St. Petersburg and Moscow Societies of Factory and Mill Owners (PSFMO and MSFMO) or the Southern Coal and Steel Producers Association, which were organized in the aftermath of the 1905 revolution specifically to defend employer interests, especially against those of organized labor; they continued to remain socially and culturally distant from those on both sides of the management-labor divide who would politicize the traditional relationships between workers and their employers.

There were other cleavages as well. St. Petersburg industrialists moved much closer to the regime in the aftermath of 1905 than their entrepreneurial colleagues in Moscow and generally avoided any political associations or positions that might be construed as confrontational, at least in public. This was largely due to the centrality of the state itself in promoting iron and steel production, especially for defense, but it was also the result of close personal interconnections between most owners of major mills and mechanical plants in the capital, the financial oligarchy that backed them, and their associates and supporters in the government, particularly the Ministry of Finance. The leading figures of St. Petersburg industry moved easily in and out of government service, serving officially at times as ministers and deputy ministers. They also channeled vast amounts of foreign capital into Russian industry through their St. Petersburg banks and performed a critical service to the state as major buyers and sales brokers for government bonds and other obligations. Disagreements were reserved for ministry meetings and boardrooms, where power still resided. It was here that state policies were worked out, and that St. Petersburg industrialists believed Russia's future would be determined.

Among the most prominent of these men were A. I. Putilov, president of the Russo-Asiatic Bank as well as of the giant Putilov metalworking complex (and a major stockholder in some 40 of the country's leading oil, electrical, mining, and railroad companies); A. I. Vyshnegradskii, head of the Petersburg International Bank and the Sormovo steel and iron works in Nizhnii Novgorod; M. M. Fedorov, director of the Azov-Don bank and a number of metallurgical and mining enterprises; and V. I. Timiriazev, who headed the Russian Bank for Foreign Trade.[26] These men controlled a vast, interlocking complex of industry, banking and trade. The Russo-Asiatic, Petersburg International, and Azov-Don banks, for example, were the three leading stockholders in the enormous Briansk Iron and Steel works, the site of major strikes and demonstrations throughout the war. Putilov himself was a major stockholder in the Baranovskii mechanical works, along with the Russo-Asiatic Bank, and presided over its annual stockholders' meeting. Vyshnegradskii and Putilov each held almost 30,000 shares in the Lena Gold Fields Cooperative, scene of the bloody massacres in 1912.

With their sense of importance so intimately tied to the welfare of the state, St. Petersburg industrialists at times displayed an almost scornful attitude to colleagues elsewhere who would "debase" themselves with common politics. They affiliated loosely in the Association of Industry and Trade, but although the Association's positions on a number of important matters were politically quite explicit and were well publicized in its journal, *Promyshlennost' i Torgovlia*, most industrialists in the capital hardly thought of it as a political organization or even as representative of class interests.[27] Consciousness on these matters, as on others, was weakly developed.

In some contrast, a number of Moscow businessmen, particularly those

[26] Rieber, *Merchants and Entrepreneurs*, p. 366. Putilov's Russo-Asiatic Bank was particularly important in the operation of major procurement syndicates, which by January 1917 involved virtually all major Petrograd industrial enterprises. The bank itself had organized a special war-industries syndicate that distributed orders to the Baranovskii works, Russian Optical, and the Gil'zovyi plant. A list of 26 syndicates and the 66 plants connected with them is in *Oktiabr'skoe vooruzhennoe vosstanie: Semnadtsatyi god v Petrograde*, 2 vols. (Leningrad, 1967), vol. 1, pp. 403–5.
[27] Roosa, "Russian Industrialists," pp. 398–411.

associated with the textile industry and grouped around the newspaper *Utro Rossii*, began in the aftermath of 1905 to promote an explicit sense of themselves as Russia's bourgeoisie. These men were generally divorced from government circles and state affairs. Unlike their Association of Industry and Trade colleagues in St. Petersburg, they tended to regard themselves as politically progressive and saw progress largely in terms of Western political and economic institutions. Many had close ties with members of Moscow's liberal intelligentsia, particularly at Moscow University; despite the experience of 1905, they eagerly sought ways to develop what they regarded as harmonious and mutually beneficial management-labor relations. They thus emerged in the aftermath of the first revolution as both political *and* confrontational, and they were tuned to party politics.

Organizationally, this group soon centered around the Moderate-Progressive Party, founded in 1906, the Progressists, who organized in 1912, and after the start of the war, the Union of Trade and Industry (*Soiuz Torgovli i Promyshlennosti*), which the regime prevented from meeting.[28] Leading figures here included S. I. Chetverikov, S. N. Tretiakov, N. D. Morozov, E. V. Morozov, A. I. Konovalov (the Provisional Government's future minister of trade and industry), and especially the Riabushinskiis, an Old Believer family that emerged at the end of the nineteenth century as one of Moscow's most modern and active groups of entrepreneurs. With those in St. Petersburg, they shared the privileges of a social elite and were deeply committed to Russia's development as a strong European power. They were also as eager as anyone to mobilize Russia's economic and social resources as effectively as possible toward these ends, especially after the start of the war. But in addition to differences in cultural backgrounds, which may have allowed those centered in Moscow some greater perspective on the autocracy than their colleagues in Petersburg, the two groups were also very different in their attitudes towards Nicholas and his ministers, their views of the state's proper role in industrial production, their ideas about the mobilization of industry, and most important, their attitudes toward workers and labor protest.

The Petersburg industrialists were generally quite tough-minded, even ruthless, in their attitudes toward workers. As Heather Hogan has shown, they seized on time clocks, piecework, and other aspects of labor rationalization in the aftermath of 1905 partly to curb worker protests and better control their factories.[29] And insofar as they disputed govern-

[28] V. Ia. Laverychev, "Vserossiiskii soiuz torgovli i promyshlennosti," *Istoricheskie Zapiski* 70 (1961), pp. 35–60.

[29] Heather Hogan, "Industrial Rationalization and the Roots of Labor Militance in the

ment policies toward labor, it was invariably out of concern that conciliatory attitudes on the state's part would lead to "limitless new demands."[30] In Moscow, Riabushinskii, Konovalov, and others regarded
brutalities toward workers with horror, and were so deeply disturbed by
the Lena gold field massacres that they moved into open opposition. The
first congress of the Progressive party in 1912 demanded the abolition of
estates and the establishment of a representative government. Shortly afterwards, Konovalov himself began to work towards a political coalition
of sorts between the Progressists, other Duma opposition parties, and revolutionary groups on the left, including the Bolsheviks. When the war
began in 1914, Riabushinskii, Konovalov, and others spearheaded efforts
to involve workers' representatives directly in the processes of industrial
mobilization.[31]

In these circumstances, the question of bourgeois identity in prerevolutionary Russia was quite problematic. The PSFMO and MSFMO like the
Association of Industry and Trade and other groups, were effectively
agents of class mobilization in a social context in which many leading
industrialists still strongly challenged the very notion of class affiliation.
Many felt no identification whatsoever with commercial leaders or the
merchantry, especially in Moscow; some regarded the very designation
"bourgeois" with indignation. As with Russia's workers, however, strong
social, sectional, and geographical differences among these diverse elements were themselves countered by the very processes of industrial conflict: social interactions reduced the importance of social differences and
created stronger unifying identities. These aggregating pressures intensified as conflicts widened, and workers themselves increasingly failed to
distinguish between "progressives" and "reactionaries" among their
bourgeois opponents.

PETROGRAD, MOSCOW, AND THE IMPLICATIONS
OF INDUSTRIAL CONCENTRATION

The great concentration of industrial production in prerevolutionary
Russia, both in terms of geographical location and plant size, was quite

St. Petersburg Metalworking Industry, 1901–1914," *Russian Review* 42 (1983), pp. 163–
90.

[30] Rieber, *Merchants and Entrepreneurs*, p. 347.

[31] See the discussion in Rieber, *Merchants and Entrepreneurs*, p. 331; V. Ia. Laverychev,
Po tu storonu barrikad (Iz istorii bor'by Moskovskoi burzhuazii s revoliutsiei) (Moscow,
1967), pp. 102–7; and Lewis H. Siegelbaum, *The Politics of Industrial Mobilization in
Russia, 1914–1917: A Study of the War-Industries Committees* (New York, 1983), chap.
3.

important in forging social bonds as well as in other respects. In 1913, more than 60 percent of the country's industrial workforce (excluding Poland) was concentrated in the Moscow and Petersburg industrial districts, regions accounting for only 18 percent of the total population.[32] By 1917, some dispersion had taken place, partly because whole plants in the western provinces were moved eastward out of the war zone: more than 100,000 workers were now located in the Volga region, for example, and some 171,000 were concentrated in the important Kharkov-Ekaterinoslav district. Yet the Central Industrial Region extending out from Moscow, the northern industrial district around Petrograd, and the southern industrial area still accounted for more than 60 percent of Russia's gross industrial production.[33]

The most important aspect of this geographical distribution had to do with the fact that the largest number of industrial workers in revolutionary Russia were thus concentrated around the country's two major centers of political administration. Russian industrial workers were in fact doubly concentrated here, since many workers within a given industry in the two capitals were also employed in very large plants. The five provinces with the largest numbers of industrial workers under factory inspection at the end of 1916 were Moscow, with 411,070; Petrograd, with 277,880; Vladimir, with its very large complement of textile workers, 205,000; Kostroma, with again, mainly textile workers, 97,430; and Kiev, with 83,710.[34] Together they accounted for more than half of all workers under the Inspectorate's supervision.

The city of Petrograd in early 1917 also presented a most remarkable picture in terms of industrial distribution. As table 1.4 indicates, of the nearly 400,000 industrial workers in the city at the beginning of 1917, some 237,000 were metalists. And among this most active group of workers, most (78 percent) were employed in plants with more than 500 workers, located largely in the Vyborg district, on Vasil'evskii Island, and in the Petrograd district between them.

According to statistics published in 1922, other industrial workers in the capital, perhaps as much as 82 percent of the workforce as a whole, were also largely employed in plants of over 500.[35] A large proportion of

[32] Tsentral'nyi statisticheskii komitet, *Statisticheskii ezhegodnik Rossii, 1913* (St. Petersburg, 1914), vol. 10, pt. 1, pp. 33–62; Kruze, *Polozhenie*, p. 47.

[33] L. S. Gaponenko, "Rossiiskii proletariat, ego chislennost' i territorial'noe razmeshchenie po osnovnym promyshlennym raionam nakanune sotsialisticheskoi revoliutsii," in *Rabochii klass i rabochee dvizhenie v Rossii v 1917 godu* (Moscow, 1964), pp. 14–48, especially pp. 41, 47. See also appendix 2, table 1.

[34] TSSU, *Trudy*, vol. 7, vyp. 1, p. 38.

[35] *Statisticheskii sbornik po Petrogradu i Petrogradskoi gubernii* (Petrograd, 1922), p. 50, as cited by Gaponenko, *Rabochii klass Rossii v 1917 godu* (Moscow, 1970), p. 106.

TABLE 1.4
Distribution of Industrial Enterprises under Factory Inspection in Petrograd and Moscow, 1917

Industry	Petrograd				Moscow			
	Number of Plants	Number of Workers	Percent of Labor Force	Average Number of Workers per Plant	Number of Plants	Number of Workers	Percent of Labor Force	Average Number of Workers per Plant
Minerals	32	3,900	1.0	122	20	1,690	0.8	85
Metals	379	237,369	60.4	626	302	56,927	27.6	189
Wood and wood products	81	6,754	1.7	83	54	1,964	1.0	36
Chemicals	58	40,087	10.2	691	52	24,220	11.8	466
Food products	70	15,773	4.0	225	82	22,856	11.1	279
Animal products (leather)	50	12,627	3.2	253	81	3,807	1.8	47
Textiles	100	44,115	11.2	441	252	76,130	37.0	302
Paper and printing	218	26,481	6.8	121	188	14,349	7.0	76
Other	23	5,722	1.5	249	28	3,976	1.9	142
Total	1,011	392,828	100.0	389	1,059	205,919	100.0	194

SOURCES: *Fabrichno-zavodskaia promyshlennost' goroda Moskvy i Moskovskoi gubernii, 1917–1927 gody* (Moscow, 1928), p. 1; Z. V. Stepanov, *Rabochie Petrograda v period podgotovki i provedeniia oktiabr' skogo vooruzhennogo vosstaniia* (Moscow and Leningrad, 1965), p. 29. Cf. Rashin, *Formirovanie*, p. 83.

new inhabitants in the decade before 1917 were peasants, many of whom took up the difficult burdens of common laborers in the hot shops of the metal plants, and many of whom continued to have access to land. (There was little difference, in fact, between the percentage of workers in the metal plants and in textiles possessing land.)[36] Others worked on the wharves, entered the textile factories, or found employment as laborers in the hazardous chemical and munitions plants. As the data on workers per plant in table 1.4 suggest, these industries also brought large numbers of workers under one roof and into direct contact with each other.

In contrast to Petrograd, Moscow in 1917 had a far greater concentration of textile workers, both in absolute and relative terms, although here, too, metalworkers had reached numerical dominance within the city limits by 1917. More important in comparison to Petrograd was the relative balance in Moscow of workers in different industries, a factor that helped cause Moscow workers to mobilize rather differently from their counterparts in Petrograd.[37]

Workers in other parts of Russia also worked in large plants, optimizing the utilization of scarce supervisory and managerial personnel, and permitting an efficient application of capital. According to A. G. Rashin, only about 7 percent of Russia's more than 11,000 industrial enterprises employed 500 or more workers in 1913, but they accounted for some 55 percent of the total work force. Particularly in the textile industry, where some manufacturers had installed the latest Western technology, enterprises tended to be quite large. Some 78 percent of the workforce in the cotton fabric sector, for example, was employed in plants of more than 1,000.[38]

Such patterns necessarily affected the labor movement. Concentration of industrial plants in Russia's major administrative centers, and within these cities in particular industrial districts like Vyborg, virtually invited industrial conflict to spread from plant to plant. News of unrest travelled almost at once through factory districts even without newspaper reports. Such concentration fostered a network of communication among workers, itself contributing to the process of class formation and a growing sense of class identity.

Moreover, the huge size of many plants intensified the nature of social interactions between workers and their employers. A shutdown of only two or three plants in the Vyborg district of Petrograd could turn thousands of workers onto the streets. When the Putilov plant closed in the

[36] S. A. Smith, *Red Petrograd: Revolution in the Factories, 1917–1918* (Cambridge, 1983), p. 18.
[37] Koenker, *Moscow Workers*, p. 94.
[38] Rashin, *Formirovanie*, pp. 98–101.

Narva district across the river, almost 30,000 workers were idled. And when the Danilov cotton spinning plant closed in Moscow for lack of fuel oil in January 1917, 5,400 workers and 6,600 dependents were suddenly without income, ostensibly because of inept planning by a handful of plant administrators. Similar processes could occur at the Sormovo complex in Nizhnii Novgorod, the locomotive works at Kharkov, or large plants like the Alafuzov leather and textile factories in Kazan.

Despite the risk of conflict, concentration clearly facilitated rapid industrial expansion, although it hardly overcame the obstacles to smooth and rapid growth. Geology, geography, and the critical problems of finance constantly intervened. Whereas most industrial production took place in the north, Russia's fuel production was concentrated in the south, far from the centers of industry. Transport, especially the railroad network, was thus a critical element in Russian development, and the very concentration of Russian industry created conditions in which strikes on the railroads themselves could threaten industrial production anywhere, as they had in 1905. Equally threatening was the danger of equipment failure or interruptions caused by bad weather. Thus Petrograd workers and others worried for good reason in wintertime, especially in the winter of 1916–1917, about supplies of raw materials necessary to keep them employed, foodstuffs, and other goods essential for personal welfare.

The Impact of the First World War on Production

Although historians are still debating the effect of World War I on the longer-term processes of Russian historical development, there is little doubt about its immediate impact. Virtually every element in Russia's social, political, and economic structure came under enormous pressure. Social movement and dislocation began to affect town and countryside alike in unprecedented magnitude. State institutions were overburdened from the start, even if few officials agreed with former Prime Minister Witte, whose "practical conclusion [was] that we must liquidate this stupid adventure as soon as possible."[39]

It is not necessary here to rehearse the war's effects in any detail. The government's lack of preparation for a long conflict is well known, and so are the main elements of Russia's growing general crisis. Central elements of the economy were affected immediately. Imports of critical raw materials like coal fell almost at once. Textile production had to turn

[39] George Maurice Paleologue, *An Ambassador's Memoirs, 1914–1917*, 3 vols. (London, 1923–25), vol. 1, p. 123.

within months to domestic supplies of cotton, already inadequate for many needs. Leather manufacturers lost their largest foreign buyer, Germany. Metal-processing plants, particularly those producing machine parts, instruments, electrical engines and the like, faced the loss of desperately needed machine tools from abroad. The statistics in virtually every category are staggering. Russian imports fell from 10.4 million tons in 1914 to some 3.8 million tons in 1915, to take just one example. Exports dropped even more.[40]

Scarcities and higher prices for imports naturally led to a rise in domestic prices and the cost of living. If workers managed to secure compensatory wage and salary increases, these in turn raised costs of production, which further increased prices. Mobilization drained some 6 million men from the urban and rural work force in the first year of hostilities alone, and led very rapidly to new problems in agrarian and industrial production and to the disruption of transport and social services. By January 1917, almost 15 million men had been inducted into the army. As many as 5.5 million may have become casualties.[41] Under the best of circumstances, Russia would have been hard pressed to overcome these losses.

Nor is it necessary to recapitulate in any detail the administrative burdens brought on by the war or the inadequacies of the regime's response. Like most other belligerents, Russia's governing apparatus was never structured to assume the enormous tasks thrust upon it. If Nicholas lacked both personal good judgment and competent advisors, he also faced a fragmented and partly antagonistic business community, as we have seen, some of whose members urgently insisted that the state come to its aid while others forcefully resisted regulatory intervention and even the smallest encroachment on established methods of doing business. The state confronted enormous needs for additional capital, but it also met determined opposition to new taxes. No one had sound or consistent fiscal advice.

At first, of course, none of these problems seemed insurmountable. In important ways the outbreak of war seemed to mitigate political and social conflict in Russia, as elsewhere. In late July 1914, virtually everyone in Moscow and Petrograd (as the capital was renamed) was momentarily a patriot. The importance of nation and citizenship was suddenly thrust to the fore, and the significance of being "Russian" seemed to overwhelm both particularistic social identities and antagonistic social relations.

Yet it was soon apparent that the war would affect different social

[40] A. L. Sidorov, *Ekonomicheskoe polozhenie*, pp. 363–67.
[41] Allan K. Wildman, *The End of the Russian Imperial Army: The Old Army and the Soldiers' Revolt* (Princeton, N.J., 1980), p. 95.

groups and different branches of production quite unevenly, even within the same industrial sector. The period between July 1914 and the spring of 1915 brought some dislocation almost everywhere, particularly as a result of fighting in Poland, mobilization, the disruption of transport, and the uncertainties of foreign trade. Within a relatively short period of time, however, the needs of the war itself began to have a strengthening effect on some industries. By the late spring of 1915, state resources were being mobilized to support defense production, and a reasonable system of deferments and exemptions for skilled workers began to be implemented. Regulatory commissions were created to supervise transport operations, fuel and food distribution, and overall defense production. The result of this state-sponsored mobilization was that a complex process of industrial segregation began to unfold, on the one hand separating favored industries from those the state was unable to protect (or that could not protect themselves), and on the other identifying for special consideration particular branches of production (and even particular plants) within the favored category itself.

The broadest patterns of segregation can be seen in terms of gross output. Although the best estimates of total industrial production for the 58 provinces of European Russia (excluding Poland), the Caucasus, Siberia, and Turkestan, made in the early 1920s, show a growth of some 1,211 million rubles between 1913 and 1916, or 21.5 percent, this was almost entirely the result of increased output in only two sectors, metals and chemicals. Metalworking plants alone accounted for an increase of 1,260 million rubles, and chemicals, for 541 million. Of the other major industries, only leather, linen, hemp and jute, and various clothing plants (including shoes) showed any increase whatsoever and accounted for only 8.3 percent of new output.

In all other industrial sectors output declined, in some branches, quite sharply. Mineral extraction and processing (including cement production, ceramics, and glassmaking) fell some 53 percent between 1913 and 1916, from an annual gross output of 154 million rubles to less than 90 million. Wood products declined 38 percent; the production of silk and paper, some 20 percent. Most dramatic and significant were the declines in Russia's two largest industrial branches, food processing and cotton textiles. In the food sector, output fell from 1,516 million rubles in 1913 to 1,176 million in 1916, or 22 percent. Cotton textiles fell from 1,091 million rubles to some 893 million, or a little more than 18 percent.[42]

[42] TSSU, *Trudy*, vol. 26, vyp. 2, "Fabrichno-zavodskaia promyshlennost' v period 1913–1918 godov" (Moscow, 1926), pp. 162–63. See also the discussion in N. Ia. Vorob'ev, "Izmeneniia v Russkoi promyshlennosti v period voiny i revoliutsii," *Vestnik Statistiki* 14 (1923), especially pp. 150–53.

Explanations for these different rates of growth and decline are not difficult to find. State resources obviously began to pour into weapons and armament production, traditionally the preserve of metalworking plants in Petrograd, and into the production of gunpowder and explosives, soon the major activity of the chemical industry. These sectors were also given priority in fuel and resource allocations and were the beneficiaries of virtually all new imports of machine tools, which came primarily from the United States (and were financed almost entirely by the state). They were also able to capitalize production with adequate loans or sales of stock. In contrast, both the output and profitability of less-favored industrial sectors suffered as resources became increasingly scarce. These sectors also became much less attractive for private investment.

These differences exacerbated the relative benefits of employment in one or another industrial branch and hence, to some extent, sharpened rather than reduced the importance of being a metalist or textile worker. Even within the metal trades the largest and most lucrative military contracts were bestowed at first by the state only on a relatively small number of major producers. In the fall of 1914, for example, contracts worth some 66 million rubles for shells and shrapnel were placed with only 16 plants, led by the Putilov, Baltic shipbuilding, Obukhov, Nevskii, and Petrograd metal works in Petrograd.[43] Small or medium-size producers were almost entirely neglected. In these circumstances, the importance of being a skilled metalist or an employee, at, say, the Nevskii or Obukhov plants, naturally increased, at least in terms of job security.

Thus in the metalworking industry alone, while gross output increased some 55 percent in plants receiving state contracts, the number of metalworking enterprises themselves shrank dramatically between 1914 and 1915, from 2,420 to 1,977, or 18.3 percent. The number of workers employed in the industry as a whole similarly declined by some 40,000. In chemicals, the number of plants went from 504 on January 1, 1914, to less than 390 one year later, and was even lower in 1916. The number of workers in chemicals declined from 82,000 to approximately 65,000 in 1916, despite increased output in the industry as a whole, and only began to increase later in the year. In South Russia, 25 percent of the blast furnaces operating in the metallurgical industry in 1915 had shut down in 1916, despite increased demand for iron and steel; of the 223 metallurgical plants operating in 1915 (excluding Poland), only 145 remained open on the eve of the revolution. According to statistics compiled by N. Vorob'ev for the Central Statistical Administration in 1926, some 356 major enterprises closed in 1914, 573 in 1915 and almost 300 in 1916.

---

[43]A. L. Sidorov, *Ekonomicheskoe polozhenie*, pp. 28–29.

Some of these, of course, reopened, but it is clear that the overall effect of the shift to military production even in favored industrial sectors remained highly destabilizing.[44]

Thus the economic bases for a sharp renewal of social conflict were created even as the war added strong state support for certain types of additional output. Demand for defense production, meanwhile, also increased more rapidly than production capacity. In the metals branch alone, for example, the state's demand for military goods on the eve of the February revolution was still some 16 percent above the industry's productive capacity. In chemicals and metallurgy, it was even higher. Hence job security for some workers also brought new pressure to increase output, and with it, a tendency to extend work hours, speed up production processes, and take additional risks with faulty equipment or unsafe working conditions. This especially affected new employees, largely women, children, and adolescents. In 1915, children and adolescents constituted a little more than 7 percent of the industrial work force but were involved in almost 15 percent of all accidents. The percent of illnesses and accidents in the large plants of the textile industry doubled between 1914 and 1916; in Ekaterinoslav, as many as 842 of every 1,000 workers became ill in the course of 1915, and 322 were injured.[45]

These distortions had other important consequences as well. It remained relatively risky, for example, and also relatively unprofitable, for mechanical plants to continue production of nonmilitary goods, despite the fact that many other plants depended on such equipment to fulfill their own military contracts. As orders for nonmilitary goods were left unfilled, and as older machinery or equipment began to wear out, not only did production itself decline, but productivity began to fall even more rapidly as workers were idled or forced to slow down as a result of inadequate equipment or supplies. Thus, while output per worker increased some 40 percent in the metal-processing and machine plants between 1915 and 1916, and some 32.5 percent in chemicals (almost entirely the result of new equipment), it fell by between 15 percent and 20 percent in almost all other industrial sectors, and more than 30 percent in the lumber mills and factories making wood products.[46]

Countervailing tendencies thus began to develop simultaneously in Russia after the outbreak of war, even within the same industrial locale. On the one hand, the particular circumstances of work and production affected different groups of workers more than they had earlier; on the

[44] TsSU, *Trudy*, vol. 26, vyp. 1, pp. 34–36.
[45] Laverychev, ed., *Rabochii klass*, pp. 268–69; Gaponenko, *Rabochii klass*, p. 202.
[46] TsSU, *Trudy*, vol. 26, vyp. 1, p. 38.

other, common pressures on all workers increased substantially, strengthening broader class identifications and focusing social conflict. A similar process occurred with employers. As industrial and manufacturing associations expanded during the war, differences between them in orientation and outlook increased, especially regarding workers. But so, too, did unifying concerns about the welfare of Russia as a whole, and hence efforts to contain social conflict, especially in Petrograd, where industrial output expanded more rapidly than any other place in the Empire. Yet the rate of factory closings expanded rapidly there also. Only the Kiev industrial region had as many plants shut down during the war as Petrograd, and nowhere did the intensity of concern about maintaining production reach the levels of the capital.[47]

CHANGING WORK ENVIRONMENTS

It is hardly surprising that these developments drastically affected the environment of work before February, although again, inconsistently, and in a variety of ways. Efforts to apply various systems of scientific management, which had long threatened workers' autonomy and their control over the pace and nature of work, now found new and concentrated application in support of the war in Russia, as they did elsewhere in Europe. The effects of rationalization on skilled armaments workers may have been somewhat less in Petrograd and Moscow than in Saxony, Berlin, or Paris, and labor discipline never became state policy in Russia as it did through the Industrial Mobilization Department in Italy, but like their comrades in the West, Russian workers everywhere felt great pressure to meet the demands of the war, and struggled with rising prices and shortages of goods.[48] By July 1916, the average prices for most items of

[47] M. M. Shmukker, *Ocherki finansov i ekonomiki zhelezno-dorozhnogo transporta Rossii za 1913–1922 gody* (Moscow, 1923), pp. 95–103; see also B. Grave, *K istorii klassovoi bor'by v Rossii v gody imperialisticheskoi voiny* (Moscow, 1926), pp. 16 ff.

[48] On Germany, see especially Heinrich Volkmann, "Modernisierung des Arbeitskampfs zum Formwandel von Streik und Aussperrung in Deutschland, 1864–1975," in *Probleme der Modernisierung in Deutschland: Sozialhistorische Studien zum 19. und 20. Jahrhundert*, ed. Hartmut Kaelble et al. (Opladen, 1978), pp. 110–70; Heinrich Potthoff, *Gewerkschaften und Politik zwischen Revolution und Inflation* (Düsseldorf, 1979); and Dick Geary, "Radicalism and the German Worker: Metalworkers and Revolution, 1914–1923," in *Society and Politics in Wilhelmine Germany*, ed. Richard J. Evans (London, 1978). Rationalization in France is discussed by Gary Cross, "Redefining Workers' Control: Rationalization, Labor Time, and Union Politics in France, 1900–1928," in *Work, Community, and Power: The Experience of Labor in Europe and America, 1900–1925*, ed. James E. Cronin and Carmen Sirianni, (Philadelphia, 1983), pp. 143–72. On state intervention in Italy, see especially L. Tomassini, "Industrial Mobilization and State Intervention in Italy during World War I: Effects on Labor Unrest," in Sapelli and Haimson, eds., *War, Strikes,*

primary necessity had more than doubled in Russia since 1913, a rate of increase greater than that of any other major belligerent.[49]

Some of the most dramatic changes took place in Petrograd and Petrograd province. The total number of industrial workers here grew by more than 50 percent during the war. Chemical workers increased by almost 75 percent; metalists, by more than 130 percent; and the number of workers in service occupations, like doormen, cab drivers, dockworkers, haulers, office employees and railroad workers, by as much as 700 percent. Thousands of garrison soldiers and hordes of new government workers swelled Petrograd even more, straining city services and stretching housing and living conditions to the limit. Moscow, Kharkov, Baku, and a number of smaller industrial towns found themselves under similar pressures, but none as serious as the capital's.[50]

The demand for work, however, was as uneven as the economic vitality of Russian industry itself, even in Petrograd. The evidence indicates that at least one-third of all employed workers left their jobs for one reason or another between 1914 and 1917. Many went to higher-paying jobs, and some were drafted (although work by the Soviet historian O. I. Shkaratan suggests that the share of the workforce lost to conscription is probably much lower than has been assumed, and in Petrograd, may have been less than 17 percent).[51] But many more changed jobs because plants they were working in shut down, or because the pressures of work became otherwise untenable. Some 9,000 left the Putilov plant alone in 1915, for instance, despite the fact that the overall size of the workforce here was expanding rapidly. At the Treugol'nik rubber plant in the nearby Narva district, the number of workers replaced in 1915 exceeded 10,000![52] If we lack precise figures on these changes, their dynamics are still quite extraordinary. In Russia as a whole, at least one-third of all workers employed in January 1914 left their jobs between the outbreak of war and February 1917. More than 300,000 workers, mostly unskilled, filed

---

and Revolution. See also Dick Geary, *European Labor Protest, 1848–1939* (New York, 1981), chap. 4.

[49] See James E. Cronin, "Labor Insurgency and Class Formation: Comparative Perspectives on the Crisis of 1917–1920 in Europe," in Cronin and Sirianni, eds., *Work, Community, and Power,* pp. 28–29; S. O. Zagorsky, *State Control of Industry in Russia during the War* (New Haven, Conn., 1928), pp. 58–63; A. L. Sidorov, *Ekonomicheskoe polozhenie,* pp. 349–423.

[50] Gaponenko, *Rabochii klass,* pp. 103–7.

[51] O. I. Shkaratan, *Problemy sotsial'noi struktury rabochego klassa SSSR* (Moscow, 1970), pp. 199–204.

[52] K. F. Sidorov, "Rabochee dvizhenie v Rossii v gody imperialisticheskoi voiny," in *Ocherki po istorii oktiabr'skoi revoliutsii,* ed. M. N. Pokrovskii (Moscow and Leningrad, 1927), vol. 1, p. 217.

through the Moscow labor exchange alone between October 1915 and June 1916, its first nine months of operation.[53]

This enormous movement was accompanied by significant changes in the social composition of the workforce, as well as major changes in factory size. In Petrograd, the handful of leading plants that first received government defense contracts expanded in almost geometric proportions. The five largest[54] soon employed more than 80,000 workers; the seventeen largest, more than 165,000.[55] By January 1, 1917, only some 7 percent of all enterprises in Petrograd employed more than 1,000 workers, but their employees still constituted more than 65 percent of the total work force, a quite remarkable degree of concentration.[56] Similar patterns developed elsewhere, although to a lesser degree. The Bromley and Dinamo plants in Moscow, the Sormovo works in Nizhnii Novgorod, the Briansk steel works in Ekaterinoslav, and other enterprises favored with large defense contracts also took on thousands of new workers almost overnight, again, with virtually no expansion whatsoever in even the most essential social services. Workers in the Vyborg and Narva districts in Petrograd, in Moscow's Zamoskvoreche district, in Baku, Kharkov, and other industrial centers literally found themselves living and working on top of each other as a result of this expansion, elbowed and shoved for apartment space, food, advantageous shift assignments, and better-paid positions. And in plants forced to shut down, even only temporarily, tens of thousands of other workers found themselves forced to pack up, leave their apartments or dormitories to look for new jobs, and worry about being drafted into the army.

Women and younger workers, meanwhile, began to enter the work force in great numbers, even though skilled trades, offering premium wages and now ever more highly concentrated in metals, metallurgy and chemicals, remained almost entirely male. Like other European countries, the largest number of Russian workers in 1917 were between the ages of 20 and 40, but it was also this age group that felt the war's impact most greatly. The best estimates of the war's effect on male workers in general were made in early 1921 by N. Vorob'ev, using 1918 data. By his calculations, the percentage of male workers between the ages of 20 and 39 fell between 1897 and 1917 from nearly 58 percent to 45 percent, while the percentage of workers 40 or over rose by more than a third. Similarly,

---

[53] Ibid., p. 226.

[54] The five were Putilov, Petrograd Pipe, Treugol'nik Rubber, Obukhov, and Okhta Explosives.

[55] A. L. Sidorov, *Ekonomicheskoe polozhenie*, p. 415.

[56] I. P. Leiberov, "Petrogradskii proletariat v bor'be za pobedu fevral'skoi burzhuazno-demokraticheskoi revoliutsii v Rossii," *Istoriia sssr* 1 (1957), p. 43.

the number of male workers under age 17 rose from 5.9 percent to 6.4 percent.[57] In Petrograd and Moscow, the percentage declines in the 20–39 age group were even greater.[58] Overall, the share of boys and girls under age 17 in the work force rose during the war from 10.5 percent in 1914 to 14 percent in 1917, as indicated in figure 1.1.

Age-distribution figures cloak somewhat the relative increase in the number of women in the workforce, however, as well as the differential

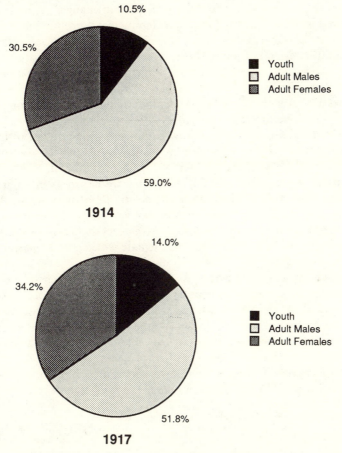

1914

1917

Figure 1.1 Age and Sex Distribution of Workers, 1914 and 1917
Source: tssu, *Trudy*, vol. 7, vyp. 1, pp. 3–39.

[57] Vorob'ev, "Izmeneniia," pp. 142–44.
[58] Ibid., p. 144; tssu, *Trudy*, vol. 7, vyp. 1, pp. 3–39. See also Smith, *Red Petrograd*, pp. 25–26.

impact of mobilization on different branches of industry. Although skilled men tended to be exempted from military service, the demand for labor power increased during the war much faster than it could be filled by males alone. In industrial production, the proportion of women among workers rose from 30.5 percent in 1914 to 34.2 percent at the start of 1917. Women also poured into nonfactory occupations, especially domestic clothing production, retail trade, and services. Textiles, chemicals, and the paper industries continued to employ the largest share of women, as they had before the war, but big changes in the sex ratio occurred in every industrial group, including metal production.[59]

The implications of this shift, however, are not entirely clear. For wives of absent soldiers, entry into the labor force may have constituted a real hardship, complicating their already difficult lives. For young unmarried women, the demand for wartime labor offered new and welcome opportunities and probably raised their standard of living. In the region around Moscow, for example, peasant girls, who before the war had earned 15 kopecks a day in textile mills, now could earn a daily wage of up to a ruble in unskilled jobs in munitions plants, and some could afford the luxury of silk dresses and perfume.[60] On the other hand, environments dominated by experienced male workers were clearly being diluted by workers new both to production and to the labor movement. And as women and youngsters began to enter the work force in great numbers, overall pressures to raise production were exacerbated by new tensions, particularly in relations between new female workers and their male supervisors.

The war also affected wages. As figure 1.2 indicates, Russian workers certainly participated in the country's increased prosperity between 1900 and 1913 through increased wages, although most of the rise observed between 1900 and 1913 took place in the first six years of the century, and the biggest increases came in 1906 and 1907 during Russia's first great wave of strikes.

Complicating the picture, however, is the relationship of money wages to the rising prices of goods and services.[61] Careful reconstruction of con-

[59] TSSU, *Trudy*, vol. 7, vyp. 1, pp. 4–37, 39.

[60] Eduard Dune, "Zapiski krasnogvardeitsa," MS, Nicolaevsky Collection, Hoover Institution, on War, Revolution, and Peace, p. 5.

[61] Unfortunately, information on prices and workers' budgets is even less straightforward than wage data. Prices varied significantly across the empire, and changes did not occur uniformly over time. Aggregate figures for all of Russia, compiled by Strumilin, suggest that real wages rose only modestly between 1900 and 1914 and that real wages actually declined during the 1905 revolution from a peak in 1903. Such aggregate figures, however, are notoriously sensitive to the choice of statistical techniques and can only be generally suggestive of trends. Moreover, regional variation was substantial but difficult to measure because of

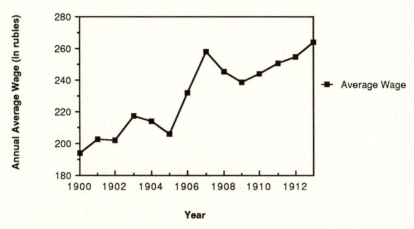

Figure 1.2 Movement of Wages, 1900–1913
SOURCE: Kruze, *Polozhenie*, p. 191.

temporary data by the Soviet historian Iu. I. Kir'ianov indicates that in aggregate terms, real wages generally increased between 1900 and 1914, only modestly in St. Petersburg before the war, but more substantially in Moscow province.[62] Many Russian workers were probably better off in 1913 than they were in 1900, even if the overall material position of the vast majority, especially in the capitals, very much worried local authorities and strained relations with the tsarist regime.[63]

The outbreak of war, however, brought new changes in wage patterns, as indicated in figure 1.3. These were also undoubtedly related to the in-

the absence of comparable data on local prices. See Kruze, *Polozhenie*, p. 215; S. G. Strumilin, "Dinamika tsen za 1918–1922," in *Izbrannye proizvedeniia* (Moscow, 1963), vol. 1, pp. 197–213.

[62] Kir'ianov, *Zhiznennyi uroven'*, p. 132. How well off Russian workers were in comparison with workers elsewhere in the capitalist world and in terms of nonpecuniary factors is, of course, another question. Wages in Russia were much lower than in Western Europe or the United States, although comparisons are difficult to make. Russian male heads of household could not support their families by their earnings alone, and a far greater proportion of married women worked for wages in Russia than in either England or Germany. (See Kir'ianov, *Zhiznennyi uroven'*, pp 147–49.) In Western Europe, women normally worked only until marriage and then dropped out of the labor force. Whether this difference represented acute need, rising budgetary expectations, or cultural differences is an interesting question, but one that cannot be answered with the evidence at hand. Nonetheless, the welfare of a working-class family in which mothers were employed outside the home—over half of women workers in Russia were married, compared to 20 percent in Germany—was likely to be inferior to that of families in which mothers worked at home.

[63] See *Usloviia byta rabochikh v dorevoliutsionnoi Rossii (po dannym biudzhetnykh obsledovanii)* (Moscow, 1958); Thurston, *Liberal City*, and Kruze, *Polozhenie*, pp. 214–42.

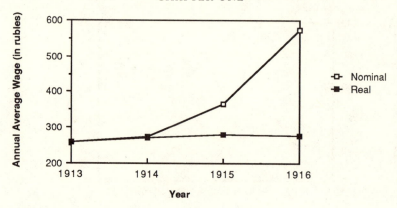

Figure 1.3 Movement of Wages, 1913–1916
SOURCE: TSSU, *Trudy*, vol. 26, vyp. 1, table 14, pp. 153–55.

flux of women and younger workers, although they reflected as well the sharp differences in economic well-being experienced by different industrial sectors.[64] Nominal wages for all workers increased some 34 percent by the end of 1915 compared to 1913 and more than doubled by the end of 1916. But real wages declined by some 15 percent overall, and by as much as 20–25 percent in mineral production, printing, silk and paper manufacturing.

Even more important, although real wages on the eve of the revolution had increased relative to 1913 in metals, chemicals, leather, and even certain branches of textile production, they had reached their peak in 1915. In 1916 real wages declined virtually across the board; with Russia's growing economic crisis, they threatened to fall even more. In the mechanical and machine-building trades, for example, real wages in 1916 were 9 percent higher than they had been in 1913, but 7 percent lower than in 1915; in leather production, they were 8 percent above 1913 levels, but 9.3 percent lower than in 1915. Only chemical workers, miners, and metallurgical industry workers enjoyed real wage increases of more than a few rubles in 1916 in comparison to the previous year, and in mining, the increase was still less than workers had earned before the war.

The years 1914–1916 were thus a time of both rising expectations and major disappointments for Russian workers even in favored industries, and a period of unremitting hardship for many printers, mineral industry workers, and workers in silk, wool, and paper manufacturing, whose real

[64] Since women in all industries received lower wages than men in the same job categories, the figures hide somewhat both the decline in real per capita wages that occurred as a result of the influx of women and the real savings achieved by manufacturers in wage costs, but the overall patterns are clear.

wages steadily declined. And both tendencies were felt keenly even in Petrograd, where average monthly real wages were estimated to be approximately the same for workers in 1916 as in 1913, but had fallen some 11 percent from what they had been in 1915.[65]

Significant variations in wage changes also occurred between different groups of workers within the same industry, and between equally skilled workers in one industry compared to another or in different geographical regions. In general, Petrograd workers received the highest wages, and highly skilled workers such as metal craftsmen received wages at rates of three to four times the level earned by the least well-paid employees within the same plant. Again, however, if wage differentials remained great during the war, the purchasing power even of relatively high wages was eroded by rising prices, the introduction of price controls, and growing scarcities, which sapped workers' time as well as money. There is also inconclusive evidence that some groups of highly skilled workers did not necessarily earn the greatest increases during the war, either in nominal or real terms, in comparison to their less-skilled comrades.[66]

Industrialists and manufacturers could (and did) forestall worker discontent in their own plants with further wage increases, but this only diverted anger over rising prices and lengthening food lines toward targets outside the factory walls. Nicholas and his ministers were not, of course, directly responsible for rising prices, but it was natural for workers to look to them for relief and reasonable to assume that more competent state officials might be able to overcome the worst problems in transport and supply.

Shortages in Moscow and Petrograd were particularly difficult for workers. According to a survey taken in Moscow at the beginning of 1915, metalworkers were spending some 74 percent of their family wages on food and clothing, and textile workers, as much as 105 percent—more, that is, than their recorded income. A third of all metalworkers did not eat meat on a daily basis; some 12 percent were living off their savings.[67] The situation in Petrograd was similar. Supplies to the capital were more uncertain, partly as a result of transport problems, particularly in the winter, partly because of the rapidly expanding urban population. If the prices of essential goods in Moscow rose 131 percent between 1914 and mid-1916, according to government figures, the increase in Petrograd exceeded 150 percent.[68] According to one account, rents and lease pay-

---

[65] B. Grave, *K istorii*, p. 53.

[66] See, e.g., R. Arskii, "Rabochii klass vo vremia voiny," *Trud v Rossii*, 1 (1925), pp. 28–29.

[67] M. Balabanov, "Rabochii klass nakanune revoliutsii," in *Professional'noe dvizhenie v Petrograde v 1917 godu*, ed. A. Anskii (Leningrad, 1928), p. 15.

[68] K. F. Sidorov, "Rabochee dvizhenie," pp. 232–34.

ments rose in some parts of the city by as much as 300 percent.[69] Defense production also meant longer hours and even compulsory overtime. Many could ill afford the time to stand in long lines for food or other essentials, or did so utterly exhausted, and, as the weather grew cold, at considerable cost to their physical well-being.

At the same time, however, wage increases could only partly deflect dissidence away from manufacturers and industrialists. The increasing harshness of work conditions everywhere, even in favored industries like the metal trades, very much undercut the status conferred by higher wages. Industrialists under pressure to fulfill state defense contracts soon introduced strict new regimens in their plants, leveling increased fines for lateness and other similar offenses, and requiring a longer workday in many places even at basic pay rates. In 1915, the PSFMO raised with the Ministry of War the possibility of militarizing certain private factories as a way of maintaining discipline; after a long and often bitter dispute, the massive Putilov works was sequestered by the War Ministry in February 1916, largely because of concerns about worker unrest.[70]

Industrialists and their plant administrators also had the power in many places to send dissident workers directly into the army, and sometimes used it against strikers, especially if they felt they could do so without great costs to productivity. A more common response, particularly to strikes, was simply to close plants down and reopen them only after a new complement of workers had been hired. There were obvious limits to this tactic, and the evidence suggests that local authorities were reluctant to condone it, despite circulars of support in 1916 from the Ministry of Internal Affairs.[71] Nevertheless, groups of dissident workers were drafted from the Putilov plant, as well as from others in 1916, and the device of dismissing and rehiring all employees was utilized especially in smaller enterprises on the eve of the revolution both in Petrograd and Moscow, as well as elsewhere. In the Gorlovsko-Shcherbinskii district of the Don region, some 1,000 striking miners of military age were arrested and sent to the front in May 1916.[72]

As elsewhere in Europe, especially Italy and Germany, all of this obviously affected Russian workers' sense of well-being during the war and raised anxieties about the future. As economic strains increased, loyalties to the government obviously weakened along with patriotic feelings and

[69] Arskii, "Rabochii klass," pp. 19–20. See also Leiberov, "Petrogradskii proletariat," pp. 45–46.

[70] See the discussion in A. L. Sidorov, *Ekonomicheskoe polozhenie*, pp. 126–32.

[71] See, e.g, *Birzhevyia Vedomosti*, April 8, 1916; V. Grave, *K istorii*, p. 10.

[72] Iu. I. Kir'ianov, *Rabochie iuga Rossii, 1914–fevral' 1917 goda* (Moscow, 1971), p. 252.

the power of common national or civic identities. The importance of changing work environments during these months was thus not simply that new circumstances created new grounds for protest, but also that they kindled or strengthened class identities, and tied a sense of well-being directly to workplace conditions. One's role in production in wartime Russia, one's source of income, access to essential goods and services, and dependency on employment all reinforced one's sense of what it meant to be a "worker," and hence strengthened the basis for new collective action.

THE GENERAL PATTERN OF WARTIME STRIKES

The sharp repression of striking Don miners in May 1916 was part of the tsarist regime's failing effort to contain what was, in effect, the third great strike wave of the prerevolutionary period, rivalling those of 1905–1907 and 1912–1914. Before the year was out, more than 957,000 industrial workers, the largest number since 1906, had left their benches in strikes over wages, hours, working conditions, and political issues.

The nature of these strikes and their relation to the broader patterns of development we have outlined is only now becoming clear. Using sophisticated statistical techniques and a painstaking strike-by-strike reconstruction of the data, Leopold Haimson is developing a vivid picture of the interconnections between industrial concentration, wage levels, and the intensity of labor protests during all three major periods of prerevolutionary unrest.[73] With his work as reference, we can limit ourselves here to the briefest of outlines, sufficient only to permit an examination in the following chapter of how the overall patterns of strikes between February and October 1917 related to those during the war.

In broadest contour one must recognize, first, that in terms of labor protests, the outbreak of war at the end of July 1914 came at a very opportune time for the tsarist regime, despite its lack of military, economic, or political preparedness. As we have noted, 1912 and 1913 were years of enormous resurgence in Russian labor protests, symptomatic of a new revolutionary crisis. The first seven months of 1914 brought strikes and protests to a pitch comparable to 1905. When the war came in July, it acted to quell a floodtide of labor protest.

One can appreciate both the absolute and relative magnitude of labor

[73] Haimson and Petrusha, "Two Strike Waves"; Leopold H. Haimson and Eric Brian, "Labor Unrest in Imperial Russia during the First World War: A Quantitative Analysis and Interpretation," in Sapelli and Haimson, eds., *War, Strikes, and Revolution*; Leopold H. Haimson with Eric Brian, "Changements démographiques et grèves ouvrières à Saint-Pétersbourg, 1905–1914," *Annales: Économies, Sociétés, Civilisations* 4 (July–August 1985), pp. 781–803.

protests in 1912–1914, and more important for our purposes, the contrasting quietude which followed, from the data assembled in table 1.5. (Additional data for the 1895–1917 period appear in appendix 2, table 2.) Most significant here are the absolute numbers of both strikes and strikers in the first half of 1914, in contrast to the period from August to December and afterwards, and the changing intensity of Russian workers' participation in strikes as the war progressed, measured as the percentage of the total industrial labor force on strike.

The absolute numbers themselves are remarkable. Table 1.5 shows that some 1,327,897 industrial workers went on strike in 1914 between January and the end of July, approximately 67 percent of the country's entire industrial workforce under the aegis of the Factory Inspectorate. In sharp contrast, 9,561 workers in a mere 41 industrial plants went on strike in the months following the outbreak of hostilities, the lowest number for any comparable period since 1904.

Table 1.5 indicates, however, that by the end of 1915, the level of strike intensity among industrial workers was moving rapidly toward prewar levels. As we will see more clearly in chapter 2, most protests in 1915 were directed against employers. But after police killed and wounded

TABLE 1.5
Strikes and Strikers in Enterprises under Factory Inspection, 1912–1916

	Number of Strikes	Number of Strikers	Strike Intensity[a]
1912	2,032	725,491	.358
1913	2,404	887,062	.452
1914 (Jan.–Jul.)	3,493	1,327,897	.677
1914 (Aug.–Dec.)	41	9,561	.005
1915	928	539,528	.280
1916	1,288	957,075	.498

SOURCES:
1912: Iakovleva, "Zabastovochnoe dvizhenie," p. 61.
1913: TSSU, *Trudy*, vol. 7, vyp. 1, pp. 132–35; *Dinamiki rossiiskoi i sovetskoi promyshlennosti*, vol. 1, pt. 3, pp. 176–77. For 1913, Iakovleva gives 887,096.
1914: TSSU, *Trudy*, vol. 7, vyp. 1, pp. 37, 142–45.
1915: Ibid., pp. 37, 152–55.
1916: Ibid., pp. 37, 162–63. See note to Appendix 2, Table A.2, for 1916 variations.
NOTE: Enterprises under factory inspection are mechanized enterprises or those employing more than 15 workers.
[a] Strike force as a percentage of workforce.

scores of striking textile workers in Kostroma in June, political protests increased.[74] September 1915 witnessed the sharpest outbreak of political strikes since the beginning of the war, involving more than 87,000 workers; whereas summer strikes in 1915 involved only textile workers and metalists, the September strikes, now overwhelmingly dominated by the metalists, also included workers from every major industrial sector except chemicals.[75] As Haimson has argued, these strikes mark the beginning of Russia's third great prerevolutionary strike wave, leading to the February revolution.

Table 1.5 shows just how extensive strike activity soon became. Considering Russia's wartime circumstances and the serious risks strikes involved, 1916 was a year of extraordinary activism. The level of strike intensity among industrial workers exceeded that of 1912 and 1913, and the rate of increase compared to the beginning of the war strongly indicated that workers were no longer willing to put the state's needs before their own. As we will see more closely in chapter 2, most workers continued to leave their plants over manifestly economic issues, insisting on wage increases or changes in factory conditions. The center of this new storm remained the politically volatile Vyborg district of Petrograd, however, where comparatively well-paid and politically conscious metalists took advantage of their more secure positions and went on strike reasonably confident their employers and the state would want them quickly back at work. And as political demonstrative strikes increased in 1916, they, too, were increasingly concentrated among militant Vyborg workers in machine-construction and metal-fabricating plants. Of the 119 political strikes reported for October 1916, for example, 115 took place in conjunction with food shortages in this district alone. These occurred between October 17 and 29 in the Langenzippen and Dinamo plants, and in the Semenov, Nobel, Aivaz, New Lessner, Phoenix, and Baranovskii metal works, many of whose workers struck two or three times each, according to detailed police accounts.[76]

Haimson's seminal work shows this concentration's fundamental im-

[74] The textilists had earlier unsuccessfully petitioned the regime to have their plants nationalized, hoping to protect themselves against further reductions in wages and deteriorating working conditions. They were now protesting increased costs for the housing controlled by their factories. According to a Duma enquiry, 12 were killed and almost 50 wounded. See M. G. Fleer, ed., *Rabochee dvizhenie v gody voiny* (Moscow, 1925), pp. 207–14.

[75] TSSU, *Trudy*, vol. 7, vyp. 1, pp. 154–55. Metalists constituted 78 percent of the September strike force.

[76] Fleer, *Rabochee dvizhenie*, pp. 95–96, 192, and especially pp. 323–26, a document entitled "Otnoshenie otdeleniia po okhraneniiu obshchestvennoi bezopasnosti i poriadka v stolitse ot 20 fevralia 1917 g. No. 5542." Most of these strikes lasted less than a day, none more than three.

portance to tsarist society and politics before 1917, and demonstrates its structural linkage to Russia's broader patterns of demographic and socio-economic change. Contrasting these strikes with those of the 1905–1907 and 1912–1914 periods also allows Haimson to show the importance of factory size, urban concentration, and especially wage levels to strike activity; his qualitative analysis, along with that of Heather Hogan, suggests the powerful role of changes in work processes, particularly efforts to rationalize and modernize metals production.[77] There can be little question that the collective action of militant and politically aware Petrograd metalworkers thus brought about Russia's revolutionary situation on the eve of 1917, however much this crisis was also the result of longer-term structural faults in Russia's socioeconomic and sociopolitical development and the remarkable political ineptitude of the tsarist regime.

At the same time, however, the implications of this situation for the future were quite unclear. Industrial conflict outside of Vyborg was not necessarily inimical to social order or political stability. Strikes and other forms of protest that focused on individual enterprises were essentially an extreme form of management-labor negotiations in tsarist Russia, as they were elsewhere, even as they grew in scope and intensity; there was certainly reason to assume, as some members of the business community themselves recognized, that if the activism of labor and management *both* could take place within mutually recognized legal boundaries, labor conflict in Russia could assume the "legitimate" forms it largely had in Western Europe and the United States.

Yet strikes and labor conflict in the months before the February revolution had necessarily sharpened class identities as well, largely in antagonistic terms. For many on both sides of the labor-management divide, the growing differences in class interests seemed much clearer than they had in 1905, even as a broad and collective interest in bringing a responsible, democratic government to Russia also gained strength. For the moment, particularistic identities and class outlooks on the part of workers and their employers alike were both largely subordinated to a more pressing common struggle against the state. That the struggle was being waged for different reasons largely defined the political tasks ahead.

[77] Haimson and Brian, "Labor Unrest"; Hogan, "Industrial Rationalization," pp. 163–90.

2

. . . .

STRIKES IN 1917:

AN OVERVIEW

Throughout the industrialized world, strikes and other forms of workplace activism invariably challenge prevailing social orders by contesting power and control within the workplace, and sometimes beyond. This is true of strikes in relatively stable political systems, in which workers often press the limits of managerial control over resources, workplace rules, and the ways wages are determined, but it is even more obvious in historical circumstances in which the prevailing contours of power and authority in society at large are fundamentally threatened, circumstances often described as "revolutionary situations." Such was the case throughout Europe in the last years of the First World War and the years immediately following, when strikes and social conflict reached unprecedented levels virtually across the continent. In most cases, the old structures and institutions bent and adjusted to the challenges of labor but ultimately held firm, in some measure because of the inherent flexibility of dominant liberal institutions. Uniquely in Russia, strikes and other forms of labor protest led to the collapse of fundamental political and social institutions.

The February revolution radically altered the context of Russian labor protest. As the Provisional Government came to power, sharing authority with a burgeoning network of workers' and soldiers' soviets, strikes and other forms of labor activism no longer simply challenged prevailing social and political systems, but contributed to the very definition of the new order itself, structuring and defining new relationships of power and authority inside the workplace and out. In one sense, everything in Russia after the fall of the tsar was "up for grabs." The February revolution brought new democratic institutions but also strengthened skepticism about their effectiveness and value from those who felt their economic and social well-being depended on a strong, supportive state. Even such a fundamental notion as "property" was ill-defined, especially in the countryside and in the huge state-owned plants that dominated defense production. Peasant conceptions about rights to land were largely unencumbered with legal notions of entitlement and conveyance; many workers whose welfare depended on continued and effective industrial production now began to feel a plant should be theirs, particularly when its owners tried to shut it down. Also, social values in revolutionary Russia were much more often expressed in actions than in words. No constitution or Magna Carta molded a collective state consciousness. And although all collective actions necessarily reflect some value system, the centrality of strikes to Russia in 1917 lay in the fact that the political process itself knew no formal or constraining boundaries. Activist workers thus created and then constantly reset the frontiers of political and social struggle, redefining norms and values at the very moment their strikes and protests were also structuring the new order's political institutions and socioeconomic relationships.

What shaped the limits of activism after February, as before, were economic circumstance, organization, tradition, and what might roughly be called a "sense of the possible."[1] Economic and social conditions, especially the availability of raw materials, orders, markets and equipment, clearly continued to affect the types of actions in which both workers and managers chose to engage, even as such activism also stimulated new protests. Memories of past strikes also carried both restraining and energizing influences. Worker and managerial organizations were important facilitators but also provided a leadership that could (and did) impose restraints. Most important, the complex tactical judgments of activists themselves necessarily mediated patterns of protest, although in ways always less obvious than their behavior.

The new institutional setting also shaped the limits of activist behavior. Workers in tsarist Russia had struggled for their rights and welfare within a system that had been alternately paternalistic and repressive, but, except at the national level of nominal Duma representation, they had no means of participation in the bureaucratic structure that addressed their grievances. Workers were likewise excluded from the limited forms of local self-government that brought landowners and the urban bourgeoisie into the arena of civic responsibility.

With the fall of the old regime, many tsarist administrators remained in their offices, but the bureaucratic system lost its monopoly of power. The notion of "dual power" shared or contested between a Provisional Government reflecting bourgeois interests and a hierarchy of soviets led by Petrograd and representing the common people portrays too neatly the burgeoning of new institutions and the resulting confusion in lines of au-

---

[1] The best discussion of collective action, and one to which we owe a substantial intellectual debt, is Charles Tilly, *From Mobilization to Revolution* (Reading, Mass., 1978).

thority and responsibility. The notion of dual power likewise poses the reality of "class struggle" too starkly, especially in the weeks immediately after February. In effect, both major contenders for power in the workplace were confronted throughout 1917 with the need to find appropriate new ways to achieve their goals, methods whose relationship to the democratic values, principles, and institutions of the new revolutionary order would critically affect its development.

In this context, strikes took on new and more complicated meaning. While in some respects they remained very much ordinary phenomena in 1917, common to all industrial societies and a central element of labor-management negotiations in all bourgeois democracies, they also continued to be part and parcel of an ongoing revolutionary process, setting the form and shape of social and political relations that were not themselves well established or even especially well defined. The difficult task historically is to discern what was "ordinary" and "revolutionary" about strikes during 1917, and to analyze how they themselves contributed to the ultimate fate of the new order.

We will attempt to do this in the following chapters by looking closely at worker mobilization, management-labor relations, strikers' demands and the rhetoric of protest, and especially the changing pattern of these elements at moments of high strike activity. Before doing so, however, we must look briefly at the year as a whole and analyse how the aggregate patterns of strikes in 1917 reflected continuities and departures from what came before.

THE STRIKE UNIVERSE IN 1917: PROBLEMS OF MEASUREMENT AND COMPARISON

As we have indicated, for the period between March 3, when the Grand Duke Mikhail Aleksandrovich refused the throne and the Provisional Government formally took power, and October 25, when the Second Congress of Soviets endorsed the Bolshevik takeover, we count 1,019 strikes of all sorts occurring in the territory under Provisional Government control. Some 60 percent involved individual enterprises. The remainder were multienterprise strikes, or strikes involving workers from a variety of different establishments. Our minimum estimate is that more than 2,441,000 strikers were involved in these protests; we calculate very conservatively the number of likely participants only in those cases in which we feel reasonable estimates of strikers can be made.

Determining how these figures compare to those of the immediate prerevolutionary period is not simple, for the two sets of data are not precisely comparable. As we detail in our Note on Methodology in appendix

1, factory inspectors before February counted as a single strike every instance in which workers in an enterprise left their benches, even if a number of factories were actually striking together for a common set of demands. (Strike statistics in Western Europe were also gathered in this fashion.) Tsarist strike data was also limited to mechanized plants or plants employing more than 15 workers and excluded mines, state-owned plants, and all nonindustrial enterprises, a very considerable number.[2] This method of accounting was well suited to the needs of the tsarist Ministry of Trade and Industry as well as to the police, since it kept close tabs on workers on a plant-by-plant basis. It made some sense as well in terms of the general nature of strikes themselves before 1917, especially during the war, when agitating for strikes was illegal, and relatively few economic strikes occurred involving more than one enterprise in a single, coordinated walkout.

After February, however, political liberties changed not only the context in which strikes could be organized, but also the ways in which they were reported. The Factory Inspectorate continued to function almost everywhere for a period of weeks, and in some places for a number of months, supervised initially by the Provisional Government's new minister of trade and industry, the liberal industrialist Alexander Ivanovich Konovalov. Where possible, inspectors continued to record strikes on an enterprise-by-enterprise basis, sending handwritten or typed accounts to the ministry. But just as workers in different plants could now readily join together to press common demands more forcefully and to ensure that comrades in different enterprises were not treated less favorably than fellow workers elsewhere, so the process of reporting strikes largely shifted from the Factory Inspectorate to the press, which might record striking tailors in Pskov, hotel workers in Piatigorsk, or leather workers from a number of different shops in Kazan as involved in single strikes if they quit work together; little effort was made by the press to ascertain precisely how many enterprises were involved. Strikes also spread rapidly into nonindustrial sectors, especially the service trades. Counting the number of enterprises here was often impossible.

As we have noted in the introduction, the most appropriate unit of measurement for strikes in 1917, and one the data itself compels us to use in drawing aggregate pictures, is thus not the individual enterprise, but

[2] On January 1, 1917, there were 12,492 enterprises subject to factory inspection, according to TSSU, *Trudy*, vol. 7, vyp. 1, "Statisticheskii sbornik za 1913–1917" (Moscow, 1921), table 4, p. 39. In contrast, the 1913 compilation of the Congress of Trade and Industry, Sovet s"ezdov predstavitelei promyshlennosti i torgovlia, Peterburg, *Fabrichno-zavodskiia predpriiatiia Rossiiskoi imperii* (Petrograd, 1914), lists 27,759 enterprises of all sorts, excluding those in Finland.

the unit commonly used at the time: a work stoppage with common goals. As Charles Tilly has suggested to us, the imputation of common goals to strikers from different enterprises can be problematic, but in most such cases workers presented a single set of demands to employers' associations and generally acted in unison. On March 12, for example, a one-day strike-demonstration celebrating the new government took place in Vladimir, involving workers from some 21 different enterprises, largely textile manufacturers. The Factory Inspectorate recorded 21 separate strikes, but we regard this incident as a single strike, as we do the strike of Petrograd dye workers that began on May 12. Here eight larger plants were involved (Danziger, Peklie, Lissner, Golaevskii, Sykin, Obukhovit, Atamonov, and Damm), each of which employed 35 to 50 workers, but also striking were a number of factory stores and many small shops. All strikers demanded a minimum wage of four rubles for women and five for men, even though individual shop owners began to bargain separately with their own workers. We also record as a single strike the more than 400 tailors who struck their shops in Perm in August, some 2,000 waiters, clerks, and hotel employees who struck in Samara in June, the tram drivers, truckers, porters and factory workers in Tsaritsyn who protested the Moscow State Conference on August 17, and the various pharmacy employees in Tomsk, Smolensk, Tiflis, Nizhnii Novgorod, and elsewhere, each of whose coordinated and organized work stoppages we consider a single citywide protest. Of the 458 strikes recorded by the Factory Inspectorate between March 3 and October 25 included in our data, we thus count only 188 separate incidents. If we were able systematically to use the Factory Inspectorate's single enterprise measure, we estimate that the 1,019 strikes in our data set might balloon more than tenfold, since so many nonindustrial enterprises were small stores or shops.

A more accurate means of comparing 1917 and prerevolutionary data would be through numbers of strikers, rather than strikes. Here, too, however, there are difficulties. Factory inspectors often knew rather precisely how many workers in a given enterprise went on strike, since it was incumbent upon employers to provide this information to the government. After February, exact figures of this sort were difficult to obtain, especially from smaller plants. Once again, we consequently use wherever possible in our data a carefully drawn *minimal* estimate of the number of workers on strike, derived both from factory employment records and a careful examination of contemporary strike reports. Since we feel confident about such estimates for only some 72 percent of our 1,019 strikes, however, comparisons here as well with prerevolutionary trends can only be approximate. Nevertheless, at the most aggregate levels biases are minimized; and if one bears in mind that our count of strikes and estimates of strikers are *always* somewhat lower than these levels must have been in fact, comparisons and generalizations can still prove informative and useful.

CONTINUITIES AND CHANGES IN STRIKES
BEFORE AND AFTER FEBRUARY

The strike wave that had been building throughout 1916 virtually exploded in January and February 1917. On January 9 alone, more than 186,000 workers, some 137,000 in Petrograd, struck to commemorate the anniversary of Bloody Sunday.[3] In the weeks that followed, the numbers of strikers continued to swell. By the time the Duma committee and the Petrograd Soviet had laid the foundations for a new Provisional government at the end of February, Russia's hardworking corps of factory inspectors had recorded strikes in 1,330 individual enterprises involving 676,000 workers, according to the data published by K. N. Iakovleva, a larger number than for all of 1916.[4] Just 190 (14 percent) of these strikes involving a little more than 101,000 strikers were over wages or workplace issues that management itself could resolve; the rest were political protests.

How does this activism contrast to the overall pattern of strikes in the months between March and October? If we examine the nature of strikes in our sample that correspond to the Factory Inspectorate's categories and approximate conservatively the number of individual enterprises that might have been involved, we can arrive at a minimal figure comparable with the Inspectorate's measure of strikes. On this basis, some 707 strike episodes for which we have collected data translate very roughly into strikes involving at least 2,977 individual industrial enterprises. At first glance, 1917 thus appears to represent a continuation of strike activity from the immediate prerevolutionary period (table 2.1).

In sharp contrast to January and February, however, after March 3, only 17 percent of strikes, involving a minimum of 507 plants, were explicitly political; some 83 percent, involving at least 2,470 plants, were

[3] M. G. Fleer, ed., *Rabochee dvizhenie v gody voiny* (Moscow, 1925), pp. 323–26.

[4] K. N. Iakovleva, "Zabastovochnoe dvizhenie v Rossii za 1885–1917 gody," in *Materialy po statistike truda*, vyp. 8 (Moscow, 1920), p. 61. Using strike lists in TsGIA, Leopold Haimson and Eric Brian count a slightly higher number of economic strikers for January than Iakovleva gives for both months, but economic strike activity in February was minimal and the differences between these two counts are not significant. See Leopold H. Haimson and Eric Brian, "Labor Unrest in Imperial Russia during the First World War: A Quantitative Analysis and Interpretation," appendix 1, in *War, Strikes and Revolution: The Impact of the War Experience on Italy, Germany, France, England, and Russia*, ed. Giulio Sapelli and Leopold H. Haimson (Milan, forthcoming).

TABLE 2.1
Strikes and Strikers in Enterprises under Factory Inspection,
March 3–October 25, 1917

	Number of Strikes	Minimum Strike Estimates Using FI Method[a]	Number of Strikers[b]
ECONOMIC			
Individual Strikes	462	462	234,710
Multienterprise strikes	223	2,008	719,220
Total	685 (97%)	2,470 (83%)	953,930 (62%)
POLITICAL			
Individual strikes	7	7	1,650
Multienterprise strikes	15	500	571,980
Total	22 (3%)	507 (17%)	573,630 (38%)
Total for all strikes	707 (100%)	2,977 (100%)	1,527,560 (100%)

NOTE: Enterprises under factory inspection are mechanized enterprises or those employing more than 15 workers.

[a] See appendix 1.

[b] Figures based on estimates for 76 percent of strikes.

over enterprise-related issues. The ratio of economic to political strikers is somewhat smaller (62 percent to 38 percent) but still indicates a real preponderance of strike participants engaged with their own employers. When we expand our purview beyond industrial strikes and analyze all work stoppages for which we have good information on the nature of demands (table 2.2), we find at least 76 percent of all strikers leaving their jobs over wage and workplace issues.[5] By our own system of counting, 975 of 1,019 common strike actions, or 96 percent, were directed against employers, 591 (61 percent) involving individual enterprises, and 384 (39 percent) involving a number of enterprises acting in concert.

It would thus appear that the eight months between the fall of the tsar and the Bolsheviks' coming to power represented a significant turnabout from late 1916 and early 1917, when political strike activism reached a wartime peak. Yet late 1916 and early 1917 were also an exceptional moment in wartime strike activity, the flashpoint of political resentments

[5] We have information on demands for 784 strikes, or 77 percent.

TABLE 2.2
Strikes and Strikers in All Enterprises and Sectors,
March 3–October 25, 1917

	Number of Strikes	Number of Strikers[a]
ECONOMIC		
Individual Strikes	591	275,708
Multienterprise strikes	384	1,587,980
Total	975 (96%)	1,863,688 (76%)
POLITICAL		
Individual strikes	14	3,342
Multienterprise strikes	30	574,820
Total	44 (4%)	578,162 (24%)
Total for all strikes	1,019 (100%)	2,441,850 (100%)

[a] Figures based on estimates for 72 percent of strikes.

that had long been building. If we take a broader view and examine the war years as a whole, it is clear that with the notable and significant exception of strikes in Petrograd (especially the Vyborg district), where political demonstrative strikes were concentrated, the dominant focus of strikes and strikers from August 1914 onward was on workplace-related issues. The 646,785 workers whom the Factory Inspectorate reported on strike over economic issues in 1916, in fact, constituted a larger army of economic strikers than in any other year in Russia's history, with the notable and symptomatic exception only of 1905. And whereas political strikes during the war and even in 1916 were squeezed into brief, intense episodes and concentrated overwhelmingly within a small but highly militant segment of the labor force, economic strikes, and especially strikes over wages, occurred in all parts of the empire, in every industrial sector, and with the participation of all types of workers, albeit in varying degrees. Only in January and February 1917 was the balance between economic and political strikes reversed, as it had been in 1914 before the outbreak of war.[6] Thus, in broader pattern, as tables 2.3 and 2.4 indicate, the eight revolutionary months of 1917 essentially reflected a continuation of workers' wartime emphasis on workplace issues, even allowing for differences in the ways of counting strikes. In percentage terms, the

[6] Haimson and Brian, "Labor Unrest."

TABLE 2.3
Wartime Economic Strikes and Strikers in Enterprises under Factory Inspection

	Number of Strikes	Percent of Total Number of Strikes	Number of Strikers	Percent of Total Number of Strikes	Estimated Number of Strikers per Strike
1914 (Aug.–Dec.)	34	83	6,716	70	198
1915	713	77	383,358	71	538
1916	1,046	81	646,785	68	618
1917 (Jan.–Feb.)[a]	190	14	101,481	15	534
1917 (Mar.–Oct.)[a]	2,470	83	953,930[b]	62	457[c]

SOURCES:
1914–1916: See table 1.5. For 1916, "Svedeniia o zabastovochnom dvizhenie," TSGIA, f. 23, op. 16, gives 908 economic strikes with 572, 278 strikers. These and other discrepancies are discussed by Haimson and Brian. See "Labor Unrest," appendix 4a.

1917 (Jan.–Feb.): Iakovleva, "Zabastovochnoe dvizhenie," p. 61.

[a] Minimum estimates for 1917 based on the Factory Inspectorate's method of counting.

[b] Minimum estimates based on 2,086 strikes (84 percent).

[c] For 2,086 strikes whose number of strikers could be estimated only.

TABLE 2.4

Wartime Political Strikes and Strikers in Enterprises under Factory Inspection

	Number of Strikes	Percent of Total Number of Strikes	Number of Strikers	Percent of Total Number of Strikes	Estimated Number of Strikers per Strike
1914 (Aug.–Dec.)	7	17	2,845	30	406
1915	215	23	156,170	29	726
1916	242	19	310,290	32	1,282
1917 (Jan.–Feb.)[a]	1,140	86	574,805	85	504
1917 (Mar.–Oct.)[a]	507	17	573,630[b]	38	1,744[c]

SOURCES:
1914–1916: See table 1.5. For 1916, "Svedeniia o zabastovochnom dvizhenie," TSGIA, f. 23, op. 16, gives 253 political strikes with 306,069 strikers. See Haimson and Brian, "Labor Unrest," appendix 4a.
1917 (Jan.–Feb.): Iakovleva, "Zabastovochnoe dvizhenie," p. 61.
[a] Minimum estimates for 1917 based on the Factory Inspectorate's method of counting.
[b] Minimum estimates based on 329 strikes (65 percent).
[c] For 329 strikes whose number of strikers could be estimated only.

division between economic and political strikes corresponds very closely with the ratio of the war years, and so does the distribution of strikers.

In absolute terms, however, the extent of economic strike activity among industrial workers also increased very substantially in 1917 as a whole compared to previous years. Comparing our very conservative estimates for the March–October period with Factory Inspectorate data for the war (table 2.3), we find that substantially more than twice the number of economic strikes occurred among industrial workers in the eight months following the tsar's abdication than in all of 1916, and that *at a minimum*, the number of strikers increased by almost 50 percent. If the change in regimes thus brought little alteration in the tendency of industrial workers to focus their strikes on workplace issues, the sheer number of strikers here also signified an exceptional and increasing degree of economic activism, not evidently retarded by the downfall of the tsar or by the increasing risk of strikes in deteriorating economic conditions. There were obvious ways, of course, in which Russia's new democratic order made it far easier for workers to engage in strikes if they wanted to, but the crucial question is how this absolute growth in the scale of economic strike activity among industrial workers related in specific ways to conjunctural economic or political factors after February, a matter to which we must return.

Political strike activism poses similar questions. Here, too, one can understand very well why strikes over issues beyond an employer's control might have subsided after the overthrow of the tsar in comparison with January and February, but table 2.4 shows a substantial increase in political strike activism relative to 1915 and 1916. The overall statistical picture itself, however, may be misleading. Political strikes during the war were illegal, were often brutally repressed, and frequently cost participants their jobs. Striking workers were also sometimes handed directly over to military authorities. As we have discussed in chapter 1, the wartime period as a whole reflected a very sharp decline in political strike activity compared to the period between 1912 and July 1914. Yet the range of grievances sparking the extraordinary wave of prewar political strikes could hardly have dissolved overnight with the outbreak of hostilities, and therefore the lessening of political strikes in 1915 and 1916 does not necessarily reflect any great lessening in political consciousness or commitments among industrial workers. One can surmise that protests were suspended for strategic or even patriotic reasons, as they were in other social sectors, or that many in the factory were intimidated by the very real threat of state repression or the likelihood of losing their jobs, especially in industries negatively affected by the war. Other explanations are also possible, but they all lead to the same conclusion: the beginning of the war witnessed what we would call an artificial calm in the activism of politically conscious workers, in the sense that the sudden and dramatic suspension of strikes could not represent any real diminution in fundamental sources of discontent.

When strike activity was renewed in 1915, we suspect that political sentiments were largely cloaked within the relative legalities of economic protest, especially outside of Petrograd; by 1916, we think it most likely that economic strikes, which still remained legal, had themselves become a major symptom of political as well as economic unrest, whether or not workers' protests were directed expressly against the state. In these terms, it is possible that January and February 1917 were exceptional months in terms of the relative balance of political and economic strikes not because workers suddenly came alive politically, but because in Petrograd and elsewhere they came to believe, along with other sectors of society, that their own personal well-being now depended so greatly on the end of the autocracy that they were willing to take new risks. Like privileged society above, workers' grievances turned squarely toward the tsarist regime, as long-term but partially suppressed commitments to radical political change now found open and active expression.

These commitments obviously carried past February. What is perhaps most important about the data presented in table 2.4 is thus not so much the relative dominance of economic over political strikes throughout 1917 as the extent to which political strike activism itself clearly continued in substantial measure after February despite the availability of other demonstrative forms of political protest. At the very least, the return in new political circumstances of the dominant wartime pattern of economic strikes does not mean either the end of political interest or the abandonment of the strike as an explicit political weapon.

At the same time, however, the political and social possibilities for workers' activism were so radically altered by the fall of the old regime and the dramatic broadening of civil liberties that one cannot automatically equate the strike process during 1917 with that which came before. In other words, despite important continuities with the past, strikes after February may well have reflected to a much greater degree than earlier the types of economic struggle common to workers in Western European political democracies, who largely pursued political interests in other arenas. We will therefore have to scrutinize the strike process very closely in the chapters that follow if we are to understand whether (and to what extent) the former political underpinnings of strikes continued to motivate strike practice between March and October. We must balance the complex relationships between labor-management conflict in the enterprise, broader patterns of social polarization, and the struggle for state power that lay at the core of the revolutionary process as a whole.

The Nature and Focus of Strikes in 1917

Workers struck in Russia between March and October for a great variety of specific goals, presenting a far richer panoply of demands than those recorded by the factory inspectors before February. As we have indicated, the Inspectorate's convention divided demands in strikes against employers into three major categories: wages, hours, and working conditions or factory order. Strikes over factory order generally involved demands for changes in work environments, but also included strikes over questions of workers' dignity (forms of address, harassment, and so forth).[7] Such categories, however, while useful for broad comparisions, were hardly precise. Our data show such wide-ranging demands as the introduction of a voluntary piecework system, the removal of Cossacks from factory grounds, and the demand that employers of domestic servants clean their own bedrooms. In all for 1917 we have catalogued more than 250 different strike demands.

In their manifest objectives, however, strikes in 1917 predominantly concerned wage-related issues, the most immediate and straightforward issue in economic conflict. More than two-thirds of all strikes directed against employers after February had to do in some way with wage relief, either for straight increases (506 strikes), a change in pay rates (122 strikes), bonuses (39 strikes), or some combination of similar goals. They involved 73.3 percent of all strikers (table 2.5). Significantly, if we employ an approximation of the Factory Inspectorate's system of measurement, the results are almost exactly the same. Using minimum estimates of the number of industrial enterprises, we find that some 67 percent struck over wage issues and, as table 2.5 indicates, involved some 57.5 percent of all strikers. Figures for 1917 reflect workers striking for more than one issue during a single strike and are not strictly comparable to those for 1914–1916. We can assume, however, that factory inspectors would have recorded virtually all strikes over wage issues in the wage category alone and that the comparisons here are valid.

Strikes of this sort generally did not press the borders of traditional labor-management conflict, at least overtly, since they did not directly challenge the right of plant owners to control their factories or otherwise manage their affairs. Here, too, one finds a basic line of continuity with the immediate prerevolutionary period. In 1916, 84 percent of all eco-

---

[7] As we shall see, a number of strikes in 1917 also related to workers' control. They included demands that employers recognize trade unions or factory committees or the right of workers to participate in hiring and firing. Such cases before February were generally catalogued as political by the Inspectorate since they could not then be decided by individual employers. For purposes of comparison with prerevolutionary strikes, we have included them here as strikes over order.

nomic strikes were essentially conflicts over wages, either in terms of re-sisting wage reductions, as was the case in Kostroma, Ivanovo-Vozne-sensk, and other textile centers in the Central Industrial Region, or for increased pay or a change in wage scales, as most often occurred in the Petrograd metal industry. Strikes over wages had always constituted the largest category of economic strikes in Russia, but in the period immedi-ately before the war their frequency had fallen dramatically: from Janu-ary to July 1914, wage strikes made up less than half of all economic strikes, and as table 2.5 depicts, involved just under 11 percent of all strikers. In contrast, 53.1 percent of the industrial strike force left their benches over wage issues in 1916. In absolute numbers, these strikes in-volved more than 508,000 workers.[8]

Although the percentage of all workers striking over wages remained relatively constant during the war, the number of wage strikes themselves increased at the expense of strikes over hours, working conditions, fac-tory order, and questions involving workers' dignity, such as the harass-ment of women, verbal abuse, or appropriate form of address. This was particularly the case with strikes over hours, as Haimson has shown, which constituted one of the most contentious points of labor-manage-ment conflict between 1905 and 1914 but fell off very substantially after July 1914 and continued to remain low throughout the remainder of the prerevolutionary period.[9] The distinctions among these types of strikes are important, since strikes over hours represented a far more serious struggle for power in the workplace than strikes over wages. Manage-ment efforts to control time impinged in many ways on the traditional autonomy cherished particularly by skilled workers, thousands of whom, in effect, continued to work as if they were artisans in the individual shops of large production combines, many under independent adminis-tration. From 36 percent of all economic strikes in 1914, however, strikes over hours dropped in 1915 and 1916 to a mere 2 percent, and involved less than 1 percent of all strikers each year. In 1916 this represented only 2,600 workers compared to 71,000 in 1914. By January and February 1917, according to Iakovleva, the Factory Inspectorate could identify only a single strike throughout Russia which concerned issues of working time.[10]

As table 2.5 shows, the percentage of industrial workers subject to in-

---

[8] TSSU, *Trudy*, vol. 7, vyp. 1, table 15, pp. 162–63.

[9] Thus, the percentage of strikes over wages increased from 56.0 percent in 1915 to 67.9 percent in 1916; strikes over factory order decreased from 18.9 percent to 11.9 percent and strikes over hours from 1.9 percent to 1.5 percent. See TSSU, *Trudy*, vol. 7, vyp. 1, tables 9, 12, 15, pp. 142–45, 152–55, 162–63.

[10] Iakovleva, "Zabastovochnoe dvizhenie," pp. 68–69.

TABLE 2.5
Strikers by Cause, 1914–1917
(in Percents)

	Wages	Hours	Order	Various Other Causes	Politics
1914 (Jan.–Jul.)[a]	10.9%	5.3%	4.1%	5.5%	74.0%
1914 (Aug.–Dec.)[a]	54.6%	3.0%	12.6%	0.0%	29.8%
1915[a]	43.0%	0.8%	27.1%	0.4%	28.6%
1916[a]	53.1%	0.3%	14.2%	0.0%	32.4%
1917 (Jan.–Feb.)[a]	9.9%	0.0%	5.0%	0.0%	84.9%

	Wages	Hours and Factory Conditions	Dignity	Workers' Control	Politics
1917 (Mar.–Oct.)[a][b]	57.5%	37.4%	32.4%	41.9%	37.5%
1917 (Mar.–Oct.)[b][c]	73.3%	55.2%	23.5%	61.3%	24.0%

SOURCES:
1914–1916: TSSU, *Trudy*, vol. 7, vyp. 1, tables 9, 12, 15, pp. 142–45, 152–55, 162–63.
Jan.–Feb. 1917: Iakovleva, "Zabastovochnoe dvizhenie," table 6, pp. 68–69.
[a] Workers subject to factory inspection only.
[b] Figures for Mar.–Oct. 1917 add to more than 100 percent because of multiple counting of strikes with principal demands in more than one category.
[c] Workers from all enterprises and sectors.

spection striking over wage issues in 1917 (57.5 percent) was entirely consistent with wartime patterns. Equally important, however, is the fact that questions of hours, working conditions, workers' dignity, and especially workers' control assumed new and far greater importance in 1917, even if the degree of industrial workers' interests here before February was obscured by the Factory Inspectorate's system of recording. According to our aggregate tabulations, almost 42 percent of all strikers in industries nominally subject to factory inspection and more than 61 percent of strikers in all economic sectors used strikes to struggle for some form of workers' control in 1917, whether to gain recognition from employers for factory or enterprise committees or as a means of securing some greater role in the actual processes of production.

As we have suggested, if one compares March–October patterns in table 2.5 with those of January and February 1917, particularly in terms of wage versus political strikers, there are strong indications that radical tendencies among strikers may have calmed somewhat after the autocracy was swept from power and that strike activism as a whole came to reflect the less overtly politicized patterns of the war period. Yet the apparent increase after February in more contentious demands over the length of the workday, how work should be organized, or even whether employers should continue to be responsible for hiring and firing their workers carried with them important implications for the broader struggle for power in 1917. The important question of what strikes and strike demands may actually have meant in Russia's revolutionary context after February thus requires further exploration.

Strike Outcomes

The changing pattern of workers' strike demands must be interpreted in part in terms of the relationship between strike goals and outcomes. There is some evidence that strikes can result more often in workers' victories in capitalist economies during periods of prosperity, but outcomes vary significantly according to the issues at stake.[11] In prewar Russia, strikes over issues of time and hours were rarely successful, even among metalists. According to one account, they failed in as many as 82 percent of the cases even in the great period of worker activism between 1912 and the start of the war.[12] Thus the shift during the war years away from hours toward wages and working conditions might indicate, at least in part, a shift from more to less contentious issues of conflict and the mobilization of active workers behind struggles that were most likely to be won, although the shift was also clearly a consequence of new and increasing pressures of inflation on wages and other sources of income.

Figures compiled by the Factory Inspectorate on strike outcomes during the war are hence of particular interest. These were divided into "totally successful," "partially successful," and "unsuccessful," from the workers' viewpoint. Because of the complexity of strike demands, the

[11] This is the implication, for example, of J. R. Hicks's argument in his *Theory of Wages* (New York, 1948). See also Edward Shorter and Charles Tilly, *Strikes in France, 1830–1968* (Cambridge, 1974), pp. 86–87, and Clark Kerr and Abraham Siegel, "The Inter-Industry Propensity to Strike," in *Industrial Conflict*, ed. Arthur Kornhauser, Robert Dubin, and Arthur M. Ross (New York, 1954), pp. 189–212. P. K. Edwards argues, however, that a lack of reliable quantitative data on the incidence of strikes and the patterns of business activity makes it impossible to establish whether correlations between strikes and prosperity are positive. See his *Conflict at Work: A Materialist Analysis of Workplace Relations* (Oxford, 1986), p. 115.

[12] K. F. Sidorov, "Rabochee dvizhenie v Rossii v gody imperialisticheskoi voiny," in *Ocherki po istorii oktiabr'skoi revoliutsii*, ed. M. N. Pokrovskii (Moscow and Leningrad, 1927), vol. 1, p. 192.

Factory Inspectorate's categories never completely reflected the reality of strike outcomes. Nonetheless, they still show rather well in aggregate terms that in contrast to the 1912–1914 period and earlier, a large percentage of economic strikes were settled in the workers' favor in Russia after the beginning of the war, as they were elsewhere in Europe. The number reported as settled totally for the workers increased from a mere 8.3 percent in 1913 and 9.2 percent in 1914 to approximately 31 percent in 1915 and almost 27 percent in 1916. Whereas almost 70 percent of all strikes brought no economic concessions whatsoever to 69 percent of all workers on strike in 1914, the figure on the eve of the revolution was quite different: only some 34 percent of all strikes in 1916, involving 31.4 percent of all strikers, did not result in some improvement in workers' economic well-being. These data are summarized in figures 2.1 and 2.2.

Analyzing strike outcomes is even more difficult for 1917 than for the war years. The definition of success or failure was no longer restricted to the employees of the Factory Inspectorate and now very much depended on the observer. Obviously, *Pravda*'s descriptions did not necessarily correspond to those of the Menshevik newspaper *Rabochaia Gazeta* or the liberal organ *Rech'*. Many factories also responded to strikes and strike threats by shutting their gates, sometimes locking workers out temporarily, sometimes for good. Many strikes were never heard about again after an initial newspaper report, their results remaining unknown to the public and the public record.

We have tried to compensate for these difficulties by carefully analyzing different accounts of a single strike and deciding for ourselves whether the strike was won or lost. We have also been rigorous in excluding from review strikes for which data about outcomes were insufficient or unconvincing. We thus come to a clear determination in only one-third of our cases, a substantially smaller sample than that available for the war years.

Still, what is most interesting about strike outcomes in aggregate terms between March and October is that so few seem to have ended in outright failure and so many were apparently settled by compromise. Even on the basis of our limited sample, the patterns of compromise for factories subject to the Factory Inspectorate were quite comparable to those for 1915 and 1916, and even the first two months of 1917. Compromise outcomes were also prevalent in France toward the end of the war and may have reflected a broad interest in preserving industrial peace as the strains of war increased. The extent to which these attitudes existed in Russia as well, and when, is thus of real interest.

So, too, is the fact that although the number of industrial workers nominally under factory inspection who participated in completely successful strikes in 1917 was almost exactly the same as that in 1916 by our estimates, the number of participants from *all* branches in strikes that were

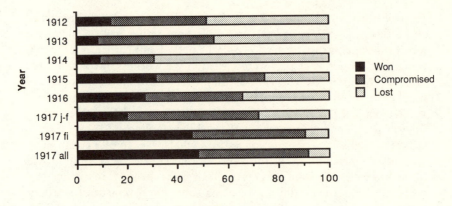

Figure 2.1 Outcomes of Economic Strikes, 1912–1917
  SOURCES: TSSU, *Trudy*, vol. 7, vyp. 1, pp. 136–39, 146–49, 156–59, 164; K. N. Iakovleva, "Zabastovochnoe dvizhenie," p. 71. Note: Statistics are for economic strikes only, for
which outcomes are reported.
KEY: 1917 j–f January–February 1917 strikes
      1917 fi   1917 all strikes reported by the Factory Inspectorate
      1917 all all 1917 strikes

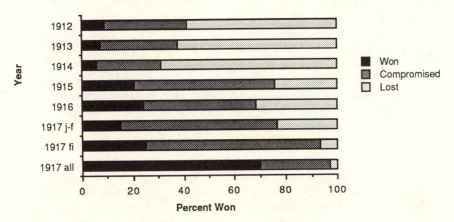

Figure 2.2 Outcomes for Economic Strikers, 1912–1917
  SOURCES: See figure 2.1.
KEY: 1917 j–f January–February 1917 strikes
      1917 fi   1917 strikes reported by the Factory Inspectorate
      1917 all all 1917 strikes

won may have been as high as 70 percent. Here, the greater willingness of employers to grant concessions when outcomes would not affect the war effort may have been a factor, and in any case, an issue we will also have to explore. Failure rates were also correspondingly low. Figure 2.2 suggests that as few as 6.8 percent of all strike participants in enterprises subject to factory inspection, and only 2.7 of all strike participants, lost strikes outright. One thus sees here the greatest shift from wartime patterns, and a pattern of real interest: the number of strikes lost outright by workers in 1917 may have been the lowest in the history of Russian labor.

Sectoral and Geographic Patterns in 1917

Other points of continuity with prewar patterns emerge when we consider the sectoral distribution of strikes in 1917. As we have noted, the Factory Inspectorate paid attention only to workers in mechanized industrial plants employing more than 15 workers. We have cast our net more widely and included in our sample strikes wherever they were reported to have occurred, whether in factories or factory offices, secondary schools or graveyards, restaurants or retail stores. Table 2.6 depicts the aggregate distribution of strikes and strikers by industrial branch, as well as those strikes in which workers from more than one industrial branch participated together. Table 2.7 depicts the distribution of strikes over four broad sectors of the economy.

The figures in table 2.6 reveal clearly when we consider 1917 as a whole the exceptional degree to which the politically charged metalworking industry continued to dominate the strike process, along with the large workforce in textiles, just as before the change of regimes in February. In terms of numbers, the textile and metal industries alone had accounted for the overwhelming majority of striking workers in both 1915 and 1916, together furnishing about 90 percent of strikers in each year. Between March 3 and October 25, 1917, almost half of all industrial strikes by branch and approximately 75 percent of all strikers (in strikes for which estimates can be made) were from these two branches! Since metalists were also active in virtually all of the large strikes involving more than one branch, like the political-demonstrative strikes accompanying the April and July Days and the protests against the Moscow State Conference in August, their dominant role in strike activity for the year as a whole was even higher than the branch figures in table 2.6 indicate.

This situation was not unique to Russia. The rationalization of work processes among the metal trades pressed skilled workers here toward increased political consciousness and activism throughout Western Europe and the United States in these years, although in varying degrees. In

TABLE 2.6
Strikes and Strikers by Industry, March 3–October 25, 1917

Industry	Number of Strikes	%	Estimated Number of Strikers[a]	%	Strike Intensity[b]	Estimated Number of Strikers per Strike[c]
Minerals	10	1.5	2,923	0.2	2.9	417
Mining	17	2.4	61,526	4.9	148.8	6,836
Metals	199	29.2	532,080	42.7	97.4	3,500
Wood and wood products	66	9.7	45,791	3.7	52.2	803
Chemicals	20	2.9	19,171	1.5	20.7	1,278
Food products	62	9.1	13,683	1.1	4.0	291
Animal products (leather)	64	9.4	135,570	10.9	193.2	2,884
Textiles	137	20.1	412,923	33.1	57.0	3,720
Paper and printing	98	14.4	21,397	1.7	26.6	260
Mixed products	8	1.2	2,436	0.2	[d]	405
Total	681	100.0	1,247,500	100.0		2,340
Total for strikes involving more than one industry	59		354,800			18,674
Total for all industrial strikes	741		1,602,300		76.5	2,902

SOURCE: Workforce figures as of January 1, 1917, from TSSU, *Trudy*, vol. 7, vyp. 1, "Statisticheskii sbornik za 1913–1917," table 4, p. 39.

[a] The estimate of strikers represents only those strikes for which satisfactory estimates could be made. The percent of strikes for which these estimates could be made by branch are as follows: mining, 53%; animal products, 73%; metals, 74%; textiles, 78%; wood and wood products, 82%; chemicals, 75%; paper and priting, 84%; food products, 76%; minerals, 70%; mixed products, 75%; all industrial stirkes, 74%.

[b] Strike force as a percentage of the workforce.

[c] Calculated only for strikes with estimates of strikers.

[d] Cannot be calculated because size of workforce is unknown.

TABLE 2.7
Strikes and Strikers by Economic Sector, March 3–October 25, 1917

Sector	Number of Strikes	%	Estimated Number of Strikers[a]	%
Industrial	741	72.7	1,602,300	65.6
Transport	64	6.3	717,590	29.4
Service	175	17.2	103,910	4.3
Other	39	3.8	18,050	0.7
Total	1,019	100.0	2,441,850	100.0

[a] Minimum estimates based on 74% of industrial strikes, 73% of transport, 69% of service, 49% of other strikes, and 72% of all strikes.

England, challenges to the traditional dominance of skilled craftsmen in the metals plants of Glasgow, Sheffield and Manchester fuelled a powerful and revolutionary workers' committee movement throughout the war.[13] Metalists in Turin and Milan reacted similarly and also saw events in Russia itself as a model for their own challenges to state and managerial authority.[14] French workers were highly patriotic, especially in defense industries, but even here metalists spearheaded major strikes as the war came to an end, especially in Paris.[15] And although extremely repressive management policies in Germany inhibited metalists and others from striking during most of the war, it was this group again that took the lead in labor activism in the face of growing food shortages and impending military defeat.[16] The continued dominance of metalists in Russian strikes after February thus had important implications not only for the political stability of the new Provisional regime, but for revolutionary politics well beyond Russia's borders. The form and content of these strikes, as well as those in other industrial branches, thus demand careful attention in the

[13] James Hinton, *The First Shop Stewards' Movement* (London, 1973), especially part 2.

[14] Stefano Musso, "Scioperi e conflitto sociale durante la prima guerra mondiale a Torino," and Giovanna Procacci, "The Changing Nature of Popular Protest and Labour Unrest in Italy, 1917–1918: The Political Content," in Sapelli and Haimson, eds., *War, Strikes, and Revolution*.

[15] Jean-Louis Robert, "Les Grèves parisiennes (août 1914–juillet 1919)," in Sapelli and Haimson, eds., *War, Strikes, and Revolution*.

[16] Gerald D. Feldman, "Labor Unrest and Strikes in Saxony, 1916–1923," and Ilse Costas, "Management and Labor in the Siemens Plant in Berlin, 1906–1920," in Sapelli and Haimson, eds., *War, Strikes, and Revolution*.

chapters that follow, especially in terms of the ways they may or may not have been compatible with the new order's own goals and values.

As table 2.7 shows, a most interesting concentration of strikes in 1917—slightly more than 17 percent—also took place in the highly diversified service sector, which included waiters and cooks, maids, chauffeurs, barbers, hospital and other public service employees, and a wide variety of porters, warehouse hands, doormen and the like. Since strikes by these workers were rarely publicized and not officially registered before 1917, it is impossible to make pre- and post-February comparisons, yet we have recorded more strikes by waiters and cooks than by coal miners or oil workers between March and October. Moreover, strikes by doormen, coachmen, and chauffeurs were publicized as part and parcel of the general labor movement throughout the year, despite the obvious social and occupational differences separating this group of workers from what one generally considers the proletarian rank and file. One important characteristic of strikes as a whole in 1917 was thus the ways in which they served implicitly to bring highly variegated worker groups into a common arena of struggle. At times these connections were quite explicit as well.

Other major concentrations of strikes in 1917 included the paper and printing industry, the leather workers, and the food processing industries (table 2.6). Among paper workers and printers, of which there were some 16,000 and 24,000 workers respectively in January 1917, employed in 90 paper plants and 211 print shops, typographers generated by far the largest number. There were also considerable numbers of strikes among workers in shoe-manufacturing plants, among tailors, and among saw mill workers. The very range of these strikes suggests the degree to which strikes became a major arena of social conflict in 1917.

The likely importance of this to the development of Russian social relations in 1917 becomes even stronger when we look more closely at the number of strikers than of strikes. It is here, in fact, despite greater problems of statistical reliability, that we can sense one of the most important aspects of strike activism as a whole during this period: its sheer number of participants, many of whom clearly struck more than once. As we have noted, the total number of all Russian industrial workers in early 1917 (including miners and railroad workers) was slightly more than 3,300,000.[17] Our own estimates of strike participants cover only a little more than 72 percent of all strikes we know occurred in 1917 (table 2.7), but even so, we count more than 2.4 million strikers between March 3 and October 25, a level of activity matched only by the "dress rehearsal"

[17] See table 1.1.

of 1905 and the period of intense political strike activity during the first seven months of 1914.[18]

Aggregate data, however, are not necessarily the best way to measure labor activism, since they say little about relative activity in different industrial sectors. Although metalists and textile workers continued to dominate the strike process overall in 1917, we need to know how their relative role may have changed from the prerevolutionary period. For this we turn to measures of strike propensity, which adjust for the different sizes of industries' work forces.[19] An industry whose share of the strike force exactly equals its share of the work force would have a strike propensity of one, regardless of the actual numbers of strikers, workers, or strikes. A propensity higher than one signals the group is more strike prone than average. These propensities and a ranking of industrial branches by strike propensity appear in table 2.8.

Although strike propensity figures for 1917 are somewhat distorted by the necessary exclusion of strikes involving workers from more than one industrial branch, they are nonetheless quite revealing. First, it is extremely interesting that although the numbers of industrial strikers in 1917 increased over previous years, the relative position (or rank order) of major industrial branches to each other changed very little for strikes in which workers in one branch of production struck alone. Table 2.8 strongly suggests, therefore, that with some exceptions, those industries that had been most active in strikes before February were also most strike prone in 1917. Metalists ranked either first or second in strike propensity throughout the period 1913–1917, and textile workers were also consistently active in both absolute and relative terms, especially if one looks at economic strike propensities apart from political strikes. Those industries with the lowest strike propensities were equally consistent: food-processing and mineral extraction remained at the bottom of the rankings.

The greatest shift occurred among animal-products workers (largely leather workers), who emerged as the single most strike-prone industry in 1917 for reasons that we will need to explore. Although metalists accounted for the largest number of strikers in 1917, animal-products workers provided only 135,000 strikers by our minimum estimates in an industry with only some 70,000 workers. The strike *intensity* of this industrial branch, measured as a ratio of strikers to the workforce, was thus more than 193 percent. A large segment of these workers was employed

[18] See appendix 2, table A.2, which gives aggregate strike data for 1901–1917.

[19] The strike propensity is defined as a ratio of an industry's share of the total strike force to its share of the labor force. The assumption underlying this measurement is that all things being equal, each industry's workers would strike in direct proportion to their share in the labor force.

Table 2.8
Strike Propensities, 1913–1917
(Measured as a Ratio of an Industry's Share of Strikers to Workers)

Industry	Type of Strike	1913 SP	1913 Rank	1914 SP	1914 Rank	1915 SP	1915 Rank	1916 SP	1916 Rank	1917[a] SP	1917[a] Rank
Animal Products (leather)	Economic	1.12		.66		.45		.27			
	Political	.38		.82		.13		.13			
	All	.07	(8)	.78	(4)	.36	(4)	.23	(4)	3.38	(1)
Metals	Economic	1.99		2.12		.99		1.43			
	Political	4.09		3.54		3.22		3.78			
	All	3.16	(1)	3.16	(1)	1.61	(1)	2.19	(1)	1.68	(2)
Textiles	Economic	1.10		.90		1.88		1.56			
	Political	.40		.42		.56		.19			
	All	.71	(4)	.55	(6)	1.48	(2)	1.12	(2)	.98	(3)
Wood and wood products	Economic	.42		.40		.34		.23			
	Political	.41		.63		.07		.03			
	All	.42	(5)	.57	(5)	.37	(5)	.17	(5)	.91	(4)
Paper and printing	Economic	.40		.49		.14		.16			
	Political	1.04		1.50		1.01		.10			
	All	.76	(3)	1.23	(2)	.38	(3)	.14	(6-7)	.46	(5)

TABLE 2.8 (*cont.*)

Industry	Type of Strike	1913		1914		1915		1916		1917[a]	
		SP	Rank	SP	Rank	SP	Rank	SP	Rank	SP	Rank
Chemicals	Economic	1.16		1.89		.01		.40			
	Political	1.41		.93		.00		.01			
	All	1.30	(2)	1.18	(3)	.01	(8)	.27	(3)	.36	(6)
Food products	Economic	.31		.20		.18		.16			
	Political	.11		.24		.18		.08			
	All	.20	(6)	.23	(7)	.18	(7)	.14	(6-7)	.07	(7)
Minerals	Economic	.19		.26		.27		.19			
	Political	.08		.10		.38		.02			
	All	.13	(7)	.15	(8)	.30	(6)	.13	(8)	.04	(8)

SOURCES:
1913–1916: TSSU, *Trudy*, vol. 7, vyp. 1, tables 2, 6, 9, 12, 15, pp. 36–37, 132–35, 142–45, 152–55, 162–63.
1917: Ibid., table 4, p. 39 and table 2.5 above.
NOTE: Calculations show relative propensities among these industrial branches only. Mining, mixed products, and other industrial sectors are excluded.
[a] Single industry strikes only. The exclusion of strikes involving more than one industry reduces in particular the strike propensity for metalists, who were especially active in multi-industry strikes.

in leather factories employing under 100 workers. Labor mobilization was consequently more difficult than for workers like the metalists in large industrial plants, or even textile workers. The leather workers' high level of strike activity is thus especially noteworthy not only because of what it suggests about the pervasiveness of labor discontent, but also because it raises questions about the forms and methods of strike mobilization, which were clearly more difficult for workers in smaller shops than for those in large industrial enterprises. The high aggregate numbers of strikers in 1917 in industries like leather working, in comparison with preceding years, may also have reflected new and different kinds of activism relatively unaffected by such factors as plant size or location. Thus the level of discontent among less visible workers in smaller industries like wood processing or leather working (animal products) may actually have been just as intense as in industries with large numbers of workers like metal processing, traditionally associated with the "vanguard" of labor politics in 1917. The "biographical" ways strikes formed and developed, their relationship to various parties and other agents of mobilization, and especially the ways that the extent and cohesiveness of strike activity may have been related to the responses of employer groups are thus additional issues very much deserving scrutiny. So, too, is the question of whether it makes conceptual sense to think of a vanguard within the labor movement in 1917, and if so, in what ways.

One common understanding of a vanguard in the prerevolutionary period related to patterns of geographical concentration. According to available data for 1916, as many as 65 percent of all strikes (and almost 75 percent of all strike participants) were located in only four provinces: Petrograd, Moscow, Vladimir, and Kostroma; these four accounted for 47 percent of the factory labor force under government inspection at the end of 1916.[20] Economic strikes of consequence obviously took place elsewhere in Russia during the war, particularly in Baku and the Ekaterinoslav mining district, but in percentage terms these did not involve much more than 1 percent of the Russian strike force as a whole, and only in Baku during 1916 were there more than a dozen or so individual work stoppages.[21]

Most significant, of course, was the degree to which political strikes were concentrated in Petrograd, a matter Leopold Haimson's work explores in detail. Aggregate figures are impressive: more than 340,000 participants in political strikes in Petrograd during 1915 and 1916, a figure seven times the number of any other locality; some 718,000 workdays

[20] TSSU, *Trudy*, vol. 7, vyp. 1, tables 3, 14, pp. 38, 160–61.
[21] Fleer, *Rabochee dvizhenie*, pp. 125–26.

lost, 76 percent of the national total; and as much as 55 percent of the total number of strikes.[22]

In sharp contrast to the months before February, strikes in 1917 extended into every province of the empire, and virtually every city and town. Our data set includes strikes from more than 170 different localities. The fewest are recorded for Western and Eastern Siberia, and for Turkestan, where most of Russia's domestic cotton was produced, but even these areas witnessed a number of work stoppages, certainly enough that strikes may be considered to have been a common experience for workers everywhere in 1917. In this respect, the pattern of strikes between March and October very much resembled that of 1905.[23]

At the same time, however, the great preponderance of strikes and strikers in 1917 still remained concentrated in the industrial and political centers of Moscow and Petrograd and the industrial regions around them. The data are summarized by region in table 2.9. Again, numbers of strikers are estimates and are known to be incomplete. The percentage of strikes on which we base our estimates of strikers for each region appears in the table notes.

The concentration of strikes and strikers in the cities of Moscow and Petrograd was probably the single most important reflection of workers' power in 1917, just as it had been before the revolution. Part of the reason for this, of course, was the continued centrality of the two capitals to Russian national politics, and the consequent magnification of labor unrest in the perceptions of unsympathetic political figures, giving strikers here a potential power far greater than their comrades elsewhere had. In other words, more than elsewhere, strike activism here directly influenced general perceptions in the nation at large about the character and content of labor protest, and hence about the intensity of social conflict and the revolutionary process. The ways strikes were reported and perceived in the capitals, in fact, may well have contributed as much to the determinant processes of political and social polarization as their objective features, since many observers clearly came to believe that the February revolution had unleashed an unprecedented wave of strikes, even though in many ways the broad patterns were not radically different than before.

We therefore need to explore the ways in which workers and the labor press thought and wrote about strikes and attempt to discern the ways in

[22] Haimson and Brian, "Labor Unrest," tables 2a, 2b, 3a, 3b, and appendices 3 and 4.

[23] On 1905, see in particular Leopold H. Haimson and Ronald Petrusha, "Two Strike Waves in Imperial Russia (1905–1907, 1912–1914): A Quantitative Analysis," in *Strikes, Wars, and Revolutions in an International Perspective: Strike Waves in the Late Nineteenth and Early Twentieth Centuries*, ed. Leopold H. Haimson and Charles Tilly (New York, 1989).

TABLE 2.9
Strikes and Probable Strikers by Region, March 3–October 25, 1917

Region[a]	Number of Strikes	%	Estimated Number of Strikers[b]	%	Estimated Number of Strikers per Strike[c]
Petrograd region[d]	74	7.3	28,446	1.2	662
Petrograd city	126	12.4	403,090	16.5	5,522
Moscow region[e]	171	16.8	423,960	17.4	3,312
Moscow city	247	24.2	450,180	18.4	2,274
Kiev region	106	10.4	75,017	3.1	807
Odessa region	28	2.7	4,418	0.2	192
Kharkov-Ekaterinoslav region	70	6.9	31,381	1.3	848
Rostov region	52	5.1	24,590	1.0	585
Transcaucasus region	29	2.8	6,086	0.2	265
Caspian region	10	1.0	55,560	2.3	9,260
Volga region	40	3.9	101,590	4.2	4,417
Urals region	25	2.5	122,270	5.0	6,435
Other	41	4.0	715,262	29.3	—
Total	1,019	100.0	2,441,850	100.1	—

[a] Provinces included within each region are noted in appendix 1.

[b] The estimate of strikers represents only those strikes for which satisfactory estimates could be made. The percentage of strikes with striker estimates by region are as follows: Petrograd, 58%; Petrograd city, 58%; Moscow, 75%; Moscow city, 80%; Kiev, 88%; Odessa, 82%; Kharkov-Ekaterinoslav, 53%; Rostov, 81%; Transcaucasus, 80%; Caspian, 60%; Volga, 58%; and Urals, 76%. Striker data for Petrograd and Petrograd city is thus very much understated. Caspian region strikes include the large Baku oil strike in September, which inflates the strikers-per-strike data. "Other" includes an estimated 700,000 railroad workers participating in the September 24 strike.

[c] Calculated only for strikes with estimates of strikers.

[d] Excluding city of Petrograd.

[e] Excluding city of Moscow.

which working-class perceptions and the representation of strikes may have influenced worker activism; we must also examine management's perceptions of striking workers, at least insofar as they were similarly reflected in the public organs of what one can roughly label Russia's trade-industrial bourgeoisie, and attempt to discern the ways in which these public images of strikers may also have contributed to the changing climate of labor-management relations.

At the same time, the spread of strikes throughout the country as a whole between March and October suggests that this form of collective action may also have provided an important common experience for various types of workers in broad numbers, in and outside of industry, perhaps establishing a basis in action on which otherwise distant political arguments could find specific, local expression. Even unsuccessful strikes by workers on the periphery in 1917 may have created at least some sense of commonality with those at the center and hence some common understanding. Striking pharmacy workers in Poltava, Kiev, and Smolensk in early October knew very well, for example, about the comparable struggles of their colleagues in Moscow and Petrograd, which were well publicized in union journals and the national press; waiters and cooks in Minsk, Voronezh, Smolensk, and Ekaterinoslav were undoubtedly aware of the major confrontation between Petrograd restaurant employers and their workers in May and June; for companies like Singer, whose employees were spread around the country, strikes initiated in the capitals soon had workers off their jobs in a number of different localities. To test the extent of this sense of commonality in workers' strike experience, we will need to explore carefully the ways in which participation in strikes themselves may have mobilized workers and the degree to which strike actions everywhere meant participation in a process of confrontation, as well as the development of at least some attributes of class consciousness.

THE RHYTHM OF STRIKE ACTIVISM IN 1917

It should now be apparent that the effort to see a great strike wave unfolding after February 1917 as part and parcel of Russia's deepening political revolution is at best a serious oversimplification. Even a quick glance at the incidence of strikes over time in 1917 indicates that the February revolution did not usher in an ever-expanding wave of strikes (figures 2.3 and 2.4). These figures also suggest it is equally inaccurate to conceptualize strikes in 1917 simply as revolutionary episodes correlating directly with political events of cardinal importance, as the Soviet historian Lisetskii and others have maintained.[24] The discontinuities as well as important continuities between strike patterns of 1917 and before indicate instead that no single explanation of the strike process can adequately interpret the patterns depicted here.

[24] See e.g., A. M. Lisetskii, *Bol'sheviki vo glave massovykh stachek (mart–oktiabr' 1917 goda)* (Kishinev, 1974), p. 280.

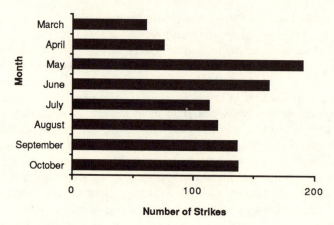

Figure 2.3 Strikes by Month, 1917

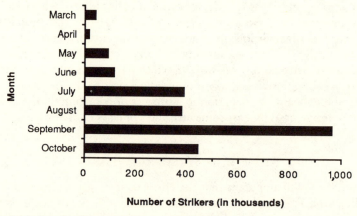

Figure 2.4 Strikers by Month, 1917 (Minimum Estimates)
NOTE: Estimates of strikers based on the following percentages of strikes: March, 80%; April, 77%; May, 75%; June, 72%; July, 75%; August, 76%; September, 72%; and October, 63%.

We would suggest, in fact, that strike activism in revolutionary Russia can best be conceptualized in terms of two distinct if complementary ways of looking at strike behavior. The first follows from observations about the content of strikes and their geographic and industrial distribution. The overwhelmingly economic orientation of strikes in 1917 suggests that in some important respects, this form of labor protest reflected patterns of activism and labor-management relations common to most capitalist socioeconomic systems. Revolutionary Russia was, after all, a free democratic society. Workers had avenues other than strikes through which to express their political grievances, and in many instances, strikes were a primary means of working out economic relations within the enterprise, just as they were in the established democracies of Western Europe. Strikes interpreted as "routine" labor conflicts in this sense might help explain why leather workers emerged in 1917 as the most strike-prone industrial group and why strikes extended so widely across economic sectors and geographic boundaries. In other words, although we can sensibly interpret the economism of strikes during the war as a way to evade government repression of essentially political protests, the political freedoms available to Russian workers after February suggest that we might take their economic demands in this period at face value. Accordingly, strikes must be thought of, at least in part, as localized economic phenomena, whose logic might largely be explained by ordinary factors like wage levels, employment opportunities, and workers' ability to mobilize resources or to organize.

At the same time, of course, even routine aspects of strike activism in 1917 did not occur in a political vacuum. Extraordinary changes obviously occurred in Russia's social, economic, and political terrain in the eight months between March and October. From conditions of relative order in March through the first coalition in May, the country found itself by late September in utter political disarray. The military offensive launched in late June failed completely, leaving the army on the verge of collapse. In early July, liberal ministers from the Kadet party resigned; after the attempt by Bolshevik soldiers to force full power on the Soviet during the July Days, the credibility of socialist moderates was sharply undermined. As the Right began to mobilize, the capacity of state authorities to maintain order disappeared, along with the ability to implement any major social reforms. An attempted coup by General Kornilov in late August only intensified social polarization and political weakness. In retrospect, Lenin's call in mid-September for the Bolsheviks to seize power is only surprising as a measure of how rapidly change was occurring.

Comparable changes affected Russia's economy and social relations. Agrarian revolution through forceful peasant seizures of land was by September an irreversible process. Private and foreign capital, hopeful in the spring about investment opportunities in a liberal capitalist economy, had by the fall virtually ceased financing production. Railroads operated fitfully, despite the best efforts in many places of responsible worker committees. Lists of apartments for rent filled whole pages of liberal newspapers like *Rech'* and *Russkiia Vedomosti*. Factory workers, doormen, cab drivers—virtually anyone, in fact, supporting even moderate socialist activists in the burgeoning hierarchy of soviets—were viewed by the "privileged" with growing fear and suspicion.

Strikes in Russia between March and October 1917 thus occurred in circumstances of great flux, in which their own content and form may have both altered these unfolding processes of revolution and been altered by them. If strikes in some ways were essentially economic in their nature and goals after February 1917, reflecting in the main the same general pattern of wage-centered demands as they had during the war, they were also inextricably linked to major aspects of the unfolding political process. They must also be seen, therefore, again at least in part, as reflecting central aspects of political struggle in and outside the workplace, even if they were not conducted expressly for political ends. Moreover, in the uncertain conditions of revolutionary flux, the acceptable boundaries even of economic conflict were under continual challenge. Strikes thus may have tended to shift even in the course of their own development from weapons of struggle and protest within boundaries initially considered appropriate to Russia's new order to weapons of protest that contested or rejected these boundaries. Whether (and how) this might have occurred can only be seen by examining the strike process in all its aspects as it unfolded during the eight months between the fall of the old regime and the onset of Soviet power.

How, then, can we characterize the way strike activism developed against the backdrop of revolutionary chronology in 1917, both in terms of the numbers of strikes, and even more importantly, considering their magnitude, the numbers of strikers? Rather than a "wave" of strikes that increased in intensity as the revolution evolved, gathering momentum more or less proportionately with specific political events, what the evidence suggests is a "clustering" of strike activity in what might be described as three periods of the revolution's social and political development.

The first emerged after seven weeks of relative quiescence in March and early April, when strike activity was generally at a very low level. Between March 3 and April 18, we record an average of only 1.6 new strikes and 940 strikers per day (on estimates for 80 percent of strikes recorded for that period). This remained an important time in the process of labor relations, as we will see in chapter 3, but the number of strikes was the lowest of any time between March and October. The upsurge began right before the April crisis, and continued through May and June until just after the July Days. This was the period, of course, of the first coalition cabinet, and a time when workers and others may have expected real gains from the newly appointed socialist ministers. New strikes occurred on an average of 4.4 per day, and the average number of strikers per day increased to just under 7,200 (on estimates for 79 percent of the strikes).

Strike activity fell off again with the suppression of the July uprising and remained relatively low for most of the month. (Between July 7 and July 28, new strikes averaged 2.4 per day; strikers, slightly fewer than

450 per day, the lowest number of the revolutionary period.) From the very end of July to mid-August, however, we can discern a second, less extensive cluster of strikes, which occurred along with a number of signs of growing political and social polarization. These included the strains accompanying the formation of the second coalition, the enormous conflict over the Moscow Conference, and the various assemblies in late July and August of former Duma representatives and public figures determined to "restore law and order." New strikes averaged almost four per day, and while this figure was not at the level of May and June, the average number of strikers was now much greater: almost 13,000 per day on estimates, again, of some 80 percent of the strikes.

Once more, however, strike activity largely subsided at the end of the summer despite the tense moments surrounding General Kornilov's attempted march on Petrograd in late August, although this episode itself sparked a number of workers to leave their jobs in demonstrative protest strikes. Late August and early September marked the beginning in many places of the fall harvest. It was during these weeks as well that Russia was again threatened militarily (Riga fell on August 21), and that further signs emerged indicating the potentially catastrophic decline of the country's economy. The greatest number of workers affected was in the textile industry, particularly cotton; the largest number of enterprises was in the food-processing sector; the highest number of enterprises per worker was in the production of wood and wood products. Each of these branches was already facing substantial production problems in 1916, as we have seen, but difficulties intensified rapidly in the summer of 1917 and spread as well to industries which had previously been fairly secure. More than 90 metal-processing plants closed their doors at least temporarily in the June–August period, largely due to a lack of fuel and raw materials, but also to lock out potential strikers. At first these were almost entirely smaller plants and shops, located for the most part outside of Petrograd and Moscow. But by midsummer, production everywhere was falling. During the first five months of the revolution alone, from March through July, more than 560 industrial enterprises shut their doors throughout Russia, leaving more than 100,000 industrial workers unemployed.[25] By early September, even metal plants in Petrograd were seriously affected. Production declined here by more than 30 percent compared to 1916. In the highly favored chemicals industry, the decline was almost 40 percent.[26]

[25] L. M. Kleinbort, *Istoriia bezrabotitsy v Rossii, 1857–1919 gody* (Moscow, 1925), p. 267. Some of these undoubtedly reopened, however. See TSSU, *Trudy*, vol. 26, "Fabrichno-zavodskaia promyshlennost' v period 1913–1918 godov," vyp. 1, pp. 35–36.

[26] TSSU, *Trudy*, vol. 26, vyp. 1, pp. 394–403. See also N. Ia. Vorob'ev, "Izmeneniia v russkoi promyshlennosti v period voiny i revoliutsii," *Vestnik Statistiki* 14 (1923), p. 153.

In these circumstances of economic crisis, social conflict, and heightened political consciousness, a final period of intensive strike activity occurred, lasting from mid-September until the Bolsheviks came to power. Now, however, the number of strikers involved rose dramatically. In September, as many as 700,000 railroad workers went on strike for a period of from one to three days, and in the third week of October, approximately 300,000 textile workers left their plants in one of the most extensive and best organized Russian strikes in history. If one sees relatively little progression in strike numbers from spring to fall, there was clearly a dramatic increase in strike intensity, measured by the number of strikers. Strikes now averaged 4.8 per day, essentially the same as in the first period of peak activity, but the daily number of strikers now averaged 30,455 (on estimates for only 68 percent of the strikes).[27]

This is most important. Among other things it suggests that it was not so much the numbers of strikes themselves that paralyzed industry or eased Lenin's transition to power, but the enormous increase in the number of strikers, many of whom pressed economic demands in circumstances in which the very act of striking was often welcomed by employers as an excuse to close their enterprises. The very nature of strikes themselves may thus have changed from March to October.

THE IMPACT OF REVOLUTION:
THE PRINCIPAL QUESTIONS AT HAND

First and foremost among the issues at hand, consequently, are the very nature of Russian strikes in 1917, their relationship to the unfolding processes of Russia's revolutionary development between March and October, and the ways in which their character may have changed, despite strong continuities with the past. If changes did occur, as our overview strongly suggests, a central question is the degree to which they were related to the internal dynamics of the strike process itself, including workers' ability to organize, and how much was due to external circumstances: to rising social conflict and to political and economic conjunctures. In other words, we must seek to understand the changing relationships be-

---

[27] This pattern essentially holds true for industrial strikes if they are measured on an enterprise basis, the method used by the Factory Inspectorate. According to our estimates, strike activity may have doubled in May and June in comparison with March and early April, subsided after July 6 to a little more than March–April levels, increased in late July and August to almost six strikes a day, the highest levels of the year, and then remained at a consistent level of approximately 3.7 strikes per day until October 25. The large number of enterprises that protested against the Moscow Conference between August 15–17 and the more than 80 plants that struck to protest the Kornilov mutiny on September 1 seem to account for the major discrepancies.

tween strikes as economic *and* political phenomena in 1917, the points of intersection between components of routine struggle in the work place and those that challenged in a radical way the evolving social and political order.

This involves exploring the complex matter of social polarization in 1917, a set of processes central to the evolution of revolutionary politics. Here our focus must be on management-labor relations and the degree to which the dynamics of these interactions themselves may have altered the nature and meaning of strikes. For if the end of autocracy brought Russian workers the unfettered opportunity to strike, a common right of workers in most industrial societies, it also brought workers and employers alike a chance to test the ability of Russia's developing new order to sustain strike activism as an appropriate means of resolving labor-management conflict. In effect, while the political structures, and indeed, the very nature of the post-tsarist order were themselves in the process of being formed, both major contenders for power in the workplace were confronted with the difficult task of finding effective methods of struggle to achieve their goals, methods whose relationship to the values, principles, and developing institutions of democratic Russia would critically affect how that order was to be defined.

We will thus have to look closely in the chapters that follow at how workers' goals, attitudes, and tactics may have changed over time, how changing strike demands may have affected the outcomes of strikes, and how both may have been affected by the broader chronology of revolutionary politics. The attitudes and actions of industrialists and other management groups are also obviously of central importance. So, too, are the matter of perceptions and the question of how strikes were reported in the daily press, especially as the issue of "who is to blame" became increasingly central to the processes of social polarization.

Finally, there is the question of the character of strikes themselves on the eve of October and the possibility that their changing character was attributable to the role of what some have called a workers' vanguard. Here we will need to return to many of the issues we have just touched in overview, examining changes in urban or industrial concentration, the role of skilled workers, and such structural factors as plant size, workers' age, and gender. If the character of strikes did indeed change in the course of 1917, as we suspect, we should learn much about the relationship between politics and social relations in revolutionary Russia. We may also find that Lenin and the Bolsheviks came to power facing a different sort of challenge from activist workers than has customarily been assumed, with important implications for what followed.

3

· · · · · · · · · · · · · · · · · · ·

THE FEBRUARY REVOLUTION AND

THE MOBILIZATION OF LABOR

The massive strikes and demonstrations engulfing the tsarist regime in Petrograd during the last days of February constituted one of the largest and most effective instances of mass activism in modern history. However clear the warning signs, and however often Duma leaders and other officials predicted the coming crisis, the enormous power of mobilized Petrograd workers and the ease with which they brought one of Europe's oldest and proudest dynasties to its end stunned observers and participants alike, whatever their politics.

What was so impressive about events in Petrograd was not simply the way in which a highly concentrated, literate, and politically conscious group of workers crushed one of Europe's great autocracies, but the degree to which they were able to control and direct the power implicit in mass strike actions towards discrete and achievable ends. We now understand, as a result of work by Leopold Haimson, how crucially important the metalworkers of the Vyborg district were in moving the February strikes toward a full-fledged political revolution, and how disproportionate their role in terms of the numbers of workers throughout the empire. The demonstrations of angry women on February 23, International Women's Day, gave a vital impetus to unfolding events, and the lockout of thousands of Putilov workers in and around the Narva district was an act of crass folly, given the volitile mood of the capital. But the real force for change came from thousands of Vyborg metalworkers, who struck that district's metal-fabricating and machine-construction plants on February 23 and effectively initiated the chain of events that would lead to the tsar's abdication eight days later.[1] Strikers in Vyborg organized meet-

[1] Leopold H. Haimson and Eric Brian, "Labor Unrest in Imperial Russia during the First World War: A Quantitative Analysis and Interpretation," in *War, Strikes, and Revolution: The Impact of the War Experience on Italy, Germany, France, England, and Russia*, ed. Giulio Sapelli and Leopold H. Haimson (Milan, forthcoming); I. P. Leiberov, "Petrogradskii proletariat v bor'be za pobedu fevral'skoi burzhuazno-demokraticheskoi revoliutsii v Ros-

ings, met their comrades when they arrived for work, and argued with those who showed signs of hesitation. And it was they who made the crucial decision to force their way across the river into the heart of the capital after troops mounted machine guns on rooftops around government buildings, erected barbed wire, and set up defenses on the bridges, hoping to seal the district off from the rest of the city. By taking their strikes to the very center of power on February 27, rather than returning to work, Vyborg metalists fundamentally changed the nature and scope of the protest and brought the uprising to a head. The strike leaders' moral authority among their comrades was translated into a political force of enormous range and power.

In the sense that they began without a central and formalized leadership, the February strikes in Petrograd were, of course, "spontaneous." (The Petrograd Soviet came into existence only on the afternoon of February 27, district soviets in Vyborg and elsewhere somewhat later.) It is common for Western historians to emphasize this and to use terms like "chaos" and "anarchy" in discussing February and subsequent labor activism in 1917 (in John Keep's view, "the words which best describe the state of Russia during 1917").[2] Yet such a view underestimates the complexity of labor mobilization in 1917—a process central to our understanding of Russia's revolutionary development between February and October—and hence the difficult tasks facing labor leaders and others hoping to harness the power of mobilized workers in support of their own (and Russia's) revolutionary objectives.

As discrete acts of protest against those in authority, whether inside the factory or out, strikes invariably forced workers to clarify their goals in objective terms. In contrast to demonstrations and other forms of protest that were not workplace related, strikes also required workers to make decisions, actively or passively, about what best served their interests. This, in turn, meant that those formally in power had either to set agendas essentially compatible with those of the strikers themselves, whose power lay in their ability to stop the processes of political or economic administration, or to develop some greater power of containment or repression. Terms like "spontaneity" and "chaos" obscure the degree of logic and consciousness the mobilization of labor involves, the importance (and rationality) of its subjective as well as objective elements, and

sii," *Istoriia* SSSR 1 (1957), pp. 41–73; and especially Tsuyoshi Hasegawa, *The February Revolution: Petrograd, 1917* (Seattle, 1981), chap. 12. Hasegawa (p. 221) reports that 59,800 Vyborg workers had struck 32 large plants in the district by the end of the day on February 23.

[2] John L. H. Keep, *The Russian Revolution: A Study in Mass Mobilization* (New York, 1976), p. ix.

the degree to which strikes in particular, as a central element of the mobilization process, were invariably related to workers' judgments about their own power and the views of others about the legitimacy of their goals.

The act of striking itself was a crucial part of workers' mobilization. The very act of leaving the factory against regulations, of risking dismissal or arrest, of raising demands to be met before work would resume, of disregarding the government's appeals—all this not only forced strikers to clarify their own objectives, but subjectively inculcated a sense of power, a sense of identity as workers, a feeling of comradeship and solidarity with others. To some extent, the accompanying street demonstrations had a similar effect. But much more so than demonstrations, strikes were discrete and to some extent "formal" actions. They involved at least some degree of organization, however rudimentary. They brought together in collective actions workers who knew each other well, who shared everyday work experience, who worked for the same foremen and owners. Many had struck together before and shared the consequences. They also knew they might well go out again. In important if less tangible ways, strikes were also "schools for collective organization," as Social Democrats had long understood. They provided object lessons in politics and class relations. They tied workers to Russia's revolutionary past, evoking memories in particular of 1905 and 1912, as well as more recent wartime protests. The very act of striking generated a "mental sediment," as Rosa Luxemburg put it, that made most strikes a memorable, even vital, experience for their participants, individually and collectively.[3] And everywhere as well, the act of striking gave workers in widely different occupations and factories the opportunity to participate directly and forcefully in the process of revolution. Strikes had lives of their own, all the more so in February when they reached for and secured unprecedented political gains.

STRIKES BEYOND PETROGRAD IN EARLY MARCH: THE LINKS BETWEEN POLITICAL AND ECONOMIC CHANGE

What helped make February such a powerful moment in the consciousness of Petrograd workers was also experienced elsewhere, where the act of striking brought diverse groups of workers together in powerful and subjectively intense associations. Like those in the capital, the strikes that swept through Moscow, Kharkov, Vladimir, and other industrial centers

[3] Rosa Luxemburg, *The Mass Strike*, trans. Patrick Lavin (Detroit, 1925), p. 33.

early in March were spontaneous only in the sense that there, too, they occurred because workers understood why and how their Petrograd comrades had succeeded, and because they recognized that strikes could bring them further political and economic gains. There were obviously other forms of protests available, and in some places they were extensively used: demonstrations that did not involve an interruption of work, petitions, evening rallies, and the dispatch of delegations to local dumas and other government offices to participate in the change of regimes. But strikes had important symbolic as well as substantive content everywhere. By demonstratively withholding their labor and disrupting production even in enterprises whose owners had no significant political connections, workers in the provinces put the muscle of direct action behind the insistence of newly formed soviets for political and social reforms and helped ensure that they would be represented in negotiations over new forms of local authority.

In Moscow, officials were able to suppress a good deal of information about the events of February 23 and 24, and the weekend was relatively calm. But word spread quickly when Petrograders refused to return to work on Monday, February 27, and workers in Moscow began to leave their own benches by afternoon. On Tuesday, February 28, Russia's second capital found itself in the throes of its own general strike, one accompanied by attacks on police stations in industrial neighborhoods, arrests of tsarist officials, and the seizure of arms. Metalworkers again played a leading role, as they had in three other recent strikes, when some 45 percent of the city's metalists had left their benches. But so did printers, tram workers, textile workers, and others, equally energized by news from Petrograd and carried as well by the momentum of recent strikes. (In January and February, almost one-third of the city's workforce, 120,000 men and women, had participated in strikes, more than twice the number for all of 1916.)[4] On March 1, delegates from 51 factories convened the first session of the Moscow Soviet. Late in the afternoon of the same day, a Committee of Social Organizations formed with Soviet participation to assume control of city affairs.[5]

A similar pattern occurred in cities and towns throughout the Central Industrial Region around Moscow, as well as in Kolpino, Kronstadt, and

[4] Diane Koenker, *Moscow Workers and the 1917 Revolution* (Princeton, N.J., 1981), pp. 95–96.

[5] A. M. Andreev, *Mestnye sovety i organy burzhuaznoi vlasti (1917 god)* (Moscow, 1983), pp. 24–33; A. Andreyev (Andreev), *The Soviets of Workers' and Soldiers' Deputies on the Eve of the October Revolution* (Moscow, 1971), pp. 32–33; William G. Rosenberg, "Les Libéraux Russes et le changement de pouvoir en Mars 1917," *Cahiers du Monde Russe et Soviétique* 9, no. 1 (1968), pp. 52–53.

the industrial suburbs around Petrograd. More than 1 million factory workers were employed in Vladimir, Kostroma, Nizhnii Novgorod, Tula, Iaroslavl', and Tver (the six provinces that made up the Central Industrial Region, along with Moscow), some 60 percent in textiles. In the country's largest textile center, Ivanovo-Voznesensk, a town of 200,000 and the scene of large bloody strikes in both 1905 and 1915, workers left their plants on March 2 and declared a general strike for the following day. In Kostroma province, another scene of wartime labor fatalities, women textilists went from factory to factory in Kineshma and other provincial towns where large plants were located in close proximity to each other. In Vladimir, which had no large enterprises and a garrison of some 25,000 troops, workers managed to prevent the garrison commander from arresting a delegation from Moscow on the night of March 3, after which regional power was vested in a provincial Executive Committee.[6] In Sormovo, outside of Nizhnii Novgorod, some 23,000 workers in the huge iron and steel complex left work on March 1.

Strikes erupted in similar fashion in Tula. Here some 40,000 workers in two large state-owned armaments plants (Oruzheinyi and Patronnyi) faced a formidable garrison of almost equal numbers, and strikes had consequently not occurred in January and February. In Baku, the Petrograd events were apparently quite unexpected, but oil workers nonetheless declared a general strike on March 3 and paraded through the center of town to the steps of the City Duma.[7] In Kharkov, some 40,000 machinists at several plants, including Helferick-Sade, an important manufacturer of artillery equipment, went on strike on March 2, the same day delegates from some 43 different enterprises organized the Kharkov Soviet.[8] The Tver Soviet held its first meeting on March 3, after a two-day strike at the Zalyginskii, Ursus and Meshchinskii, Morozov, and Bergov factories. Even in Saratov, which had no large industry, a workers' soviet organized on March 2 with more than 80 delegates from 49 enterprises. It immediately declared a one-day general strike.[9] Only in the

---

[6] *Tysiacha deviatsot semnadtsatyi god vo Vladimirskoi gubernii.*, ed. N. Shakhanov (Vladimir, 1927), pp. 16–17; G. Korolev, *Ivanovo-Kineshemskie tekstil'shchiki v 1917 godu* (Moscow, 1927), pp. 12–13; E. N. Burdzhalov, *Vtoraia russkaia revoliutsiia*, vol. 2, *Moskva, front, periferiia* (Moscow, 1971), pp. 180–86; D. A. Furmanov, *Sobranie sochineniia*, 5 vols. (Moscow, 1928), vol. 5, pp. 184–85; there were some 280 enterprises in the Ivanovo-Kineshma region, which included the districts of Shuia, Sereda, Teikovo, Rodniaki, Vichuga, Iur'evets, and Kokhma, in addition to Ivanovo-Voznesensk and Kineshma (Korolev, p. 20).

[7] Burdzhalov, *Vtoraia russkaia revoliutsiia*, vol. 2, p. 288.

[8] Ibid., pp. 220–21.

[9] Ibid., pp. 178, 206–8; Donald J. Raleigh, *Revolution on the Volga: 1917 in Saratov* (Ithaca, N.Y., 1986), pp. 80–81.

Urals and the Don basin were workers apparently content to greet the new regime with smaller demonstrations, partly because the pattern of work in the mines and foundries made strikes of this sort more difficult to organize, partly because most miners and foundry workers, particularly in the Urals, lived in small villages at some distance from their neighbors. Even so, workers in Ekaterinburg demonstrated on March 2 and participated in the organization of a Committee of Social Organizations similar to the one in Moscow; in the Donbass, where some 280,000 miners worked in the Krivoi Rog area, local soviets also formed in every major center. A regional soviet conference in mid-March, the first such gathering in the country, brought together representatives from 48 separate organizations.[10]

Virtually all these strikes were classified by the Factory Inspectorate as political. The designation is appropriate in that strikes were directed not against management but against the old regime (or in support of the new order). Many workers clearly saw the end of tsarism as the chance for significant improvement in their welfare, however, both in terms of the end of factory despotism (especially in state-owned plants) and in terms of higher wages and other direct benefits. The Menshevik leader and new Petrograd Soviet chairman Nikolai Chkheidze put the matter succinctly in a speech reported on March 6 in *Izvestiia*, the Soviet's new daily, when he suggested it would be "absurd" for workers to return to their benches under former conditions. When *Izvestiia* did urge Petrograd workers to resume production on March 7, it encouraged them to demand control over factory and shop administration through workers' committees, to insist on collective agreements ("and see to it that they are put into force at once"), to insist that women's and children's work be regulated, and to demand immediate pay for the days spent on strike ("This is their right, and he who dares to deny it covers himself with shame forever").[11]

In fact, the Petrograd Soviet reflected workers' sentiments as much as or more than it encouraged them. From the moment the political victory was won, Petrograd workers, particularly in the Vyborg district, turned the thrust of their protests against management. The end of autocracy meant political freedoms, of course, but the importance of these was embedded for many in the opportunities thus opened for economic betterment.

---

[10] F. P. Bystrykh, "Rabochee stachechnoe dvizhenie na Urale v period podgotovki velikoi oktiabr'skoi sotsialisticheskoi revoliutsii," in *Rabochii klass i rabochee dvizhenie v Rossii v 1917 godu* (Moscow, 1964), especially pp. 117–19; V. Ia. Borshchevskii, "Stachechnoe dvizhenie v Donbasse v period podgotovki oktiabria," in ibid., pp. 136 ff; Burdzhalov, *Vtoraia russkaia revoliutsiia*, vol. 2, pp. 234–35.

[11] *Izvestiia* (Petrograd), March 6, 7, 1917.

Thus 7,000 workers of New Lessner noisily opposed the end of their strike on March 7 until firm guarantees of the sort listed by *Izvestiia* were made. At the United Cable factory, Langenzippen, Tudor, Shchetinin, and elsewhere, workers agreed to return on March 9 to an eight-hour shift, introduced on their own accord over management opposition. In some cases, like those of the Vulcan machine-construction works and the James Beck textile factory across the Nevka tributary from Vyborg, work was resumed for the time being "under old conditions," but clearly with the expectation that improvements would be forthcoming.[12]

Elsewhere, workers forcefully ejected particularly offensive foremen and managers from plants and factories, sometimes carting them symbolically out of the factory in a wheelbarrow. In Arkhangel, according to reports of the Factory Inspectorate, workers accused an engineer and two of his technical assistants of illegalities at the port and prevented them from continuing their duties. In Vladimir, a newly formed workers' militia at the Sobinskaia textile plant arrested the English manager K. K. Smith and sent him to the Soviet. Similar instances occurred in other textile plants of the district, in Viatka (at the Dolgushkin and Laptev leather works), at several large textile plants in Kaluga and Kostroma, and especially in Moscow, where the Inspectorate recorded some 16 cases.[13] As many as 60 members of the Baltic shipyard administration in Petrograd may have been treated this way.[14] According to a later account, workers at the huge Putilov complex murdered the plant director and his aide and threw their bodies into the Obvodnyi canal.[15] These actions were obviously of enormous concern to plant owners, soviet leaders, and government officials alike. On March 7, the PSFMO gathered in an emergency session to discuss them and initiated the series of meetings and negotiations that led to the well-known agreement of March 10 recognizing factory committees as legitimate institutions, establishing a network of conciliation boards, and instituting the eight-hour working day. Thereafter work in the capital returned more or less to normal.[16]

The issues at hand varied somewhat from place to place, but everywhere strikers seemed to associate political change with improvements in the workplace and other economic gains. Industrial workers in Moscow were most concerned with the eight-hour working day, particularly after

[12] *Revoliutsionnoe dvizhenie v Rossii posle sverzheniia samoderzhaviia* (Moscow, 1957), pp. 229–31.

[13] TsGIA SSSR, f. 23, op. 27, d. 360, ll. 7–14.

[14] S. A. Smith, *Red Petrograd: Revolution in the Factories, 1917–1918* (Cambridge, 1983), p. 55, citing LGIA, f. 416, op. 5, d. 30, l. 24.

[15] N. Paialin, "Putilovskii zavod v 1917 godu," *Krasnaia Letopis'* 3 (1932), p. 172.

[16] See the factory-by-factory review in *Revoliutsionnoe dvizheniia posle sverzheniia samoderzhaviia*, pp. 229–30; the agreement itself is on p. 242.

the March 10 agreement in Petrograd. Here the Soviet at first tried only to mediate between workers and their employers, referring disputes to its newly created conflict commission.[17] By March 18, when pressured Moscow Soviet leaders convened to discuss the question, reports indicated that workers at as many as one-third of the city's enterprises had already instituted an eight-hour day on their own (*iavochnym poriadkom*).[18] In Tula and at Sormovo, near Nizhnii Novgorod, workers also insisted on an eight-hour day and returned to work only when they felt that their local soviets agreed it was necessary.[19]

In Vladimir province, and among textile workers generally in the Ivanovo-Voznesensk district, the pressing question had to do more with food than with hours. Workers demanded flour rations, some of which had been promised for weeks but not delivered because of short supplies, although they returned to their jobs without their demands being met as the new regime took power.[20] Elsewhere the immediate issue was money. In Kovrov, Saratov, and Kherson, workers demanded higher wages; at the Tarnopol Brothers plant in Odessa, which manufactured artillery shells and proximity fuses, workers struck on March 3 for an increase in piece rates.[21]

THE FORMATION OF FACTORY COMMITTEES, TRADE UNIONS, AND OTHER ORGANS OF MOBILIZATION

Largely because their strikes and demonstrations required some organization, workers almost everywhere formed factory committees in the first days of the revolution. In some cases, especially in larger Petrograd and Moscow plants, they also formed their own factory militias, sometimes complementing, sometimes replacing, district police. Workers' committees were necessary to lead and coordinate protests and to act as spokesmen for striking workers with factory administrations. Such committees had organized in 1905. They also had more recent antecedents in groups encouraged by the WICs as part of the broad effort here as elsewhere to enlist workers in rationalizing production to support the war.[22] Militias

[17] See *Izvestiia Moskovskogo Soveta Rabochikh Deputatov* (hereafter *Izvestiia* (Moscow)), March 14, 1917.

[18] See the discussion in Koenker, *Moscow Workers*, pp. 107–9.

[19] TsGIA, f. 23, op. 16, d. 271, l. 11; Burdzhalov, *Vtoraia russkaia revoliutsiia*, vol. 2, pp. 177, 168–69.

[20] TsGIA, f. 23, op. 16, d. 235, l. 10, 12.

[21] Ibid., d. 235, l. 14, d. 259, l. 4, d. 271, l. 11.

[22] See Lewis H. Siegelbaum, *The Politics of Industrial Mobilization in Russia, 1914–1917: A Study of the War-Industries Committees* (London, 1983), especially chap. 7.

were formed primarily as a defense against what was expected to be a brutal counterattack by tsarist troops (the force of which in Russia's earlier revolutionary moments was still, for many, a vivid memory). In Petrograd, armed bands appeared in numbers during the day on Monday, February 27, as garrison troops joined the demonstrations and local militias were disarmed.[23]

Historians tend to stress the role of these groups, as well as of trade unions and other similar organizations, as "organs of mass mobilization," reflecting in John Keep's words again, the "processes underway amidst the confusion . . . which determined the shape of the new order."[24] They were certainly important structural components in the politicization of labor in 1917 and served from the first, as Keep and others have suggested, to link Bolsheviks and other socialist parties to the rank and file. Yet it does not necessarily follow that the real impact of such groups was to organize, direct, or even mobilize activist workers.

This was so because constant tension and conflict also surrounded their work, directly relating to strikes. There was tension, for example, among the various organizing groups themselves: between factory committees and the trade union bodies that soon formed to lead them (and whose local cells they became), and between party representatives and groups like the soviet executive committees, many of whose leaders considered the creation of a stable political order to be their primary goal. Even in early March, conflicts emerged among these groups over the appropriateness of continuing strikes or initiating new ones, and over the question of institutional (or representational) legitimacy.

Additional tensions had to do with the way in which the political order of the "revolutionary democracy," was to be defined, and hence the committees' own institutional definition. Problems here stemmed from both potential and real conflicts among different levels of leadership, and between factory spokesmen and their own rank and file, especially in larger plants. These had to do with issues such as the role of factory meetings as opposed to committees themselves in setting policies; the scope or boundaries of committee authority; the rights and powers of factory militias; and of course, political orientations. At the Obukhov metal works, the Sestroretsk armament complex, and scores of other plants in Petrograd, many workers were performing militia service as often as two or three days a week while at the same time receiving their factory wages. Plant committees found themselves negotiating with owners on the one hand and militia leaders on the other over compensation, problems of staffing,

---

[23] Rex A. Wade, *Red Guards and Workers' Militias in the Russian Revolution* (Stanford, Calif., 1984), especially chap. 2.
[24] Keep, *The Russian Revolution*, p. ix.

and questions of future production, especially after the PSFMO insisted factory militias be disbanded. Such internal conflicts affected the development of organizations attempting to impose some direction on workers' activism every bit as much as conflicts between different organizations themselves.

Still, factory committees and similar groups emerged in early March as vital elements in the mobilization of labor. On the railroads and in state defense plants, particularly Petrograd metal works, committees quickly assumed responsibility for restoring order, maintaining production, and in the case of the railroads, tackling certain basic administrative problems long seen as barriers to line efficiency. With the flight of tsarist administrators, workers' committees in these state enterprises assumed quasimanagerial status. But more important for our purposes is the manner in which here and elsewhere, as the movement rapidly spread outwards from Petrograd, these new organizations reflected workers' revolutionary commitments and aspirations at the most elemental level.[25]

This "primary" quality of the new committees burdened them from the start with extremely difficult (and perhaps insoluble) problems. One was to satisfy in some meaningful way the diverse and at times contradictory aspirations of their constituents, a task made enormously difficult by the committees' very democratic foundations and by the consequent frequent turnover in their membership. Factory meetings soon became a regular part of the workday in most enterprises. Committees explained and justified their actions at these meetings, heard suggestions and criticisms, committed themselves to new goals, and submitted to new elections. On the major railroads in both Petrograd and Moscow, for example, full-scale line congresses began to meet toward the end of March to advise the Main (*Glavnyi*) Line Committees on how to perform their tasks. The most important of these, as the first congress of worker delegates on the Moscow-Kazan Railroad put it, was "improving our welfare—the first order of the day!"[26] Elsewhere, committees struggled over the very ques-

---

[25] D. A. Kovalenko, "Bor'ba fabrichno-zavodskikh komitetov Petrograda za rabochii kontrol' nad proizvodstvom (mart–oktiabr' 1917 goda)," *Istoricheskie Zapiski* 61 (1957), pp. 66–111; D. A. Tseitlin, "Fabrichno-zavodskie komitety Petrograda v fevrale–oktiabre 1917 goda," *Voprosy Istorii* 11 (1956), p. 86, surveys committee activity; *Golos Zheleznodorozhnika*, June 4, 7, 1917; *Vestnik Omskoi Zheleznoi Dorogi*, 12 (March 25, 1917); *Vestnik Ekaterininskoi Zheleznoi Dorogi*, 489–90 (March 4–17, 1917); *Vestnik Iuzhnykh Zheleznykh Dorog*, 13 (March 27, 1917). By the end of the first week of March, there were hundreds of such committees in Russia's industrial plants and railroads, sometimes several representing workers in different shops within a single large enterprise. See L. S. Gaponenko, *Rabochii klass Rossii v 1917 godu* (Moscow, 1970), pp. 290–300.

[26] *Izvestiia Ispolnitel'nago Komiteta Moskovskogo Uzla, Moskovsko-Kazanskoi Zheleznoi Dorogi*, 1 (May 30, 1917).

tion of submitting to the decisions of the Petrograd Soviet and its Executive Committee, whose leaders emerged largely from the ranks of the Menshevik intelligentsia.[27]

Factory committees also struggled to gain the broader legitimacy needed to enhance their authority with plant owners, as well as among their own rank and file. Their powerful endorsement by the Petrograd Soviet on March 5, followed shortly by the March 10 agreement with Petrograd manufacturers authorizing committees "in all factories and mills, elected on the basis of universal, equal and direct suffrage," were major steps in this regard, but the most important event was the promulgation of Provisional Government legislation on April 23 legitimizing their creation nationwide.[28] Yet the committees' task of sustaining their authority actually *increased* as the weeks went by, despite this legislation, as Russia's economy deteriorated and the strains of revolutionary polarization increased.

Committees also faced the need to overcome their relative weakness as individual enterprise units in the struggle with management and the state. This led naturally to efforts beginning in March to coordinate committee activities through central councils, trade unions, and local soviets, but this process simultaneously engendered new tensions over individual enterprise needs and objectives as opposed to those of more broadly based institutions. In Moscow, many factory committees were closely related to (and in some enterprises even organized by) the Labor Section of the city Soviet.[29] This was true in many other places as well; even in Petrograd, where the elements of spontaneity and autonomy were so strong, close links were quickly forged with district (*raionnyi*) soviets.[30] The issue of whether committees were essentially the primary cells for broader associations like trade unions (and hence subordinate to broader interests), or autonomous representatives of their own worker constituents, caused bitter debate at gatherings like the first Petrograd Conference of Factory

[27] See especially Ziva Galili y Garcia, *The Menshevik Leaders of the Petrograd Soviet, 1917: Social Realities and Political Strategies in the Russian Revolution* (Princeton, 1989); Wade, *Red Guards*, chap. 3, especially pp. 60–66; G. I. Zlokazov, *Petrogradskii sovet rabochikh i soldatskikh deputatov v period mirnogo razvitiia revoliutsii* (Moscow, 1969), chap. 1; B. M. Freidlin, *Ocherki istorii rabochego dvizheniia v Rossii v 1917 godu* (Moscow, 1967), pp. 63ff.

[28] See *Izvestiia* (Petrograd), March 6, 11, 1917; *Vestnik Vremennago Pravitel'stva*, April 25, 1917; also Robert P. Browder and Alexander F. Kerensky, eds., *The Russian Provisional Government 1917: Documents*, 3 vols. (Stanford, Calif., 1961), vol. 2, pp. 709–20.

[29] D. V. Antoshkin, *Professional'noe dvizhenie sluzhashchikh, 1917–1924 gody* (Moscow, 1927), pp. 385–86; Koenker, *Moscow Workers*, pp. 144–49.

[30] *Organizatsiia i stroitel'stvo sovetov rabochikh deputatov v 1917 godu. Sbornik dokumentov*, ed. P. O. Gorin (Moscow, 1928), p. 144 (misprinted as p. 134 in this edition).

Committees, held in late May, as well as within the labor movement more generally.[31]

All of these problems directly related to strikes. Factory committees were obviously the logical leadership organs for strikes, and indeed, their members risked being replaced by new members or supplanted by specially elected strike committees if they resisted rank-and-file pressure. But factory committees also risked losing their legitimacy if they pressed strikes with little chance of success or took other actions that workers deemed too risky. At the same time, the very process necessary to legitimize committee authority tended to identify committees with those supporting social order (and particularly those advocating the orderly resolution of grievances), rather than with radicalism or the militant activism often felt by those wanting to strike. The consolidation of committee authority within the managerial structure of an enterprise thus tended to contradict efforts at consolidating committee authority among workers. Finally, problems associated with coordinating the actions of an individual enterprise with goals or policies of broader associations like the trade unions meant that factory committees could not always play the role in strikes that even some of their own members desired. The Petrograd Central Council of Factory Committees attempted to distinguish between conflicts within enterprises (the purview of factory committees) and broader, industrywide conflicts between labor and management (the province of trade unions).[32] The line, of course, was impossible to draw clearly.

A similar set of contradictions faced the trade unions. Although many union figures had continued to play an important role in the labor movement after 1905, when most union activities were repressed, the task of organizing national unions had to begin virtually from scratch with the fall of the tsarist regime; because of the rapid formation of factory committees and soviets, the new union leadership had to work hard in the early weeks of the revolution to develop rank-and-file support.[33] Still, unions "sprang up like mushrooms" in March, as *Rabochaia Gazeta* put it.[34] A meeting in Petrograd of the newly organized Central Bureau of

---

[31] *Pervaia rabochaia konferentsiia fabrichno-zavodskikh komitetov* (Petrograd, 1917); see the discussion in S. Schwarz, *Fabrichno-zavodskie komitety i profsoiuzy v pervye gody revoliutsii*, MS, Hoover Institution on War, Revolution, and Peace. 1935, pp. 3–5.

[32] Schwarz, *Fabrichno-zavodskie komitety*, pp. 3–5. See also the discussion in Antoshkin, *Professional'noe dvizhenie sluzhashchikh*, pp. 383–86; *Pervaia rabochaia konferentsiia fabrichno-zavodskikh komitetov.*

[33] Antoshkin, *Professional'noe dvizhenie sluzhashchikh*, pp. 376ff; Koenker, *Moscow Workers*, pp. 147–49; see Victoria E. Bonnell, *Roots of Rebellion: Workers' Politics and Organizations in St. Petersburg and Moscow, 1900–1914* (Berkeley, 1983).

[34] *Rabochaia Gazeta*, March 25, 1917.

Trade Unions on March 20 drew representatives from the printers, construction workers, post and telegraph employees, gold, silver, and bronze workers, clerks and shop assistants, barbers, pharmacists, bank workers, and medical personnel, as well as metalists, bakers, and leather workers.[35] By one count, more than 70 different unions had organized by the end of April.[36] Among the most active were the leather workers, whose first constituent conferences were held in Petrograd on March 5 and in Moscow six days later. (An organizational assembly of leather workers on Vasil'evskii Island in Petrograd drew as many as 2,000 people on March 12.)[37] The metalists, whose union had remained relatively strong and politically developed throughout the years of reaction, were also active early, as were the printers, whose Menshevik attachments were strong. In contrast, the chemical workers union did not formally organize until May.[38]

As they organized in 1917, trade union leaders, too, faced a myriad of problems, some similar to those of the factory committees. They competed for worker loyalty with the committees and with local soviets, and insofar as the basis of union membership was often dues payments, they frequently found themselves at a disadvantage. When the paper workers' union organized at the Golodaevskii factory, for example, the elected treasurer absconded with the first 2,500 rubles of collected dues. Workers refused to pay more, preferring to do without the union's "help."[39] Questions of trade union goals in Russia's new democratic order also had to be resolved, along with difficult issues about the unions' role in developing the country's economy. Among these various problems, the most important in terms of strikes had to do with principles of organization, administrative structure, and relations with the Provisional regime.

The central organizational issue, in Russia as elsewhere, was whether a union should be organized on a craft or production basis: whether it should represent a particular specialty within an industrial branch, in other words, or all workers involved with branch production. In practice, workers tended to organize by craft, especially in highly stratified indus-

[35] Ibid.

[36] Antoshkin, *Professional'noe dvizhenie sluzhashchikh*, p 374. See also A. M. Pankratova, *Politicheskaia bor'ba v Rossiiskom profdvizhenii. 1917–1918 gody* (Leningrad, 1927); A. Anskii, ed., *Professional'noe dvizhenie v Petrograde v 1917 godu* (Leningrad, 1928); Koenker, *Moscow Workers*, pp. 374–75.

[37] *Revoliutsionnoe dvizhenie v Rossii posle sverzheniia samoderzhaviia*, pp. 530–31.

[38] *Rabochii Khimik*, 1 (February 1918). The first gathering of the metalist union in Petrograd was on March 12, and although the delegates had not been formally elected, they established a commission of 21 members with the right to govern the union temporarily until a constituent congress could be convened (*Pravda*, March 15, 1917).

[39] *Piat' let raboty* (Moscow, 1922), p. 18 (publication of the Union of Paperworkers).

tries like the railroads. Most early unions formed on this basis in 1917; although many eventually became "sections" of national organizations based on production principles, craft loyalties remained particularly strong among printers, textile workers, railroaders, and food industry workers, and they were a force to be reckoned with everywhere. The woodworkers' union, for example, came to represent some 25,000 workers in the capital, employed in the most diverse branches of production, from munitions (where they constructed the shipping crates) to railroad cars, airplane manufacture, construction, docks, and furniture. It soon found itself contending with other powerful unions whose members would be directly affected by woodworker strikes.

Since different groups of workers had different working conditions, rates of pay, and political agendas even within a single factory, the relationship between union organization and strikes was hardly predictable or consistent. Pressures by engine drivers and their union to strike Petrograd railroads in April were resented, for example, by members of other railroad craft unions who saw the engine drivers as a highly paid elite, eager to preserve their privileges rather than advance the cause of railroaders as a whole.[40] Among postal workers, higher-ranking employees resented efforts of ordinary clerks to increase wages to their own "Grade Four" salary level and organized their own "Union of the Postal Employees' Intelligentsia" (*Soiuz Intelligentnykh Sluzhashchikh*) to protect their privileged position.[41] And when the printers' union began to negotiate its first contract with Petrograd employers and attempted to engineer substantial gains for its lowest paid members by giving them raises of 90 to 100 percent (compared to 50 percent for skilled workers), its efforts were stoutly resisted by the aristocratic typesetters. They revolted when confronted with a pay differential of only 1.4 to one, angered at the apparent undervaluation of their relative worth.[42]

It is hardly surprising in these circumstances that as scores of different unions began to organize on all levels in March and early April, they faced difficulties in establishing boundaries between their own activities and interests and those of other institutions. Like the factory committees they were attempting to coordinate, they remained a central element of

---

[40] *Volia i Dumy Zheleznodorozhnika*, April 22, 1917. See the discussion in William G. Rosenberg, "The Democratization of Russia's Railroads in 1917," *American Historical Review* 86, no. 5 (December 1981), pp. 986–94.

[41] K. V. Bazilevich, *Professional'noe dvizhenie rabotnikov sviazi (1917–1918 gody)* (Moscow, 1927), pp. 34–35.

[42] A. Tikhanov, "Rabochie-pechatniki v 1917 godu," in *Materialy po istorii professional'nogo dvizheniia*, vol. 4 (Moscow, 1925), pp. 185–87; *Izvestiia* (Petrograd), August 3, 5, 11, 1917.

labor mobilization. But, also like the committees, they had to contend with an even more powerful element in the mobilization process—the strike itself— which continued to bring workers directly into the struggle for economic and political change.

THE LIFE OF THE STRIKE

One of the most important contributions of Michelle Perrot's superb study of late nineteenth-century strikes in France is her appreciation of the strike as a "fête of liberation," an outburst of collective human feelings as important or more so to our understanding of historical experience as any abstract statistical formulations.[43] To insist on the notion of festival is not to minimize in any way the tensions, anger, anxieties, or personal suffering that were also part of most strikers' experience, but to prompt instead a broadly organic and humanistic conception of the strike phenomenon, one that allows us to recognize what Perrot describes as its life cycle: its origins, initial actions, structuring, maturation, and eventual denouement. Strikes tend to follow a pattern of development, in other words, that is both mobilizing agent and process, and that both shapes and is itself shaped by the personal experiences of the strikers. However difficult to measure, the totality of such elements in any given strike constitutes a complex subjective reality that may in the end have as great or greater an influence on the broader course of events as such familiar (and more readily measured) objective elements as interrupted production, cost and price fluctuations, or shifts in the composition of the work force.

HOW STRIKES BEGAN:
WORKERS ON THE OFFENSIVE

It is common to think of strikes beginning suddenly, born of spontaneous anger or frustration. One of the Russian words for "strike," *zabastovka*, derives in fact from the Italian *basta*, meaning "enough!"[44] And, to be sure, strikes begin at a point beyond which workers are not prepared to accept further restrictions or assaults on their well-being, their dignity, or their claims to justice. But in understanding the origins of strikes it is important to recognize that even seemingly spontaneous strikes almost

[43] Michelle Perrot, *Les Ouvriers en grève: France, 1871–1890* (Paris, 1974), vol. 2, pp. 548ff.

[44] The word *zabastovka* seems to predate the modern labor movement. It occurs in the works of the nineteenth-century writer Lermontov, and Gogol uses it in *The Inspector General (Revizor)*. See Akademiia nauk SSSR, *Slovar' Russkogo iazyka* (Moscow, 1984), vol. 2, pt. 3.

always involve at least some degree of forethought and organization, even if this is not apparent to outsiders. One must also recognize that although all strikes obviously do not begin in the same way, they can generally be understood in terms of two broad categories, even if the line between them cannot always be clearly drawn in practice.

Some strikes are deliberate, offensive actions, designed to achieve specific goals. Often strikers have assessed the risks and weighed the alternatives with some care, recognizing, especially in prerevolutionary Russia, that there were few safeguards against managerial retribution, and cognizant that striking might cost them their jobs. Other strikes, in contrast, develop as a consequence of actions by an employer. These are not so much an offensive tactic as a defensive response to what is perceived as intolerable or unacceptable management behavior. Defensive strikes would presumably not occur if the terms or conditions governing the workplace had not been changed by the owners. They often involve relatively little planning, although the arbitrary acts to which they are a response are almost always part of a longer pattern of management behavior, and workers have either struck before, or thought and talked about walking out.[45]

The strikes that occurred immediately following the formation of the Provisional Government in March were largely offensive, just as they would prove to be throughout the year. They began, according to most sources, because "management refused to meet worker demands." We estimate that some 80 percent of the strikes we have recorded in the weeks between March 3 and April 18, and approximately 85 percent of all strikes between March 3 and October 25, were of this sort. Some 70 percent of these were strikes for higher wages. They included nonindustrial workers as well as those in factories. Appearances notwithstanding, strikes thus rarely began suddenly, without warning or preparation, either in March and April or throughout the rest of 1917. Wage strikes in particular, the overwhelming number of cases, were almost always preceded by some formal presentation of demands to plant owners. They frequently involved at least some degree of negotiation.

The mood of strikers in offensive strikes was also commonly enthusiastic, even ebullient, in the weeks immediately following the February uprising, reflecting its tremendous success. Strike reports refer to the "good

[45] Most labor activism, of course, is the result of at least some interaction with management; what one party might consider "offensive" is therefore often understood by the other as a defensive response to provocation. In addition, information about the course of events is very often unclear even to the participants. Misinterpretation is commonplace. For the historian, the evidence itself is even more ambiguous, even if understanding how strikes began is central to understanding the nature of worker activism.

humor" of strikers, their enthusiasm and high spirit. Metalworkers at one of Moscow's two Rozental plants joined strikers at their sister plant on March 21 in such spirit, pledging to return to work only if their management satisfied the other workers' grievances. And at the same meeting that authorized this strike, the metalists instructed their factory committee to send greetings to the Bolshevik newspaper *Sotsial Demokrat*.[46] This and similar examples of enthusiasm undoubtedly occurred because workers on the offensive saw themselves taking the initiative in a new political environment where strikes now were not only considered legal (even though no formal legislation to this effect had been passed), but also broadly recognized as a legitimate, even admirable means of struggle. To strike was risky, but it was also a means of associating with a rich and heroic tradition, of identifying broadly with Russia's revolutionary past and present. Offensive strikes signified commitment as well as challenge.

A somewhat different picture emerges when one looks at strikes that began defensively, as a consequence of management actions of one sort or another or other events that workers perceived as provocations. Strikes of this sort were much closer to being spontaneous, even if considered beforehand. They were also rarely well organized, at least at the start. They tended to occur most frequently in industrial enterprises rather than in the nonindustrial sector (although this pattern may also reflect a bias in reporting). In larger plants, they frequently began in a particular section or shop, sometimes spreading throughout the whole enterprise, sometimes not. In contrast to offensive strikes, work stoppages of this sort also tended to be much less controlled, as workers vented their anger over whatever (or whomever) they felt was acting against them.

The most common defensive strike occurred in reaction to workers being fired. Although this was overwhelmingly a phenomenon of the later spring, particularly the period between mid-April and the end of June, it occurred frequently enough in the period immediately following the February revolution to stir angry memories and great bitterness. During the war, strikes were very often followed by mass layoffs, and fired workers found themselves pressed into the army, especially in state plants. More than 1,500 persons were sent to the front from the Briansk metal works in Orel province, for example, after strikes in April and May of 1916; and as recently as the beginning of February 1917, 2,100 workers were discharged at the Tula armament works after a strike, 100 of whom were sent immediately to the army.[47] When owners reacted to the February strikes in a similar way, workers were outraged and staunch in their resistance.

[46] *Sotsial Demokrat*, March 23, 1917.
[47] *Rabochee dvizhenie v gody voiny*, ed. M. G. Fleer (Moscow, 1925), p. 163; *Oktiabr' v Tule. Sbornik dokumentov i materialov* (Tula, 1957), p. 7.

Thus when owners of the Shevrokhrom shoe factory announced on March 14 that they were laying off 300 workers because of "declining productivity," the news drew angry denunciations from workers and Soviet spokesmen alike, and precipitated a 17-day strike by all 2,000 employees. Strike leaders were adamant about management's apparent intention to rehire its workforce after a careful screening, a common prewar tactic.[48] Similar strikes occurred at the Phoenix-Kobriner plant, the Gurevich textile factory, and elsewhere.[49] Such strikes also occurred, however, when only one or two employees were fired. Fifty workers left their benches at the Serpinskii metals plant in Moscow's Butyrki district, for instance, to protest the dismissal of only one of their comrades.[50]

As the weeks unfolded, an increasing number of defensive strikes also began because production was curtailed, workers were locked out, or owners announced their intention to shut down, events that also resulted, of course, in workers losing (or fearing to lose) their jobs. The first instance of this sort we know of occurred as early as March 7, when owners of the S. E. Maitop tobacco factory on Lazaretnaia street in Feodosia locked workers out. At the Moscow envelope factory Shabat, the owner announced he would fire five workers as a result of increased costs after February, provoking a strike in which workers demanded their hours be cut back instead. At the Levi clothing shop, also in Moscow, some 25 tailors were locked out when the owner felt he could not make wage concessions.[51]

What was important in these first weeks of the revolution, and the range of strike origins suggests this, was that workers were ready to use strikes freely either to promote or defend their interests, even without any national economic agenda or central coordinating institutions. On the contrary, both the agenda and the institutions themselves were emerging in response to (and in interaction with) the cumulative experiences of strikes and strikers. Labor mobilization through strikes from below paralleled and complemented political and social organization above, as did, of course, workers' committees and other kinds of social formations in the factories. This interaction could be seen already in March and April in the ways individual strikes evolved after they had begun, as the experience of striking made mobilization from below a broad and powerful reality for politically conscious workers and their less alert comrades alike.

[48] *Sotsial Demokrat*, March 17, 23, 1917.

[49] *Sotsial Demokrat*, April 16, May 4, 1917; *Izvestiia* (Moscow), April 18, 1917; *Torgovo-Promyshlennaia Gazeta*, May 4, 1917; *Proletarii* (Moscow), May 5, 1917.

[50] *Vpered*, April 15, 1917; *Izvestiia* (Moscow), April 21, 1917.

[51] *Rabochaia Gazeta*, March 9, 1917; *Sotsial Demokrat*, April 26, May 2, 1917; *Vpered*, April 26, May 3, 1917; *Zemlia i Volia*, April 27, 1917; *Trudovaia Kopeika*, April 29, 1917.

WORKERS' MEETINGS AND ORGANIZATIONS:
THE FOUNDATIONS OF SOLIDARITY

Whatever their origin, Russian strikes derived most of their enormous energy early in 1917 from large and often boisterous meetings, or rallies. The gathering of workers with flags and banners in factory yards or city theaters was not only a great part of the Russian revolutionary spectacle, but a vital part of the process of labor mobilization. If strikes were fetes of liberation, as Michelle Perrot suggests, in which exuberant workers felt suddenly free from constraining routines, the "rally" (*miting*) was a crucial catalyst and precipitant. On strike during the March revolution, workers at the Provodnik factory near Moscow seemed to do nothing but hold meetings. Instructions came from the city to elect deputies to the Soviet: "another excuse for a meeting." And these meetings attracted not only workers "but even their wives and children . . . the meetings continued for hours; some people would leave, others would arrive, but there was never a shortage of speakers in the front of the hall."[52]

Meetings served first to inform workers in a factory or profession about what was going on. If a small group of laborers walked out of a metal shop to protest new factory regulations, a mass meeting might take place to spread the word and mobilize support. If trade unions or factory committees decided themselves to call a strike, the first step was to gather workers together to explain their goals and plans. A series of meetings preceded the strike of gold- and silversmiths in a shop in Moscow's luxury commercial district in May. Workers first presented their demands, then met again four days later to listen to the owner's reply. He claimed poverty: the firm had been losing 15,000 rubles a year on its filigree handbags since the start of the war. Discussion at the meeting was lively. One worker proposed a collection to help make up the owner's losses, but the majority reiterated their demands of a 30 percent increase in pay and a two-week paid annual vacation. A subsequent meeting listened to a new response from the owner and voted to strike, adding to the list of demands recognition of the factory committee and the trade union.[53]

Meetings also served to mobilize workers in a number of different factories or workshops and to assure small groups of workers that much larger numbers were struggling with them. This was especially true of women and of service personnel like laundresses, retail clerks, restaurant workers, and even tailors, who often found themselves in the difficult position of confronting managers or shop owners in very small numbers.

---

[52] Eduard Dune, "Zapiski krasnogvardeitsa," MS, Nicolaevsky Collection, Hoover Institution on War, Revolution, and Peace, p. 28.

[53] *Proletarii* (Moscow), May 18, 1917.

One such instance occurred early on in Moscow, where frequent meetings allowed workers in a dozen or more tailor shops in the Tverskoi district to coordinate a strike against a well-organized owners' union.[54] Among woodworkers, scattered among a wide variety of different manufacturing plants and elsewhere, such gatherings served to spread feelings of solidarity, even among groups not accustomed to interacting with each other. In addition, it was at these meetings that workers either organized their strike committees or endorsed the desires of their factory committees or unions about their strike. In either case, meetings served to legitimize formal strike leadership and to coordinate and strengthen strike organization. After the strike had begun, assemblies and rallies served to inform and to keep spirits high.

Factory committees, specially organized strike committees, and trade unions all played important roles in strikes, but in varying ways and to varying degrees, particularly early in the year. Our file has information about the involvement of some type of organization for a little more than 360 strikes in 1917, although for only 19 in the period between March 3 and April 18. Few of these contain explicit information about the presence of strike committees. Still, such organizations played a crucial role in a number of strikes, particularly in the retail sector and in the chemical industry, where other forms of organization were relatively weak. The more familiar factory committees, at times serving as trade union organizations within an individual enterprise, played a leadership role most frequently in strikes in the highly concentrated metal industry, but also among construction workers, wood workers, and railroad workers.

Strike committees were not, of course, permanent organizations, but they served indirectly as a means of drawing activists into the trade union movement, expecially in March and early April. And certainly the unions themselves played an increasingly important role in small strikes, formulating demands, providing various kinds of support, and serving at times themselves in a leadership role, especially where the scale of industry was small or traditions and organizational experience were weak. Union representatives were especially active in strikes of chemical workers, printers, textile workers, and retail employees. On the other hand, strikes among metalworkers showed relatively little union involvement, either in the weeks immediately after February or throughout the year. Metalists were used to acting on their own.[55]

Factory committees did not support strike actions in every instance in

---

[54] *Izvestiia* (Moscow), May 7, 1917.

[55] Only 25 percent of strikes in the industry reported any union presence, compared to more than 35 percent in printing and paper manufacturing, and 33 percent in plants manufacturing leather goods and other animal products.

March and early April, nor did they later in the year. Neither, of course, did trade unions. There was a deliberate effort in the spring on the part of some of these organizations to try to contain strike tendencies, in order "to protect the image of the Soviet," as the metalist union leadership in Kharkov expressed it, and otherwise demonstrate proletarian responsibility.[56] Railroad union leaders in Kiev, for example, wired their comrades in Moscow to "show an example of sacrifice of personal interests for the sake of the general good," while the food workers' union put tremendous pressure on striking flour mill workers to continue to work even though their strike would officially continue.[57] This was true elsewhere as well throughout the year, and in different industries and circumstances: both among politically conscious printers in Moscow, for example, and among women workers at the large Girault textile plant. Here some 4,000 women wanted higher wages but were ambivalent about striking; they were ultimately persuaded not to strike when textile union representatives told them a walkout would hurt the union as a whole.[58]

MOBILIZING SUPPORT

Once a strike was organized, one of the leadership's first tasks was to try to secure outside support, especially when it was clear that the conflict would not be settled quickly. Most strikes between the February revolution and the crisis that broke on April 20 over the new government's war aims lasted for only one or two days. But some, like the strike of 575 cotton cloth workers at Novinki in Vladimir province, or the Minsk woodworkers' strike on March 16, lasted a week, and a walkout at Lebedev textiles on March 13 went on for almost two weeks.[59] The Lebedev strike concerned management's refusal to pay workers for time lost striking, an issue of obvious importance in defining the boundaries of future

---

[56] *Pobeda velikoi oktiabr'skoi sotsialisticheskoi revoliutsiia i ustanovlenie sovetskoi vlasti na Ukraine* (Kiev, 1957), p. 514.

[57] *Volia i Dumy Zheleznodorozhnika*, June 1, 1917; *Delo Naroda*, July 3, 1917; *Rabochaia Gazeta*, July 12, 1917.

[58] *Pechatnik* 1 (June 11, 1917; *Zemlia i Volia*, June 9, 1917; *Vpered*, June 15, 1917. Overall, our data show only 13 cases between March and October in which trade unions specifically opposed strikes, most occurring after the July Days. (In contrast, we also find that trade unions supported strikers almost half the time when strikes were provoked in some way by management.) Further, almost 20 percent of all strikes reported active trade union support for the months of April, May, June, and July, but only some 12 percent of the strikes in each month between August and October reported such support. (If we add to the category of overt "support" the strikes for which reports noted union "presence" but said nothing about an active role in support of strike activity, all figures rise, but the months of May to July are still characterized by much greater union involvement in support of strikes than the last three months before the October revolution.)

[59] TsGIA, f. 23, op. 16, d. 235, l. 14; d. 248, l. 6; *Sotsial Demokrat*, March 17, 25, 1917.

conflict, and one in dispute at many other plants as well. In strikes of this sort, workers had few resources to carry them through without great hardship, particularly when inadequate wages or foodstuffs were the initial reasons for striking.

Realizing that the power of the strike as a weapon against management depended in large measure on the strikers' ability to maintain themselves without regular wages or other means, strike leaders often had to scramble for help at the very moment workers were leaving their jobs. Strike committees asked most often for contributions to a strike fund. They also pleaded with other workers to join their protest with strikes of their own. In approximately 10 percent of the cases in our file for the year as a whole, striking workers actually did receive some type of help, but the most common assistance came in the form of "endorsements," rather than material aid. The latter generally came from other unions, factory committees at larger plants, or local soviets. In fewer than 5 percent of the cases did other workers actually join strikers from another plant in response to such appeals by initiating strikes of their own.

On the other hand, as trade unions organized in March and early April, they immediately began collecting internal funds to prepare for future walkouts; when strike funds were collected from other factories, they were often well publicized, particularly in *Pravda*. When 100 workers at the Anglo-Russian Telephone factory went on strike in Petrograd on March 14, for example, *Pravda* reported that Dinamo workers had collected 29 rubles toward a strike fund and hoped to gather more.[60] Commonly, workers also authorized deductions for strike funds from their regular pay through factory committees, again publicizing their contributions in newspapers and the trade union press.[61]

There were, of course, powerful subjective aspects of this appeal for support, and these suggest how important the strike process itself was in mobilizing labor generally in 1917, and in developing components of proletarian identity and class consciousness. Striking workers clearly worried a great deal about risking their jobs and their personal safety, even in the weeks immediately following the triumphs of February and early March. They consequently sought the help of newly formed district and city soviets to keep strikebreakers from taking their places. At the Mercury boot manufacturer in Moscow, for example, workers struck on March 14 after plant owners, expecting that the revolution would lead to a drastic reduc-

[60] *Rabochaia Gazeta*, March 15, 1917; *Pravda*, March 15, 1917.

[61] Moscow's workers, for example, reported upwards of 400,000 rubles in contributions to strike funds for all of 1917. See Koenker, *Moscow Workers*, p. 274, and chap. 7. Moscow leather workers accumulated a 19,000 ruble strike chest before their big strike began in August (ibid., p. 321). The strike fund of tavern and restaurant workers was reported in early July to hold some 20,000 rubles (*Zemlia i Volia*, July 9, 1917).

tion in orders from the army, cut wages in half. The newly organized leather workers' union appealed in *Izvestiia* for others to stay away and used the Mercury strike to broaden its membership.[62] Similar patterns emerged when retail clerks struck in Petrograd on April 11. The clerks in particular feared that shop owners might easily hire replacements. Their strike angered merchants and potential customers alike and had the incidental effect of bringing the strike weapon out of factory districts like Vyborg to the city's most fashionable neighborhoods. When Petrograd laundry workers struck in early May, they had to entreat to the city Soviet to help protect them against physical abuse.[63]

As we have seen, the laundry workers' strike was closely followed in the press, partly because it, too, caused great inconvenience for residents of the affluent central districts, partly because it was the first major service-sector strike in Petrograd that mobilized large numbers of previously passive workers, most of whom were women. At a series of meetings, striking workers repeatedly asked for help. They worried publicly about others taking their places and asked other trade unions to prevent anyone from being hired in the future who could be identified as a strikebreaker. Lists of strikebreakers' names were published in the press, along with expressions of deep gratitude for the moral and material support that was allowing them to continue their struggle "with confidence and determination."[64]

Participation in strikes of this sort was clearly a momentous event for those concerned. Support from outsiders bolstered morale and helped workers overcome their initial fears and inhibitions, but it also communicated clearly the importance of "proletarian solidarity," a phrase that was often used by labor activists in Petrograd and elsewhere but that sounded slightly foreign to many. Strike experience could not be taught. For women laundry workers and others long on the periphery of Russia's labor movement, strikes brought dignity and a sense of social identity. Strikes demystified employers' power. And once mobilized, strikers were often ready to press again, if need be, for further change.

THE CHOICE OF STRIKE TACTICS

The life of any strike included decisive moments when workers had to make critical tactical decisions. The Vyborg workers' decision to cross the

[62] *Izvestiia* (Moscow), March 17, 1917.
[63] *Rabochaia Gazeta*, April 12, 1917; *Novaia Zhizn'*, May 12, 1917.
[64] *Zemlia i Volia*, May 10, 1917; *Novaia Zhizn'*, May 11, 12, 13, 17, 1917; *Izvestiia* (Petrograd), May 11, 16, 17, 19, 21, 1917; *Rabochaia Gazeta*, May 14, 17, 18, 24, 26, 1917; *Pravda*, May 20, 22, 23, 25, 27, 29, 30, June 1, 3, 1917 (n.s.).

Neva on February 27 instead of staying near their factories or even returning to work was perhaps the most dramatic example of this sort, but similar kinds of choices were made in every work stoppage throughout 1917.

One of the first had to do with what *kind* of strike workers wanted to conduct. In most cases, employees simply decided to leave their positions and force an enterprise to close. But in some instances workers decided to conduct what they called an "Italian strike" (*italianskaia zabastovka*). This could signify either a work slowdown or a sit-down, during which workers stayed inside the plant but did not work.[65] In the former case, a short Italian strike might precede a conventional strike, as at the Putilov wharf, where woodworkers staged a one-day Italian strike before joining a broader strike in October. More commonly, workers chose an Italian strike as a way of pressuring management without risking their jobs or

[65] *Tret'ya vserossiiskaya konferentsiya professional'nykh soyuzov, 1917 goda. Stenografícheskii otchet*, ed. Diane Koenker (1927; reprint, Millwood, N.Y., 1982), pp. 244, 503. The derivation of the term "Italian strike" is unclear. The practice of the slowdown, "ca'canny," or "folded-arms strike" was widespread in England and France in the 1890s and later. A 1920 British labor relations study confirms the prevalence of the tactic during World War I: "that demoralising doctrine, so harmful to the State, the employer, and the man himself, commonly called by the name 'Ca'canny,' or 'Go slow,' to limit work to the level of the slowest man, to restrict production when the world is crying out for goods, has before, during, and after the War been a great influence in setting class against class" (George Ranken Askwith, *Industrial Problems and Disputes* (1920; reprint, Freeport, N.Y., 1971), p. 299). S. A. Smith contends that the term was borrowed from the well-known slowdowns on the Italian railways in February 1905 (*Red Petrograd*, p. 275–76, n. 88; see also Daniel L. Horowitz, *The Italian Labor Movement* (Cambridge, Mass., 1963), p. 69, who dates these episodes to 1904; the railroaders called their tactic "noncollaboration," or "working-to-rule.")

It is difficult to pinpoint more precisely the origin of the term in Russia, or the moment (if ever) when it changed from a slowdown to a more militant sit-down or factory occupation. A. Aleksandrov, *Polnyi Russko-angliski slovar'* (St. Petersburg), gives no reference to "Italian strike" in his 1885, 1917, 1919, or 1923 editions. D. N. Ushakov, *Tol'kovyi slovar' Russkogo iazyka*, vol. 1 (Moscow, 1935), gives the first published definition of *italianskaia zabastovka*: "the type of strike when the striking workers remain in the workplace, and either do not commence work or work only according to the rules and obey them to the point of absurdity [*do bessmyslitsy*]" (col. 1265). A. I. Smirnitskii, *Russko-angliiski slovar'* (Moscow, 1949), translates the term as "ca'canny strike, underhand sabotage, stay-in strike, sit-down strike" (p. 280). By the 1965 edition, the definition had been shortened (and radicalized) to "stay-in strike, sit-down strike" (p. 227). The authoritative dictionary of the Academy of Sciences in 1957 also adopted the more radical definition: "a type of strike in which the strikers appear at the work place but either do not work or only go through the motions of working" (Akademiia nauka. Institut iazykoznanie, *Slovar' Russkogo iazyka* (Moscow, 1957), p. 961). The term may have passed into Russian usage via the interaction of Russian and Italian activists at the Russian Social Democratic party workers' school at Capri; no other country's labor movement uses the term.

their wages, especially when employers let it be known they might close an enterprise for a time to conserve materials or hire a new, less costly workforce. Workers at the Menshikov machine-construction plant in Moscow began an Italian strike on March 25, for example, when their foremen began to penalize workers elected as representatives to the soviets, calling them "graft takers" (*podkuplenki*), and the plant owners refused to pay workers their former wages for a reduced (eight-hour) workday. A wholesale firing (*raschet*) was also announced for March 29, with new hirings after Easter. It was thus extremely risky for workers to leave the plant or to otherwise try to shut production down completely.[66]

Explicit sit-downs, or factory occupations, occurred much less often, and rarely in March and April. (In fact, this tactic was seldom employed anywhere in industrialized Europe before the notable Italian factory occupations in 1920, although there were a few cases of "Italian strikes" in the Petersburg metal industry in 1912 and 1913 that involved factory occupations and not just slowdowns.) A veteran trade union leader, D. A. Kol'tsov, suggests part of the reason: "Such methods of struggle as an Italian strike, or sabotage, . . . introduce only irritation among workers, and do not organize the working class." But the printers' union accepted the Italian strike as a suitable weapon of class struggle, along with strikes, boycotts, sympathy strikes, and participation on conciliation boards.[67]

Once a strike was under way, workers frequently declared the struck firm under boycott (*boikot*). Usually this served as an appeal to other workers not to take the place of the strikers. In other cases, particularly in the printing trades, it was a way of asking other shops not to take jobs originally contracted to the shop on strike. Such an appeal was made in April by workers at the Iakovlev printshop in Moscow, for example, and received prominent notice in the press.[68] Less frequently, the term referred to a boycott of the products or services of a struck establishment. Waiters and waitresses in Petrograd tea shops urged "citizens" not to patronize tea rooms on strike.[69] Striking Petrograd chauffeurs marked automobiles *not* under boycott with special passes.[70] Boycotts were also directed against individuals. (Indeed, the term was coined through the

---

[66] *Sotsial Demokrat*, March 25, 1917.

[67] See Paolo Spriano, *The Occupation of the Factories*, trans. Gwyn Williams (London, 1975), and Iu. I. Korablev, ed., *Rabochee dvizhenie v Petrograda v 1912–1917 godakh. Dokumenty i materialy* (Leningrad, 1958), pp. 54, 138–40. We are indebted to Heather Hogan for the latter reference.

[68] See, e.g., *Sotsial Demokrat*, April 25, 1917.

[69] *Rabochaia Gazeta*, July 13, 1917.

[70] *Rabochaia Gazeta*, July 19, 1917.

ostracism of Captain William Boycott by his Irish subjects.)[71] Striking Petrograd housepainters named one Petr Ivanovich Smirnov as a strikebreaker and promised to "boycott" him as well as their contractor.[72] The Moscow precious metals trade union leadership voted to boycott a worker at the Bovdzei factory for not submitting to the decisions of the factory's general meeting and for not joining the trade union. The worker was declared a "harmful element" and driven from his job as well as ostracized.[73]

Although the boycott appeared to be a common adjunct to strikes, the use of pickets to warn off strikebreakers and to publicize the strike was not. Sometimes groups of workers clustered around entrances to make entry difficult; often in these circumstances strikers argued with those attempting to pass or otherwise attempted to explain and promote their cause. Factory militias and the Red Guard units that later replaced them also often stood guard, preventing suppliers or other traffic from entering or leaving a plant. During a strike at the Tver Iron Foundry in March, workers placed guards at the gates to prevent the owners from removing valuables or other factory documents, fearing this might jeopardize the plant's ability to continue in operation once the strike was settled.[74]

At the same time, workers rarely made an explicit decision about the legality of their tactics: we have found no evidence at all in the documents of factory meetings of specific questions in this regard. Undoubtedly, this was partly due to the very centrality of "illegal" strikes to the February revolution as a whole. It may also have related to the fact that the legality of strikes themselves continued to remain unclear, since no formal legislation was forthcoming from the new regime. Certainly workers thought of strikes as legitimate weapons from the very first. On the other hand, once violence against foremen and managers subsided in early March and the authority of factory committees' was consolidated, striking workers seem to have generally conducted themselves in an orderly fashion, largely avoiding provocative acts or unnecessary conflict, several well-publicized cases to the contrary notwithstanding.[75]

Likewise, direct acts of sabotage or violence did not accompany these

---

[71] See Michael A. Gordon, "The Labor Boycott in New York City, 1880–1886," *Labor History* 16, no. 2 (Spring 1975), pp. 184–229.

[72] *Rabochaia Gazeta*, May 16, 1917; *Zemlia i Volia*, May 10, 1917.

[73] *Izvestiia* (Moscow), October 18, 1917.

[74] *Velikaia oktiabr'skaia sotsialisticheskaia revoliutsiia. Khronika sobytii*, 4 vols. (Moscow, 1957–61), vol. 1, p. 281 (henceforth VOSR. *Khronika sobytii*).

[75] See William G. Rosenberg and Diane P. Koenker, "The Limits of Formal Protest: Worker Activism and Social Polarization in Petrograd and Moscow, March to October, 1917," *American Historical Review* 92, no. 2 (April 1987), pp. 296–326.

strikes. Not a single case appears in our files in which strikers deliberately sabotaged machinery or otherwise interfered in a destructive way with equipment or tools needed for production. (Some glass was broken in an early strike involving Petrograd sales clerks, and damage was reported in a strike of miners in the Donbass. But in a third case, at the Khanzhonkov film factory in Moscow, workers claimed their employer himself vandalized his property, called in police, and blamed the damage on the workers in order to discredit their cause.)[76] Nor were Russian workers incendiaries or otherwise inclined to destroy property, despite the prevalence of such acts in the countryside.[77] Despite images to the contrary, striking workers seem instead to have recognized that their own well-being depended on their ability, ultimately, to resume production with a minimum degree of disruption. As we shall see in the following chapter, acts of violence took place in other contexts, apart from strikes. Indeed, episodes of violence by workers were also balanced by reports of violence *against* workers, particularly early in the year.[78]

INTERVENTIONS, OUTCOMES, AND THE LIFE OF THE STRIKE IN WORKERS' POLITICAL EXPERIENCE

The life of a strike in 1917 was sometimes affected by the intervention of outsiders, especially after Lenin's return to Petrograd on April 3 and the rapid politicization of Russian economic life thereafter. Speakers from various factories and parties often addressed strikers' meetings, particularly in Petrograd and Moscow, pressing workers to action or offering moral or material support. Delegations also made their way to striking factories in the countryside, especially in the Central Industrial Region around Moscow. Obviously strikes presented rich opportunities to polit-

---

[76] *Russkaia Volia*, May 18, 1917; *Volia Naroda*, October 17, 1917; *Sotsial Demokrat*, April 22, 1917.

[77] For the year as a whole we record in our file only 28 cases involving some associated violence. Six involved personal assaults, six involved property, and the rest do not distinguish clearly between repressive violence directed against strikers and violence by strikers. Most violent acts initiated by strikers, moreover, occurred in September and October.

[78] In seven strikes, workers reported repressive actions against them by employers, the police, and sometimes the public. During the October pharmacists' strike in Petrograd, a pharmacy owner fired his revolver at a member of the strike committee but was then left free by the militia (*Novaia Zhizn'*, October 12, 1917). Another pharmacy proprietor was taken into custody after his gunshot wounded a striker (*Rabochaia Gazeta*, October 14, 1917). Petrograd laundresses faced a barrage of opposition as they held out for higher wages. One laundry proprietor received a four-day jail term for threatening his striking workers with an axe (*Novaia Zhizn'*, May 20, 1917).

ical organizers, but workers struck overwhelmingly in 1917 for their own economic betterment, and not because outsiders urged them forward.

To some extent, *every* supportive newspaper commentary could be seen as a form of outside intervention. By this criterion, virtually all strikes in our file involved outsiders, even in March and April. As the year unfolded, institutions like the soviets and the state ministries played increasing roles in the strike process, but the available evidence gives no indication that groups of workers ever felt they were losing control over their own activities. On the other hand, through their participation in strikes, the collection and allocation of strike funds, and the often heated discussions over the course of negotiations or other strike-related matters, workers almost certainly developed an awareness of the complex political and economic dimensions of Russia's revolutionary conjuncture, as well as some sensitivity to problems of organization, political method, and the relations of production. In a phrase, workers always learned from strikes, even if what they learned was not what they or others expected.

Perhaps the most important lesson was that *gains of some sort were almost always forthcoming from strikes*, however much they also involved hardship. Between March 3 and the April crisis, fewer than 5 percent of the cases in our file ended in outright failure, and these were mostly in rural textile plants, where striking workers found themselves relatively isolated. Only a single struck enterprise closed during these weeks, as far as we can determine. In the overwhelming majority of cases, strikes resulted in real gains, even if workers' demands were not completely satisfied. Over the entire year, as we have indicated in chapter 2, fewer than 9 percent of the strikes between March 3 and October 25 for which we have clear information regarding outcomes resulted in outright defeats for workers, and in only 15 cases were factories forced to close. This held true for every major industrial or service sector, including textiles.

We will return more than once in the following chapters to these remarkable patterns and consider their various implications for Russia's revolutionary development in 1917. Given the rapid deterioration of Russia's economy in these months, workers had abundant reason to be wary of strikes in their struggle for economic betterment, since work stoppages obviously threatened their wages. Also, few social services were available outside the workplace. Unemployment support was minimal, even after trade unions developed substantial reserve funds. Yet the risk clearly proved worth taking; in the process, strikers in every branch of industry and commerce learned first-hand the benefits of collective action more surely than they could have through even the most accomplished political agitators.

TOWARD A "ROUTINE" PATTERN
OF STRIKE ACTIVITY

Whether this remarkable pattern of success emerged in the immediate post-February period because strikes and strikers carried by the momentum of the revolution intimidated employers, or whether gains resulted because plant owners recognized the strikers' legitimate economic needs, the effect of these early successes was to encourage workers from the start to see strikes as a more-or-less routine way of negotiating their demands. The largest group of strikes in these weeks occurred at the textile plants around Kovrov and Ivanovo-Voznesensk in Vladimir province, where many, especially women, found themselves in desperate conditions. As early as March 5, a three-day strike at the Kolmaznik cotton-spinning plant in the village of Cheritsy won 12 yards of free cloth for workers and an Easter bonus equalling 10 percent of their annual wage. A two-day strike shortly afterward at the Malinin textile plant brought 1,500 workers a 20 percent Easter bonus. So did a series of subsequent strikes at manufacturers throughout the province: at the Buzinyi Linen Manufacturer beginning on March 7, where more than 800 workers won bonuses and new apartment and bath privileges in a six-day strike, and at a group of linen plants in Vladimir on March 9, where workers in the first major economic strike of the revolutionary period involving more than one enterprise won a 15 percent increase in wages as well as an additional stipend for lodging. On March 10, workers from these plants and others organized a large, one-day "victory" strike to celebrate their achievements. Parades and demonstrations brought scores of workers together from schools, offices, and retail stores, as well as other factories and workshops.[79] Similar demonstrations took place in Moscow, Kursk, Ekaterinoslav (an important industrial center in the Ukraine with more than 100 enterprises), and even distant Vladivostok on Sunday, March 12.[80]

Obviously not, every strike was a success. In Tula, workers at the Litvak textile manufacturer called off a three-day strike when owners refused their demands for an eight-hour workday.[81] So did woodworkers in Minsk and other groups of workers elsewhere (although many returned to work expecting the issue to be worked out in negotiations).[82]

---

[79] TSGIA, f. 23, op. 16, d. 235, ll. 10, 12; *Tysiacha deviatsot semnadtsatyi god vo Vladimirskoi*, p. 26.

[80] VOSR. *Khronika sobytii*, vol. 1, pp. 169–81.

[81] TSGIA, f. 23, op. 16, d. 268, l. 3.

[82] TSGIA, f. 23, op. 16, d. 248, l. 8; *Velikaia oktiabr'skaia sotsialisticheskaia revoliutsiia v Belorussii* (Minsk, 1957), vol. 1, p. 168.

What is important about these few failures, however, is not only that they were rare exceptions to the rule in March and early April, but that factory inspectors consistently described them as "orderly" or "peaceful," despite their relative lack of success. Clearly the political climate favored gains for workers willing to strike in the first weeks of the revolution, and many obviously knew it. Virtually every one of the strikes reported by the Factory Inspectorate for early April also recorded significant gains. At the Dedovkin chemical works in Ivanovo-Voznesensk, strikers refused an initial offer for a 20 percent pay increase, and won on April 13 gains of from 60 to 150 percent. At Melenkovskii textiles in Vladimir, some 5,000 strikers won a 100 percent wage increase.[83]

Newly organized soviets clearly aided workers in these efforts, even as many organizers also warned workers against unrealistic expectations and urged restraint. At the Tobol'ka plant of the huge Prokhorov Manufacturing Company, for example, Tver Soviet leaders persuaded almost 2,000 striking workers to return to work pending a review of their demands by the company's central administration. (They won a 33 percent increase in wages and an increase of from two to five rubles in living allowance.)[84] In Revel', the Soviet secured an eight-hour working day for workers at the city's two largest plants, the Northern (Becker) and the Russko-Baltic Steel Works, which produced railroad equipment and freight cars as well as armaments. Workers here were also promised a 50 percent wage hike.[85] Additionally, plant owners largely conceded an eight-hour workday to strikers in many areas, even if the question of overtime work and wages remained a subject of dispute. The number of strikes and strikers consequently began to decline toward the end of March.

Strikes themselves gradually lost much of the anger and militance associated with the February events and the subsequent purge of particularly offensive foremen. As the Factory Inspectorate reported to A. I. Konovalov, the minister of trade and industry, on March 28, work everywhere was returning more or less to normal. The labor movement in the factories was settling down, even if "not yet completely orderly," and more important, the situation was clearly improving. Even the intensity of labor productivity seemed to be increasing, partly, in the Inspectorate's view, under the influence of the approaching holidays, partly because of the efforts of many factory committees.

[83] TSGIA, f. 23, op. 16, d. 235, ll. 42, 44, 39.
[84] TSGIA, f. 23, op. 16, d. 266, l. 7.
[85] *Velikaia oktiabr'skaia sotsialisticheskaia revoliutsiia v Estonii* (Tallin, 1958), pp. 20–21.

With regard to the actions in many plants of factory committees, it must be pointed out that in a number (*tselyi riad*) of instances, these committees have succeeded in instituting a certain degree of order and discipline among the workforce, and in general, it can be seen that their influence and importance is related to the number of conscious (*soznatel'nye*) workers in a given plant. Their authority is rather significant, therefore, at the metal plants, and almost non-existent in enterprises with relatively 'under-cultured' (*malokul'-turnye*) employees.[86]

In this very routinization of strikes in late March and early April, however, one can discern the sources of future conflict. The most important lay, paradoxically, in the extraordinary rates of success. Given the tenuous nature of Russia's economy, and particularly the shortages of goods and raw materials that had so badly affected production over the winter, workers' gains could only be temporary unless the larger problems could be effectively addressed. The delivery of fuel between March 10 and April 9 to the very region where textile workers had just won a major wage increase was less than half of what was needed, for instance, and similar shortfalls were occurring elsewhere.[87] This required, in effect, an end to the war in reasonably quick order, either through complete victory, as Foreign Minister Miliukov and others in the new cabinet assumed, or, as the Soviet leaders argued, through a firm and resilient "revolutionary defense," leading to a European settlement "without annexations or indemnities." Neither was likely. Yet the success of these early strikes naturally bred expectations that comparable gains could be won elsewhere with similar tactics, if negotiations or other methods failed. Such a view tended to ignore both economic realities and the ways in which plant owners and others were themselves reacting to these early strikes with increasing hostility and resistance.

In addition, the extent to which many early strikes were settled with large monetary bonuses and special allocations toward subsistance created, in effect, a reservoir of need. Bonuses were one-time payments, quickly expended. Many workers consequently faced the prospect of reverting to previous rates that they had already claimed were inadequate or demanding new bonuses through additional strike actions. At best, in other words, the bonus system was a short-term palliative. Insofar as it

[86] TSGIA, f. 23, op. 27, d. 360, ll. 59, 61.

[87] G. A. Trukan, "O nekotorykh voprosakh rabochego dvizheniia v tsentral'nom promyshlennom raione," in *Rabochii klass i rabochee dvizhenie v Rossii v 1917 godu*, pp. 106–7.

contributed in some places to rising prices, it necessarily left an increasingly problematic shortfall and serious problems for the future.

The role played by local soviets also created sources for future conflict. Their initial support and encouragement to strikers, particularly in Petrograd, tended again to raise workers' expectations to problematic heights. So did the soviets' initial successes in securing owners' concessions. For a time, of course, this was all to the good, especially insofar as soviets used their influence to persuade workers and manufacturers to organize and utilize conciliation boards or other mediation mechanisms. But again, it was far easier for soviets to assist in organizing mediation boards than it was for them to ensure favorable settlements. Also, soviet leaders in many places were promising workers more than they could probably deliver. In Baku, for example, the soviet executive committee specifically asked local oil workers to refrain from separate strike actions since it would itself formulate demands and negotiate a collective contract.[88] And insofar as this latter power was bound to diminish over time, Mensheviks, Socialist Revolutionaries, and other relatively moderate members of the early soviet leadership blocs were inadvertently (but also inescapably) jeopardizing their future credibility and authority.

Finally, these early strikes still left major issues unresolved. In important ways, economic concessions were the easiest for owners to make. The eight-hour workday caused some difficulties, particularly as it affected military production, and the response of some owners in challenging workers' patriotism even stirred concern among the troops.[89] But an eight-hour workday simply meant in many places an adjustment of wages for overtime.[90] By focusing, understandably enough, on wage and hour issues, early strikes tested rather tentatively the boundaries of labor-management conflict. Although there were notable exceptions, striking workers largely left aside for the moment issues that challenged traditional managerial prerogatives, like the right to hire and fire employees, and even important matters concerning managerial authority on the shop floor and factory social relations, especially as they related to women. To some extent, this had to do with the formation of factory committees and the fact that legislation formally legalizing these organizations and defining their competence was being prepared for early promulgation by the

---

[88] Burdzhalov, *Vtoraia Russkaia revoliutsiia*, vol. 2, p. 293.

[89] *Revoliutsionnoe dvizhenie v Rossii posle sverzheniia samoderzhaniia*, pp. 534, 564; Allan K. Wildman, *The End of the Russian Imperial Army: The Old Army and the Soldiers' Revolt (March–April 1917)* (Princeton, N.J., 1980), pp. 315–21.

[90] Overtime work could not be mandatory by law, but the decline in productivity caused by a shorter workday led the management of some plants, like the Gorlovskii artillery works, to require it anyway (TSGIA, f. 23, op. 27, d. 360, l. 3).

government and the Petrograd Soviet. In part, it was also the result of workers forcefully dispatching the most offensive foremen and managerial personnel and settling what they regarded as the most egregious cases of "managerial autocracy" on their own. But however extensive these instances were in the first weeks of the revolution, the boundaries of managerial authority remained to be defined. So did the difficult complementary issue of workers' prerogatives. Meantime, the very success of early strikes and their obvious effectiveness as a means of mobilizing even "under-cultured" workers, as the factory inspectors described them, made it more than likely that strikes would again be the tactic of choice as the labor offensive continued and the boundaries of conflict were extended.

4

. . . .

MANAGEMENT-LABOR RELATIONS IN
THE WEEKS OF CONCILIATION

The mobilization of labor was, of course, only one element in the complex processes of class conflict and social polarization in 1917. Paralleling the adjustment of Russian workers to new conditions of political democracy and their efforts to find appropriate new ways to achieve workplace goals was the struggle of Russia's plant owners and factory managers to determine their own attitudes and strategies, and to define in the process their own relationships to Russia's new order. If strikes played a major role in the mobilization of labor, worker activism of all sorts was itself a central element in the mobilization of management, and labor-management relations more generally underlay broader processes of social polarization, at least in urban areas.

"Social polarization" is a complex concept, involving multiple relationships between workers' activism in all of its complex forms, and the equally complex (and complementary) activism of industrialists and other members of the business community. The phenomenon is hardly unique to Russia. As Lawrence Stone has suggested, the coalescence "into two coherent groups or alliances of what are naturally and normally a series of fractional and shifting tensions within society" can be found in many revolutionary contexts.[1] Nor was social polarization in any way restricted to urban Russia in 1917. In the countryside, it involved the emergence of irreconcilable conflict between peasant and gentry interests, and a broad rejection on the peasants' part of state-supported systems of land use, taxation, and agricultural development.

Wherever one addresses the issue, however, it is necessary to deal with a range of qualitative as well as numerical data. By "social polarization," we refer not only to the emergence of contending power blocs, but to

---

[1] Lawrence Stone, "Theories of Revolution," *World Politics* 18 (1966), p. 165. The notion also underlies Crane Brinton's theorized clash between French moderates and extremists in 1789, and it can be found as well in the French and German revolutions of 1848. See Crane Brinton, *The Anatomy of Revolution* (1938; reprint, New York, 1965), and Peter Amman, "Revolution: A Redefinition," *Political Science Quarterly* 77 (1962), pp. 36–53.

mentalities, to competing and incompatible sets of values, and to the emergence of broadly different conceptions about fundamental elements of social order. In this regard, what is most important about the February revolution is that it radically changed the environment of protest without engendering a clear sense of what was "appropriate" or "legitimate," or producing a constraining mechanism by which the state itself could keep activism within such bounds. Political demonstrations or demonstrative strikes against the tsarist regime were clearly acceptable in broad social circles in ways that comparable actions against a struggling political democracy were not; strikes over economic issues seemed similarly appropriate when industrialists were thought to be profiting from the war, but would obviously appear much less so after February, when they involved the risk of new social and political conflict or seemed to threaten economic collapse. The processes of social polarization thus involved a sorting out of values and interests throughout Russian society in 1917, not in the least measure among industrialists and other members of the business community.

One notion of legitimacy, however, was implicit from the start in the general conceptualization of "bourgeois democracy" shared by Provisional Government figures and soviet leaders alike: democratic Russia would move forward as a Western industrial nation guided by principles and laws similar to those of Western Europe and North America. Rights gained by workers in the West would finally be recognized in Russia as a necessary first step toward social stability based on the orderly resolution of labor-management conflicts. Trade unions and other labor organizations, including factory committees, would be welcomed as a means for labor's legitimate involvement in matters of primary concern, factory despotism would disappear along with other vestiges of tsarist rule, and the right to strike would become not only an appropriate part of labor's struggle for material betterment, and hence an integral part of democratic worker-management relations, but also one of the key civil liberties achieved by the revolution.

These views dominated public discourse during the first weeks of the new order, a time when major changes were introduced in Petrograd and Moscow factories as a result of the workers' own initiatives and the March 10 accord on an eight-hour working day and factory committees. On that date, representatives from more than 300 Petrograd enterprises agreed at a general session of the PSFMO to accept the eight-hour workday as a general standard, without wage reductions, and to sanction factory committees as organs to represent workers' interests.[2] Under great pres-

[2] *Ekonomicheskoe polozhenie Rossii nakanune velikoi oktiabr'skoi sotsialisticheskoi revoliutsii. Dokumenty i materialy*, 3 pts. (Moscow, 1957–67), pt. 1, pp. 511–13.

sure, PSFMO leaders saw the value of concessions in terms of improving productivity and restoring a semblance of industrial order.[3]

The March 10 agreement was also a means of securing what the new minister of trade and industry Konovalov and others regarded as an even more fundamental workplace reform, the creation of conciliation boards (*primiritel'nye kamery*). The boards were intended to resolve labor-management disputes without costly strikes. They were to be established on the basis of worker-management parity within each enterprise that subscribed to the agreement. Initially they had no formal legal status, could impose no penalties for noncompliance, and were hence only consultative organs whose success depended on the good will of both parties. Nonetheless, Konovalov and his supporters clearly hoped that they would lead to the rapid settlement of disputes "free from any sort of external pressure," and in particular, would help restrain coercive acts like the expulsion of foremen and other administrative personnel without at least some review.[4] (Paragraph 7 of the March 10 agreement precluded the removal of foremen or other administrative officals without examination by the boards.)[5] For particularly contentious issues, or issues "of general interest to all Petrograd enterprises or a particular group of enterprises," a Central Conciliation Board was created, composed of representatives in equal numbers from the PSFMO and the Petrograd Soviet.[6]

The creation of the Central Board was symbolically quite important. In effect, the political and moral authority of the Petrograd Soviet, dominated by moderate socialists, was being enlisted from the start for the task of resolving industrial disputes in an orderly, regular manner, no minor task. The Central Board began to function on March 31 with 16 worker and management representatives and the Soviet's blessing. In this, moreover, its goals were exactly the same as Konovalov's Ministry of Trade and Industry, whose Labor Section set as its basic goal on March 6 the mediation and reduction of labor-management conflict.[7] The new mediation machinery also had the support of such an historically antilabor management group as the employers' association of the Petrograd metal-

---

[3] *Promyshlennost' i Torgovlia*, 8–9 (1917), p. 214.

[4] *Ekonomicheskoe polozhenie*, pt. 1, p. 512.

[5] See *Izvestiia* (Petrograd), March 11, 1917; N. Dmitriev, "Primiritel'nye kamery v 1917 godu," in *Professional'noe dvizhenie v Petrograde v 1917 godu*, ed. A. Anskii (Leningrad, 1928), pp. 77–78; and *Ekonomicheskoe polozhenie*, pt. 1, p. 512. Conciliation boards had emerged briefly in Russia with the 1905 revolution and were proposed again by the Central WIC in 1916. See Lewis H. Siegelbaum, *The Politics of Industrial Mobilization in Russia: A Study of the War-Industries Committees* (New York, 1983), pp. 176–78.

[6] Dmitriev, "Primiritel'nye kamery," pp. 77–78.

[7] V. L. Meller and A. M. Pankratova, eds., *Rabochee dvizhenie v 1917 godu* (Moscow, 1926), p. 561.

working industry, which asked its membership on April 6 to send all disputes to these bodies.[8]

Similar institutions were soon organized elsewhere. The Moscow Soviet enacted a general policy on conciliation boards in early April and organized its own Central Conciliation Board in May.[9] In most places the size of such groups varied from between two and six members from each side. Workers' representatives were most commonly elected by factory meetings, those from management appointed from above. An examination of some 72 firms in which boards began to function in the spring of 1917 shows that a little more than half had "permanent" worker representatives, while the remainder were elected each time a conflict emerged, a system that also helped institutionalize the factory meeting.[10]

One can thus discern at the upper reaches of the new society, among soviet leaders, the new Provisional regime, and at least some representatives of the trade-industrial community, the emergence of a general consensus in the first weeks of the new order on both the appropriate means for resolving labor-management conflict and the general boundaries of legitimate labor activism, even if there was no effective way to ensure that these boundaries were respected. Many on the shop floor and in commercial establishments undoubtedly shared these views, even as they waited to see if the new regime would actually serve their interests. Their hopes, too, for economic and social security seemed initially to depend on a satisfactory resolution of grievances, increased production and better access to goods, a lessening of social conflict, and an end to the war—the stated goals, in effect, of Russia's new but unsettled "bourgeois" order.

THE MOBILIZATION OF MANAGEMENT

As they had before, however, major differences continued to divide Russia's manufacturers and industrialists after February, especially on the question of what the new order was to be like. As Ziva Galili y Garcia has argued, the emergence of progressive Moscow entrepreneurs like Konovalov in positions of political responsibility was partly the result of special circumstances, rather than broad support among Moscow and es-

[8] *Ekonomicheskoe polozhenie*, pt. 1, p. 164.

[9] The legal constitution of the boards received formal state approval in August, when the Provisional Government created a commission to draft appropriate legislation. The best discussion of the conciliation boards is Heather Hogan, "Conciliation Boards in Revolutionary Petrograd: Aspects of the Crisis of Labor-Management Relations in 1917," *Russian History* 9, no. 1 (1982), pp. 49–66. See also K. A. Pazhitnov, *Primiritel'nyia kamery i treteiskii sud v promyshlennosti* (Petrograd, 1917), p. 25; I. Rubin, *Primiritel'naia kamera i treteiskii sud* (Moscow, 1917), pp. 20–26.

[10] Dmitriev, "Primiritel'nye kamery," pp. 87–88.

pecially Petrograd industrialists. Konovalov in particular had developed a national reputation through his work in the WICs. Establishing close ties in the WIC with affiliated workers' groups, he had also developed a certain amount of patronage as a result of the committees' involvement in the distribution of government contracts.[11] He and others also strengthened relations with leading Kadets, representatives of Russia's strongest liberal party. According to Irakli Tsereteli, soon the dominant force of socialist moderation in the Petrograd Soviet, Konovalov's special interest before 1917 in social legislation and his efforts to work closely with democratic circles reflected a desire to "Europeanize" worker-management relations in Russia.[12] These attributes also made him generally acceptable at first to Soviet leaders as minister of trade and industry, if it also opened him to sharp attacks from those who continued to believe harsh policies toward workers were the only way to increase production.

In Petrograd, industrialists and bankers like M. M. Fedorov, A. I. Putilov, N. N. Kutler and G. Kh. Maidel continued to insist right up until February that the strictest possible measures be used against labor protests, including the militarization of labor, the replacement of strikers with prisoners of war, and the wholesale drafting of worker activists. In the spring of 1916, members of the Petrograd-based Association of Industry and Trade rejected efforts of Riabushinskii and others to draw them into a broader and more conciliatory national organization. Instead, the Putilov plant in particular became a showplace of tough regulations and harsh discipline culminating in the massive lockout of late February. In May 1916, as a result of the industrialists' pressure, the question of militarizing labor was taken up by the Special Council for Defense. Militarization was thought to be especially important for the Putilov complex and for the Parviainen works, which was emerging along with other Vyborg firms as a stronghold of worker unrest. Parviainen and others were also seeking huge interest-free loans from the tsarist regime in order to relocate from Petrograd to the Donbass region, a measure also thought likely to restrain labor militants.[13]

In response, the tsarist regime agreed to sequester Putilov in 1916, although militarization itself was not actually imposed because of Duma

---

[11] Ziva Galili y Garcia, "Commercial-Industrial Circles in War and Revolution: The Failure of 'Industrial Progressivism'," unpublished paper presented at Hebrew University, Jerusalem, January, 1988. See also the discussion in Alfred J. Rieber, *Merchants and Entrepreneurs in Imperial Russia* (Chapel Hill, N.C., 1982).

[12] I. G. Tsereteli, *Vospominaniia o fevral'skoi revoliutsii*, 2 vols. (Paris, 1963), vol. 1, p. 439.

[13] A. L. Sidorov, *Ekonomicheskoe polozhenie Rossii v gody pervoi mirovoi voiny* (Moscow, 1973), pp. 171–72, 240–41.

opposition. It continued to be discussed, however, and the discussions themselves facilitated the imposition of still harsher disciplinary measures in plants under the control of Petrograd banking and industrial circles, including the city's major railroad lines. Prisoners of war also began working in several South Russian mines and metallurgical complexes, whose owners were organized in their own Council of South Russian Industrialists (*Sovet S"ezdov Gornopromyshlennikov Iuga Rossii*) and kept very close ties to the capital.[14]

It was precisely these measures that the more progressive Moscow industrialists found so objectionable. P. P. Riabushinkii, S. I. Chetverikov, S. N. Tret'iakov, A. I. Konovalov and others in this group all had extensive industrial holdings, largely in the textile industry, but they argued forcefully against what they regarded as excessive state involvement in defense production and the narrow and reactionary viewpoints dominating Petrograd. Their concern was over not only the state's ineptitude, nor even the unconscionable profits that the Petrograd banks and industrial barons seemed to be reaping from the war with the regime's support, but also Russia's very ability to survive the war as a great industrial power, fully competitive with Western Europe.

Partly through Riabushinskii's newspaper *Utro Rossii*, and partly through their spokesmen in the Duma and at two conferences of the WICs, members of this group pressed the tsarist regime before 1917 to reduce labor-management conflict and to reform its own economic and administrative practices. They also worked to facilitate production and goods distribution through local WICs, formally organized at the ninth Congress of Representatives of Industry and Trade in May of 1915. These worked fitfully at first, but by 1916, Konovalov and the WIC leadership had managed to place contracts with some 350 enterprises in Moscow and almost twice that number in the country at large, worth some 816 million rubles.[15] They also succeeded in forming so-called Workers' Groups in some 58 of the committees as a means of involving labor directly in the problems of production, and in the process, to reduce labor-management tensions.[16]

These measures brought Riabushinskii, Konovalov, and their colleagues into new conflicts with Putilov, Vyshnegradskii, and other Petrograd and Moscow industrialists. Defense contractors dominated both the PSFMO and the MSFMO. Both groups opposed the very idea of Workers' Groups in the WICs, and before February, the Petrograd Society went so

[14] P. A. Buryshkin, *Moskva kupecheskaia* (New York, 1954), p. 77.

[15] *Rossiia v mirovoi voine, 1914–1918 goda (v tsifrakh)* (Moscow, 1925), p. 58.

[16] See the discussion in Siegelbaum, *Politics*, chap. 7.

far as to refuse even to discuss the possibility of creating conciliation boards to mediate labor-management conflicts, even though the boards were favored by its own central council. The tsarist regime was also antagonistic. Vice-Minister of Trade and Industry Varzar told Konovalov and other members of the Central Council in 1916 that although the government favored "social peace," it opposed "voluntarism" in labor-management relations and rejected conciliation boards because "industrialists and workers find themselves at the present time in completely abnormal circumstances, which exclude the possibility of harmonious relations between them."[17]

In turn, *Utro Rossii* and the Moscow entrepreneurs in 1916 moved forcefully to organize the "progressive bourgeoisie." Riabushinskii's Moscow apartment became the scene for a number of angry meetings at which the textile magnate spoke forcefully about these progressive elements "taking steps toward the complete seizure of executive and legislative power."[18] By the end of 1916, he and others were fully prepared for the "inevitable conflict" between the regime and society and hoped to enter the struggle with a substantial measure of workers' support.[19]

The Moscow industrialists had also succeeded by the end of 1916 in laying the foundations for a new Union of Trade and Industry (*Soiuz Torgovli i Promyshlennosti*) as a counterweight to the Association of Industry and Trade. Riabushinskii, Tret'iakov, and others hoped to unify trade industrialists into a liberal, nonparty organization and "to transform the merchant estate," in Riabushinskii's words, "into a trade-industrial class with a strong state consciousness," even though the tsarist regime remained deeply suspicious and blocked efforts to hold a founding congress in January.[20]

With the collapse of the regime in February, this group moved quickly to the center of political activity. On February 28, representatives from

[17] *Birzhevyia Vedomosti*, February 24, 1916.

[18] B. B. Grave, ed., *Burzhuaziia nakanune fevral'skoi revoliutsii* (Moscow and Leningrad, 1927), pp. 21, 93–96.

[19] See the discussion in V. S. Diakin, *Russkaia burzhuaziia i tsarizm v gody pervoi mirovoi voiny (1914–1917)* (Leningrad, 1967), pp. 195ff.

[20] *Utro Rossii*, December 16, 1916. Instead of a founding congress, a private conference held in Riabushinskii's apartment approved a plan to create an All-Russian Trade-Industrial Union and formed a "Provisional Organizing Committee" consisting of Riabushinskii (president), Tret'iakov, Konovalov, S. A. Smirnov, and D. V. Sirotkin. See V. Ia. Laverychev, "Vserossiiskii soiuz torgovli i promyshlennosti," *Istoricheskie Zapiski* 70 (1961), p. 38. Smirnov had extensive textile interests in Orekhovo-Zuevo and Bogorodsko-Glukhovsk; Sirotkin was a State Duma member and mayor of Nizhnii Novgorod, as well as vice-president of the Central Committee of the All-Russian Union of Cities and president of the Nizhnii region WIC.

eleven Moscow trade-industrialist organizations met at the Moscow Stock Exchange and made plans under the Provisional Committee's leadership to hold their founding congress in March. A. I. Konovalov accepted the portfolio of minister of trade and industry, recognizing that an independent Ministry of Labor would soon have to be created as well.[21] On March 19, the first All-Russian Trade-Industrialist Congress opened in the physics auditorium of Moscow University, drawing more than 1,000 persons and representing itself as the political (but nonparty) voice of Russia's national bourgeoisie. The congress formally organized an All-Russian Trade-Industrialist Union headed by a union council (*Sovet Soiuza*) and began an active campaign to affiliate local and regional associations.[22] By late spring its member groups numbered more than 500.[23] The Congress also organized a political committee including N. A. Berdiaev, Ia. A. Galishkin, I. G. Kogan, S. A. Kotliarevskii, S. V. Lur'e, and S. I. Chetverikov, along with Riabushinskii, Tret'iakov, and S. A. Smirnov, a Moscow Kadet, editor of *Utro Rossii*, and head of the Moscow WICS, who became the political committee's chairman.[24]

These men found Konovalov an eloquent spokesman for their views. "Labor is the basic productive force of the country," the new minister optimistically insisted on assuming his post. "The welfare of the motherland depends upon labor's achievements. The minister of trade and industry believes that a correct approach to and proper solution of the labor question is a most urgent problem. . . . [He] will strive wholeheartedly to satisfy, as much as possible, the needs of the workers, hoping, however, for vigorous cooperation on their part."[25] Konovalov was especially buoyed by the March 10 agreement between the PSFMO and the Soviet, which came about partly because he was able to get PSFMO leaders to meet with Soviet Executive Committee members at the ministry.[26] For

---

[21] A special Labor Section was set up in the meantime to address "urgent problems." See *Zhurnal Zasedanii Vremennago Pravitel'stva* 5 (March 5, 1917), 7 (March 7, 1917); *Vestnik Vremennago Pravitel'stva*, March 7, 1917.

[22] *Promyshlennost' i Torgovlia* 10–11 (April 1, 1917).

[23] P. P. Riabushinskii was elected Council president, with S. N. Tret'iakov as his assistant.

[24] The committee soon co-opted a number of leading Moscow liberals to its ranks, and worked closely with others. Included were N. S. Trubetskoi, P. I. Astrov, T. I. Polner, E. N. Trubetskoi, V. M. Ustinov, P. A. Buryshkin, A. M. Polianskii, and L. A. Katuar, all of whom were active in Kadet party circles, L. A. Mikhel'son, owner of the important Sudzhenskii coal mines in Tomsk province, and A. G. Karpov, member of the council of the Society of Textile Producers in Orekhovo-Zuevo and Bogorodsko-Glukhovskii districts, and a prominent member of the Moscow bank council.

[25] See *Vestnik Vremennago Pravitel'stva*, March 7, 1917, *Revoliutsionnoe dvizhenie v Rossii posle sverzheniia samoderzhaviia* (Moscow, 1957), p. 438, and the discussion in L. S. Gaponenko, *Rabochii klass Rossii v 1917 godu* (Moscow, 1970), pp. 226ff.

[26] A report appears in *Promyshlennost' i Torgovlia*, 8–9 (1917), p. 214. PSFMO leaders

him, as for Tret'iakov, Riabushinskii and others, as well as for Russian workers, the February events were also the culmination of long years of struggle: Russia would finally take its rightful place among civilized and progressive European democracies.

Yet it was not Konovalov's eloquence or values that had pressed the PSFMO into concessions, but the forceful and direct action of Petrograd workers; despite the belated recognition by PSFMO leaders that concilia-tion boards were now an important means of mediating labor-manage-ment conflict, the new minister's base of support was thin. V. D. Zhukov, L. I. Shpergadze, A. A. Bachmanov, and other PSFMO leaders understood very well Russia's new political realities, but at best their alliance with the new regime was uneasy. Their future support depended on whether con-ciliationists like Konovalov could actually restore social peace, put an end to labor activism, and strengthen factory discipline.

Assaults on Management and other Forms of Labor Protest

The urgency of these tasks for industrialists in March and early April had not only to do with strikes. Other types of assaults on management and managerial authority, some quite violent, had also occurred during the February revolution. The most visible and most frightening involved di-rect physical attacks. Less obviously, workers also began to challenge the whole system of power in the industrial workplace, which in many ways replicated the now-discredited patterns of tsarist authority, especially in the arbitrary manner in which foremen and others could fine workers or submit them to humiliating searches. What most concerned Minister Ko-novalov and his supporters in the business community during these weeks, in fact, was not that Russia's economy might be paralyzed by strikes, but that other sorts of attacks on management would strengthen reactionary positions among Petrograd and Moscow industrialists, fuel-ing the very flames of conflict the conciliationists were trying to stamp out.

The extent of direct attacks on factory administrators is impossible to measure. We know that during the first three weeks of March foremen and other managerial personnel were forcefully expelled in Petrograd from Langenzippen, Treugol'nik, the Russian-American Rubber plant, Pressovoi metal works, Puvanov and Galkin, Putilov, Peter the Great Arsenal, the Lafetno stamping plant, and the heel shop of Skorokhod

---

attending included V. D. Zhukov from the Petrograd Metal Works, L. I. Shpergadze from Erikson, and A. A. Bachmanov from the Lessner complex.

leather, among other enterprises, and in Moscow, from major plants like Trekhgornaia, Erikson, the Pavlov mechanical works, and Bromley. Some of those attacked had German names. They were likely targets of attack more because of the way they ran their shops, however, than because of their presumed origins, although Moscow workers at the Provodnik chemical works, which manufactured gunpowder and other military supplies, did arrest several engineers whom they thought were against the war. More common were the actions of workers at Kauchuk rubber, Putilov, and Treugol'nik, who threatened management with violence over wage issues and blocked some administrators from entering the factory, although without formally expelling them or demanding they be fired. A few of these expulsions led to strikes, either by workers or by white-collar employees, colleagues of the targeted supervisor, but the impression left by fragmentary records suggests that the removal of such persons constituted a stream of protest parallel to but separate from strikes.[27]

Judging by reports from Petrograd and Moscow, incidents of this kind occurred much less frequently than strikes, yet one can hardly underestimate their effect on labor-management relations, particularly in March and early April.[28] For one thing, such events served to carry traditions of prerevolutionary activism forcefully into what was supposed to be a very different social and political order. A sack nailed to a foreman's office door or pulled over his head from behind, or the act of carting a foreman out of the factory and dumping him in a manure pile to the accompani-

[27] See, e.g., the reports in VOSR. Khronika sobytii, vol. 1, pp. 86, 129, 163, 248; Russkiia Vedomosti, May 30, 1917; Raionnye sovety Petrograda v 1917 godu, 3 vols. (Moscow and Leningrad, 1964–66), vol. 2, pp. 95, 98; Fabrichno-zavodskie komitety Petrograda v 1917 godu. Protokoly, 2 vols. (Moscow, 1979–82), vol. 2, p. 23; and Rabochaia Gazeta, March 19, 29, 1917.

[28] We have catalogued along with strikes some 350 additional incidents that were not strike related between March 3 and October 25 in Moscow and Petrograd. Our data are limited to incidents that we think involved workers reported in the contemporary press or in subsequent Soviet documentary publications. (These two cities employed about 33 percent of the Russian factory labor force in 1917. [Gaponenko, Rabochii klass, p. 116; Diane Koenker, Moscow Workers and the 1917 Revolution (Princeton, N.J., 1981), chap. 1].) By comparison, our data on strikes include reports on some 373 separate work stoppages between March and October in the two capitals, many of which involved more than one enterprise. One has to be quite wary of the unsystematic way in which nonstrike incidents were reported, since countless labor protests of all sorts did not, of course, find their way into the contemporary press. This material cannot, therefore, be used with statistical precision, but it still constitutes an extensive sample. See William G. Rosenberg and Diane P. Koenker, "The Limits of Formal Protest: Worker Activism and Social Polarization in Petrograd and Moscow, March to October, 1917," American Historical Review 92, no. 2 (April 1987), pp. 296–326, for further discussion of this material.

ment of workers' hoots and jeers—these had long been treasured weapons in the workers' arsenal.[29] For another, such actions invariably raised the spectre of unrestrained, coercive violence. In the case of expulsions and cartings out, foremen were usually removed with little more than symbolic violence. (In one case, a threatened manager sat himself in the wheelbarrow and invited workers to cart him out.)[30] But there were also cases of beatings and even murder. An ousted foreman at the Respirator gas mask factory, for example, was beaten severely after he tried to resist the wheelbarrow by shooting his revolver at the protesting workers.[31] Elsewhere a sniper attempted to shoot the director of the Dinamo factory, wounding instead the factory committee chairman who was engaged in negotiations in the director's office at the time.[32]

Understandably, most such assaults were directed against management personnel directly responsible for controlling workers' wages or work routines. In the system of administration generally used in Russian industry in 1917, foremen were the most visible representatives of industrial management and appeared to many workers to be the most powerful, even though they had little control over the enterprise operations as a whole. Foremen (*mastery*) and their assistants (*podmastery*) normally had their desks or offices on the shop floor, rather than in separate administrative sections or buildings, and they interacted constantly with workers. Under the decentralized system of factory management in effect in most large enterprises, they were responsible for assigning rate or wage schedules to individual workers, checking the quality of work, recording worktime, searching workers as they left the plant, and in some places distributing wages. They also made individual hiring and firing decisions, implementing overall enterprise policy. Although nominally white-collar workers (*sluzhashchie*), they were a variegated group. Most were promoted from the ranks, and hardly white-collar in any but figurative terms.

A worker's relationship with his or her foreman was thus of enormous importance, so much so that in many places workers simply could not find employment unless some family or village contact had been made or

[29] On this, see especially Eduard Dune, "Zapiski krasnogvardeitsa," MS, Nicolaevsky Collection, Hoover Institution on War, Revolution, and Peace, chap. 1. For Petrograd and Moscow, we have found only six recorded cases of "carting out" in 1917, substantially fewer than we had expected, but again, such intimate and traditional actions may often have gone unreported.

[30] They did. This occurred at the Sampsonievskaia textile mill, in a dispute over pay. See *Novaia Zhizn'*, July 7, 1917.

[31] *Novaia Zhizn'*, May 7, 1917; also *Rech'*, May 7, 1917, which omits the detail about the revolver.

[32] *Russkiia Vedomosti*, September 8, 1917.

other personal relationship established.[33] Keeping one's job also involved pleasing the "boss," who before February could easily fire workers for virtually any reason or send their names to the plant director for impressment into the army. It is thus hardly surprising that workers in many plants used the early weeks of conciliation to settle grievances with these people, often in wholesale fashion. At the Treugol'nik rubber plant, for example, a largely female work force threw out more than twenty female foremen who had apparently been promoted during the war and who had used their new authority with excessive zeal. Workers also resisted efforts to allow them to return as ordinary shop employees.[34] In south Russia, miners attacked a number of engineers whom they held responsible for lax safety standards and industrial accidents.[35]

Although incidents of this sort always involved some form of violence, they did not directly challenge the overall system of factory administration or even the basic prerogatives of management as a whole away from the shop floor. For the time being, the ways in which men like Zhukov, Bachmanov, and other leading figures of the various industrial associations directed enterprise operations were still beyond the workers' reach, and perhaps even their sense of how plant administration could be reformed. Joint-stock companies were generally run by private boards of directors, who exercised authority through plant engineers or individual plant directors. Plants under state control like Obukhov, Baltic Shipbuilding, Petrograd Pipe, or the Sestroretsk powder works were run by the Naval Ministry and the Artillery Administration. Investment and production decisions, decisions about the procurement of supplies or contracts, and especially decisions about the development of overall factory policies, rules, and regulations thus occurred without any form of worker participation, as was the case everywhere in Europe at this time. In smaller plants, of course, and in most nonindustrial enterprises, owners themselves took a direct role in hiring and firing and had a good deal more interaction with workers, although in them, too, there was still little effort

[33] I. Gordienko describes coming to Sormovo to find work, for example, and having trouble being hired because of the lack of the proper recommendations or a "*rekomendatel'naia zapiska.*" He eventually secured a job only after calling the foreman of the boiler shop and saying that he had come from Nikolaev at the direction of the foreman's brother. See his *Iz boevogo proshlogo* (Moscow, 1957), pp. 17–18. See also Robert Eugene Johnson, *Peasant and Proletarian: The Working Class of Moscow in the Late Nineteenth Century* (New Brunswick, N.J., 1979), pp. 72–74.

[34] *Birzhevyia Vedomosti*, June 24, 1917.

[35] See D. Shlosberg, "Iz istorii ekonomicheskoi bor'by rabochikh v Donbasse, fevral'–oktiabr' 1917 goda," *Letopis' Revoliutsii* 2 (1927), p. 191; D. A. Tseitlin, "Fabrichno-zavodskie komitety Petrograda v fevrale–oktiabre 1917 goda," *Voprosy Istorii* 11 (1956), p. 86.

on the part of employees to concern themselves with basic management issues.

Yet the assaults of workers forced many at lower levels of factory administration to reconsider their position in the managerial hierarchy. With the organization of local soviets, and especially with the formation of factory committees, ideas about responsibility for enterprise policy began to change. Foremen and other supervisory personnel began to find themselves squeezed by pressures from above and below, so much so that in some places, like the Kulotinskaia textile plant in Nizhnii Novgorod, they declared publicly that they could not "serve two masters" and set a three-week period for the problem to be resolved before they themselves went on strike.[36] In effect, the revolution was beginning to force factory administrators at various levels to confront fundamental issues about their own professional identities. Some began to organize their own unions, strengthening their sense of themselves as secretaries, bookkeepers, accountants, and the like. Others soon joined forces with workers' unions and the factory committees themselves, encouraging these groups to think further about their own role in factory administration and control.

All of this was obviously a source of great concern to plant owners and boards of directors. It also implicitly challenged the policies of progressive industrialists like Tret'iakov and Konovalov, neither of whom thought worker participation in factory affairs should threaten the rights of ownership. Attacks on foremen were seen essentially as criminal acts, issues for the civil authorities. They outraged company directors and plant owners and provoked angry protests, but generally did not bring these people into the struggle to reconcile fundamental labor-management differences.

In contrast, strikes themselves were almost always an engagement with enterprise management at this higher level, a means by which workers became involved with larger issues of factory organization and production, and hence with questions concerning basic managerial prerogatives. So, too, were other coercive acts, especially those that involved threats to confiscate enterprise property or seize plants outright. As far as we can determine, few episodes of this sort occurred early in the year, and those that did were of the type that occurred at the Schlusselburg munitions factory, where workers seized a nearby estate and all its livestock to provide themselves with milk, an antidote to the poisons ingested in gunpowder production.[37] Most incidents of this sort took place later in places

[36] *Rabochaia Gazeta*, October 18, 1917.
[37] See *Novaia Zhizn'*, May 19, 1917.

where plants had already closed, as workers attempted to resume production on their own authority.[38] In these instances, the actual violence involved appears to have been minimal. Yet the threat of violence was itself coercive from the first days of March onward, a further element of real importance in structuring labor-management relations.

Meanwhile, of course, the streets were now free, and various other kinds of labor activism also occurred outside the enclosure of the workplace, in working-class neighborhoods, in the market place, and at other popular gathering points. These involved every manner of protest, overt and implicit: from mob justice to secondary boycotts, from searches of managers' apartments and company warehouses to threats on the lives of well-dressed passersby. Such street actions most often took the form of crowd justice, *samosudy*.[39] As Tsuyoshi Hasegawa has pointed out in an interesting essay, crime increased significantly in Petrograd (and elsewhere) immediately after February, partly because many ordinary criminals were released from city jails, partly because of deteriorating economic conditions and a growing sense of fear and desperation.[40] A number of criminal colonies were formed, particularly around the Olympia amusement park and on Vasil'evskii Island. The city's militia, meantime, was relatively ineffective in combatting crime. Criminals themselves were well armed, and the militia also had difficulty in detaining those who were arrested.[41] In some cases, crowds apprehending a thief attacked and beat the culprit severely; sometimes the suspect was killed on the spot. In other cases, the victims were local officials, or shopkeepers and peddlers accused of speculation and hoarding. Here, too, "justice" was dispensed quickly and harshly, although not usually with the severity reserved for criminals. Although the crowd's identity in such reports is almost always vague, there is no lack of detail about its angry and violent behavior.

Protest in the setting of the community also took the form of demonstrations, incidents involving the search for and seizure of weapons by workers, seizure of property unrelated to factories, product boycotts (especially of newspapers), political arrests (and the liberating of political prisoners), and food riots or other disorders over scarce goods. Most of

[38] We have catalogued only one case, in fact, of an outright expropriation of a going concern.

[39] Translated in some dictionaries as "lynching," but meaning rather "lynch-law."

[40] According to Tsuyoshi Hasegawa, "Crime and Revolution in Petrograd, 1917," unpublished paper, 1981, published in Japanese as "Hanzai, keisatsu, samosudo: roshia kakumeika no petorogurado no shukaishi eno ichishiron," *Surabu Kenkyu [Slavic Research]* 34 (1987), pp. 27–55. The newspaper *Petrogradskii Listok*, April 24, 1917, estimated that as many as 20,000 ordinary criminals may have been set free in early March.

[41] Hasegawa, "Crime and Revolution in Petrograd, 1917," pp. 5–8.

these, like factory seizures, took place later in the year, and we will look at them more closely in subsequent chapters. But precisely this form of activism was a matter of great concern to many industrialists and other members of the business community even in the first weeks of March, when PSFMO and MSFMO leaders feared "unbridled" civil freedoms would wreak havoc with efforts to maintain orderly production. Within weeks of the Provisional Government coming to power, the PSFMO issued a statement forcefully condemning workers' violent tendencies and began to accuse those in the factories of "ignoring Russia's vital needs" and "abandoning" their comrades at the front.[42]

It is extremely difficult to analyze the import of such incidents, although they surely influenced popular perceptions of disorder and violence and may well have affected the ways the owners of industrial plants and other enterprises began to look at strikes. Under what circumstances, for example, could crowd actions properly be construed as "protests"? While the collective beating of a thief might be seen as an implicit protest against a state power powerless to preserve order, and the collective destruction of a bread store or food stall could be regarded as a protest against economic conditions or the prevailing economic system, both actions are qualitatively different from strikes, as well as from formal political demonstrations. The nature of the crowds themselves in most instances is far from clear to us now; and in any case, the relationship between the "mob" and the "working class" has historically been a difficult one to clarify.[43]

Also, in contrast to factory-related incidents, the setting of street actions is usually of little help in understanding their composition. Incidents of crowd justice occurred throughout Petrograd (and in Moscow, although apparently less frequently). Open markets, fertile territory for

[42] See, e.g., *Izvestiia* (Petrograd), March 21, 1917, et seq., and especially April 7, 1917.

[43] Two theoretical paradigms illustrate the conceptual problem. On one hand is the identification of the "laboring classes" as the "dangerous classes," a common nineteenth-century assumption and one reflected in Louis Chevalier's important work on Parisian life, *Classes laborieuses et classes dangereuses* (Paris, 1958). On the other is the paradigm that distinguishes the "proletariat"—class-conscious workers—from what Marx and Engels called in "The Communist Manifesto" the " 'dangerous class,' the social scum" (*Selected Works of Marx and Engels* [New York, 1968], p. 44). The proletariat protests in the factory, facilitated by the organization of work, while the "scum" constitutes the mob. Both views, however, are faulty. As Tilly and Lees have pointed out, in the first, workers are assumed a priori to be criminals because of their habits, their poverty, and their lack of a stake in the social order (Charles Tilly and Lynn Lees, "Le Peuple de juin 1848," *Annales: Économies, Sociétés, Civilisations* 29 (1974), pp. 1061–91, and Charles Tilly, Louise Tilly, and Richard Tilly, *The Rebellious Century, 1830–1930* (Cambridge, Mass., 1975). The second ignores the reality of urban life, in which workers live in a heterogeneous community and often mingle with the poor, the pickpockets, the street hawkers, and the deserters.

pickpockets and easily mobilized crowds, were the scene of several incidents. Crowd justice was dispensed often in central districts, but even more frequently in outlying areas. Perhaps such incidents occurred especially often in neighborhoods with high concentrations of soldiers; they do not appear to be frequent in predominantly industrial neighborhoods. Many episodes of crowd justice, for example, were reported in the southern and eastern districts of Petrograd, and only two in the Vyborg region, a center of working-class autonomy and militancy.

DEVELOPING TENSIONS

For all this, however, there is little question that such episodes raised further doubts among PSFMO industrialists and others about the values and commitments of many in the factories during these early weeks. At a meeting of industrialists on March 16, Konovalov again went out of his way to urge accommodation, emphasizing that "freedom and order" within the framework of the existing economic system would be basic goals of the new regime, but for many industrialists the practical meaning of these concepts was quite unclear.[44] Also, as the leading trade-industrial journal, *Promyshlennost' i Torgovlia*, editorialized early in April, workers were beginning to put forward "their own, narrow, class viewpoints" not only in matters relating to production, but in terms of the operation of the whole economy. Workers obviously did not understand how fixed prices would limit profits, or how wage increases threatened them altogether.[45] Government figures like Konovalov and even moderate soviet leaders were also clearly worried about their ability to maintain social order. In effect, the progressives' entire plan for industrial peace was threatened by the growing strength of "narrow class viewpoints" on both sides, clear signs of polarization.

Still, as we have indicated, management in general had much to gain in the early weeks of the revolution from a peaceful resolution of factory grievances. What was necessary first and foremost to industrialists and manufacturers was economic security, political stability, and social peace: a climate in which investment and management decisions could be made with some degree of confidence in the future of the state and a pan-European capitalist order. "The pressing task of the moment," *Promyshlennost' i Torgovlia* further editorialized, was "the creation in the country of a firm legal order and a solid government, acting on the basis of strict legality."[46]

[44] *Revoliutsionnoe dvizhenie v Rossii posle sverzheniia samoderzhaviia*, p. 438.
[45] *Promyshlennost' i Torgovlia* 12–13 (April 15, 1917), p. 244.
[46] Ibid., 8–9 (March 18, 1917), pp. 186–88.

By early April there were also signs of improvement. As we have seen, fewer strikes occurred in the first weeks of April than at any other comparable time in the revolutionary period, and assaults on foremen and similar episodes seem to have greatly decreased as well, at least in Petrograd and Moscow. On March 23, the Iaroslavl' Soviet reached an agreement with the local society of factory and mill owners following the Petrograd model; Saratov, Rostov, Odessa, and other cities followed soon thereafter.[47] And although some Moscow industrial groups insisted that the workday remain at least nine hours until the end of the war, many firms had agreed to the eight-hour working day by the beginning of April.[48] In the Danilov cotton-spinning manufacture, directors proposed a compromise: a nine-hour working day, but with the extra hour to be paid double, and a 12.5 percent wage raise in addition.[49]

On the other hand, when industrialists resisted conciliation, workers continued to press their own program. In Kazan, for example, the local Soviet unilaterially introduced an eight-hour working day.[50] And in Moscow, although commercial and industrial leaders reacted sharply to a similar effort by that city's Soviet on March 18, workers in many larger plants managed to resolve on their own a number of pressing issues, including the organization of conciliation boards.[51] When these boards themselves began to function, moreover, they acted overwhelmingly in favor of the workers, especially in those grievances involving fines, rudeness, and inappropriate searches, but also in cases involving the expulsion of foremen or even the recovery of wages lost during the February revolution. At the central conciliation boards, the majority of issues in these weeks concerned wage disputes, but here, too, awards were generally to the workers' advantage.[52]

Although the implications of all this on the nature of labor-management relations in these weeks of conciliation are impossible to measure clearly, we think it quite likely that these initial successes may have engendered in workers generally a somewhat grandiose sense of what it was possible to achieve by various forms of direct collective action, strengthening, in effect, the powerful residues of February. Petrograd workers *had*, after all, overthrown one of Europe's oldest and most entrenched

[47] Meller and Pankratova, eds., *Rabochee dvizhenie v 1917 godu*, p. 49.

[48] The Moscow Society of Typo-Lithography Owners resolved on March 14 that the eight-hour work day was too dangerous for the country under current circumstances (*Russkiia Vedomosti*, March 15, 1917; *Russkoe Slovo*, March 15, April 13, 1917).

[49] *Russkoe Slovo*, April 13, 1917.

[50] Ibid.

[51] Koenker, *Moscow Workers*, pp. 107–8.

[52] Dmitriev, "Primiritel'nye kamery," pp. 92–94.

regimes, and the very experience of success in February must have left many in the factories feeling confident that if they wanted to, they could overthrow the new government as well. Certainly factory workers were not intimidated by the new state's authority, by the army, or by the local police, which had virtually ceased to function in industrial areas like the Vyborg district, across the Neva from the city's center.[53] Nor is there any indication that the even more substantial authority of plant and shop managers (to fire workers or impose fines, for example) was an effective restraint. For some owners, the only remaining measure was a lockout, which at this early stage of the revolution was both risky and quite drastic. Shutting down production hardly served the nation's interests, and when lockouts occurred in March and early April, they provoked broad-based and vociferous protests.

Yet the task of balancing the nation's interests with their own was also becoming increasingly difficult for PSFMO members and others in the business community, and if workers were becoming more confident about what they might be able to achieve, many industrialists were clearly becoming more anxious. Settlements uniformly favorable to workers in late March led many industrialists to expect that productivity would increase as labor unrest subsided, but by early April, few thought this was occurring. On the contrary, concessions only seemed in the view of many plant owners to fuel *new* expectations among workers, increasingly hard to meet. When wage concessions at Parviainen or the Skorokhod shoe plant averted new strikes in Petrograd, metal and leather workers elsewhere thought they should be granted similar raises. In the Central Industrial Region as a whole, where textile strikes brought workers substantial Easter bonuses, the problem became one of finding a means to maintain these higher levels of income. On the railroads, workers were given various assurances that a special commission in the Ministry of Communications would soon review wage scales across the board; in a number of individual enterprises, like the Felzer machine-construction works in Nizhnii Novgorod, plant managers began to worry that the bonuses they were granting workers would soon form the basis for new wage demands that they would find impossible to grant.[54] The Petrograd leather manufacturer I. A. Osipov and Company, on Vasil'evskii Island, granted shareholders a 10 percent dividend for 1916 and suddenly found workers expecting a comparable payout.[55]

Equally important to the attitudes of management in these early weeks

---

[53] See Rex A. Wade, *Red Guards and Workers' Militias in the Russian Revolution* (Stanford, Calif., 1985), especially chaps. 3–4.

[54] TsGAOR, f. 4100, op. 1, d. 19, p. 1.

[55] TsGAOR, f. 4100, op. 1, d. 7, p. 1b.

were the decisions of the conciliation boards, both within individual enterprises and at the higher level of the central boards. At the Petrograd Mechanical works and elsewhere, direct actions by workers against foremen and engineers made it almost impossible to organize the boards; in other plants, board members seemed uninterested in giving complex or especially contentious issues careful review.[56] For their part, some industrialists themselves simply refused at first to sanction the boards at all, rightly believing decisions would consistently be in the workers' favor. Although evidence that the boards worked reasonably well in smaller plants soon began to accumulate, and although several well-publicized decisions at major enterprises, including the Putilov wharf, helped avert conflicts, many industrialists clearly felt these institutions were only legitimizing direct worker action in the factories, rather than restoring social order, as Konovalov and his supporters had promised. When the central board in Petrograd agreed in a series of cases to accept increased wage norms for certain categories of workers, the owners of small and middle enterprises (with generally fewer than 200 workers) categorically refused to adopt them, arguing through spokesmen in the Petrograd Committee of Medium and Small Industry[57] that to impose uniform wage levels based on the finances of large plants like Putilov and Parviainen would destroy smaller enterprises and only advance the interests of the Petrograd industrial barons.[58] When the PSFMO similarly agreed in early April to raise the wages of unskilled laborers in the city's dye factories from two to five rubles a day, the owners and managers of most smaller dyeworks resolutely refused to agree.[59]

A backlash of sorts consequently began to grow, not only against Konovalov and the conciliationists in early April, but against the leadership of the PSFMO as well, for making concessions to workers too hastily and at too great a cost. Groups of employers in particular industries moved to strengthen their own industrial associations, partly to exercise more leverage on their leadership, partly to strengthen and coordinate their resistance to workers.[60] On April 6, the metalists' association threatened new shutdowns if "financial and moral support" was not forthcoming from the regime. The Union of Petrograd Wood Products Manufacturers also began drafting a report for Konovalov to show how the eight-hour

---

[56] Dmitriev, "Primiritel'nye kamery," p. 81.

[57] *Petrogradskii Komitet Srednei i Melko Promyshlennosti.*

[58] Dmitriev, "Primiritel'nye kamery," pp. 83–89, 94; Hogan, "Conciliation Boards," pp. 53–56.

[59] F. Bulkin, "Ekonomicheskoe polozhenie rabochikh Petrograda nakanune oktiabria 1917 goda," in Anskii, ed., *Professional'noe dvizhenie*, p. 39.

[60] *Ekonomicheskoe polozhenie*, pt. 1, pp. 162–63.

working day was resulting in a "colossal fall" in productivity, as much as 60 percent in some woodworking plants.[61]

It was also increasingly clear that civil authorities were powerless to prevent workers from attacking foremen or settling other grievances in a similar way, however much these incidents were decreasing. What was soon most important about them, in fact, was not simply that they were illegal according to any standard that recognized property rights or the inviolability of person, but that they were both coercive *and* successful from the workers' point of view, weakening respect for authority. In virtually every reported instance, workers found themselves able to resolve grievances by means of their own choosing, with little apparent adverse effect on their own well-being. No major factories apparently closed in response to worker militance in March and early April, as far as we can determine, nor were any workers arrested for violating managers' rights.[62]

If strikes were infrequent by mid-April, consequently, and if there was also a decrease in nonstrike actions as conciliation boards consistently rendered decisions in favor of workers, it is nonetheless quite unlikely that tensions between management and labor generally in Russia had subsided very much, or that Konovalov and his supporters were making much headway in muting the fears of many industrialists, especially in the associations of factory and mill owners in the capitals. Moderate members of the Association of Industry and Trade continued to assure their colleagues that a conciliatory posture would help avoid strikes and insisted in particular that all factory disputes be sent to conciliation boards. But resistance to concessions seems clearly to have been increasing, and with it, antagonism toward Minister Konovalov, particularly in Petrograd, but in South Russia and the Urals as well.[63] When striking Petrograd pharmacy workers proposed in mid-April to submit their dispute to the arbitration board set up by the labor section of the Petrograd Soviet, shop owners refused to show up for talks.[64] In the Don region, mine and metallurgical workers became so incensed at management's refusal to introduce basic safety reforms despite clear commitments to do so that they began a broad-scale assault on foremen and others responsible for the

[61] Ibid., pp. 162–64, 514–17.

[62] We record some 40 factory-based protests between March 7 and April 18 in Petrograd and Moscow in textile, food-processing, leather, printing, construction, chemical (rubber) and service enterprises, although the heaviest concentration was in Petrograd metal plants.

[63] See, e.g., *Ekonomicheskoe polozhenie*, pt. 1, p. 164; *Rabochaia Gazeta*, April 25, 1917.

[64] *Rabochaia Gazeta*, April 25, 1917.

risk, enraging owners who thought the revolution was over.[65] Such was the extent of these attacks in the Don that mine owners drafted an insurance plan in April "to protect administrative employees in South Russian mines who are injured as a result of worker excesses."[66]

Many leading industrialists, particularly in the defense sector, wanted something else from the regime as well: assistance in meeting wage demands through an increase in state procurement prices. On March 27, leading Petrograd metalists petitioned the regime toward this end, and secured the cabinet's agreement to form a special commission to study the issue.[67] At the same time, however, there was great wariness about any tendency on the regime's part to increase state regulation of industry or otherwise adopt policies that might compromise private interests. Pressure instead was entirely in the opposite direction, toward deregulation of the economy and decentralization of decision-making, especially in state-run enterprises and on the railroads.[68] In effect, while industrialists in Petrograd and elsewhere were girding themselves for an imminent two-front struggle against the regime for price increases and against workers over wages, they were also mustering forces against what they saw more distantly as the growing socialist danger and taking steps to increase their own economic and political power.

The number of formal trade-industrial associations thus multiplied rapidly as industrialists intensified their own organizational efforts. The PSFMO and its Moscow counterpart extended their activities through industrial "sections" (otdely) organized by branch, and both new and ongoing national organizations like the All-Russian Association of Sugar Manufacturers and the All-Russian Society of Leather Manufacturers expanded their activities. As with Russia's workers, industrialists and manufacturers took eager advantage of newly established civil liberties to hold meetings, publish, organize, and otherwise mobilize their own resources.

This, in turn, naturally worried factory and soviet leaders alike, particularly those who believed a liberal regime was the workers' best defense

---

[65] Petrogradskii sovet rabochikh i soldatskikh deputatov, *Protokoly zasedanii ispolnitel'-nogo komiteta i biuro* (Moscow and Leningrad, 1925), p. 151; Shlosberg, "Iz istorii," pp. 191–92.

[66] Shlosberg, "Iz istorii," pp. 194–95. The insurance covered death and injury from assault, loss of working capacity due to worker-inflicted injuries, and salary losses for those forced by workers to leave their jobs.

[67] *Ekonomicheskoe polozhenie*, pt. 1, p. 322.

[68] See especially the discussions at the first All-Russian Trade-Industrial Conference, March 19–21, 1917, in this regard, and William G. Rosenberg, "The Democratization of Russia's Railroads in 1917," *American Historical Review* 86, no. 5 (December 1981), pp. 983–1008.

for the moment against reactionary capital. Despite the fact that newly created institutions like the conciliation boards consistently ruled in labor's favor, many in the workshop still needed to be persuaded of the *rationality* of the new bourgeois order —its ability to resolve fundamental grievances (especially about wages) in ways that brought real benefits for workers. At the same time, Russia's leading industrialists and manufacturers had themselves to be convinced that the government would be able to protect *their* interests. Despite Konovalov's assurance that the new regime would "preserve and strengthen the existing order," as he and others put it, many in the new industrial associations remained doubtful that the government had the power to enforce its own principles and commitments or to make its procedures work.

Conciliation was consequently not an end in itself, and if it failed to protect what both parties to labor-management disputes saw as vital interests, the strategy could be readily discarded. The role of the state as the arbiter of these interests was likewise problematic, and therefore the composition of the regime was critically important. The Provisional Government had fashioned a fragile political equilibrium in these early weeks, one that was not strengthened by the consolidation of opinion and forces among industrialists and workers alike. Conflict in any number of areas could destroy the balance. In mid-April, the issue of the war emerged as the catalyst for political crisis.

5

. . . .

SPRING STRIKES AND

THE FIRST COALITION

The weeks of conciliation came abruptly to an end on April 20, when thousands of demonstrators took to the streets to protest the Provisional Government's declared war policy of "war to a decisive victory." The basic incompatibility between the revolutionary defensist position of the Petrograd Soviet, which insisted on peace "without annexations or indemnities," and the expansionist aims of Foreign Minister Miliukov and others in the Provisional Government had contributed to growing tension between the two poles of power since the overthrow of the monarchy. On March 27, the government declared its official war aims, which abjured "domination over other nations, or seizure of their national possessions, or forcible occupation of foreign territories."[1] But in transmitting this position to the allies on April 18, Miliukov reinserted his own views. According to the Soviet leader Sukhanov, "The new Note completely annulled everything the revolution had accomplished on behalf of peace up to then. It assured the Allies that Russia's aims in the war remained as before."[2] For Miliukov, this meant Russian control of Constantinople and the Dardanelles straits.

, When the note was published in the newspapers on April 20, workers and soldiers took to the streets to denounce the government and its policy. Armed workers and soldiers from the Vyborg district moved toward Nevskii Prospekt, marching under the slogans, "Down with Miliukov-Dardanel'skii," and "Down with the Provisional Government!" Local meetings took place in Moscow as well as Petrograd. Demonstrators on the next day, however, were met by soldiers and counterdemonstrators supporting the regime: their slogans endorsed Miliukov and denounced

---

[1] Robert P. Browder and Alexander F. Kerensky, eds., *The Russian Provisional Government, 1917: Documents*, 3 vols. (Stanford, Calif., 1961), vol. 2, p. 1046.

[2] N. N. Sukhanov, *The Russian Revolution*, ed. Joel Carmichael (Princeton, N.J., 1985), p. 314.

anarchy, Lenin, and German militarism.[3] There were several violent clashes. Within the Soviet, a cry went up for Miliukov's resignation, and in response, Prime Minister Lvov and others demanded Soviet representatives themselves assume government posts. When Miliukov and War Minister Guchkov announced their intention to quit, a divided Soviet leadership agreed after bitter debate to allow socialists to enter the cabinet.

The coalition was approved by the Soviet on May 1, after ten days of political crisis. Miliukov and Guchkov were gone, but ten "capitalist" ministers remained, to be joined by six socialists: Kerensky, now minister of war; Irakli Tsereteli, who was emerging as the dominant Menshevik voice among soviet leaders; the Popular Socialist A. V. Peshekhonov; Viktor Chernov, the new Socialist Revolutionary minister of agriculture; P. N. Pereverzev, minister of justice; and Mikhail Ivanovich Skobelev, a member of the Soviet Executive Committee and the new minister of labor. Most novel in the shakeup was the creation of Skobelev's Labor Ministry as an independent part of the new regime, rather than as only a section of the Ministry of Trade and Industry. Skobelev took the portfolio with some eagerness, pledging to use his new powers to fulfill the legal promises of the February revolution: the expansion of trade unions, revision of old laws on hiring, workers' meetings, and strikes (which had yet to be written), new laws on the length of the working day, comprehensive protection of labor, improvement and expansion of workers' insurance, and labor exchanges for the unemployed.[4] The new labor minister essentially saw his role as that of workers' tribune: he would bring to the cabinet programs to ensure workers' rights and well-being.[5]

The formation of the coalition was a critical event in the history of 1917. Many socialists opposed it, arguing that the Soviet held real power and should not dilute it in the government, that the Soviet would discredit itself by participating in the coalition, that the class struggle would be blunted.[6] But for others, like the left Kadet minister of transport N. V. Nekrasov, the coalition between the two power blocs of the February revolution offered a way to carry the revolution forward by providing a forum for discussion of policy differences and by symbolizing a new spirit of cooperation between workers and employers, one that placed state interests above the interests of particular classes.[7]

[3] Ibid., pp. 316–18.
[4] *Vestnik Vremennago Pravitel'stva*, March 7, 1917; *Izvestiia* (Petrograd), May 19, 1917.
[5] Ziva Galili y Garcia, *The Menshevik Leaders of the Petrograd Soviet, 1917: Social Realities and Political Strategies in the Russian Revolution* (Princeton, N.J., 1989), chap. 7.
[6] Sukhanov, *Russian Revolution*, pp. 331–32.
[7] See the discussion in William G. Rosenberg, *Liberals in the Russian Revolution* (Princeton, N.J., 1974), chap. 5.

The expectations generated by the new coalition must nevertheless be understood in terms of the climate of social relations that had been developing since well before the publication of the Miliukov note, indeed, since the February revolution itself. These expectations were not uniform within or between classes and were sometimes contradictory. The Moscow liberal daily *Russkiia Vedomosti* was optimistic, commenting on May 11, "The Ministry of Labor may not be able to remedy at once by decree the economic difficulties of Russian workers, but its work may bring changes considerably closer, and there are many lesser measures that can be enacted quickly to improve workers' lives which industrialists do not oppose, and even in some cases support."[8] This reinforced the position of Konovalov and other moderates who continued to believe that compromise rather than confrontation could best put Russia's faltering economy (and war effort) back on the rails.

But dissatisfaction with the politics and policies of conciliation had in fact been growing even before the April crisis and the formation of the coalition. For many industrialists, the coalition meant not a forum for compromise, but a more effective mechanism for reining in workers' demands. Increased government regulation would ensure labor discipline and prevent "complete financial ruin."[9] The PSFMO complained about workers' high wages and rising costs of materials, and demanded, "The Provisional Government must urgently adopt measures that can avert the impending catastrophe."[10] Entrepreneurial organizations in the south also looked to the government to put a ceiling on workers' wages or to renegotiate contracts to compensate for higher wage costs.[11]

For Mensheviks who supported the coalition, socialist participation in government meant that state power would be used in the other direction: to protect workers' interests through a minimum program of reforms and to pressure management into new concessions in the interests of social harmony and Russia's national good. State regulation of the economy would rationalize the conflicting interests of workers and management and optimize both efficiency and social justice. One of the conditions on which Soviet leaders agreed to enter the coalition had been the implementation of the regulatory plan worked out by V. G. Groman in the Soviet's Economic Commission. Regulation would limit profits, guarantee a minimum standard of living for workers, and bring state planning and regulation into all spheres of economic activity: production, trade, transport,

[8] *Russkiia Vedomosti*, May 11, 1917.
[9] *Ekonomicheskoe polozhenie Rossii nakanune velikoi oktiabr'skoi sotsialisticheskoi revoliutsii. Dokumenty i materialy*, 3 pts. (Moscow, 1957–67), pt. 1, pp. 165–68.
[10] Ibid. See also Galili y Garcia, *Menshevik Leaders*, chap. 6.
[11] *Ekonomicheskoe polozhenie*, pt. 1, pp. 173–80.

and consumption.[12] At the same time, Skobelev took steps to organize his Labor Ministry to carry out the Mensheviks' program of labor legislation.

For workers on the shop floor, as well as the tens of thousands who worked at low-paying jobs in the service or transport sectors, coalition promised the material rewards of revolution that many felt they had been awaiting with patience and restraint. Patience reigned at Sormovo, for example, while shop committee leaders worked to draft new rate schedules and to develop a strong factorywide organization.[13] Restraint paid dividends in the Urals, where workers won the eight-hour working day and succeeded in removing the most objectionable foremen; they then pledged to continue war production without interruption, actually surpassing their prerevolutionary rate of output.[14]

There were tangible grounds for workers' increased expectations as well. Transport had improved in March, partly because of the weather, partly because of new energy and operation efficiencies applied by railroad workers themselves.[15] Food supplies became more plentiful along with stores of other goods and raw materials. Even nominal wages increased for many workers in late March and April, in some places, like Petrograd, as a result of a reduction in hours; elsewhere, through bonuses and changes in basic rates.[16] The wages of Vladimir province textile workers may have increased as much as 100 percent between January and April 1917, and for skilled workers in the metal trades, the rise may have been even steeper. In the Moscow Electromechanical factory, which employed approximately 1,500 workers, the average daily wage increased from 5 rubles 40 kopecks in February to 7 rubles 70 kopecks in March, a rise of more than 40 percent.[17]

At the same time, what might be called a second round of workers' expectations was also emerging, fuelled in large measure by the relative ease with which initial gains had been won, by a growing sense that these gains were still inadequate, and by strengthened confidence in the power of workers' committees and groups at all levels. This confidence was encouraged in no small measure by Lenin's return to Russia on April 3 and

[12] Galili y Garcia, *Menshevik Leaders*, chap. 6.

[13] *Ekonomicheskoe polozhenie*, pt. 1, pp. 476–77.

[14] F. P. Bystrykh, "Rabochee stachechnoe dvizhenie na Urale v period podgotovki velikoi oktiabr'skoi sotsialisticheskoi revoliutsii," in *Rabochii klass i rabochee dvizhenie v Rossii v 1917 godu* (Moscow, 1964), pp. 117–19.

[15] See William G. Rosenberg, "The Democratization of Russia's Railroads in 1917," *American Historical Review* 88, no. 5 (December 1981), pp. 989–91.

[16] See especially the discussion in L. S. Gaponenko, *Rabochii klass Rossii v 1917 godu* (Moscow, 1970), pp. 173–207.

[17] Ibid., p. 194.

the resurgence of Bolshevik politics. It was also stimulated by the relatively conciliatory attitudes shown by many plant owners and factory managers in March and April. But it was also undoubtedly spurred by the promises of socialist entry into the coalition. The state-bourgeois tie had been weakened; workers' aspirations were fully legitimized as their own representatives assumed government posts, especially in the Ministry of Labor.

In these circumstances the strike now became the principal tactic of workers, who in virtually every commercial and industrial sector seized the moment to press for higher wages and better working conditions, goals that most had expected to follow the collapse of the tsarist regime in February. Was it the coalition itself or broader developments that spurred workers to confront their employers so massively in late April and May? The socialist ministers had pledged to support workers' interests, and workers could expect that a socialist minister would never authorize military force to prevent their use of the strike weapon no matter how much he regretted disruptions in production. In any event, the rate of strike activity escalated at the end of April, at precisely the moment the socialists joined the Provisional regime.

CHARACTERISTICS OF THE SPRING STRIKE CLUSTER

Beginning on April 19, when the number of new strikes per day increased rapidly, and ending on July 6, we have recorded 421 strikes involving a minimum of 573,160 strikers (by estimates involving 74 percent of strikes). This can be compared to only 78 strikes and some 44,000 strikers in the weeks of March and early April. Table 5.1 shows that most strikers—over 485,000—were industrial workers; many of the remainder, such as the Petrograd laundresses whose strike coincided with the formation of the coalition government, were employed in the service sector. Table 5.2 indicates that among these industrial workers, the most active industrial group by far was the metalworkers, with more than 400,000 workers on strike in these 12 weeks. Metalworkers accounted for some 84 percent of all industrial strikers in this period; their share of the workforce was only about 27 percent. Consequently, their strike propensity was more than three times higher than that of the next most strike-prone branch of industry, leather workers.

What is most interesting about the metalists' strikes is not so much the metalworkers' continued relative predominance in this form of activism, but the fact that in contrast to March and April, relatively few metalist strikes occurred in Petrograd. Most took place in Moscow and Moscow

TABLE 5.1

Strikes and Strikers in the Spring Cluster by Economic Sector

Sector	Number of Strikes	%	Estimated Number of Strikers[a]	%
Industrial[b]	303	72.0	485,970	84.8
Transport	18	4.3	5,240	0.9
Service	88	20.9	80,080	14.0
Other[c]	12	2.9	1,870	0.3
Total	421	100.1	573,160	100.0

[a] Minimum estimates based on 75% of industrial strikes, 78% of transport, 69% of service, and 75% of other strikes.

[b] Includes strikes involving more than one industrial branch.

[c] Includes strikes by construction and agricultural workers, professional groups, and others.

province; perhaps more importantly, the remainder occurred in some 23 additional provinces around the country, from Lithuania to the Amur in Siberia. At the same time, strikes among leather workers underwent a threefold increase under the first coalition in comparison with the weeks after February, and the rate of increase was even higher among chemical and woodworkers, as well as workers in the food-processing industries. A notable development concerned printers, a group whose political sympathies were strongly Menshevik: more strikes by typographers occurred during the weeks of the first coalition than in any other comparable time of the revolutionary period. These occurred, moreover, in 15 different provinces and constituted more than 10 percent of all strikes in these weeks nationwide.

Strikers in the spring cluster were concentrated overwhelmingly in the two capital cities of Petrograd and Moscow (table 5.3), which together account for 85 percent of the estimated number of strikers in our file. Petrograd's total was attributable partly to the 275,000 strikers we estimate were involved in the massive July Days strike, but even without these strikers, Petrograd's share of the strike force was second only to Moscow. The picture is more diverse with respect to numbers of strikes: Moscow and Petrograd account for less than one-half of the total. The remainder were scattered.

Moscow region's strikes were concentrated in the area's metal and textile industries but included strikes in diverse other sectors, such as a strike

TABLE 5.2

Strikes and Strikers in the Spring Cluster by Industry
(Single-Industry Strikes Only)

Industry	Number of Strikes	Minimum Number of Enterprises Involved[a]	Estimated Number of Strikers[b]	Strike Propensity[c]
Metals	88	183	409,560	3.20
Animal products (leather)	27	90	12,645	.76
Wood and wood products	29	106	6,380	.30
Paper and printing	43	168	4,985	.26
Textiles	58	414	37,765	.22
Chemicals	11	19	1,790	.09
Food products	20	64	3,415	.04
Minerals	4	18	830	.04

[a] Minimum estimates based on fragmentary factory inspector reports and accounts from other sources.

[b] Minimum estimates based on the following percentages of industry strikes: metals, 77%; animal products, 67%; wood and wood products, 90%; paper and printing, 88%; textiles, 79%; chemicals, 64%; food and products 85%; minerals, 75%.

[c] The exclusion of strikes involving more than one industry reduces in particular the strike propensity for metalists, who were active in multi-industry strikes.

by 400 waiters in Penza restaurants on May 19.[18] The Kiev region's numerous strikes included many small-scale walkouts, such as those of Minsk laundresses and stocking-knitters in Poltava. They also encompassed the 1,300 strikers at the G. N. Gurarii tobacco plant in Kremenchug, Poltava province, which began on May 1.[19] The Volga region accounted for ten strikes between the April crisis and July Days, including two at Kazan's large Alafuzov military equipment manufacture. For Kharkov, estimates of strikers are based on only 37 percent of known strikes, so the actual level of activism here may well have been substantially higher than table 5.3 suggests.[20]

The large majority of strikes in this spring cluster tended to be single-

[18] *Izvestiia* (Moscow), May 27, 1917.

[19] *Velikaia oktiabr'skaia sotsialisticheskaia revoliutsiia v Belorussii* (Minsk, 1957), vol. 1, p. 311; *Izvestiia* (Moscow), May 18, 1917; TSGIA SSSR, f. 23, op. 16, d. 256, l. 13.

[20] VOSR. *Khronika sobytii*, vol. 2, pp. 155, 256; *Novaia Zhizn'*, June 9, 1917.

TABLE 5.3
Strikes and Strikers in the Spring Cluster by Region

Region[a]	Number of Strikes	%[b]	Estimated Number of Strikers[c]	%	Estimated Number of Strikers per Strike[d]
Moscow city	130	30.9	137,770	24.0	1,325
Petrograd city	59	14.0	349,040	60.9	9,435
Moscow region[e]	55	13.1	45,835	8.0	1,090
Kiev region	44	10.5	8,480	1.5	220
Petrograd region[f]	31	7.4	2,315	0.4	135
Kharkov-Ekaterinoslav region	30	7.1	4,910	0.9	445
Rostov region	14	3.3	1,290	0.2	100
Siberia and Central Asia regions	15	3.6	1,480	0.3	113
Transcaucasus region	12	2.9	720	0.1	65
Odessa region	11	2.6	2,580	0.5	290
Volga region	10	2.4	16,790	2.9	2,100
Urals region	6	1.4	1,640	0.3	330
Caspian region	4	1.0	310	0.1	155
Total	421	100.2	573,160	100.1	

[a] Provinces included within each region are noted in appendix 1.

[b] Percentages add to more than 100 because of rounding.

[c] The estimate of strikers represents only those strikes for which satisfactory estimates could be made. The percentage of strikes with striker estimates by region are as follows: Moscow city, 80%; Petrograd city, 63%; Moscow region, 76%; Kiev, 89%; Petrograd region, 55%; Kharkov-Ekaterinoslav, 37%; Rostov, 93%; Transcaucasus, 92%; Odessa, 82%; Volga, 80%; Urals, 83%; Siberia and Central Asia, 87%; Caspian, 50%.

[d] Calculated only for strikes with estimates of strikers.

[e] Excluding city of Moscow.

[f] Excluding city of Petrograd.

factory strikes or strikes called in more than one enterprise within the same industry or trade, rather than citywide or interindustry strikes, both of which required higher levels of organization. Some 75 percent of all strikes between April 19 and July 6 fit into these categories, partly, we suspect, because trade unions and even factory committee organizations were still rudimentary, particularly outside Moscow and Petrograd. For Russia as a whole we still find factory committees identified during these weeks in less than one-tenth of all strike reports, even while the evidence is clear that where factory committees did exist, they were overwhelmingly supportive of strike actions. There are obviously biases in reporting here, but this pattern would soon be reversed, with important and interesting implications.

The relative absence of reports about factory committee leadership is also partly a reflection of the large number of nonindustrial strikes in this period, particularly in the service sector—among retail clerks, employees in commercial establishments, waiters, cooks, and even janitors and porters. More than 120 Petrograd shops in the Gostinnyi and Apraksin markets were closed in mid-May, for example, as clerks attempted to negotiate new working hours and wages;[21] in distant Piatigorsk, a resort town in the northern Caucasus, almost every hotel and restaurant was shut down at the beginning of May as waiters, maids, and porters demanded improvements in wage and working conditions.[22] Even clerks at the Russian-Asiatic bank struck on May 8 for higher wages.[23] Strikes were thus much more than a weapon of Russia's industrial proletariat in this period, more than a broad aspect of the country's general political democratization. They were also clearly a symbol of social resistance, since service people like the bank clerks and the Piatigorsk hotel employees were engaging in what was for them an unprecedented act of self-assertion, rejecting traditional patterns of subservience and their associated ethics. Interestingly, these strikes also reflected a much higher degree of cooperation between workers in different enterprises than did strikes in factories or industrial places. More than 60 percent of all nonindustrial strikes in May and June involved more than one enterprise, according to our data, compared to less than 30 percent for industrial strikes.

Several further general points about strikes in these weeks are worth making. First, the mean length of strikes tended to be twice as long in the spring cluster as earlier in the year: the average early strike (of those for which we know the length) lasted about six days, and the average strike between April 19 and July 6 lasted almost twelve days. This would seem to reflect both workers' commitment to their cause in this period and perhaps also the growing resistance of plant owners to carrying through the implicit promises of February.

Second, strikes in this period were remarkably successful, from the workers' point of view. Although we found evidence of success, failure, or compromise in less than half of the strikes in our sample, even this

---

[21] *Birzhevyia Vedomosti*, May 18, 1917.
[22] *Vlast' Naroda*, May 3, 1917; *Edinstvo*, May 4, 1917; *Novaia Zhizn'*, May 26, 1917.
[23] *Edinstvo*, May 9, 1917; *Russkaia Volia*, May 9, 1917; *Novaia Zhizn'*, May 10, 1917.

fragmentary information indicates interesting patterns: during March and April, only some 21 percent of all strikes were labeled "won," and over 6 percent were clearly "lost." But success rates rose with the rise in strike activity at the end of April. Roughly one-quarter of all strikes ended in workers' victories in this April–July cluster, and something near 40 percent of all strikes ended in either outright victory or compromise, suggesting one of the highest rates of success of any period in the revolutionary year. Conversely, only 2 percent of all strikes were publicly labeled as failures, the lowest rate of defeat of any of the three major strike clusters in 1917.

Finally, only a handful of strikes can be identified in May and June as occurring in state-run enterprises, or as being expressly against Russia's new state order per se. Few strikes involved explicit political demands; none, to our knowledge, called for the breakup of the coalition. It is clear that such sentiments were expressed by both striking and nonstriking workers in various political demonstrations in this period, particularly the great demonstration in Petrograd on June 18, and it may well be that these sentiments were simply not reported as elements of strike actions proper. But it also seems likely that as far as strikes in the aggregate were concerned, the spring cluster essentially reflected an effort to test the viability of strikes as a weapon of struggle against management, an effort, in other words, to see if the "routine" forms of labor struggle in a bourgeois democracy could finally bring Russian workers the benefits they desired.

WORKERS' GOALS IN THE SPRING CLUSTER: STRIKE DEMANDS

What did Russia's workers really want in the spring of 1917, and how were their goals reflected in strikes and other forms of collective action? Such questions are impossible to answer with precision, of course, and not only because there were no Gallup or Roper organizations in revolutionary Russia to conduct survey research. Russian labor remained highly variegated, and significant differences continued to exist between the social organization and political outlooks say, of skilled typographers in their small and scattered printshops, and common laborers in large iron and steel works. The range of attitudes among workers was thus very broad, varying to a substantial degree even between individuals in the same professions in different parts of the country. More important in terms of historical analysis, the evidence about such matters as attitudes and goals is always partly indirect. Strike demands reflect attitudinal realities, but these are necessarily mediated by rhetorical and political style, as are other forms of collective action. "Wheelbarrowing" or "carting out" is always symbolic, perhaps reflecting a range of attitudes that is more or less severe than its stylized form connotes.

Social historians cannot hope to resolve these epistemological problems, nor is there even sufficient evidence available to analyze the attitudes embedded in collective actions or strike activity in 1917 in a completely systematic and comprehensive way. On the other hand, newspapers and other sources do provide a reasonably good catalog of nonstrike actions for Moscow and Petrograd for this period; with the help of the computer, strike demands for the country as a whole can also be broken apart and analyzed with a reasonable degree of sophistication. Even if we may not be able to come to firm conclusions in all of its aspects, we can consequently explore the question of workers' attitudes and goals with some care, both in the remainder of this chapter and in chapter 6. And we can try to discern important elements of rhetoric and style. In the process, we may be able to learn something about the ways in which a variety of workers' attitudes and goals were represented publicly, and what their less apparent meaning might have been, particularly in political terms. From this vantage point, it may then be possible to understand more fully the nature and import of management's response.

For all strikes we have studied, we have recorded more than 250 separate demands. To evaluate broad trends, and particularly changes over time, however, it is necessary to aggregate these particular demands into a more manageable set of categories. The most simple method of aggregation is the system used by the Factory Inspectorate, which as noted in chapter 2, grouped all demands into four major categories: wages, hours, factory order (or job control), and strikes over political issues.[24] We have found this simple division useful for certain purposes and use it with one modification, categorizing strikes over personal treatment as "dignity" strikes, rather than as strikes over factory order, which are closely related. We also refer to strikes over factory order as "control" strikes to better reflect the terminology and objectives of 1917, and we broaden the "hours" category to include strikes over other work conditions as well.

[24] As noted earlier, this division is also utilized by Haimson in his work on prerevolutionary strikes and is dictated by the available data (Leopold H. Haimson and Ronald Petrusha, "Two Strike Waves in Imperial Russia (1905–07, 1912–14): A Quantitative Analysis," in *Strikes, Wars, and Revolutions in an International Perspective: Strike Waves in the Late Nineteenth and Early Twentieth Centuries*, ed. Leopold H. Haimson and Charles Tilly (New York, 1989). Edward Shorter and Charles Tilly employ essentially two groups, wages and organization, in their study *Strikes in France, 1830–1968* (Cambridge, 1974). Other studies rely in a similar way on the categories utilized by the data collectors. See, e.g., P. K. Edwards, *Strikes in the United States, 1881–1974* (Oxford, 1981).

Thus in the analysis which follows, our major demand categories are strikes over wages, conditions (hours), workers' dignity, and job control, as well as strikes with explicit political objectives. Because we have collected raw strike material ourselves, however, we are able to refine this division into much more detailed categories. We can distinguish, for example, between strikes for an eight-hour workday and those for a six-hour day; we can distinguish demands for higher basic wages from demands for vacation pay, sick pay, a change in payment forms, or ratios between different work classifications. Here we have found that all strikes for which we have data can be divided into some 40 categories, including eight that are distinctive but have only one or two cases.[25] Hence we are also able to use a second, more detailed aggregation in our analysis, one that allows us to look more closely at the different types of strike demands themselves, as well as their relationship to other aspects of the revolutionary process.

A Quantitative Review of Spring Strike Demands

1. Wage Demands

We have seen in chapter 2 how wage demands occupied the premier place in the vocabulary of strikes throughout the revolutionary period, as before. Wage demands were present in two-thirds of all strikes in our data file for the year as a whole; in terms of workers on strike, of over 2.4 million strikers that can be counted, approximately 1.76 million made such economic demands. During the first half of 1917, to early July, just over 70 percent of strikes included wage demands. Figures 5.1 and 5.2 indicate the frequency of strikes and strikers by demand for this period. Proportions were essentially the same in the period of intense strike activity from April 19 through July 6. Of 421 strikes beginning in these weeks, 301 included wage demands. In terms of estimated strikers, these 301 wage strikes involved a minimum of 280,090 strikers, or just under half of the known strikers in the period (see table 5.4).

In these strikes over wages, reports often stated simply, "workers made economic demands." We can assume that such strikers had more specific goals to lay on the bargaining table; they undoubtedly indicated to their adversaries (if not to the newspapers) the range or magnitude of the wage increases they sought or the specific changes they demanded in rates of

---

[25] See appendix 2, table A.3.

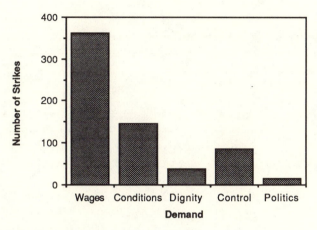

Figure 5.1 Strikes by Demands, March 3–July 6, 1917

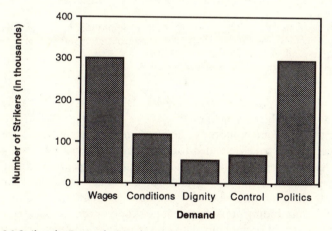

Figure 5.2 Strikers by Demands, March 3–July 6, 1917

pay, which effectively amounted to the same thing.[26] Frequently, of course, workers publicized the size of their wage demands quite extensively, asking for across-the-board percentage increases or graduated percent raises based on skill levels, experience, or gender. They also demanded specific ruble increases, either graduated or with one scale for all. In early June, for example, approximately 3,000 Kharkov metalworkers

[26] Such brevity of reporting was perhaps a carryover from the days of the underground and of police surveillance over labor protest. Strikes that were not "political" were "economic."

TABLE 5.4
Strikes and Strikers in the Spring Cluster by Demand Group

Demand Group	Number of Strikes	%	Estimated Number of Strikers[a]	%	Estimated Number of Strikers per Strike[b]
Wages	301	71.5	280,090	48.9	1,157
Conditions	108	25.7	107,200	18.7	1,204
Dignity	33	7.8	52,760	9.2	1,884
Control	73	17.3	66,570	11.6	1,024
Politics	9	2.1	276,000	48.2	55,200
All strikes	421		573,160		2,115

NOTE: Strikes and strikes are overlapped for strikes with principal demands in more than one category.

[a] Estimates based on 80% of wage strikes, 82% of conditions strikes; 85% of strikes over issues relating to workers' dignity; 89% of workers' control strikes; 56% of known political strikes; and 64% of all strikes.

[b] Calculated only for strikes with estimates of strikers.

demanded for unskilled workers a new daily wage of five rubles for women and six rubles for men.[27]

There was, of course, more to the economic compensation issue than just wage levels. Strike demands for pay included severance pay, which was an issue of special concern since so many plants were announcing shutdowns during 1917. Such demands also included allowances for food or housing: in a number of enterprises, management provided barracks accomodations, rudimentary canteens, or food shops on factory premises. For workers at such plants who rented private lodgings, firms would pay a supplement for housing in order to equalize compensation for all workers, and the level of these supplements frequently became strike issues. Workers at the Anokhin factory in Sudogda, near Vladimir, struck in March for a two-ruble apartment supplement because the factory management failed to provide housing, and workers were forced to live in a settlement nearby. They also demanded 60 kopecks a month for baths.[28] Elsewhere workers asked as well for pay during holidays, during illnesses, and also for the time they were out on strike. This last demand occurred with great frequency, often after strikes had otherwise been settled. Al-

[27] *Russkiia Vedomosti*, June 13, 1917.
[28] *Pravda*, March 12, 1917 (o.s.).

though essentially a demand for wages, it was also an issue of workers' dignity, since workers clearly wanted owners to admit that the responsibility for the strike was theirs.

Most wage demands, although usually characterized as "moderate" because they did not challenge the prerogatives of the factory management, could nonetheless become quite bitter, especially in the context of rapidly rising prices. One such group (which we catalog under the heading of "rate systems"), concerned the ways in which wages were paid, rather than how high they were, and also provoked bitterness. The piece-rate system of payment was especially detrimental to workers in times of economic contraction, as in 1917, when the work available, and hence the pieces to fabricate, was reduced. After 1905, piece-rates had also begun to carry overtones of scientific management and the intensification of labor, two elements industrial workers understandably regarded with apprehension. Hence the piece-rate system was a particular source of grievance in the spring of 1917 and led to several angry work stoppages. Employees of Petrograd dyeing and dry-cleaning establishments began a long strike in mid-May partly over this issue, for example.[29] Petrograd coopers insisted that piecework be strictly optional, and pipefitters in Moscow struck for over three weeks to establish a minimum daily wage and eliminate piece wages, among other issues.[30] Conflicts over rates figured in a number of less-publicized strikes as well, and in disputes centering on union contract packages. Sales workers in many places wanted to be put on salary instead of the prevailing commission system; waiters demanded regular salaries instead of forced reliance on tips.

Strikes were also fought over complete schedules of job categories and appropriate compensation, called tarifs. These demands were frequently the product of trade union involvement and often represented lengthy periods of internal discussions and negotiations about appropriate and fair wage differentials for various categories of skill. The process of tarif preparation is well documented in trade union journals in 1917, especially for metalworkers, printers, leather workers, and woodworkers; the demand for tarif reform is especially important, because it reintroduced the principle of collective bargaining into the labor scene in 1917.[31]

[29] *Pravda*, May 31, 1917 (n.s.); *Rabochaia Gazeta*, October 20, 1917.

[30] *Rabochaia Gazeta*, July 4, 1917; *Izvestiia* (Moscow), April 29, 1917.

[31] See *Metallist, Moskovskii Metallist, Pechatnik, Golos Kozhevnikov*, and *Ekho Derevoobdelochnika*; S. A. Smith discusses the tarif question for Petrograd in *Red Petrograd: Revolution in the Factories, 1917–1918* (Cambridge, 1983), pp. 119–21; see also Diane Koenker and William G. Rosenberg, "Skilled Workers and the Strike Movement in Revolutionary Russia," *Journal of Social History* 19, no. 4 (Summer 1986), pp. 605–29, and Victoria E. Bonnell, *Roots of Rebellion: Workers' Politics and Organizations in St. Peters-*

Wage demands of one sort or another dominated strike discourse in almost every region of Russia. In the northeast region, excluding the city of Petrograd, in the Kharkov region, in the city of Moscow, and in strikes in the Volga region, nearly every worker on strike advanced economic demands during this spring upsurge, as far as we can determine. Wage demand frequencies were relatively low in the city of Petrograd, where the strike force was dominated by 275,000 political strikers who came out during the July Days, but in aggregate numbers, Petrograd's 71,000 wage strikers were second only to Moscow, where an estimated 132,000 workers claimed wage improvements. In terms of strikes themselves, rather than strikers, the picture across the country is more uniform. Three-quarters of strikes in Petrograd city, Moscow city, the Moscow industrial region, and the Volga concerned wage issues. The lowest level of wage strike activity among regions with relatively frequent strikes may have been the Kharkov-Ekaterinoslav region, encompassing the provinces of Kharkov, Kursk, Voronezh, and Ekaterinoslav.

The frequency of wage strikes among industrial branches shows some variation but confirms the overall high level of wage strikes. Ninety percent and more of workers in the service and retail sectors, railroad workers, woodworkers, chemical workers, and paper workers included wages as part of their strike demands. Metalworkers struck more for political issues than for wages, but even so, nearly 130,000 metal workers across the country participated in wage strikes in the weeks between April 19 and July 6.

One obvious reason for the frequency of wage strikes in this early period was quite simply that strikes were traditional tools of economic bargaining. But the economic freedom unloosed by the February revolution had also stimulated prices, and wage strikes can be seen as an early and immediate response to rapidly increasing inflation. The rate of inflation doubled between March and April; prices were 28 percent higher in June than in May. This can be seen in table 5.5, which indicates the relationship in the first four months of the year between the share of workers demanding higher wages and the rise in the price index. Rapidly escalating prices clearly put real pressures on workers to balance their family budgets, so it is hardly surprising that May and June saw such huge increases in the number of workers making wage demands.

Finally, the success rate of strikes in this period may have had something to do as well with workers' choice of contestable issues. Whereas some 23 percent of all strikes concluded in this period with full victory

burg and Moscow, 1900–1914 (Berkeley, 1983), for some early attempts to win collective contracts in the 1905–1907 period (e.g., p. 188).

TABLE 5.5
Economic Demands and Inflation, March–June, 1917

	Minimum Estimated Number of Strikers[a]	Percent of Strikers Making Economic Demands	Percent Change in Price Index
March	41,640	38	6
April	17,700	92	13
May	91,140	96	18
June	114,270	91	28

SOURCE: Kokhn, *Russkie indektsy tsen* (Moscow, 1926), p. 10. The index is constructed from the market basket of goods consumed by an average unskilled worker as of 1918 (Kokhn, pp. 23–26). These figures are for all industries in Russia, but the rate of change follows closely the prices reported for Moscow alone in 1917. See, however, Diane Koenker, *Moscow Workers and the 1917 Revolution* (Princeton, N.J., 1981), p. 130n, for a discussion of discrepancies.

[a] Minimum estimates based on reports as follows: March, 80% of strikes; April, 77%; May, 75%; June, 72%.

for the workers, and 2 percent with failure, wage strikes emerged as relatively more successful. Just over 27 percent of wage strikes ended in victory, and nearly 50 percent ended in either victory or compromise. Only 1.5 percent of all wage strikes were recorded as defeats.

2. Demands for Improved Conditions

If wage issues constituted the standard demand for strikes in the spring, the pattern was more varied for strikes and strikers raising demands about working conditions. Hours and conditions in Russian factories and workshops were notoriously bad before the revolution, even relative to Western Europe and the United States. Long hours, poorly lighted and unventilated work spaces, hazardous machinery, and the use of child labor had all shocked reformers and fuelled both liberal reform movements and revolutionary activism.[32] Prerevolutionary government legislation

[32] M. I. Tugan-Baranovsky, *The Russian Factory in the Nineteenth Century*, trans. Arthur and Claora S. Levin (Homewood, Ill., 1970); E. E. Kruze, *Polozhenie rabochego klassa Rossii v 1900–1914 godakh* (Leningrad, 1976) and *Usloviia truda i byta rabochego klassa Rossii v 1900–1914 godakh* (Leningrad, 1981); Iu. I. Kir'ianov, *Zhiznennyi uroven' rabochikh Rossii* (Moscow, 1979); Rose L. Glickman, *Russian Factory Women: Workplace and Society, 1880–1914* (Berkeley, 1984).

had placed limits on the employment of women and children and had provided for state factory inspectors to enforce factory reforms, but the autocratic nature of capital-labor relations and the lack of any kind of countervailing powers belonging to workers made improvements slow in coming, if at all.

The strike weapon provided workers in 1917 with real power to negotiate for improved conditions, and they took advantage of it extensively. Overall in the spring, some 25 percent of strikes and approximately one-fifth of all strikers raised demands about conditions of work. These issues were especially important in the Moscow and Petrograd industrial regions, in Western Siberia, and along the Volga. In these areas, 50 percent and more of the strikers in the April–July period demanded improvements in working and living conditions. Such workers struck for medical care and factory clinics, improved sanitary conditions, ventilation, and especially better living quarters. The provision for baths figured in a strike in Minsk; soap and boiling water for tea were demanded by strikers in Nikolaev.[33] Strikers at Krasnoiarsk leather factories, where the manufacturing process required the use of water and humid conditions, demanded special clothing as well as a general improvement in sanitary conditions.[34] Other strike demands included improved eating facilities and factory distribution of bread (so workers would not have to stand in long lines on their own time). Such issues were significantly less frequent among strikers in the capital cities of Petrograd and Moscow, however. Here, municipal authorities had come to provide alternative services for industrial and other workers: housing and food supply were not nearly so dependent on factory authorities as in the industrial settlements of the provinces.[35]

A large category of strikes over working conditions involved hours. Strikes over hours—for an eight-hour workday, a six-hour workday (frequent in strikes of white-collar employees), or shorter hours generally—accounted for 68 strikes in this period and involved over 110,000 strikers. The significance of such demands was complex. In some ways, demands about hours can be seen as a pay demand: workers typically wanted the shorter hours to carry no reduction in pay, and hence a higher hourly rate. These demands also relate to job conditions; just as heat, ventilation, and adequate eating facilities made a worker's job easier, so did shorter

---

[33] *Velikaia oktiabr'skaia sotsialisticheskaia revoliutsiia v Belorussii*, vol. 1, pp. 389–90; TSGIA, f. 23, op. 16, d. 27, l. 17.

[34] *VOSR. Khronika sobytii*, vol. 1, p. 693.

[35] See James H. Bater, *St. Petersburg: Industrialization and Change* (London, 1976); Robert W. Thurston, *Liberal City, Conservative State: Moscow and Russia's Urban Crisis, 1906–1914* (New York, 1987).

hours and more rest time. As such, we might consider demands about hours to be acceptable and traditional claims, much on the order of wage demands. But hours also concerned control, control over the allocation between factory and nonfactory time. Hours were an extremely contentious issue in the prewar strike experience, and they constitute therefore an important liminal demand, between normal and, to employers, excessive claims for the distribution of workplace power.

The specific demand for an eight-hour workday illustrates the multiple meaning of the hours issue, reflecting political awareness as well as what labor historians call "job consciousness." Along with a few others, this demand linked Russian strikers to the broader international revolutionary labor movement and served as an important symbol of revolutionary commitment, one that would later be cited when revolutionary strikes swept factories in Germany, Italy, and elsewhere in Western Europe.[36] As we have seen, the eight-hour workday was placed by rank-and-file workers squarely on the agenda of revolution immediately after the fall of the tsar, when Petrograd workers refused to return to work until the issue had been resolved. In Moscow, the eight-hour workday was the source of great friction between local workers and the Moscow Soviet of Workers' Deputies until the latter unilaterally decreed the eight-hour workday on March 18.[37]

Throughout the spring, it was clear that the eight-hour workday had not always been implemented even when an overarching agreement had

[36] Historically, the eight-hour workday was a key issue of the international labor movement. First proposed in 1848, and then included as a part of the Marxist program after the 1866 Geneva Congress, it became broadly popular in the 1890s. By 1905, the eight-hour workday had become an integral demand of the Russian labor movement and occupied an important place in the petition carried by Father Gapon's followers on Bloody Sunday. (A copy of the petition is published in Sablinsky, *Road to Bloody Sunday: Father Gapon and the St. Petersburg Massacre of 1905* (Princeton, N.J., 1976), pp. 344–49.) See Sidney Webb and Harold Cox, *The Eight Hour Day* (London, n.d.); G.D.H. Cole, *History of Socialist Thought*, 2 vols. (London, 1954), vol. 1, pp. 108, 432; O. V–skii, "Vos'michasovoi rabochii den'," *Ekonomicheskii Zhurnal* 5 (1891); Iu. Zhukovskii, "Vos'michasovoi rabochii den'," *Iuridicheskii Vestnik* 9–10 (1891); A. I. Stul'ginskii, "K 10–letiiu vos'michasovogo rabochego dnia na Dobrushskoi kn. Paskevicha pishchebumazhnoi fabrike," *Pishchebumazhnoe Delo* 6–8 (1905), pp. 235–42, 276–82, 316–19; "Opyt vvedeniia 8–chasovogo rabochego dnia na Dneprskom metallicheskom zavode, sela Kamenka, 1897," *Gornozavodskii Listok* (Kharkov), 15 (1897), p. 3014; *Tret'ya vserossiiskaya konferentsiya professional'nykh soyuzov, 1917 goda. Stenograficheskii otchet*, ed. Diane Koenker (1927; reprint, Millwood, N.Y., 1982), p. 421 (a report that the eight-hour workday was in effect in Groznyi from 1896); Kir'ianov, *Zhiznennyi uroven'*, pp. 39–63.

[37] See Smith, *Red Petrograd*, pp. 65–68; M. David Mandel, *The Petrograd Workers and the Fall of the Old Regime* (London, 1983), pp. 86–89; Koenker, *Moscow Workers*, pp. 107–9, 238–39.

been reached. The issue consequently remained the subject of angry debates, resolutions, and of course strikes. Its potency as a strike demand arose in part because of the multiple symbols it conveyed. It was implicitly a political demand, a symbol of the justice of workers' revolutionary achievements, of their equality in the new society. It was also often explicitly political: workers argued that they needed shorter hours in order to have time to devote to political activity. At the same time, it was a demand about working conditions: workers wanted "eight hours to sleep, and eight hours for recreation and culture" after their eight hours of work.[38] It also, in effect, functioned as an economic demand, since workers used the eight-hour day as the norm upon which to add overtime pay at higher rates.[39] In the process of the continuing collapse of the Russian economy, the demand also evolved into a principle of labor solidarity, a way to combat unemployment. With the eight-hour workday, each worker labored less and the available work was spread out among more workers.[40] Because the issue of the eight-hour workday touched on so many bases of workers' goals and expectations in 1917, it received a great deal of attention from labor organizations and management groups alike. Among workers, it figured in 13 percent of the strikes in the spring cluster and involved at least 63,000 strikers.

Another popular goal that symbolized workers' hopes for a more just society but that provoked much less contention was the demand for paid annual vacations. Although not as symbolic and emotional an issue as the eight-hour workday, the frequency with which strikers demanded adequate vacations and the relative suddenness with which this demand appeared on the agenda of Russian strikes illustrates some of the forward-looking aspects of workers' strike demands in 1917. Moreover, it anticipates issues raised by workers elsewhere in Europe only after the end of the war, and therefore provides another example of the concrete ways in which the Russian revolution provided a symbol as well as a model for revolutionary movements elsewhere.

The paid vacation was not a traditional socialist demand. It cannot be found in the Erfurt program or the St. Petersburg workers' petition in 1905 and seems to have arisen as an issue of importance only after 1905, perhaps as an adjunct to new methods of scientific management that were introduced in the first decades of the new century. Regular annual rest

---

[38] *Gazeta Kopeika*, April 8, 1917. A discussion of the eight-hour workday in the context of workers' leisure in the United States can be found in Roy Rosenzweig, *Eight Hours For What We Will: Workers and Leisure in an Industrial City, 1870–1920* (Cambridge, 1983).

[39] *Tret'ya vserossiiskaya konferentsiya*, p. 418.

[40] Ibid., and F. Shipulinskii, *Trud i otdykh (Vos'michasovoi rabochii den')* (Moscow, 1917).

was advocated by industrial specialists as a way for management to raise productivity, and after World War I, labor unions took up the cause. Either through collective contracts or by government legislation, the paid vacation for workers had become a widespread achievement of labor in Western Europe by the 1920s.[41]

The issue arose in at least one instance in Russia in 1905; St. Petersburg printers negotiated for an annual vacation as part of their collective contract, but other evidence of the demand is scanty.[42] It is known that the paid vacation before the war was not a right or a benefit enjoyed by all workers, but a special privilege to be granted only to loyal workers of long service. The award of a vacation, as Lenin himself argued in 1913, could thus be used to depoliticize workers (Lenin said "enserf") by making such benefits contingent on subservience and loyalty. The activist worker who stood up for his or her rights was not likely to receive the valued time off.[43]

Statistics on the extent of paid vacations for Russian workers are sketchy at best. A study of factory workers in the Moscow industrial region in 1908 showed that about 2 percent of sampled textile workers received paid vacations of six or more days, and less than one-half of 1 percent of metalworkers enjoyed paid leave.[44] (A German study showed 2 percent of metalworkers had received vacations in 1912.)[45] Moreover, with the exception of the article by Lenin and one in the metal workers' union journal, the issue does not seem to have received much attention from the trade union press before 1917.[46]

It is especially surprising then that the issue became so important in the spring of 1917. In 38 strikes in our strike file involving at least 38,000 strikers, workers demanded paid two-week or four-week vacations. Those that specified a term of eligibility usually demanded that such vacations be given to workers after one year of service in the plant. In addition, the issue was often part of the tarif package presented by unions. The union of domestic servants in Chita, for example, included a paid one-month vacation after one year of service as one of 15 points in their collective contract.[47] Published factory committee protocols from Petro-

---

[41] Charles M. Mills, *Vacations for Industrial Workers* (New York, 1927), p. 15.

[42] Mark David Steinberg, "Consciousness and Conflict in a Russian Industry: The Printers of St. Petersburg and Moscow, 1855–1905," Ph.D. dissertation, University of California, Berkeley, 1987, p. 624.

[43] V. I. Lenin, "Ob otpuskakh dlia rabochikh," in *Polnoe sobranie sochineniia*, 5th ed. (Moscow, 1958–65), vol. 23, pp. 191–92 (originally in *Pravda*, no. 124, May 20, 1913).

[44] I. M. Koz'minykh-Lanin, *Semeinyi sostav rabochikh* (Moscow, 1912).

[45] Lenin, *Polnoe sobranie sochineniia*, vol. 23, p. 209.

[46] *Metallist* 3, no. 27, June 15, 1913, p. 9.

[47] *Professional'nyi Vestnik*, December 20, 1917, p. 11.

grad also provide a glimpse of how the demand was popularized and implemented outside the strike process itself. The factory committee at the Baltic Shipbuilding plant, for example, heard on June 28 that skilled and unskilled workers at the Grebnyi port had unilaterally won the right to paid vacations; under the assumption that soon all plants under the administration of the Naval Ministry would follow suit, the Baltic workers decided to introduce vacations at their plant immediately.[48] The Petrograd Cartridge plant's committee also initiated paid vacations of from two weeks to one month for one to three years' service, on the grounds that some private factories had already received the same concession.[49]

The question of working conditions in general seemed to be most pressing in this period to workers in small-scale manufacturing and trade, those whose working conditions had not been protected before the revolution by the factory inspectors. As many as nine out of ten strikers in retail shops may have demanded better working conditions, along with eight of ten construction workers, two-thirds of all striking printers, and better than 40 percent of strikers in mineral factories, in woodworking enterprises, on the railways, and in the service sector as a whole. Geographically, the Moscow and Petrograd regions, the Rostov area, and the Volga appeared relatively more concerned about such issues, but the variations among regions are small. Work conditions, like wages, concerned strikers everywhere.

Tactically, strikes over conditions in this period were just as likely to generate success as strikes over wages. Some 30 percent of all strikes about conditions were reported as full victories, and full or partial success came in nearly 50 percent of all instances. The outright failure rate for strikes about conditions was a little greater than that for wage strikes, but the numbers are quite small: by our count, only five of 301 wage strikes failed to produce results for workers, compared to three of 108 strikes over conditions.

3. Demands Concerning Workers' Dignity

Strikes over issues of dignity and personal respect revealed a new and distinct set of demands in 1917, conveying a level of grievance obscured by the Factory Inspectorate's method of data collection. In some of these cases, workers struck over the form of address used by supervisors. Traditionally, supervisors had used the familiar "thou" (*ty*), equating workers with serfs, children, and animals. Now in 1917, workers expected to

[48] *Fabrichno-zavodskie komitety Petrograda v 1917 godu. Protokoly*, 2 vols. (Moscow, 1979–82), vol. 1, pp. 276, 278.
[49] Ibid., p. 299.

1. Workers from the Dinamo machine works presenting Red regimental banners to representatives of the Fourteenth Siberian Infantry regiment.

2. Demonstrating restaurant and cafe workers with banners demanding "respect for waiters as human beings" and an end to the practice of tipping.

3. May Day demonstrators with banners reading "Long Live the International Holiday of Labor," "Long Live Socialism," "Long Live the Constituent Assembly," and "Long Live the Democratic Republic."

4. Employees of the Ministry of Labor.

5. "Agitators" urging subscription to the government's Liberty Loan in late May or early June, 1917.

6. Workers' living quarters (early twentieth century).

7. Workers' room in a Petrograd factory dormitory (early twentieth century).

8. Workers' living quarters (early twentieth century).

9. Workers' room in a Petrograd factory dormitory (early twentieth century).

10. Kitchen of a workers' apartment (1925).

11. Female workers' quarters in Petrograd.

12. View of the Putilov works (1915).

13. View of the Russian Renault (Reno) plant.

be addressed with the formal "you" (*vy*) and demanded also that supervisors cease other forms of verbal abuse. At the "De Paris" restaurant in the Crimea, for example, striking waiters in late April demanded a dressing room, a table where they could sit and eat their meals, and address in polite form by supervisors.[50] It may well be that disputes of this sort rarely led to strikes and were settled instead by negotiation.[51] Of the whole catalog of workers' demands in the spring of 1917, those over questions of dignity were certainly the least costly to resolve, however irritating to management. Thus, strikes that did include demands over such questions are an impressive indication of just how deeply workers felt about these issues; since we know dignity questions were often settled through negotiation, they testify indirectly to a far broader range of concern than the reports themselves document.

Demands were raised in a number of strikes in the spring about self-respect for particular groups of workers as well as for all employees. Strikes calling for equal pay for men and women, for better conditions (such as maternity leave) for women, for special work rules for apprentices and underage workers—these describe a world of solidarity among workers, a concern for those less able to defend themselves. The demand for equal pay for men and women, to be sure, was a double-edged weapon; there were surely cases in which male strikers pushed this demand in order to make women too expensive to hire. But implicit in the demand for workers' dignity in general is at least some degree of egalitarian sentiment, however difficult to evidence.

Most interesting is the kind of workers who included these demands in their strikes. Dignity issues emerged almost exclusively in strikes of clerical and service workers rather than in industrial work places. Nearly one-fifth of all striking retail and clerical workers in this period advanced demands of this sort, compared to an overall share of approximately 9 percent of all strikers. As many as two-thirds of striking service workers may have demanded greater respect from their employers in this way. Workers in the service sector struck much more frequently over matters of dignity than over either conditions or worker control, again testimony to the depth of feeling among Russian employees. On the other hand, the relative quiet of industrial workers on this issue suggests that industrial workers may have already perceived themselves, and were perceived by their adversaries, as equal combatants in shop floor struggle, that past strike conflict had already diluted the older paternalistic mode of rela-

[50] *Sotsial Demokrat*, April 28, 1917 (n.s.).

[51] The issues raised in conciliation boards in Petrograd are examined by Heather Hogan, "Conciliation Boards in Revolutionary Petrograd: Aspects of the Crisis of Labor-Management Relations in 1917," *Russian History* 9, no. 1 (1982), pp. 49–66.

tions and gained industrial workers a substantial degree of self-respect, if not social or economic parity. Service and clerical workers were still seen and treated as menials, as domestics, as personal servants; the intensity of demands for personal respect from this sector in these months testifies forcefully to the hopes many of Russia's most exploited employees had about the revolution creating a radically new social order.

Evidence on the outcome of such dignity strikes would suggest that management readily agreed to this aspect of the new order. Of 33 strikes over dignity issues in the spring cluster, none was reported to be lost, 15 (45 percent) were fully victorious for workers, and 20 (60 percent) were either fully or partially successful.

4. Demands Concerning Job Control and Factory Organization

Demands like the collective tarif, the eight-hour workday, and paid vacations occupied a gray area between what might be considered traditional grievances, whose satisfaction depended more on a firm's balance sheet than on the social attitudes of management, and those that tended to challenge traditional prerogatives of decision-making and control by management. In their own way, these intermediate demands helped to shape workers' expectations about controlling their work environments as much as specific demands for "workers' control," in which workers insisted on being allowed to organize their own committees to supervise enterprise activities. Still, between demands for the eight-hour workday and for outright worker self-management, a large set of demands set forth workers' aspirations to expand the limits of their autonomy inside the factory.

Some concerned control of factory time in ways more specific than just shortened hours. Strikers insisted on changes in work schedules, on rearranging dinner breaks, on grace minutes for tardiness. They demanded time off for holidays and a weekly day of rest (more common among nonfactory workers such as waiters or domestic servants). The "English week," with its half-day holiday on Saturday, was rarely if ever a specific issue, but some tarif proposals requested early closings, by one hour, on Saturday and before holidays. Workers also struck over the organization of the labor process, demanding changes in work rules, job descriptions, and production norms. There were strikes over how many workers should be assigned to a particular task, and over who would make entries into work-record books. As we have seen, supervisory personnel in general were often targets of workers' anger; many strikes, particularly in the early part of the revolutionary period, demanded the firing of individual supervisors.

A number of demands under the categories "workplace rights" and "rehiring of fired workers" attest to the great concern of Russian workers in 1917 about job security as shortages, the threat of demobilization, inflation, and Russia's general political instability all generated real anxieties in the workplace. We thus find strikers seeking a guaranteed number of work days a month and demanding explanations for production cutbacks. As the weeks wore on, there were also an increasing number of strikes protesting threatened or actual plant closings, either temporary or permanent, even though in these instances strikes were generally ineffective weapons. They were not always ineffective, however. At the Chepurin metalworking and mechanical plant in Blagoveshchensk, for example, shortly after the first coalition was formed, workers were charged with beginning a slowdown ("Italian strike") when management threatened to close the plant in response to wage demands. The Chepurin works was an important shell producer, with an outstanding contract of more than a half-million rubles, at 25 rubles and 48 kopecks for each projectile. Workers demanded that 4 rubles and 65 kopecks from each piece be applied toward wages. Whether or not a slowdown actually occurred—the charge was heatedly denied as "a cursed provocation"—the conflict mobilized local soviet and civic leaders, who formed a "neutral commission" to review the situation.[52]

These strikes were in many respects political strikes, seeking to reallocate decision-making power at the locus most immediate to workers, the shop floor. Control of the workplace—of rules, of employment decisions, of the pace of work and of discipline—was very much contested terrain, as Richard Edwards puts it, especially after February, when employers no longer had the tsarist police available to enforce their dominance in the workplace.[53] Hence 1917 was a particularly fluid period in determining what has been labeled "the frontier of control." "The real frontier, like most lines in industry, is more a matter of accepted custom than of precisely stated principle."[54] How far workers would or could go in pushing this frontier was an open question for workers and managers alike, but the struggle to establish a new custom generated important political lessons for partisans on both sides of the barrier.

The struggle to extend the limits of workers' control was led in most cases by representative workers' organizations, and it is no surprise that differences over the rights and powers of factory committees and trade unions provoked numerous clashes. Although factory committees formed

[52] *Edinstvo*, May 11, 1917.

[53] Richard Edwards, *Contested Terrain: The Transformation of the Workplace in the Twentieth Century* (New York, 1979).

[54] Carter L. Goodrich, *The Frontier of Control: A Study in British Workshop Politics* (New York, 1920), p. 56.

much more quickly after February than the larger and organizationally more complex trade unions, and tended to take up workers' grievances immediately, the question of trade union rights figured in a surprisingly large number of strikes. The specific demands involving either trade unions or factory committees tended, however, to be the same: recognition of the elected committee, the union, or its delegates, and union or committee participation in decisions about hiring and firing.[55]

Overall, the frequencies of strikes over issues of control lagged behind wage and conditions strikes in the spring of 1917. Only some 17.3 percent of strikes, and 11.6 percent of strikers, included these demands, as table 5.4 indicates. But variations across region and industry were sizeable. Scarcely 3 percent of the 46,000 strikers in the Moscow region concerned themselves with such issues, whereas almost one-fifth of the strikers in the Petrograd region were involved with issues of control. The cities of Petrograd and Moscow produced the most strikers for control issues, a total of 63,000: 10 percent of the estimated strikers in Petrograd, 20 percent in Moscow. But generally, with the exception of the two capitals, the control issue was not widespread in the early part of the year, at least in terms of strike demands.

The picture is also varied in terms of industry. Historical experience would suggest that metalworkers would be most willing to contest these shop-related political issues because of their political experience and economic strength. But quite surprisingly, metalworkers struck scarcely at all over control issues in these weeks. Rather, among industrial workers, leather, wood, and food workers, and printers sent between 20 percent and 40 percent of their strikers out over these issues. Among nonindustrial workers, construction, retail, service, and transport workers also generated disproportionate numbers of strikers over these demands. The key is that all these workers labored in small-scale enterprises. In all likelihood, workers in large industry were able to achieve sufficient autonomy outside the strike process, even before strikes over other issues were organized. For example, the expulsion of an authoritarian foreman might do more to expand shop floor autonomy than any bargainable work rules, and such expulsions, we know, were common among metal work-

---

[55] Demands involving trade unions were made in 15 strikes in the spring cluster (3.5 percent of the total of 421), involving at least 18,700 strikers, 3 percent of our estimated total. Demands about factory committees occurred in 12 strikes (3 percent), but involved at a minimum 11,000 strikers, or just about 2 percent of strikers in the period. Demands about hiring and firing, either through the trade unions or factory committees, engaged an additional 45,000 workers (8 percent) in 21 strikes. In all, then, some 11 percent of strikes between April 19 and July 6, and 13 percent of the strikers, were involved with organizational issues.

ers and others employed in large plants. In this light, workers in small work settings may have used strikes over control to catch up in early 1917 to the rights and freedoms already arrogated by workers in such industries as metals and chemicals.

Whatever their motivation, such strikers achieved substantial success. Although the failure rate for control strikes in this period is relatively high, about 5 percent, well over one-third of all such strikes ended in victory, and over half ended either in victory or compromise.

5. Political Demands and Their Implications

We have already noted how the kind of political strike so frequent in the weeks before the February revolution played a minimal role in March and early April once the new regime was formed. Prior to April 19, some 20,000 workers struck over political issues, but in the period of increasing strike frequency after April 19 and before July 1, demands referring to national or local political decisions seldom appeared in strike reports. Only nine such strikes, spread evenly across seven regions, were recorded in these weeks. Among economic sectors, nonindustrial workers were more active than industrial workers. Horse-drawn cabbies in Odessa and Rostov protested new tax treatments of their businesses, Kharkov university students demanded a voice in running school affairs, and a general strike swept Finland in late April over the issue of Social Democratic representation in local government.[56]

If explicit political strikes were relatively infrequent, however, they were not absent and hardly insignificant. In fact, the two end points of this period of intense economic strike activity were characterized by mass political strikes in Petrograd associated with the April crisis and the July Days. We have seen already that uncounted thousands of Petrograd workers and soldiers took to the streets on April 20 and 21 to protest the Miliukov note. And in the course of an attempt by Bolshevik radicals to force the Petrograd Soviet to seize power on July 3 and 4, an estimated 275,000 strikers from nearly all of Petrograd's metal and other industries halted work to demonstrate their political support for a change in regime. With this strike taken into account, political strikers accounted for nearly half of the total number of strikers in the spring period, nearly as many as strikers for wage issues (table 5.4). Because this huge political strike occurred at the very end of this period, the figures in table 5.4 are misleading. The overwhelming concerns for most of the spring were job re-

[56] *Russkiia Vedomosti*, May 25, 1917; *Delo Naroda*, April 26, May 13, 25, 1917; *Vlast' Naroda*, May 27, June 1, 1917; *Izvestiia* (Moscow), June 8, 1917; *Vpered*, May 18, 1917.

lated, negotiable at the shop level, reflecting some sense of separation between factory life and the broader political arena. Yet the explosion of
protest in July, expressed once again through strikes, suggests that no
single strike could be considered an isolated phenomenon, that the
boundaries of struggle were expanding, and that strikes taken as a whole
reflected serious and growing political grievances within the Russian labor force.

Two distinct patterns thus emerge from a review of strike demands in
this first intense period of activity. In important respects, the picture is
one of ebullient and confident workers asserting their claims to a better
life, demanding their employers fulfill the promises of February. Whether
or not strikers now asserted these demands because socialists held new
power in the coalition regime, their tactic—economic strikes—was essentially a traditional one, common to labor movements elsewhere and now
fully legitimized by Russia's new democratic order. Industrial workers
everywhere organized and negotiated with their employers in an atmo-
sphere of freedom, as citizens fully entitled to pursue their particular interests; employees in nonindustrial sectors of the economy were notable
in joining their proletarian comrades in using this weapon, their particular emphasis on personal dignity reflecting the nature of their own workplace situations. The overwhelming concern for wages and working conditions among strikers and the relative absence of strikes contesting more
fundamental political issues all suggest that a substantial degree of mutual tolerance still existed in labor relations during May and June, allowing even discouraged conciliationists like Konovalov some hope for the
future. At the same time, however, an undercurrent of more serious challenge can clearly be perceived as well. In Petrograd especially, workers
did not hesitate to employ strikes as weapons against adversaries other
than those in their enterprises, and the broader challenges raised by
strikes of all kinds—workers stopping production in order to win benefits—did little to alleviate concerns of industrialists and others that workers could not be trusted to restrain their ambitions.

We can see in these strikes, then, two central aspects of labor activism
in the spring. Although strikes in many places emerged as part of what
might be called the "routine" processes of labor relations in free enterprise economies, they also bore elements of far more radical change. And
given that the norms of these relations were themselves in the process of
definition, strikes shaped in their very occurrence both hopes and fears
about where such activism might lead. These complex dimensions of the
strike process now need to be explored in more detail.

6

COLLECTIVE ACTION

AND SOCIAL ORDER

The demands presented by workers in the course of their disputes are among the most interesting data we have on strikes in 1917. In the richness and variety of the complaints they represent, they reflect in complex ways an authentic voice of proletarian discontent, a point of entry into the subjective world of workers throughout Russia during the revolutionary crisis. They also reflect the nature of workplace conditions, workers' views about themselves and their employers, and in some ways, their visions of the future. In effect, strike demands as a whole constitute a complex and variegated prism refracting all the important relationships between Russian workers and revolutionary social realities.[1]

What sorts of realities? For analytic purposes, it is useful to bear in mind that the revolutionary process in 1917 involved both the phenomena of everyday experience and less explicit but quite powerful psychological and structural phenomena, experienced indirectly through political relations and the exercise of power as well as through various forms of social interaction. On an everyday basis, workers experienced directly the concrete realities of work conditions, the actions of foremen, fines, and the disparity between the contents of their pay envelopes and the costs of essential goods. They also read newspapers, experienced day-to-day political events, and saw notices posted about factory shutdowns. But equally important, workers experienced—if more indirectly—the effects of changing patterns of power and authority in 1917. They developed

[1] In these respects, strike demands compare favorably to another reflection of workers' attitudes and goals in 1917, the many resolutions passed by workers at various meetings and congresses and published extensively in the working-class press. Analyses of these resolutions may be found in M. David Mandel, *The Petrograd Workers and the Fall of the Old Regime* (London, 1983), pp. 6–7, and especially Diane Koenker, *Moscow Workers and the 1917 Revolution* (Princeton, N.J., 1981), pp. 228–68. See also S. A. Smith, *Red Petrograd: Revolution in the Factories, 1917–1918* (Cambridge, 1983), and Marc Ferro, *La Révolution de 1917: La chute du tsarisme et les origines d'octobre* (Paris, 1967), chap. 4.

ideas and concerns about the quality of life generally and experienced the feelings of solidarity that accompanied various forms of collective action. These more abstract elements of an evolving world view, political culture, mentality, were also a vital element of the workers' world in 1917 and defined the broader boundaries of labor-management discourse.

We emphasize this distinction because strike demands, like other aspects of worker protest, reflected a range of realities in 1917 and need to be understood in broader as well as more explicit terms. On the face of it, as we have seen in chapter 5, workers explicitly demanded higher wages, better treatment from foremen, union and factory committee recognition, and such workplace amenities as fully heated shops in the morning and boiling water for tea. They demanded playgrounds for their children, the right to sit down during slack time in restaurants, and more free time. They insisted on vacations and demanded accident insurance coverage. Characteristically, striking workers presented a number of demands of this sort to employers at once. In Kaluga, to take just one example, coal workers struck in April for 1) a change from daily wages to monthly salaries; 2) an eight-hour workday beginning at nine A.M., with one-and-a-half hours for midday dinner and a half-hour tea break; 3) a two-week vacation; 4) three-month sick leave (with one month at normal wages); 5) two-week notice and wages for dismissals; 6) tea service after dinner; 7) full wages paid for time lost as a result of the strike, and no retributive dismissals; and 8) improved conditions for those studying in area institutes, including their exemption from manual labor (for example, cutting wood for the stove).[2]

Yet strike demands of this sort often represent more than first appears. Strikes over wages in particular may disguise other pressing demands, which for one reason or another, perhaps relating to strategy or tactics, were not presented to management.[3] Where detailed lists were formulated, as in Kaluga, it is reasonable to assume they reflected workers' goals with some accuracy. Similarly, carefully enumerated demands for formal or polite address by supervisors, for an end to the demeaning custom of tipping, or for free time of some sort (vacations or rest periods), surely describe real expectations. In other circumstances, overt demands may not be more precise indicators of workers' attitudes or goals than the fact of the strike itself, even if they relate in some direct way to workers' everyday experiences; like the very act of striking, their underlying mean-

[2] *Pravda*, June 8, 1917 (n.s.).

[3] See the discussion in Edward Shorter and Charles Tilly, *Strikes in France, 1830–1968* (Cambridge, 1974), p. 68, and Rolande Trempé, *Les Mineurs de Carmaux, 1848–1914* (Paris, 1971), especially p. 743. Compare Peter N. Stearns, *Revolutionary Syndicalism and French Labor* (New Brunswick, N.J., 1971), pp. 36–39, 74.

ing or significance can only be deduced from the context of the strike, from the circumstances surrounding it.[4]

One way to probe beneath the surface is thus to pay attention to the less explicit phenomena of revolutionary experience, look closely at specific contexts, and categorize strike demands in terms of the ways they reflected social relations in the workplace or the contest for power. Where the evidence is rich enough, disputes can be analyzed for the ways in which workers themselves treated employers rudely, tried to increase their own role in production at the expense of management, or used strikes to involve themselves in nonpolitical issues that were not directly related to their own enterprise, such as the wages of other types of workers. The role of trade unions or other such agencies can also be scrutinized in some cases, as can other aspects of the strike experience, especially to determine at what point a roster of demands was actually formulated, and how workers came to adopt it.

We have consequently attempted an additional aggregation of our data on strike demands, reevaluating each of the more than 250 explicit demands in our data set, and where appropriate, regrouping them into three further categories that parallel the more familiar divisions (wages, conditions, dignity, factory control, and politics) analyzed in chapter 5. The first includes all strikes in which workers clearly challenged established managerial powers and attempted to assume for themselves prerogatives that had traditionally been management's alone. Most obvious here were strikes over issues of workers' control, an explicit category of demands which, as we have discussed, always sought to enhance the collective power of workers at the expense of management and sometimes sought as well to gain workers new responsibilities for supervising or maintaining production. At the same time, strikes in which workers demanded that plant owners share profits with employees, guarantee a certain number of work days per month regardless of actual production, cancel cutbacks in production, or replace foreign directors with Russians all clearly involved challenges to traditional managerial powers in the workplace in areas not directly associated with workers' control, even if accompanied by demands for higher wages. For example, postal workers in one instance insisted on "equal rights" with management along with an increase in wages;[5] elsewhere, textile and woodworkers wanted to keep

---

[4] This approach is most easily taken, of course, in studies of particular strike episodes. See especially the discussion about strikers' "vocabularies" and the context of strike action by Eric Batstone, Ian Boraston, and Stephen Frenkel in *The Social Organization of Strikes* (Oxford, 1978), which examines the evolution of a strike in a single engineering plant over a four-month period.

[5] *Volia Naroda*, July 4, 1917. See also *Birzhevyia Vedomosti*, July 4, 1917; *Vpered*, July 6, 1917; *Novaia Zhizn'*, July 13, 1917.

their own records of piecework production or set wage rates themselves rather than leave this responsibility to foremen.[6] In Kremenchug and Poltava, printers and food workers in early May demanded that no workers be hired or dismissed without their explicit approval, and such demands began to increase in some places with the spread of unions.[7] Such strikes clearly sought a new balance of power within the enterprise, however much the strikers' primary goal may have been increased earnings and improved welfare.

Two further categories of strikes involving less apparent struggles in the workplace involved protests over intraclass issues (rather than conflicts between broader aggregations of management and labor) and strikes over the question of whether management would honor previously made agreements. Strikes of these sorts are of particular interest in probing the question of workers' solidarity and consciousness in 1917, as well as in exploring different perceptions about the value of resolving labor-management conflict through negotiations or mediation. They thus lie at the heart of what many began to think in the spring was *the* central question of Russia's developing revolution, the relationship between collective action and social order.

ADDITIONAL CHALLENGES OF THE STRIKE MOVEMENT IN MAY AND JUNE

We have seen that strikes over control issues in the spring strike cluster occurred at a rate far below that for more conventional wage issues. If we add to these strikes cases in which wage or conditions demands also implicitly challenged the limits of workplace authority, however, we discover a much broader current of challenges to managerial prerogatives normally associated with a free-enterprise economy. As tables 6.1 and 6.2 indicate, whereas only some 17.3 percent of all strikes clearly demanded some direct form of workers' control (usually recognition for factory committees) in their engagements with management during the spring, more than twice as many (37.8 percent) challenged other kinds of managerial authority as well: the setting of hours, including the eight-hour day, the granting of vacations as a matter of right instead of privilege, the power to set forms of wage payments, the payment of wages for time workers spent on strike. Moreover, these challenges involved at a minimum almost a quarter of all strikers, a percentage twice as large again as that for workers' control issues alone. Although only estimates, our fig-

[6] *Vlast' Naroda*, May 17, 1917; *Izvestiia* (Petrograd), April 30, 1917; *Sotsial Demokrat*, April 30, 1917.
[7] TSGIA f. 23, op. 16, d. 256, ll. 11–13.

TABLE 6.1
Strikes Challenging Managerial Authority
in the Spring Cluster by Industry and Sector
(As Percentages of the Group's Total Number of Strikes)

Sector	Workers Control Issues	All Challenges
Industrial		
Metals	21.6	43.2
Wood and wood products	27.6	55.2
Chemicals	27.3	45.5
Food products	30.0	60.0
Animal products (leather)	11.1	37.2
Textiles	8.6	34.5
Paper and printing	16.3	39.5
All Industrial	18.2	41.3
Transport	5.6	22.2
Service	17.0	29.5
All Strikes	17.3	37.8

ures suggest a sizable undercurrent of protest within a variety of enterprises over issues of workplace authority in these weeks, one much larger than is evident using more conventional schema of strike causes or workers' demands.

Extremely interesting here is the relative distribution of strikers involved in both "control" and other "challenge" strikes among different economic sectors, especially between industrial workers and service sector employees. Table 6.2 indicates that overall, relatively few industrial workers (4.3 percent) struck over workers' control issues alone in these weeks, compared to more than half of all service sector employees; in contrast to only some 13 percent of the industrial strike force, as many as 85 percent of all service sector strikers between April 19 and July 6 may have engaged their employers in ways challenging established patterns of enterprise authority.

The comparative percentages are explainable in several ways. Industrial workers in many of Russia's largest plants had organized their factory committees during the first weeks of the revolution and had little need to engage owners further on this specific issue. The question in these

TABLE 6.2
Strikers Challenging Managerial Authority
in the Spring Cluster by Industry and Sector
(Minimal Estimates, as Percentages of the
Group's Total Number of Striking Workers)

	Workers' Control Issues	All Challenges
Industrial		
Metals	0.6	6.9
Wood and wood products	47.9	81.4
Chemical	8.8	36.8
Food products	20.7	33.0
Animal products (leather)	21.5	27.5
Textiles	7.9	35.6
Paper and printing	23.4	72.3
All Industrial	4.3	13.2
Transport	18.6	58.0
Service	54.9	85.2
All Strikers	11.6	23.8

enterprises became one of defining committee rights, a matter the Provisional Government attempted to work out with its statute of April 23, but with legislation intended only for industrial enterprises.[8] Railroad workers also organized their own line committees soon after February, encouraged to do so by Minister Nekrasov.[9] Service sector employees, on the other hand, struggled for the most part with individual owners in small and diverse shops, with little attention from the ministries or even the soviets. Table 6.2 suggests how very strongly they felt the elements of workers' control allowed their industrial comrades should be theirs as well.

The degree to which this was conscious emulation, stimulated perhaps by broader political concerns, or a consequence in part of agitation by

[8] The statute is in Robert P. Browder and Alexander F. Kerensky, eds., *The Russian Provisional Government, 1917: Documents*, 3 vols. (Stanford, Calif., 1961), vol. 2, pp. 718–20.

[9] See the discussion in William G. Rosenberg, "The Democratization of Russia's Railroads in 1917," *American Historical Review* 86, no. 5 (December 1981), pp. 988–90.

Bolsheviks or other radical labor organizers is impossible to measure. The most extensive efforts at unionization among service sector employees in these weeks was in the public sector, especially the postal system,[10] but service sector strikes were strongly concentrated among waiters and other restaurant employees, thousands of whom struck in May and June to force owners to give up their traditional reliance on tips instead of wages, and among laundry workers, many of whom drew close to the Bolsheviks during the Petrograd strike in May, and who demanded new powers over hiring and firing. In any event the result is clear: large numbers of service-sector employees willing to strike during May and June clearly identified this form of protest as a means of altering the traditional balance of power within their establishments.

The distribution of challenges to managerial authority within different industrial branches also deserves attention. As tables 6.1 and 6.2 indicate, the largest percentage of both "control" and "all challenge" strikes occurred in the wood and paper industries, where the percentage of strikers challenging managerial authority was significantly higher than the average, ranging from an estimated 72.3 percent of all paper workers and printers to more than 81 percent of all woodworkers. By contrast, metalworkers, who constituted the largest numerical group of strikers in these weeks, ranked low in the share of strikers challenging managerial power within the enterprise.

In part this pattern probably reflects the fact that metalists, and to a lesser extent the textile workers, were also far more active politically than other branches: metalists and textile workers were the only two industrial groups to have participated in any numbers in open political strikes between March and July, as we have seen, and the number of metalists involved in the July Days strikes in particular dilutes in statistical terms their percentage of "challenge" strikers.[11] But more important, we think, is the way these patterns reflect the spread of concern about the nature of managerial authority from larger and more politically active groups like the metalists to hitherto less active groups like the woodworkers: tables 6.1 and 6.2 suggest that as with service sector employees, industrial workers less actively involved in the overt political struggle in the spring began

[10] As early as mid-March a central organizing committee had been formed in Moscow; by late spring, postal employees in many places had formed "shop" committees similar to those in industry. See K. V. Bazilevich, *Professional'noe dvizhenie rabotnikov sviazi (1917–18 gody)* (Moscow, 1927), pp. 44–56.

[11] Still, during either May or June, in relative terms fewer metalists appear to have been involved in these strikes than almost all other types of industrial workers, although the range in June between metalists, animal products workers, textilists, and workers in paper and printing enterprises is quite narrow.

to use the strike weapon intensively as a means of changing workplace relations.

Also, many strikes in these branches, especially among printers, tended to be small-scale, as they were again in the service sector. Employers here may have been more reluctant than in large firms to allow their workers new powers, partly because of economics, but probably also because many small enterprises were traditionally run in a very authoritarian manner, with little attention to such issues as workers' rights. The broader political implications of the revolution may thus have had particular resonance here in the spring of 1917. At the same time, although they were less *active* politically, printers were clearly among Russia's most politically *aware* workers, and may have used their strikes more deliberately in May and June to alter traditional workplace patterns because of expectations raised by the formation of the coalition. In any case, there seems little doubt that the strike process itself facilitated an extention of workers' challenges to managerial power across industrial as well as sectoral boundaries in these weeks.

There is some indication that the spread was extending geographically as well. While our data here are incomplete, more than 60 percent of the strike force we can record for the Kievan region and almost half the strikers in the Volga region, encompassing principally the provinces of Kazan, Samara, Saratov, and Simbirsk, may have been involved in strikes of this sort. Waiters in distant Kazan, for example, declared a strike on May 17, when restaurant and tavern owners refused to begin paying a monthly salary of 25 rubles instead of having their employees depend on tips, and began their protest with a parade through town carrying banners declaring "Down with Slavery and Humiliation!"[12] In Cheliabinsk, printers demanded in June that hiring take place only through their union and refused to be paid for piecework.[13] By comparison, data for the cities of Moscow and Petrograd indicate much lower ratios of "challenge" strikers (approximately 37 and 11 percent, respectively), and each is substantially lower than the surrounding regions. Although the contours of this strike activism in the provinces are still quite vague, we can see an analogy between workers away from the capitals generally and those service workers and small shop craftsmen not hitherto linked with the traditions of direct political struggle. In any event, the extent to which these new workers appear to have begun to challenge their employers' traditional powers is impressive, further testimony to the strong social pressures beginning to fuel the revolution nationwide.

A closer look at the weeks of the spring strike cluster, and particularly

[12] *Kazanskii oktiabr'. Materialy i dokumenty*, ed. E. Grachev (Kazan, 1926), pp. 65–68.
[13] *Bor'ba za sovetskuiu vlast' na iuzhnom Urale (1917–1918 gody)* (Cheliabinsk, 1957) p. 62.

at the month of May, provides an essential key to understanding how these challenges were manifested. As we have seen in chapter 5, these weeks saw a sharp rise in the number of strikes and strikers overall, compared to preceding weeks. The number of strikes that began in May—190—was the largest of any month in the revolutionary period; the jump from a minimal estimate of 18,000 strikers in April to over 90,000 in May signaled the beginning of the wholesale expansion of strike activism. But just as important as the quantitative growth in strikes in May is the change in the nature of demands within the broader categories we have examined in chapter 5.

As we have seen, economic matters continued to dominate strike issues in May, as they did throughout this entire period. But only in May did issues about rate *determination*—issues as much about power as about levels of income—occupy a total number of strikers second only to wages per se among all economic issues. We estimate that over half of all strikers left their jobs partly over this issue in May, in some instances demanding management alter wage scales or methods of calculation, and in others, demanding workers' representatives themselves play a role in the process. On May 8, for example, a "nearly general" strike of needleworkers in Samara began in an effort to shift wages from piecework to a daily or monthly basis after employers indicated they would only allow piece rates to rise 10 to 25 percent. Strikes elsewhere followed similar patterns.[14]

Comparing the share of strikers over time-related issues also reveals a sharp discontinuity in May. Strikes in our file over the eight-hour workday jumped from approximately 13 percent of strikers in March and April to 30 percent in May and June. Strikes in which workers demanded that their own organizations determine who would be hired and fired (an important component of the "challenge to authority" strikes) likewise took a sharp rise: this single demand was made by one-third of all strikers in May. Strikes demanding recognition of trade unions or factory committees (two additional challenges to managerial power) also rose markedly after the formation of the first coalition, but in many places essentially because of wage concerns. In Pskov, for example, a number of small firms refused in early May to recognize the needleworkers' union because owners feared they would have to pay wage rates agreed upon between the union and larger establishments, and a strike began on May 5.[15]

What we have, then, is a most interesting if rather complicated picture: on the one hand, as we have seen in chapter 5, the inclination to use strikes as overt political weapons concentrated almost exclusively among

[14] *Revoliutsiia 1917–1918 godov v Samarskoi gubernii*, ed. I. I. Bliumental' (Samara, 1927), vol. 1, p. 100.

[15] *Ustanovlenie i uprochenie sovetskoi vlasti v Pskovskoi gubernii, 1917–1918 gody* (Pskov, 1957), p. 92.

Petrograd and Moscow metalists in the late spring, erupting in force only during the July Days, and on the other, an extensive use of "economic" or "nonpolitical" strikes by other industrial branches and economic sectors throughout the country to press the frontiers of factory authority and contest traditional managerial prerogatives.[16] Indeed, the significance of demands challenging managerial authority in these weeks seems to lie precisely in the identity of the groups of workers who pressed them most intensely: as far as we can tell, they were not the more overtly radical workers associated with metal-fabricating or defense industries, but workers in small-scale industry and in retail stores and service establishments, whom the tsarist legal system had placed at the greatest disadvantage vis-à-vis their employers, whose strikes were the most easily repressed, whose personal relationship to their employers the most closely monitored, and who had not had political influence before February. The overall picture in these weeks still suggests patterns of strike activism conforming in broad contour to those common in Western "bourgeois democracies," and one not necessarily inimical to the mutual efforts of soviet figures, employer associations, and government officials to establish a firm and stable social order. Yet a forceful undercurrent of opposition to the ways power was distributed in the workplace, at odds with these goals, clearly strengthened after the formation of the first coalition.

STRIKE ORIGINS AND LEADERSHIP IN THE SPRING

Why did these changes occur? One reason clearly had to do with Russia's changing economic circumstances in May and June 1917. The weeks immediately after the revolution had seen a sudden rise in workers' incomes, especially in the capitals. Wages for Petrograd machinists as a whole jumped 35 to 50 percent in March alone, and at some industrial plants, like the Parviainen works, employees doubled their wages between February and April.[17] Many manufacturers also agreed to Easter bonuses, as we have seen, especially in the textile industry, where payments of this sort were often used in the past to keep labor peace. With workers now free to strike with little fear of reprisal, many agreements were reached simply because strikes provided extra leverage. In Penza, for example, workers at the Peremyshlin match factory were given raises in the form of new piece and day rates despite the fact that their factory committee

[16] The term "frontier of control" has been conceptualized and developed most thoroughly by Carter L. Goodrich. See his *The Frontier of Control: A Study in British Workshop Politics* (New York, 1920).

[17] S. G. Strumilin, *Zarabotnaia plata i proizvoditel'nost' truda v Russkoi promyshlennosti za 1913–1922 gody* (Moscow, 1923), pp. 11–13; Smith, *Red Petrograd*, p. 70.

demanded the firing of two foremen, one accused of bribery, the other of rudeness. Owners were eager to keep the peace, and in the general context of the moment, were even reported to feel these demands were reasonable.[18]

In May, however, there were several important changes in the economy. One was that with so much more money in circulation (both because of higher wage bills and because of the hardworking government printing presses), price increases began to catch up to wage increases; workers who felt they had won real gains in March and April began to fall behind again, and many must have become concerned that the revolution had not really improved their standard of living as much as they expected it would. Workers may therefore have demanded changes in the rate system and more power for their elected representatives to adjudicate wage distributions in order to protect themselves against rising prices. Further, there were undoubtedly members of the workforce who had not shared in the initial round of wage increases, presumably because they were unorganized or farther away from the major cities. Such workers thus began to engage in strikes at a time when the economy had already begun to falter. Since management could not so easily afford to satisfy wage demands at this point, demands turned more to issues of power and workplace control.

Yet the changing political situation undoubtedly played a central role as well. For many industrialists, especially those skeptical from the start about the efficacy of Konovalov's conciliationist policies, the formation of the first coalition raised serious concerns about their future relationship to the regime. Government subsidies for military production appeared threatened. Owners like N. N. Alafuzov, the head of the important manufacturing complex in Kazan which now made boots for the army, felt that even the imposition of more limited working hours would threaten their contracts and expressed their concerns directly to the ministry; although manufacturers like Alafuzov may have agreed to wage demands in March and April because they expected to pass costs on to government purchasers, the presence of socialists in the coalition raised strong doubts about the regime's willingness or ability to absorb them.[19] Some clearly worried further that socialist power would spread, that new government policies would further threaten free enterprise, especially those associated with the PSFMO and MSFMO. On the other hand, some workers themselves might have sought more control over their enterprises

---

[18] *Postanovka i pobeda velikoi oktiabr'skoi sotsialisticheskoi revoliutsii v Penzenskoi gubernii. Sbornik dokumentov i materialov* (Penza, 1957), pp. 68–69.

[19] *Kazanskii oktiabr'*, pp. 25–32.

in order to ensure their share in whatever resources government or soviet leaders might still make available.

Whether from economic or political concerns, however, most strikes began in May and June because workers themselves decided to go on the offensive: they occurred because strikers thought they could win. And although they often involved some degree of organization, the process of collective action itself still remained the major impetus for mobilization. Even those strikes that began in May and June at the instruction of a trade union group or factory committee did so without much planning. The Petrograd laundry workers' strike began on May 1 when a newly organized Union of Petrograd Laundry Workers declared workers "everywhere" were leaving their jobs, but fewer than half of the city's approximately 5,500 laundry employees initially quit work. It was only after strikers appeared at the shops of their working comrades that the strike spread rapidly throughout the city. Strikes began in a similar way from "below" almost everywhere in May and June: in the Caucasus town of Piatigorsk, where health resort and food service workers struck early in May for higher wages; in Kharkov, where unskilled metalists struck in June; in Yalta, where printers struck from June 4 to 21 in an effort to boost their wages.[20]

Cases of this sort soon began to raise new questions about the proper role of trade unions, especially after Skobelev was appointed to head the new Ministry of Labor and the socialist complexion of the coalition became more pronounced. Difficulties turned both on the degree of control national union figures should have over local groups, which were most often factory committees, and on the prerogatives of various central trade union councils over their constituent memberships. By the late spring, the most important of these councils were the Petrograd and Moscow Central Bureaus, which had organized in March, and the Central Council of Trade Unions elected at the Third All-Russian Trade Union Conference in June.

For the most part, trade unionists in these leadership positions had by June a vivid sense of the potential danger from strikes. Just as earlier, many did not support every strike initiative in these weeks and sometimes expressed genuine concern that workers might jeopardize the policies and tactics of the soviets, which continued to be dominated almost everywhere by socialist moderates, especially Mensheviks. Many were also quite concerned that what they regarded as spontaneous activism on the workers' part could breach the efforts of Minister Skobelev and others to

[20] See, e.g., *Vlast' Naroda*, May 3, 1917; *Vpered*, June 5, 1917; *Novaia Zhizn'*, June 7, 11, 1917; *Birzhevyia Vedomosti*, June 28, 1917.

achieve gains from above; for the most part, they saw their primary task as one of strengthening labor organization and erecting structures and procedures to channel the remarkable energy of their constituents in what they defined as a "constructive" way. The secretary of the All-Russian Central Council, A. Lozovskii (Solomon Dridzo), put it this way: "We can compare the strike to a 42-inch cannon. There are other, lighter weapons of struggle. Not only a strike, but even the threat of a strike can sometimes show results, and therefore preparation for the waging of a strike is also one of the methods of economic struggle."[21]

Lozovskii at this time was an independent Social Democrat (although he soon joined the Bolsheviks), and hardly an opponent of strikes. But like others he was convinced that one of the major tasks of the Central Council was to gain control over "anarchistic and spontaneous" elements within the union movement as a whole, a task which naturally placed the Central Council, along with most national unions, in a position of opposition to most work stoppages initiated by workers themselves.[22] "Proletarian responsibility" thus continued to be a common theme in labor discourse, as important in some quarters as "solidarity."[23]

In these circumstances it is not surprising that unions on all levels also had difficulty establishing boundaries between their own activities and interests and those of various governing institutions: soviets on the one hand and the government itself on the other. The Central Council struggled in particular under the first coalition against what it perceived as the "hegemonization" by the soviet network, a struggle which led by early July to deep differences with the Soviets' Central Executive Committee. The Council pressed for "full independence in the area of economic policies" and demanded a policy of "noninterference" on the part of the soviets.[24] Similarly, the all-Russian railroad union insisted responsibility for transport policies be largely left in its hands, a stance which led to charges of cooptation ("statization") from the rank and file and of meddling in government business on the part of railroad management.[25]

At the same time, however, although trade union influence was clearly increasing, the paramount leadership role within industrial enterprises was played by factory committees, which may or may not have thought of themselves as local union cells. The committees frequently led strikes themselves in individual enterprises, even if they appointed a subordinate

[21] *Tret'ya vserossiiskaya konferentsiya profsoyuzov, 1917 goda. Stenograficheskii otchet*, ed. Diane Koenker (1927; reprint, Millwood, N.Y., 1982), p. 256.

[22] See, e.g., *Rabochaia Gazeta*, June 7, 1917; *Novaia Zhizn'*, May 13, 1917.

[23] See, e.g., *Volia i Dumy Zheleznodorozhnika*, June 1, 1917.

[24] *Professional'nyi Vestnik* 8 (December 20, 1917), pp. 1–2.

[25] Rosenberg, "Democratization," pp. 995–97.

strike committee. (Where independent strike committees played a leading role, strikers generally came from more than one enterprise, and sometimes more than one industrial branch.) Trade union representatives were increasingly active in strikes of chemical and woodworkers, printers, textilists, and retail employees, as well as in the general activities of many larger enterprises, especially in Moscow and Petrograd, where much was at stake in terms of workers' loyalties and affiliations. In Arkhangel province, the woodworkers' union even called a strike in late April "for educational reasons, in the sense of creating solidarity and discipline among its members";[26] when a number of shops in the massive Putilov works went on strike during the third week of June, a factorywide meeting voted to charge the metalists' union with responsibility for leading the strike, but the union was reluctant to accept and bent its efforts instead to bring the scattered work stoppages to a halt. Union leaders felt strongly that new wage norms should be worked out through negotiations for the industry as a whole. Perhaps because of its growing size—itself a sign of one kind of success—the metalworkers' union was more centralized than most other unions and appears to have been somewhat less responsive to local protests, although metalists' strikes reported more factory committee leadership than any other industry.[27]

Yet trade unions clearly remained a vital source of direction and support for striking workers in May and June, even if union officials themselves often did not serve as strike leaders. These were confusing times for many workers, and unions sometimes helped clarify positions and formulate their demands. In Tsaritsyn, for example, workers at the armaments plant voted initially in late April to support the Liberty Loan (*Zaem Svobody*), without apparently understanding its meaning. Six days later they emphatically changed their minds.[28] The availability of strike funds or other forms of relief were also of great importance, as was the ability of national or production union leaders to negotiate at high levels with industry representatives. Along with the soviets, the unions also provided important opportunities for mediation, using union members somewhat detached from turmoil of day-to-day strike action as workers' representatives on conciliation boards.

As one might expect, undirected work stoppages in May and June seem to have occurred much more frequently outside the two capitals than

[26] *Bor'ba za ustanovlenie i uprochenie sovetskoi vlasti na Severe* (Arkhangel, 1959), p. 56.

[27] See, e.g., *Edinstvo*, June 22, 1917. The activities of the Petrograd union are discussed extensively by Smith, *Red Petrograd*, pp. 121–29.

[28] *Tysiacha deviatsat semnadtsatyi god v Stalingradskoi gubernii*, ed. G. T. Gavrilov (Stalingrad, 1927), p. 37.

within, where factory committees and particularly trade union organizations were stronger. Our evidence also suggests that strikes without union involvement began more frequently in the service sector than in industry, a consequence as well, no doubt, of the stronger role of committees and unions in the factories. A disruptive and contentious strike by some 2,000 Petrograd postal workers in early July, for example, caught the strong communications workers' union entirely by surprise.[29] And the kind of small and disorderly strikes that broke out in the Putilov plant in June undoubtedly occurred quite frequently throughout the country in these weeks, even if they tended to be both small and short-lived. For the year as a whole, according to our limited data, the average size of an organized strike may have been as high as 6,500, while the average size of strikes that began without any reported organization was probably under 2,000.

It should not be surprising that so many strikes in the spring proceeded without union initiation, and these estimates should not be taken to suggest a revolt against union leadership or a preference for wildcat (*dikie*) spontaneity. Clearly, some locally initiated strikes, such as the well-publicized Putilov actions, were wildcat actions in defiance of union wishes. But union organization was simply too thin in May and June to monitor all cases of labor unrest and factory conflicts, and often enough it was a locally inspired strike that first brought workers into contact with union organizers. Such was the case, for example, with the brushmakers of Minsk, who "formed a union during the course of the strike."[30] In such cases, strike actions themselves served as a school for trade unionism.

In other instances, however, strikes in May and June proved to be schools of a different sort. As we have indicated in chapter 3, there were often marked contrasts between strikes that began as deliberate, offensive actions on the workers' part, designed to achieve certain goals, and those that occurred as "defensive" reactions against some activity of management. Offensive strikes tended to be relatively peaceful and were frequently upbeat in mood. Those beginning defensively were frequently angry and reflexive, with workers showing little patience toward any pleas for moderation.

Despite the presence of socialists in the cabinet, or perhaps, in some measure at least, because of the business community's concern after Skobelev assumed the minister of labor's post that he and others might move too rapidly to improve workers' welfare at their expense, the weeks of the first coalition were also a time when large numbers of strikes began over unacceptable management actions. Overwhelmingly, these had to do

---

[29] *Vpered*, July 6, 1917.

[30] *Velikaia oktiabr'skaia sotsialisticheskaia revoliutsiia v Belorussii*, 2 vols. (Minsk, 1957), vol. 1, p. 407.

with workers being fired. Most were in large industrial enterprises, almost half in our data file were in metalworking plants, and almost all occurred between mid-April and the end of June. In cases in which strikes broke out because two or three workers had been fired, employers had typically moved against especially activist workers, either for political agitation of some sort (usually on enterprise time), or for other forms of organizational activity. When larger groups of workers were fired, it was frequently as a reaction of management to workers' demands for higher wages. In effect, workers in these instances were essentially *forced* to strike, even if they had not intended to do so when they initially presented their grievances.

Reports in our file of strikes beginning in this way in May and June generally come from provincial areas, where owners may have felt less inhibited in these matters, rather than Petrograd or Moscow, although they certainly occurred in the capitals as well. Thus a strike at the Smoliakov foundry in Iaroslavl' began at the end of May after a group of "worker-agitators" was fired for demanding the removal of employees they thought had "brought disorganization to the worker's ranks," and the remainder of the workforce was fired when they walked off in sympathy.[31] Instances of this sort occurred among metalists, woodworkers, printers, rubber workers, waiters, insurance company clerks, workers in an envelope plant, and food service employees, among others.[32]

A number of strikes also began shortly after the socialists entered the government, when factory owners locked workers out rather than accept their demands or even their terms for negotiating. Some employers, like the owner of the Levi clothing shop in Moscow, refused concessions or even negotiation with workers without the approval of employers' associations.[33] At the Kornev electro-technical works in early June, the owners fired a boy for smoking and then shut the shop down entirely rather than allow other employees to protest.[34] At the Kal'meier boxmaking works in Moscow late in mid-June, 50 workers were locked out because the owner refused to equalize wages for different categories of workers who were, in fact, performing the same jobs.[35] In larger enterprises, like

[31] VOSR. *Khronika sobytii*, vol. 2, p. 197; *Ustanovlenie sovetskoi vlasti v Iaroslavskoi gubernii* (Iaroslavl', 1957), p. 123.

[32] See, e.g., *Vpered*, May 7, 11, 1917; *Trud*, May 12, 1917; *Izvestiia* (Petrograd), May 16, 1917; *Sotsial Demokrat*, April 26, May 7, June 3, 8, 1917; *Zemlia i Volia*, June 15, 1917; *Delo Naroda*, June 7, 1917; *Trudovaia Kopeika*, April 29, 1917.

[33] *Sotsial Demokrat*, May 2, 1917; *Vpered*, May 3, 1917.

[34] *Trud*, June 1, 1917; *Vpered*, June 3, 1917.

[35] *Izvestiia* (Petrograd), June 22, 1917; *Vpered*, June 22, 1917; *Sotsial Demokrat*, June 24, 1917.

the tailor, bootmaker, and capmaker shops of the Officers' Economic Society in Moscow, strikes often spread or began in different shops as a result of lockouts when owners shut production down rather than settle a dispute with a particular shop or section.[36] In some cases, it is clear that workers were locked out by plant owners attempting to enforce their own political views on the workplace, angry at the political implications of worker protest. At the Chepurin metal works in Blagoveshchensk, where workers began a slowdown in early May to gain higher wages, as we have noted, the plant's owners ultimately accused the ringleaders of treason, discharged the entire workforce, and announced the plant had been closed because of the workers' "irresponsibility" and "lack of patriotism." Enraged, the Chepurin workers refused to leave the grounds and angrily declared themselves on strike, demanding management relinquish control of the plant to them.[37] By late spring, lockouts had become a fairly common practice, as owners took advantage of labor unrest to halt unprofitable production or to stop production because of inadequate supplies or high costs.

Three additional patterns of strikes that began defensively in May and June can also be discerned in the data, although here, too, one cannot analyze the materials quantitatively in any very systematic way. These involved strikes beginning in response to wage reductions or changes in systems of wage payments, strikes in response to management's refusal to bargain or to accept agreements worked out in mediation or conciliation commissions, and strikes that occurred as protests against some form of harassment or repression.

As we will see, strikes over wage reductions tended to occur later in 1917, rather than during the spring, and were closely tied to growing production difficulties. But already in May and June there were several publicized instances of plant and shop owners refusing to pay higher wages or implement new rate systems that workers thought they had agreed to; in other instances, plant managers withheld wages or raised the prices of goods or services provided to workers by the company. Strikes also began in these weeks when workers were docked pay for time lost in political meetings or demonstrations or when bonuses or other supplementary payments in kind were withheld. Striking workers in these instances were both figuratively and literally on the defensive, since a strike to protest reduced or withheld wages often played to management

[36] *Proletarii* (Moscow), May 24, 1917; *Sotsial Demokrat*, May 26, 1917. See also *Birzhevyia Vedomosti*, May 19, 1917.

[37] See the reports in *Vlast' Naroda*, May 11, 1917; *Russkiia Vedomosti*, May 11, 1917.

desires to reduce or stop production, and the strike itself, reactive and unplanned, deprived workers even of unacceptable wages.

The same was true with instances in which management refused to submit disputes to mediation or conciliation commissions or rejected outright agreements a negotiating team had achieved. When service workers at Gostinnyi Dvor and other Petrograd markets attempted to have the minister of labor mediate a long dispute, market owners failed to show up for talks at the Ministry because they rejected the notion that any outside body might have authority in the matter.[38] In Moscow, metalworkers at the Kerting plant went on strike in late June when management refused to enroll the plant in an industrywide disability and illness fund.[39]

Other types of incidents—physical or verbal abuse, or a recurrence of incidents like the famous "maggots in the soup" case on the battleship *Potemkin*—almost never appear in strike reports as direct causes of work stoppages. A rare example is a strike of workers in a small metal-stamping shop on the outskirts of Moscow. Here 19 workers struck "on the grounds of the cruel treatment towards workers by the wife of the owner" as well as because of delays in wage payments. Besides several wage-related demands, workers insisted the wife withdraw from the factory.[40] Such instances, however, did not normally turn into strikes, at least not ones that found their way into the public record, since workers could find other ways to correct abusive behavior if they felt strongly enough, without jeopardizing their own wages or jobs. In large industrial plants, especially in Petrograd and Moscow, the wheelbarrow was always at the ready.

NONSTRIKE ACTIONS IN MAY AND JUNE

How much was the wheelbarrow used in May and June? As we have indicated, our catalog of nonstrike incidents is limited to Petrograd and Moscow and is necessarily incomplete, but for the capitals, at least, the evidence makes it clear that along with strikes, other forms of activism also increased substantially in May. Although it is sensible to divide these incidents between those that took place within or around individual enterprises and those that occurred on the streets and were not clearly enterprise-related, we estimate that more incidents of both types may have occurred in May than in all of March and April, especially if one sets aside episodes connected with the April crisis.

According to available accounts, most enterprise-related incidents in

[38] *Izvestiia* (Petrograd), August 23, 1917; *Russkiia Vedomosti*, August 23, 1917.
[39] *Trud*, July 13, 14, 1917; *Izvestiia* (Petrograd), July 13, 1917.
[40] *Izvestiia* (Petrograd), April 26, 1917.

the capitals during these weeks were directed toward owners or administrators in an effort to settle particular grievances. But from March to May an important shift occurred, away from attacks on individual foremen and plant administrative or engineering personnel toward more comprehensive forms of collective action, such as seizing control of the enterprise. More than a dozen such cases were reported for May and early June in both Petrograd and Moscow, affecting such major plants as the Gulavi machine and boiler works, the Brenner mechanical works, Petrograd Aviation (Lebedev), and the Schlüsselburg gunpowder works, where workers put all managerial personnel on salaries under their control.

Collective action in almost all of these instances, moreover, was designed to keep the enterprises operating and to prevent lockouts or closings. Thus the Brenner factory committee took control of the factory on May 24 and immediately secured orders from the Petrograd gun works to keep production going, the Gulavi workers took over on May 26 because their plant was owned by Germans and its future uncertain, and workers at the Prokhorovskaia Trekhgornaia textile plant in Moscow, alarmed by reports that as many as 33 textile plants in the Moscow region had shut down for lack of fuel, resolved in June to take control over fuel and raw materials and give supervisory responsibility in this area to their Control Commission. Similar events occurred at the Sestroretsk plant, among others, where concerted workers' protests kept production going.[41]

It is most interesting that very few of these enterprises were also involved in strikes in May and June. Of the more than 40 enterprises in Moscow and Petrograd in which we know some direct action took place in this period, only six also went out on strike.[42] At Siemens-Schuckert, workers threatened on April 23 to remove the factory administration forcibly if demands for higher wages and improved conditions were not met, but succeeded in winning these goals only as a result of a one-day strike on May 23. Treugol'nik rubber workers likewise threatened administrators over back pay and wage-increase issues at the end of April but had to strike in June to achieve their demands.[43] But these cases were the exceptions.

It is also worth observing that in comparison to actions involving in-

[41] *Oktiabr'skaia revoliutsiia i fabzavkomy* (Moscow, 1927), pt. 1, p. 147; *Revoliutsionnoe dvizhenie v Rossii v mae–iiune 1917 goda. Iiun'skaia demonstratsiia* (Moscow, 1959), pp. 283–84; *vosr. Khronika sobytii,* vol. 2, pp. 120, 172.

[42] These were the Treugol'nik rubber plant, Aivaz metals, the Pavlov mechanical works, Siemens-Schuckert, the Liaskovskii tarpaulin factory and AMO.

[43] *Revoliutsionnoe dvizhenie v Rossii v aprele 1917 goda. Aprel'skii krizis* (Moscow, 1958), pp. 444, 455–57; *Birzhevyia Vedomosti,* May 18, June 24, 1917; *Novaia Zhizn',* June 24, 1917.

dividual enterprises, there were relatively few reports of street actions (*samosudy*) in Moscow and Petrograd during these weeks.[44] Only a dozen or so cases appeared in the Moscow and Petrograd press between the beginning of May and the end of June, and almost none before. All but two involved attacks on thieves or burglars caught in robberies; in most instances, according to both liberal and socialist newspaper reports, the culprits were set upon by their attackers and beaten "cruelly." In several instances, like the attack in Petrograd in mid-June on a man caught robbing a charity box, the thieves were killed. In others, militia attempting to protect the suspects from the crowd's wrath were also beaten.[45]

It is also interesting that such actions seem to have been almost entirely *against* the violators of social order in these weeks, rather than against the institutions or persons representing or supporting that order. No attacks on government (or soviet) offices, for example, and only occasionally attacks against militiamen of the sort just mentioned, are reported. There were also no major food riots or attacks on salespeople reported. On the contrary, workers and antigovernment political demonstrators were themselves the objects of attack in several cases, most notably during the April crisis, and the thieves and burglars assaulted in most instances were hardly representatives of propertied groups. While incidents of samosudy, of taking matters into one's own hands, were clearly growing during these weeks of the first coalition, they thus seemed to reflect different attitudes toward social order inside the factory and out.

Yet the significance of such differences should not be exaggerated. Individual street actions offered some contrast to the large Petrograd demonstrations against the government and its war policy in April, as well as to Bolshevik-led protests against the regime on June 10, which were kept to a minimum because of pressure from the Soviet.[46] Acts of civic-minded crowd justice also contrasted with well-publicized events during these weeks at Kronstadt, where radical sailors established their own control over the naval fortress. In Petrograd, street actions contrasted as well with the anarchists' celebrated seizure of the Durnovo mansion in early June, accompanied by an attack on the reactionary newspaper *Russkaia Volia*.[47] But taken together, all such incidents obviously raised questions

[44] We specifically exclude from this category political demonstrations such as those occurring in April, although obviously "street actions" sometimes occurred in connection with them.

[45] See, e.g., the reports in *Novaia Zhizn'*, May 13, 19, 24, June 14, 18, 1917.

[46] See the reports in *Izvestiia* (Petrograd), June 10, 1917, and the documents in Browder and Kerensky, eds., *Russian Provisional Government*, vol. 3, pp. 1311–23.

[47] See *Izvestiia* (Petrograd), June 9, 1917; *Vestnik Vremennago Pravitel'stva*, June 20, 1917.

about the orderliness of civic life and the tactics of moderation at this point in the revolution, and when combined with the ways we now know strikers were also challenging managerial authority, clearly threatened hopes for a stable social order, especially in the business community.

CONTINUED EFFORTS AT MEDIATION

The stability of public order came into question in no small measure because of expectations cultivated by Konovalov and the "progressives" after February, and also because of the commitments of the first coalition to secure appropriate gains for workers without unduly disrupting the economy. How, then, did increasing labor activism affect efforts at conciliation and mediation? Direct negotiations between management and labor began in earnest in many sectors in late May and early June in an effort to avoid strikes. Silk workers in Moscow, Petrograd warehouse workers, engravers, glass workers, metalists, and others all entered into talks after indicating their intentions to strike, and many agreed for a time to postpone their walkouts. A survey of 66 enterprises in Saratov revealed that workers in 41 had presented economic demands to owners since the February revolution, and in 21, they were completely satisfied. Owners in only ten enterprises had rejected their employees' demands outright; the rest made some concessions.[48] Similar patterns occurred elsewhere. At the Alafuzov complex in Kazan, management personnel attempted to talk to representatives of each shop individually after a strike began over bonuses in early June, although the walkout continued largely as a result of pressure from the larger shops.[49]

It is impossible to know exactly how often negotiations resulted in settlements that completely avoided strikes, but it does seem clear that in many instances in May and June, talks themselves did not generally postpone conflict very long. In a little more than half of the cases in our file for this period, negotiations lasted 21 days or less before workers went out on strike. Most lasted one week or less. Even more important, in only two or three instances in which negotiation began in late April or May did workers postpone their strikes beyond the end of June, even in those cases in which negotiations were carried on for more than three weeks. Although workers and managers were thus clearly willing to discuss their differences at the enterprise level in May and June, perhaps even more so than before the April crisis, the weeks of the first coalition were clearly

[48] *Tysiacha deviatsot semnadtsatyi god v Saratovskoi gubernii* (Saratov, 1957), p. 77.
[48] *Kazanskii oktiabr'*, pp. 85–86.

marked by a shift from relative patience to relative impatience in the workplace.

One dramatic instance of this sort that gained national prominence involved the huge Sormovo defense plant in Nizhnii Novogorod, which employed some 25,000 workers. A joint-stock company owned almost entirely by Petrograd banking interests,[50] the Sormovo complex operated in 1917 largely on the basis of defense orders. It was one of the country's biggest producers of artillery and shells. In July 1916, soldiers and police had repressed a large strike, and a number of those arrested were put on trial shortly before the February revolution. New protests led to new arrests, as well as sympathy strikes from other Nizhnii plants. By the revolution, Sormovo workers felt they had many scores to settle; in early March, as we have seen, a substantial list of demands was drawn together. There was little response, however, from the plant's Petrograd owners.[51]

Shortly after the formation of the first coalition, the central factory committee presented a new schedule of wage norms to the plant's headquarters. A principal complaint was that the average wage of Sormovo workers was now 50 percent less than for comparable work in Petrograd.[52] On May 12, the Sormovo management telegraphed back to Nizhnii Novgorod that no additional increases were even "thinkable," a response that infuriated the plant's rank and file. A 22–person strike committee, including several members of the large Bolshevik contingent at the complex, took the issue immediately to the local soviet, which wired Labor Minister Skobelev that the situation was extremely tense. Under soviet and ministerial pressure a workers' delegation was also dispatched to Petrograd to continue negotiations.

On May 23, the Sormovo management agreed to increase wages if the state would raise its procurement prices and if workers agreed both to the return of management personnel expelled in early March and to complete managerial control over production. Not surprisingly, workers rejected these conditions outright. A strike was set for May 31. By now, reports of the Sormovo negotiations were appearing in every major newspaper. The country waited to see whether one of its largest and most important defense plants would shut down.

---

[50] According to *Birzhevyia Vedomosti*, May 18, 1916, the largest holders were the Petrograd Discount and Loan Bank (Uchetnyi i Ssudnyi), the Petrograd International Commercial Bank, the I. V. Junker Commercial Bank, the Dzhamgarovye Banking House, and the Russian Bank for Foreign Trade.

[51] *Dokumenty velikoi oktiabr'skoi sotsialisticheskoi revoliutsii v Nizhegorodskoi gubernii* (Gorki, 1945), pp. 22–24.

[52] Ibid., p. 152.

The conflict brought the new labor minister Skobelev and his assistant (and later successor), Koz'ma Gvozdev, their baptism of fire. Like Skobelev, Gvozdev was a prominent Menshevik and member of the Soviet Executive Committee. He was also a former chairman of the Workers' Group of the Central WIC, a position through which he had familiar relationships with a number of leading industrialists. Both men were fully aware of the problems posed by the Sormovo case and their possible implications for future conflicts. Each was also eager to avoid compromising his own political position, or in any way weakening the new coalition. Skobelev put the matter this way:

> The law on the freedom to strike . . . secures full freedom for the workers' class struggle. The trade unions . . . will lend a rational and planned character to this struggle. . . . At the present time, however, spontaneous actions often take the upper hand over organized action; they are taken without consideration for the conditions of the enterprise involved, . . . and bring damage to the class movement of the proletariat. [Strikers] are sometimes trying to achieve a wage increase of such proportions that it would disrupt industry and deplete the treasury.[53]

Intervention in these circumstances was at best a tricky business, and Skobelev's experience was already discouraging. Early in May he had convened a conference of workers and owners from the Donbass mining and metallurgical industries, where conflict over wages and working conditions had strengthened the industrialists' reluctance to maintain unprofitable production and threatened a major crisis. One week's arguing had ended without a settlement, partly, it was felt, because of Skobelev's own reluctance to take a firm position. The best the minister could do was to appoint a special investigating team to go to the Donbass region and examine the situation directly.[54]

As the Sormovo conflict intensified, Soviet pressure increased on Skobelev and Gvozdev both. Many in Nizhnii Novgorod insisted the new socialist minister and his assistant use their power to force the plant's administration to settle. Soviet leaders and others also pressured Kerensky, now the minister of war, some demanding that the plant be nation-

---

[53] *Vestnik Vremennago Pravitel'stva*, June 18, 1917, as cited in Browder and Kerensky, eds., *Russian Provisional Government*, vol. 2, p. 731.

[54] I. Sh. Chernomaz, "Bor'ba rabochikh Ukrainy za povyshenie zarabotnoi platy v marte–oktiabre 1917 goda," in *Nekotorye problemy sotsial'no-ekonomicheskogo i politicheskogo razvitiia Ukrainskoi SSR* (Dnepropetrovsk, 1972), p. 107; *Ekonomicheskoe polozhenie Rossii nakanune velikoi oktiabr'skoi sotsialisticheskoi revoliutsii. Dokumenty i materialy*, 3 pts. (Moscow and Leningrad, 1957–67), pt. 2, pp. 94ff.

alized to assure an adequate flow of artillery supplies to the front. But the managing director Meshcherskii was outraged at what he regarded as the workers' "concessions or strike" ultimatum. Apparently with the support of the Petrograd banks, he rejected it out of hand, threatening to lock the gates if workers refused to accept his conditions. Negotiations were suspended. On June 20, 25,000 workers walked off the job.[55]

These well-publicized events were notable for several reasons. Sormovo workers were strongly supported by local soviet authorities, and their protest was part of a broader pattern of regional unrest, apparently fueled in part by growing antiwar sentiment and increasing support for the Bolsheviks. Perhaps for this reason, neither management nor the Sormovo workers themselves appeared willing to put the state's defense interests above their own, despite Kerensky's and others' concerted efforts during these weeks to rally the country in support of the war, and more pointedly, despite the start of the crucial offensive on June 18. What appeared to be the primacy of partisan interests among Petrograd industrial and banking interests could not have been more dramatically broadcast, even if Meshcherskii and others insisted that regaining direct control over production *was* the only way to assure the plant's ability to meet national need. Furthermore, negotiations hardly mitigated labor-management antagonism, nor did the fact that workers interested in presenting their grievances had to travel from Nizhnii Novgorod to Petrograd to do so.

The Sormovo strike was thus a real challenge for Skobelev. His approach was to lean heavily on both parties to accept mediation, particularly since the role of a conciliation board in the conflict was prominent by its absence. Under Ministry pressure, an agreement was reached on wage issues, largely because Skobelev himself promised some state support for wage concessions. But it was not until early July that Sormovo workers returned to their jobs, agreeing with a reluctant ownership that the remaining issues in dispute, including the contentious issue of pay for days lost during the strike itself, would be given over to a government commission.[56]

The unwillingness of both parties in the Sormovo dispute to submit to mediation was symptomatic of a broader pattern. In the case of the Petrograd laundry workers, shop owners not only refused mediation, but imposed fines, arranged to have workers thrown out of their apartments, promised strikers a 100 ruble bonus if they returned to work on the basis

[55] *Dokumenty Nizhegorodskoi gub.*, pp. 147–52. See also the discussion in A. M. Lisetskii, *Bol'sheviki vo glave massovykh stachek (mart–oktiabr' 1917 goda)* (Kishinev, 1974), pp. 43–49.

[56] *Dokumenty Nizhegorodskoi gub.*, pp. 152–53; *Edinstvo*, July 2, 1917; Lisetskii, *Bol'sheviki vo glave*, p. 49.

of former conditions, and, as we have noted, organized their own "Union of the Reasonable" (*Soiuz Blagorazumnymi*) for strikebreakers.[57] Although negotiations in most industrial enterprises were conducted during May by factory-based boards, the willingness of both sides to use this mechanism decreased substantially from early May to late June, and the boards were increasingly utilized only as a consequence of substantial pressure to do so from outside the factory, either from government officials like Skobelev, or from local soviets.

Management reluctance undoubtedly had to do with the boards' overwhelming tendency to favor workers. We know of only two cases in April, May, and June in which disputes mediated by a factory-based conciliation board resulted in an outright defeat for workers. There is also some evidence that even simple resistance to using the boards on the part of management resulted more often than not in a compromise settlement, rather than outright worker victory. In these weeks, at least, a hard line by owners seemed to bring them some advantage. On the other hand, workers' reluctance to use the boards may have had several more problematic causes. There is some evidence of a growing frustration on the part of many workers with the amount of time and energy negotiations required, particularly as many boards in May and June resolved to reinstate foremen and others whom workers had summarily expelled, as in the case of Treugol'nik. Here and elsewhere in May, workers seemed to feel confident that gains could be achieved more quickly by direct action. Major victories were being scored through strikes in a matter of days, generally with little apparent hardship for the strikers. Workers were also achieving major changes without strikes, and many undoubtedly felt little need to arbitrate disputes their own direct actions had already "resolved." At the Petrograd tram park, for example, workers apparently wheelbarrowed three administrators out of the shops in early May to prevent a conciliation board from hearing their case.[58]

Similar and more portentous reactions to the use of mediation occurred elsewhere as well in May, as at the Moscow Metal Works (Guzhon), a large and important defense plant in Moscow's Rogozhskii district. Moscow Metals was owned by Jules Guzhon, a transplanted Frenchman and an active member of both the WIC and the MSFMO.[59] On March 23, workers here had unilaterally introduced an eight-hour day over management protests, and soon after the formation of the first co-

[57] *Rabochaia Gazeta*, May 14, 1917; *Pravda*, May 25, 1917 (n.s.).
[58] *Novaia Zhizn'*, May 20, 1917.
[59] We appreciate Lewis Siegelbaum's providing us with this description of Jules Guzhon.

alition, workers in the castings and bolt shops expelled their foremen for not performing their duties in a "proper" way. Others were threatened.

An aroused administration, led by the chairman of the board of directors, V. I. Arandarenko, tried to stand firm, insisting to the Guzhon factory committee that any disputes of this sort had to be presented to the board and submitted to the conciliation commission if they could not be resolved. Arandarenko threatened to close the factory if the factory committee could not "guarantee" the safety of foremen and other administrators. Representing some 4,000 workers, the factory committee responded that such guarantees were impossible, and in any event, unnecessary if administrators did their jobs properly. It insisted further that the workers' decisions in these two cases was "final," that it was therefore not necessary to submit the conflict for arbitration, and, adding insult to injury, announced that the administrator in charge of passport registration and plant security was also being summarily expelled.

The Guzhon administration responded by threatening to close the plant unless workers followed a legal course of action. At a factory conference on May 24 attended by representives of the Moscow Soviet as well as Guzhon directors, Soviet spokesmen admitted problems were being caused by "workers with little sense of organization or consciousness" (*malosoznatel'nye i neorganizovannye elementov rabochei massy*) and recognized that the "sole legal route" for the resolution of disputes was through the conciliation board. The directors then decided not to close the plant immediately, although the administrators remained "suspended."[60]

This retreat caused tremendous agitation among Guzhon's managerial personnel, however, and on the afternoon on May 25 they quit the plant en masse. While the directors appealed through the MSFMO for militia protection, workers seized the plant themselves and announced that work would continue. On May 26, management tacitly admitted defeat. As they returned to their posts, the plant's directors acknowledged they had no effective defense against violations of their legal rights. Arandarenko put their view succinctly: "[I hear repeated] accusations of lockouts and desertion. Industrialists are not foolhardy, and they know very well that workers thrown into the streets will not remain calm. The fact of the matter is that the very foundations of private enterprise are being destroyed."[61] Rank-and-file workers, of course, may have felt differently about what had transpired. Their actions had removed objectionable foremen, blocked the plant's closing, and seemingly secured their control

[60] *Ekonomicheskoe polozhenie*, pt. 1, pp. 433–35.
[61] Ibid., p 436.

over future Guzhon operations, all of which were more immediately important than the "foundations of private enterprise."

Social Polarization and Class Consciousness in the Spring

The events at Guzhon show quite clearly the close interactions that continued to exist between strikes and other forms of direct action in the late spring of 1917, despite the ardent efforts of Skobelev, Gvozdev, and others to keep labor-management conflict within orderly bounds. What made this range of activity so important was that it confronted directly the fundamental principles on which Russia's new democratic order was being structured, and on which private enterprise was relying for its own and Russia's prosperity. To observers like Arandarenko, accustomed to regarding Russian labor as a single undifferentiated and uncultured social whole, "workers" simply did not understand how important political and social stability was for their own well-being. Their demands were "excessive," "outrageous"; strikes reflected "parochial" interests, jeopardizing not only the viability of the coalition regime, but the place of democratic Russia in a postwar European order, which depended entirely on avoiding military defeat. In elections in May and early June to local city dumas and soviets, moderate socialists allied in various "blocs" generally returned substantial majorities, and some of their support came from working-class districts. But electoral returns also indicate that even in this early test of political strength, support for the Bolsheviks was especially concentrated in working-class neighborhoods, particularly in Petrograd and Moscow.[62] It seems extremely likely, therefore, that the issues revealed in management-labor struggles also propelled workers toward the Bolshevik camp and would have done so at this point in the revolutionary process even had the party's own agitation efforts been less intense. The process of labor radicalization, in other words, was firmly rooted in workplace relations.

To what extent, then, can we say that the nature of these relations reflected a strengthening of more coherent class identities and mentalities in these weeks? Did they contribute to a growing importance of one's sense of him or herself as a worker, rather than (or perhaps as well as) waiter, metalist, laundress, or printer? Did they also foster a sense on the part of industrialists and shop owners alike that their vital interests were

---

[62] See the discussion in Kh. M. Astrakhan, "Partiinost' naseleniia Rossii nakanune oktiabria (po materialam vyborov v gorodskie dumy v mae–oktiabre 1917 goda)," *Istoriia SSSR* 6 (1987), pp. 134–55; William G. Rosenberg, "The Russian Municipal Duma Elections of 1917," *Soviet Studies* 21, no. 2 (1969), pp. 131–63; Koenker, *Moscow Workers*, chap. 5.

increasingly at odds with the demands of their employees? Whether or not the various forms of labor activism we have analyzed indicated as sharp an assault on social stability in May and June as some newspapers maintained, many entrepreneurs and businessmen were clearly shocked and frightened. "The workers have retreated behind their narrow class-based viewpoints," *Promyshlennost' i Torgovlia* asserted, not only as producers, but also as consumers and as citizens. They demanded higher wages while simultaneously insisting on lower fixed prices; they wanted material improvements but were undermining social and political stability. Limits had to be set: "Otherwise, all profits will disappear." The task of the commercial and industrial community was thus to unify and coordinate its interests, "which, with sufficient mass activity on the part of industrialists and businessmen, and with the existence in the country of elementary principles of law and order, must lead the nation out of the blind alley into which the revolutionary tornado has driven her."[63]

The month of May thus saw business and industrial circles mount a major effort to mobilize further their forces. A steady stream of delegations began to arrive at the Ministry of Trade and Industry to press employers' interests. On May 4, the Petrograd Association of Wood Products Manufacturers demanded an official end to the eight-hour workday:

> There is a fundamental psychological significance to the fact that workers have gained this "victory" under extreme circumstances, which have forced leading industrialist organizations like the PSFMO to move too hurriedly to meet a whole series of ill-considered demands. Having seen how easily they can have their colossal demands granted, workers have naturally abandoned all interest in anything resembling a serious increase in [productivity through] the intensification of labor.[64]

On May 9, the PSFMO presented a detailed report to Prime Minister Lvov on the "disastrous" consequences of workers' wage demands on industry;[65] one day later, representatives from the industrialists' Association of Metallurgical and Iron Works presented Konovalov with a similar report on their financial difficulties, insisting that labor's demands were entirely out of bounds and that they threatened all possibility of profitable production. The government had to decide between capitalism or socialism, and the decision had to be made quickly if Konovalov and others ex-

[63] *Promyshlennost' i Torgovlia*, 12–13 (April 15, 1917), p. 244; 20–21 (June 10, 1917), pp. 378–81.

[64] *Ekonomicheskoe polozhenie*, pt. 1, p. 514.

[65] Ibid., pp. 165–68.

pected these important plants to remain open.[66] In Kharkov, Ekaterinoslav, Rostov, and other towns of South Russia, in the Urals and the Caucasus, as well as in Moscow and Petrograd, industrialists, shop owners, manufacturers and other employers met together and expressed their "outrage," as Moscow textile manufacturers put it, at the course of events.[67] The organization of Kineshma textile manufacturers agreed on May 12 not to allow any concessions on questions involving factory politics that the association as a whole did not agree to.[68] On May 17, a delegation of leading South Russian industrialists from all branches of industry appeared in Petrograd to confer with Konovalov, Skobelev, and workers' representatives themselves. The sessions succeeded primarily in sharpening battle lines.[69]

There can be little doubt that strikes and other forms of direct action by workers contributed greatly to the mobilization of management in these weeks. In specific instances, like the strike of Petrograd laundry workers or the strike of salesclerks at the Gostinnyi Dvor, Apraksin, and Aleksandrov markets, and the Mariinskii shops, traders and shop owners were essentially *forced* to organize themselves into an employers' association in order to bargain with the strikers, much as workers here and elsewhere were themselves forced to organize in order to keep their enterprises open. The Shopowners' Association that developed as a result of the Petrograd salesclerk strike began at the end of May, for example, to attempt to extend itself to *all* Petrograd commercial firms, as well as to meet with representatives of sympathetic political parties on the question of defending their interests.[70] In Petrograd's Vyborg district, the heart of the city's (and Russia's) metalworking industry, industrialists from 13 major plants met to discuss the current situation generally and to press in particular for an increase in the prices of their goods.[71] Strikes had occurred at five of their plants: Nobel, Erikson, Reikhel, Renault, and Phoenix. At the Baranovskii works, two large meetings of workers on May 11 and May 16 resolved to establish an economic "control commission" to supervise the receipt of all raw materials, the shipping of finished goods, factory food supplies, and all monetary receipts and expenditures.[72] The

[66] Ibid., pp. 169, 403.

[67] Ibid., p. 171.

[68] *Tysiacha deviatsot semnadtsatyi god v Ivanovo-Voznesenskom raione: Khronika* (Ivanovo-Voznesensk, 1927), pp. 90–91.

[69] *Ekonomicheskoe polozhenie*, pt. 1, pp. 174–80, 334.

[70] *Russkaia Volia*, May 27, 1917.

[71] Included were Nobel, Erikson, Geisler, Phoenix (Feniks), Russian Renault (Reno), Lebedev, Reikhel, Erlich, Struk, Zelenov and Zimin, Martens, Gallik, and Baranovskii.

[72] *VOSR. Khronika sobytii*, vol. 2, p. 109; *Ekonomicheskoe polozhenie*, pt. 1, p. 184.

Vyborg group appealed to other organizations in the employers' associations to assist them in fighting these "totally inadmissable" actions.[73]

A conference of trade and industrial leaders in early June further clarified these positions and strategies. The meetings were an outgrowth of earlier efforts by Tretiakov and others to organize Russian industrialists nationally, efforts that had taken hold in March, as we have seen, to help end social conflict. What they revealed instead was that many participants had by now abandoned most of the conciliatory attitudes that had characterized earlier gatherings. The Trade-Industrial Union by this time encompassed some 500 different industrial and trade societies, and the main objective of the June conference was to forge a single national organization.[74] Although this effort failed, largely as a result of continued opposition from major Petrograd industrialists, the conference produced instead a "Committee to Defend Industry," designed to coordinate and strengthen the efforts of some 13 major industrial associations. Delegates also passed a strongly worded set of resolutions on the "obligation" of the government to protect capitalism and to crush workers' control, removing any lingering ambiguities about these matters. Under the "existing conditions of the world economy, there can be no other economic order in Russia besides capitalism." For this reason, as well as because of the rampant anarchy that threatened to destroy all of industry and especially the "fruitless and unqualified harm consequent to all attempts to create some sort of socialist order in individual enterprises," there could be no question of "allowing workers to interfere in the management of industrial enterprises, or any sort of factual subordination of factory administration to workers or employees."[75]

Four discrete policies toward labor emerged from these hardened viewpoints, policies which although not formally articulated, were clearly designed to structure management-labor relations as the revolution continued. First, owners would take steps to negotiate wage contracts or other disputes only with established trade union representatives, rather than with individual workers' committees or other ad hoc groups. This would assure some order in the negotiating process, and perhaps, given the educational levels and the general political sophistication of trade union leaders in central organizations, provide some ground for reasonable settlements. Second, efforts would be strengthened to reach *industrywide* wage agreements through collective contracts (*tarifs*), rather than by allowing for individual settlements. Negotiations toward this end had be-

[73] *Ekonomicheskoe polozhenie*, pt. 1, p. 523.
[74] See ibid., pp. 181–82. See also the discussion in V. Ia. Laverychev, "Vserossiiskii soiuz torgovli i promyshlennosti," *Istoricheskie Zapiski* 70 (1961), pp. 41–42.
[75] See *Ekonomicheskoe polozhenie*, pt. 1, pp. 181–84.

gun with metalists in late May and were extended in June to textilists, woodworkers, printers, and others. Third, industrialists would step up their pressure on the government to raise procurement prices and otherwise provide additional subsidies to industry in the form of guaranteed loans or contracts. And finally, strikes and other forms of labor protest were now to be resisted as forcefully as possible, despite the fact that businessmen and industrialists all recognized the legitimate place of strikes in the social relations of a free enterprise economy.

Meanwhile, the very nature of the strike process itself could not help but solidify common "proletarian" feelings as much as or more than it strengthened the solidarity of management. As we have seen, very few strikes for which we have information in this period were initiated "from above," on directions from trade unions or similar groups outside the enterprise. The overwhelming majority began as workers themselves gathered together to discuss their conditions or to react to discharge notices or other management actions, occurrences that necessarily reinforced an awareness of social position.

Factory meetings thus became an even stronger component of everyday life for workers in May and June than they were during the revolution's first weeks. In industrial enterprises, meetings of this sort were now called regularly by factory committees, which had been formed almost everywhere. Among service-sector employees and those in other nonindustrial firms, it was the meeting itself that allowed employees to organize themselves. And once a strike began, those on strike gathered together almost every day, even if they rarely organized formal picketing.

The Petrograd laundry workers' strike in May and the strike of restaurant and tavern workers in early July visibly thrived, for example, on daily meetings. Workers gathered at places like the Cirque Moderne to hear reports about the progress of the strike and to formulate and reformulate their strategy. Laundry workers used the meetings at first to target shops that had not shut down and to dispatch delegations to try to halt work. The restaurant workers used them as well as a means of building up citywide support and of making sure their demands were noted and understood in the press. After a large meeting on June 30, several thousand striking waiters and waitresses marched down Nevskii Prospekt and up Liteinyi to the Petrograd Soviet at the Tauride Palace, waving placards and banners, determined that the "bourgeoisie" and Soviet leadership both should understand their cause.

Such gatherings, often addressed by Bolsheviks or other socialist radicals, could only heighten a striker's sense of him- or herself as a "worker," whatever one's occupation or background. They also could not help but spread feelings of class solidarity, even among groups unaccustomed to interacting with each other, however vaguely formed such notions of class identity actually were. In early May, the nascent Moscow union of yard-keepers (*dvorniki*) held a "grandiose rally" outdoors in Miusskii square, a gathering organized by the Moscow trade union council. Here yardkeep-ers were informed about a set of demands being prepared to present to homeowners, and they were encouraged in the process to think of them-selves as members of a much wider army of militant workers. However different their occupations and outlooks, their actions were similar to those underway in scores of industrial factories and mills, as well as in offices, commercial establishments, and service enterprises throughout the country. The yardkeepers assembled again at Miusskii Square on May 24, this time 10,000 strong. Hearing that the homeowners' association refused to meet their demands, the dvorniki authorized a strike. The crowd then proceeded to march almost two miles to the headquarters of the Moscow Soviet, located coincidently, if appropriately, on Skobelev Square.[76] Two weeks later, having apparently won their demands, yard-keepers were back on strike. Again they gathered at Miusskii Square, but this time they marched even farther to the offices of the municipal govern-ment, carrying banners with the slogans, "Down with the chains of slav-ery!", "Long live socialism!", and "Proletarians of the world, unite!"[77]

Strike committees also played an important role in cultivating such feelings of solidarity. In laundry workers' strikes, or walkouts of phar-macists, hotel workers, retail clerks, or other kinds of salespeople, which occurred in such numbers in May and June, problems of organization and coordination were formidable. Individual enterprises, each with relatively few employees, were scattered around the city. These strikes also involved large numbers of women and stirred up a great deal of animosity on the part of both employers and those inconvenienced by the shutdowns. Composed in each of these cases of striking workers themselves, rather than representatives from outside union groups, committees were able to centralize decision-making and overcome the formidable problems of communication and misinformation with remarkable success. Workers relied on committees to formulate demands coherently and to prevent workers in one enterprise from undercutting their comrades by settling individually. In the sales clerks' strike, for example, which involved some

[76] This Skobelev, however, was not the minister of labor but the hero of the conquest of Central Asia in the 1870s.

[77] *Proletarii* (Moscow), May 23, 25, 1917; *Trud*, June 6, September 17, 1917; *Vpered*, May 21, 24, June 3, 1917; *Izvestiia* (Moscow), May 25, 1917. See also *Utro Rossii*, May 25, 1917; *Russkoe Slovo*, June 2, 4, 6, 1917. After merging with the unions of house porters and domestic servants, the yardkeepers struck yet again in October. See *Izvestiia* (Moscow), October 14, 21, 1917; *Russkoe Slovo*, October 22, 1917; *Trud*, October 21, 1917.

6,000 employees in more than 500 different shops, strikers decided that *all* discussions with shop owners were to be conducted by strike committee representatives, thwarting efforts of individual shop owners to play on the personal loyalities of their employees and break the strike shop by shop. The strike committee alone was also vested with the responsibility for accepting or rejecting settlement offers and used this power rather cleverly to lever favorable offers from several larger stores into better terms for everyone.[78]

Although such complex matters can hardly be addressed with precision, our statistical data also yield some interesting if scattered clues about workers' consciousness in the spring. When we catalog strike demands according to the way in which they reflected workers' concerns for other workers, for example, we find that approximately 11 percent of all industrial strikes and 14 percent of all service-sector strikes (involving at least 16 and somewhat more than 26 percent of all strikers respectively) had something to do with a change in relationships among employees themselves. These cases do not lend themselves well to quantitative comparison since expressions of concern about other workers were often the accidental result of strike reporting. Still, it is clear that the plight particularly of unskilled workers and women received considerable attention in strike demands in the spring, especially in the textile, paper, and printing industries; the need to increase the consistently lower wages women received was a concern of metalists as well. At least 14,000 strikers for whom we have information raised the issue of women's wages (and less often, women's rights); more than 16,000 demanded improvements for unskilled workers. Apprentices figured explicitly in five strikes involving some 68,000 strikers. Strikes of this sort commonly demanded equal wages or specific differentials for men and women, better conditions or wages for minors, or a minimum wage for laborers or apprentices.

Strikes also occurred in May and June that reflected a more general sense of solidarity and egalitarianism among workers *within* an enterprise. At Moscow's Shevrokhrom boot factory, workers demanded that the administration reduce shifts to six hours rather than follow through with its threatened layoff of 300 of the plant's 2,000 workers. These workers also argued that layoffs would reduce the output of boots. Since the strikers settled for shorter hours (and hence reduced output), they appear to have placed solidarity with workers above solidarity with soldiers.[79] We find cases as well in which workers struck to equalize the pay

---

[78] See, e.g., the reports in *Izvestiia* (Petrograd), May 11, 1917; *Birzhevyia Vedomosti*, May 19, 1917; *Russkaia Volia*, May 21, 27, 1917; *Pravda*, May 25, 1917.

[79] *Sotsial Demokrat*, March 23, 1917; *Trud*, April 15, 1917.

between shifts, to fire "spies" in their shops, or to equalize wages in one factory with those in another. Overall, we estimate that a minimum of 110,000 strikers participated in strikes of this sort, whose demands reflected some sort of bond among workers themselves.

In several instances, however, strike demands also indicate an indifference to inequalities and a degree of competition or conflict among workers. Most workers demanded larger raises for male than female workers, for example, maintaining traditional patterns of gender discrimination. Some also demanded an end to the bonus system, which greatly benefitted certain kinds of workers and not others, especially on the railroads. Elsewhere, skilled workers like those employed in Moscow's precious metal trades attempted to restrict the mobility and perquisites of apprentices. Understandably, however, explicit statements of conflict among workers were quite rare in strike reports: strikes by their very nature symbolized solidarity, not divisiveness, and even in those instances in which strike leaders had to tread delicately between the sectional demands of their constituents, workers had an obvious need to present a united front externally.

More important, the *overall* pattern of strikes involving concerns about other workers in the spring suggests a process of proletarian cohesion, not conflict. In all likelihood, strengthening class identities were therefore reinforcing the strong undercurrent of protest we have seen challenging traditional forms of managerial authority, just as the clear resistance to these challenges on the part of employers, especially those in smaller enterprises, suggests an increasing coalescence of both industrial and nonindustrial employers, at least in their common concern about eroding enterprise power. In any event, while moderate soviet leaders, especially in the provinces, continued to stress the importance of organization and restraint, of keeping impulsive behavior in check in favor of cooperation or "legitimate" struggle, values they shared with other, nonsocialist members of the political elite (*verkhi*), workers throughout the economy struggled to situate themselves effectively in an intensifying struggle with their bosses. Wrestling with fundamental questions about the nature and distribution of authority and power, they became involved in large numbers of collective actions. In these circumstances, class consciousness surely deepened on both sides of the labor-management divide, to a great degree as a result of strikes. The ways in which these and other workers' actions were already concerned in May and June with the distribution of workplace power suggests how difficult it was becoming to contain routine labor protests within the bounds of free enterprise and political democracy.

7

. . . .

PERCEPTIONS OF STRIKES AND
THE NATURE OF STRIKE REPORTING:
SOCIAL IDENTITIES AND
MORAL VALUATIONS

THE JULY DAYS

The events of late June and early July in Petrograd drew a sharp rein on even the most hopeful members of the capital's business community. Swayed, perhaps, by the unrealistic enthusiasm of liberal party leaders like Paul Miliukov and the unrestrained rhetoric of Alexander Kerensky, the minister of war, many thought that the military offensive begun on June 18 might bring a quick end to the war. Reports soon indicated that the offensive was in trouble. Troops were refusing in many places to leave their trenches. Soldiers' committees were reluctant to follow up initial successes. Skobelev himself left hurriedly for the front on June 30, hoping to rally the Fifth Army, but few by this time had much confidence that the minister of labor could succeed where the army's leadership itself could not. Some even resented his meddling.[1]

There was other disturbing news as well. The Moscow city duma elections of June 25 returned huge socialist majorities, even in districts generally considered nonsocialist strongholds. The liberal Kadet party ran behind Socialist Revolutionaries in every section of the city. Kadet leaders here had close ties to moderate trade-industrial groups and were strong supporters of coalition, unlike their colleagues in the capital. Still, they garnered only two-thirds as many votes as the Social Democrats, whose support divided almost equally between Mensheviks and Bolsheviks.[2] Ac-

---

[1] See, e.g., *Novoe Vremia*, July 1, 1917; *Narodnoe Slovo*, July 1, 1917; *Rech'*, July 2, 1917.

[2] The figures are in Diane Koenker, *Moscow Workers and the 1917 Revolution* (Princeton, 1981), Appendix D.

counts from the countryside, meanwhile, described an increasing number of peasant attacks on landlords and the seizure of estates. *Novoe Vremia* suggested that "hordes of Bolshevik agitators" were partially responsible for these excesses.[3]

Miliukov and others were also deeply disturbed by indications from Finland that the Diet would soon declare full independence, without waiting for an orderly resolution of the question by a Constituent Assembly, and by even more ominous indications from the Ukraine, where a separatist-minded Rada had declared on June 10 its "exclusive competence" in Ukrainian affairs, not excluding authority over some 900,000 Ukrainian soldiers. Petrograd industrialists joined Miliukov, Konovalov, and others in condemning these actions. Unlike many of their Moscow colleagues, they also felt Soviet leaders were largely responsible for these growing signs of government weakness. While the Kadet paper *Rech'* demanded Soviet leaders take immediate steps to restore order in the countryside, the PSFMO indicated that its members would close a number of additional enterprises if the Soviet could not curb workers' committees.[4] The lines between state and factory politics were becoming increasingly blurred.

In response, Soviet figures talked instead about the need to press ahead with nationalization rather than weaken the role of the committees; on July 1, *Izvestiia* reported in connection with the Finnish problem that the views of Huttunen and Finnish Diet leaders "generally corresponded" to those of the All-Russian Soviet Congress.[5] When a government delegation led by Kerensky returned from Kiev on July 2 with an agreement conceding most of the Ukrainian Rada's principal demands, the Kadet ministers resigned from the cabinet, forcing an end to the first coalition. The next morning, in an unrelated series of events, Bolshevik-led troops from the First Machine Gun Regiment moved on the Tauride Palace, demanding the Soviet take full power. They were joined within hours by tens of thousands of workers from Vyborg, Vasil'evskii Island, and other parts of the city. Strikes and demonstrations again engulfed the capital, as they had at the end of February.[6]

[3] *Novoe Vremia*, June 21, 1917.

[4] *Rech'*, June 24, 1917; *Russkiia Vedomosti*, July 1, 1917.

[5] *Izvestiia* (Petrograd), July 1, 1917.

[6] The best account of the July Days remains Alexander Rabinowitch, *Prelude to Revolution: The Petrograd Bolsheviks and the July 1917 Uprising* (Bloomington, Ind., 1968), especially chaps. 5 and 6. There is no evidence that the Bolshevik mutiny was directly affected by the Kadet resignations, or vice versa. For disaffected soldiers and workers, the ministerial crisis was simply one more sign of government weakness. The Kadets acted without knowing the demonstrations were about to occur. See William G. Rosenberg, *Liberals in the Russian Revolution* (Princeton, N.J., 1974), pp. 174–78.

The July Days were disturbing in many ways to Russian industrialists and businessmen, not least of all because militant metalworkers again seemed to be dominating the course of events, transforming their central role in industrial and defense production through the use of strikes into a political force of the first magnitude. Historical memories were well tuned to this issue, both in and outside Petrograd. And Bolshevik ideology had rarely seemed so relevant. By now Lenin's conception of a proletarian "vanguard" was well known. So were the uses to which he and other party figures hoped it might be put. As the Bolshevik leader had expressed it earlier in the year, the experience of 1905 showed clearly that

> the vanguard, the select [*otbornye*] elements of hired workers, led the struggle with the greatest tenacity and with the greatest self-sacrifice. The larger the plants involved, the more persistent were the strikes, the more often they recurred through the course of the year. The larger the city involved, the more significant the role of the proletariat in the struggle. . . . And in Russia, as in other capitalist countries in all likelihood, it is the metalworkers who constitute the most advanced segment of the proletariat.[7]

It was Lenin's view that this "advanced segment" could bring about revolution everywhere. They had led the Russian strike movement in 1905 and hence the revolutionary movement as well. The same was true in February. The pattern could surely reoccur.[8]

It now appeared to many that metalworkers throughout Russia, and particularly in Petrograd and Moscow, were fulfilling Lenin's historical expectations, that the February revolution was about to be repeated, but with the Provisional Government and Russia's national economy as its victims. Metalists dominated the July Days strikes in overwhelming numbers. Indeed, worker protest during the July Days suggested a picture very similar to that which had brought down the tsar.

Factory unrest in Petrograd centered in the Narva and Vyborg districts. On July 3, about one thousand Putilov workers assembled between two and four in the afternoon to hear appeals from the First Machine Gun Regiment to join the uprising. Ignoring their own factory committee, which urged restraint, the Putilovtsy left their plant late in the day and marched slowly toward the city center, eventually arriving at the offices of the Petrograd Soviet. There they stayed until almost four in the morning, before returning in the summer twilight to their home district. Once

---

[7] V. I. Lenin, *Polnoe sobranie sochineniia*, 5th ed., 55 vols. (Moscow, 1958–65), vol. 30, pp. 312–13.

[8] Ibid., vol. 10, pp. 31–32; vol. 16, pp. 301, 384, 393–421; vol. 21, pp. 175–76.

back, they reassembled, and after more meetings and dicussions, dispersed at ten A.M., "on strike," but with no demands.[9]

On July 4, other factory workers met to consider the Bolshevik appeal to continue the demonstrations. By David Mandel's assessment of the evidence, between two-thirds and three-quarters of the city's industrial workers walked off their jobs. Most of these July 4 strikers did not march on the city center, but, according to press reports, city life was at a standstill by midmorning.[10] For the first time since February, Petrograd was in the grip of a general strike. The best estimates are that more than 275,000 workers were involved, most of them metalists.

Petrograd by no means set an example of labor protest for the rest of Russia in early July, but this was hardly apparent to Petrograd industrialists and others who found their plants deserted and the city awash in protest. In contrast to what we now know about the importance of enterprise relations in structuring labor activism throughout the spring, events in the capital reinforced a growing perception of workers as unsophisticated and gullible, and of a strike movement politicized by Bolshevik militants, who brought workers out of their factories without regard to their own economic or political welfare, or Russia's. In this respect as in others, the massive July Days strike helped determine the events of subsequent months as fully as the cabinet crisis itself.

STRIKES AND THE ROLE
OF THE METALISTS, MARCH TO JULY

How accurate, in fact, were these perceptions? To what extent did metalworkers actually dominate strikes as a whole between March and July? The question cannot be answered solely in statistical terms. Impressions left everywhere by the massive February strikes gave Vyborg workers in particular a place of prominence in the revolutionary struggle in and outside the workplace. All the same, one cannot say if Tiflis warehousemen or Pskov leatherworkers had the example of their Petrograd comrades in mind when they went on strike in the spring, or felt in other ways that they were following the metalists' lead. During the July Days, participants in other strikes in the capital may well have felt a strong connection to the broader events around them. As we have seen, some 10,000 restaurant workers had gone on strike on June 30 for reasons quite different from the metalists; on July 3, as the machine-gunners' mutiny began, a

[9] M. David Mandel, *The Petrograd Workers and the Fall of the Old Regime* (London, 1983), especially p. 163; "Piterskie rabochie ob iiul'skikh dniakh," *Krasnaia Letopis'* 9 (1924), pp. 19–41.

[10] See, e.g., *Rech'*, July 5, 1917, and *Novaia Zhizn'*, July 6, 1917.

group of postal workers also left their jobs demanding higher wages. The postal strike was not specifically tied to the July Days, but strikers were identified as Bolsheviks, and one of their principal points of protest was the Menshevik minister of posts and telegraph, Irakli Tsereteli, whose policies were said to reflect those of the old regime and "counterrevolution."[11] On July 3, Petrograd pharmaceutical-manufacturing workers and retail clerks also began a bitter strike accompanied by antisemitic provocations, for higher wages and shorter hours. Hostilities here as well were undoubtedly sharpened by what was happening elsewhere in the city.[12]

We can, however, look with some care at overall strike patterns for the entire period between March 3 and the July Days and explore the extent to which objective indices, at least, suggest a preeminent metalist role. When we do so we find that although strikes by industrial workers as a whole dominated labor activism overwhelmingly between March and July, constituting 70 percent of the total, the number of metals strikes was far less prominent, even in Petrograd. For the country at large, some 29 percent of all industrial strikes in this period involved metalworkers alone. By contrast, 22 percent were textile strikes, 12 percent occurred in the printing and paper industry, and 9 percent involved animal-products workers (largely in the leather trades). The remainder were well scattered in other branches, although metalists and others also participated in a number of strikes together, as during the July Days.

Within this group, however, it was not so much Petrograd as Moscow that dominated strike activism, at least in terms of numbers of strikes. Although some 61 percent of all strikes in our data (and more than 73 percent of all industrial strikes) took place in the Petrograd and Moscow industrial regions together during the entire period between March 3 and July 6, only some 13.5 percent took place in the city of Petrograd, compared to 32 percent for Moscow. If we look only at industrial strikes, the disparity is even greater; only 9 percent occurred in Petrograd, while slightly more than 37 percent took place in Moscow.

The gap widens still further if we look only at metals strikes. Slightly fewer than 13 percent of these strikes took place in Petrograd between March 3 and July 6, compared to some 52 percent in the city of Moscow. Most of these (79 percent) occurred in individual enterprises, and a few involved only one or two shops from a larger complex, as at Putilov. In this respect as in others, the July Days strike was exceptional.

[11] *Volia Naroda*, July 4, 1917.

[12] See *Novaia Zhizn'*, July 7, 1917. The pharmaceutical workers' strike lasted well into the month of July.

Interestingly, and in contrast to many views of strike activism in early July, it was in the service sector that Petrograd dominated strike participation in the first half of the year, if we measure "dominance" solely in terms of numbers of strikes. Although laundry workers, waiters, cooks, postal employees, and others were involved in only about one-fifth of the work stoppages we have been able to record for the country at large, more than 27 percent of these took place in Petrograd, compared to some 16 percent for Moscow. Most were strikes by waiters and cooks (36 percent), but they ran the gamut in service professions from church employees and police to medical personnel, doormen, tradespeople, and bath attendants. Clearly this form of activism was not restricted in any significant way to either metalists or industrial workers as a whole in Petrograd: strikes were a much broader and hence potentially a much more significant social phenomenon than many in the PSFMO and elsewhere understood.

As we have discussed earlier, however, the number of strikes is in some ways a less reliable index in analyzing activism than the number of strikers, both because it distorts the role of enterprise and enterprise size, and because strike figures alone do not allow measures of propensity, the relative tendencies of groups of workers to strike. Again, we are not able to estimate numbers of strikers in every instance, but our data are more than sufficient to indicate overall patterns. These are quite revealing.[13]

Most importantly, it turns out that even before the July Days, the number of Petrograd strikers did indeed constitute a far greater share of all workers on strike than did the city's number of strikes, and was roughly equal in size to the number of strikers in Moscow. Petrograd's total share of all strikers *before* the July Days was 42 percent; Moscow's, 43.5 percent. In either case, however, with the July events included or left out, workers in the cities of Moscow and Petrograd together clearly dominated strikes in overwhelming terms, even if one allows for geographical biases in the data.

How many of these strikers were metalists? For strikes throughout the country as a whole for which estimates can be made, quite a large proportion: approximately 26 percent between March 3 and June 30, as many as 67 percent between March 3 and July 6![14] And what about Petrograd metalists? *Before* the July Days, the evidence indicates that Petrograd metalworkers alone were, in fact, a numerically significant proportion of all Russian workers on strike, some 10 percent. The Petrograd

[13] For the entire March–July period, we have estimates for 75 percent of all cases, and for slightly more than 81 percent of all industrial strikes (compared to 68 percent of those in the service sector).

[14] Estimates here are based on 75 percent of the relevant strikes in our file.

metalists' share of the industrial strike force was even larger, 14.6 percent. By contrast, Moscow metalists made up 5 percent of all strikers and approximately 7.3 percent of all industrial strikers. Yet both these figures pale when one adds the 275,000 participants in the July Days to the Petrograd totals. For the period of March 3 through July 6 as a whole, the Petrograd figure zooms to 58 percent of all industrial strikers and 48.6 percent of those on strike in all branches and sectors, industrial and non-industrial alike, a startling share of the whole in both instances. And when the propensity of strikers by industrial branch is calculated for the country as a whole, the dominance of the Petrograd metalists in the March 3–July 6 period is simply overwhelming. As table 7.1 indicates, the strike propensity of Petrograd metalists was twice as large as the next most active group. And as the second column in table 7.1 indicates, Petrograd metalists were more prone to strike than their comrades in every other industrial sector but one in this first period of the revolution even if one excludes the July Days strikes from the calculus.

In some ways, strike propensity calculations can be misleading. If 200 workers in an enterprise of 2,000 leave their jobs and shut down produc-

TABLE 7.1

Strike Propensities by Industry, March 3–July 6, 1917
(Measured as a Ratio of an Industry's Share of Strikers to Workers)

Industry	Propensity	Propensity Excluding July Days[a]
Petrograd metals	5.02	.94
All metals (including Petrograd)	2.98	2.12
Animal products (leather)	.88	1.85
Textiles	.38	.82
Wood and wood products	.33	.70
Paper and printing	.23	.54
Chemicals	.09	.16
Food products	.04	.08
Minerals	.04	.06

NOTE: Calculations show relative propensities among these industrial branches only. Mining, mixed products, and other industrial sectors are excluded.

[a] Single industry strikes only. The exclusion of strikes involving more than one industry reduces in particular the strike propensity for metalists, who were active in multibranch strikes.

tion, all workers must be considered on strike even though 1,800 may not actually have been inclined to go out. Nevertheless, the concern of industrialists and others about the propensity of metalists to strike was not misplaced in early July, even if strikes themselves were also broadly spread throughout the economy, and even though many failed to appreciate as well their importance as elements of "routine" labor struggle in Russia's new conditions of freedom. The July Days revealed clearly the degree to which entire complements of workers in Petrograd metal plants were willing to use this weapon again for overtly political ends, just as they had in February and many times in the past. If the episode was thus an unusually politicized moment in the history of Russian strikes in 1917, it still cast a long shadow over labor-management relations everywhere, ominously for those like Labor Minister Skobelev and others who still saw the foundations of social and political democracy in the peaceful resolution of conflict.

PERCEPTIONS AND REPRESENTATIONS

At the same time, it does not necessarily follow that the perceptions many had of strikes and strikers as a whole in this period were entirely accurate ones, in terms of either their relationship to social stability or the future of Russia's democratic order. This was so in part because of the ways in which strikes reflected workers' power, and because few in the capital after February doubted the uses to which this power could be put. But it was also so because of the ways in which strikes were being represented during these weeks in the press, an important aspect of the labor movement as a whole.

To some extent, of course, the issues of perception and representation affect all history and all historical writing, as does the related question of the relationships between perceptions and historical action. But the importance of the issue of perception to revolutionary Russia has to do with the way in which perceptions themselves, especially of strikes and the nature of labor protest, contributed to the determinant processes of political and social polarization. The issue is complicated by the fact that all social groups in revolutionary Russia continued in 1917 to have, in effect, multiple and often competing identities, stemming from their professions, locations, social backgrounds, self-conceptions, and even such ideological formulations as their ideas about the nature of the state. Tensions continued to exist between one's role as a patriotic citizen, for example, and as an industrialist or businessman concerned about profits, as a peasant from a village in Poltava concerned about getting a share of the land, or as a loom operator in a Moscow textile mill worried about staying employed. Whether one or another identity played a dominant or passive role in shaping both perceptions and activist behavior obviously depended on political and social circumstances, as well as the arena in which group aspirations were played out.

At the same time, the February revolution encouraged even the most particularistic workers to identify with larger collectives, especially the soviets. And with the emergence of the concept *demokratiia*, used increasingly by soviet leaders and others to distinguish "nonprivileged" social groups from the urban "bourgeoisie" and the gentry, rather than to describe political institutions, workers found themselves represented as the key element of an even broader community, one which the revolution had made fully equal to those who formerly held rank and wealth. The very periodization of revolutionary change, in fact, might be set at least in part in terms of the moments when the balance between sectional, class, and national identities shifted, the moment when one or another of these multilayered identities became, in effect, the dominant impulse underlying social action.

This was true not only with Russia's diverse workers, but also with industrialists and businessmen, who were simultaneously part of local communities with their own rich and individual traditions and members of broader collectives, increasingly aggregated in 1917 both in outlook and organizational form. In some ways Moscow's merchants and manufacturers still remained as different socially from Petrograd industrialists and bankers in 1917 as they were from their own employees. Yet the politics of revolutionary change increasingly forced them into common stereotypical categories and identities and very much strengthened associations like the PSFMO and MSFMO, even if many also saw themselves as reflecting universalized national interests, the identity of Russia as a whole.

Strikes clearly played several important roles in the evolution of these social identities, as we have suggested. The experience of going on strike itself helped overcome sectional divisions and induced broader identifications: for many workers the very act of participating in strikes was a means of identifying with a broader collective based firmly on the relationship to the means of production. Also, strikes always evoked some sort of response from plant owners and managers, most often hostility. The process of squaring off in strikes thus helped to define each participant's sense of their adversary, as well as ideas about settlements and their possible relationship to different forms of enterprise organization or management. This in turn naturally affected perceptions about the possible paths of Russia's future development.

Closely related here is the question of bias, and the ways in which different newspapers, reflecting the views of particular political or social groups, may have differently represented strikes and strikers to their publics. On the one hand, the perspective offered by some strike reporting went beyond class mobilization to affirm the parity of the working class within the larger society. In extreme form, it conveyed a sense that workers had become obligated to dominate society by the default of other social groups. On the other hand, differences in reporting (and the conflicting identities emphasized in different newspaper accounts) suggest the ways in which those on both sides of the labor-management divide were sorting out a sense of themselves and their place in the broader society, and hence, their relationship to unfolding events.

STRIKE REPORTING IN 1917

Although one must be cautious about overgeneralization, particularly in terms of the ways in which different patterns of reporting may have represented deliberate efforts to shape the news, it is apparent from even a cursory review that strikes were reflected quite differently in different newspapers, and that the conservative ("right"), moderate liberal, moderate socialist, and radical ("left") press regarded strikes and strikers in significantly different ways.[15]

Of particular interest, first, is the almost studied indifference, at least in the early weeks of the revolution, of the bourgeois press in general to strikes and the labor movement as a whole. With the end of the February revolution, *Rech'*, *Russkiia Vedomosti*, *Birzhevyia Vedomosti*, *Russkaia Volia*, *Novoe Vremia*, and other comparable newspapers concentrated their reporting almost entirely on activities of the Provisional Govern-

---

[15] We include among conservative or "right" newspapers *Russkaia Volia*, *Novoe Vremia*, and *Utro Rossii*; among "moderate liberal": *Rech'*, *Birzhevyia Vedomosti*, *Russkiia Vedomosti*, *Torgovo-Promyshlennaia Gazeta*, *Russkoe Slovo* and the so-called "boulevard" press; among "moderate socialist" papers, the press of the Menshevik, Socialist Revolutionary, and Popular Socialist parties, as well as publications of the soviets: *Rabochaia Gazeta*, *Den'*, *Vpered*, *Delo Naroda*, *Trud*, *Zemlia i Volia*, *Volia Naroda*, *Novaia Zhizn'*, *Proletarii* (Moscow), *Vlast' Naroda*, *Vpered*, *Edinstvo*, *Narodnoe Slovo*, *Izvestiia Petrogradskogo Soveta Rabochikh Deputatov*, *Izvestiia Moskovskogo Soveta Rabochikh Deputatov*; on the "left", the Bolshevik press: *Pravda*, *Proletarii*, *Rabochii Put* (Petrograd), and *Sotsial Demokrat* (Moscow). We include the Menshevik-Internationalist press, *Novaia Zhizn'* and *Proletarii* (Moscow), with the moderate socialists because on issues of labor relations, their line was generally conciliatory, like that of the mainstream Mensheviks. *Utro Rossii*, Riabushinskii's Progressist organ in Moscow, might best be categorized as "conservative-liberal," since it early reflected conciliationist tendencies, but rapidly became more resistant in its commentaries and editorial viewpoint. The divisions we make here in any case are general ones. Also, because only partial runs were available, not all papers were systematically canvassed throughout the year.

ment and the soviets. One finds virtually no strike reports whatsoever, for example, in such major newspapers as *Rech'*, *Russkiia Vedomosti*, *Novoe Vremia*, or *Russkaia Volia* from approximately the second week of March through the April crisis. Such reports as appeared in the moderate liberal press were almost entirely in boulevard newspapers like *Trudovaia Kopeika*, whose readership among the liberal parties' constituents was at best uncertain.[16]

It is impossible to know precisely the reasons for this apparent indifference. There were most probably several, ranging from editors' judgments about their readers' interests to limits on the type of assignments reporters could readily undertake, and possibly even a deliberate suppression of some reports in an effort either to protect individual firms or to avoid encouraging strikes elsewhere, although we have no direct evidence to these effects. But overall it seems evident that in these early weeks, at least, strikes were not especially notable events to newspapers with liberal or conservative viewpoints, and there seemed to be no particular concern about the development of the labor movement more generally. At least through the early months of the revolutionary period, the focus of the nonsocialist press was on political events, defined rather narrowly.

There was almost no reporting in the right or liberal press, for example, of the Petrograd laundry workers' strike, which began on May 1, and to which *Pravda, Rabochaia Gazeta, Novaia Zhizn'*, and other socialist papers devoted great attention. Indeed, on May 3, *Russkaia Volia* had a long article on "The Tasks of the Citizen-Woman," lauding the "important roles" women "had long fulfilled" in bringing up children as mothers and educators. The article suggested the time had now come to extend the responsibility for these vital functions to society at large so that women could become more socially active and fulfill their civic duties as electors and representatives in local government, even in the Constitutent Assembly. The laundresses, however, were virtually ignored, although a report on May 25 did indicate that some owners had offered concessions which workers refused.[17] A similar pattern occurred with early strikes in Petrograd and Moscow by coopers, woodworkers in industrial shops, leather workers, and even Petrograd metalists, although strikes by the latter did get some attention because of their potential impact on the country's defense effort.[18]

---

[16] On the kopeck press, see Jeffrey Brooks, *When Russia Learned To Read: Literacy and Popular Literature, 1861–1917* (Princeton, 1985), chap. 4, and Jeffrey Brooks, "The Breakdown in the Production and Distribution of Printed Material, 1917–1927," in *Bolshevik Culture*, ed. Abbott Gleason, Peter Kenez, and Richard Stites (Bloomington, Ind., 1985), pp. 151–74.

[17] *Russkaia Volia*, May 3, 25, 1917.

[18] See, e.g., *Russkiia Vedomosti*, May 24, 1917

On the other hand, the liberal and right press did pay considerable attention to strikes outside the capitals. Many provincial conflicts, such as among the Odessa cabmen or the Baku oilworkers, were conveyed to the capital by the Russian Telegraph Agency, and although their reports tended to be terse and factual, they did serve to inform the readers of the right and liberal press of the scope of labor conflict throughout the country.

Over time, several themes of conflict emerged in the liberal press: the ways in which strikes and other forms of labor protest were infringing on management prerogatives, generally reported as "rights"; strikes that appeared to have a strong impact on the country's economy; strikes that potentially affected government activities, such as those of paper workers and printers that threatened orderly elections; and strikes that involved direct government intervention, which increased as the year progressed. One of the earliest strikes to gain the attention of newspapers like *Birzhevyia Vedomosti*, for example, was not a workers' strike at all, but that of foremen at Treugol'nik Rubber, who quit work on June 23 to protest the dismissal on June 21 of some 20 female colleagues at the insistance of rank-and-file workers.[19] This assault on the prerogatives of foremen also captured the attention of the Kadet paper *Rech'*, which published a letter to the editor about the situation on June 21 and followed subsequent events closely. What is particularly interesting about the reporting in *Rech'* is that the developing conflict at Sormovo, which directly threatened military production, was almost entirely ignored. Although *Novaia Zhizn'*, *Vpered*, and other socialist papers took up the Sormovo story in the third week of June, substantive accounts did not appear in the liberal papers until early July, when they emphasized the mediating role of the Ministry of Labor.[20]

Similarly, *Russkoe Slovo* reported on the strike of Moscow doormen and janitors, dvorniki, in early June by emphasizing that only some 20 percent actually wanted a strike, but the remaining 80 percent had been "terrorized" into submission and now would not even let homeowners sweep their own sidewalks.[21] When Moscow envelope makers went on strike in late May, *Russkoe Slovo* worried whether this would prevent the proper distribution of ballots for the city duma election; similar concerns were expressed about the threat to Constituent Assembly balloting by Moscow and Petrograd printers' strikes in the fall.[22] And increasingly,

---

[19] *Birzhevyia Vedomosti*, June 24, 25, and especially June 28, 1917.

[20] Compare, e.g., *Rech'*, June 21–28, 1917; *Birzhevyia Vedomosti*, July 2, 1917; *Vpered*, June 22, 1917, et seq.; *Novaia Zhizn'*, June 23, 1917, et seq.

[21] *Russkoe Slovo*, June 4, 1917.

[22] Ibid.

reiterating the importance of settlements to Russia's national interest, *Rech', Birzhevyia Vedomosti, Russkiia Vedomosti*, and other liberal papers followed the activities of the Ministry of Labor as it involved itself in settling strikes.

Occasionally there were serious discrepancies in reporting as the liberal press emphasized the plight of management in strikes: *Russkoe Slovo* indicated that tobacco-plant owners had offered their workers an 80 percent wage increase, for example, but that workers were "holding out" for 120 percent; according to *Izvestiia*, the difference was an offer of a 15 percent increase against a demand for 43 percent.[23] At other times there were noticeable errors of omission, such as a failure to indicate that Moscow rubber workers were striking because management refused to take the dispute to arbitration, or to report that a strike at the Nobel complex near Petrograd broke out because management refused categorically to answer worker demands.[24]

These rather predictable biases and concerns were certainly not absent from strike reports in the moderate socialist press, but the approach to strikes in newspapers like *Rabochaia Gazeta, Novaia Zhizn'*, and the official press of the Moscow and Petrograd Soviets was still quite different. Strikes here were newsworthy events, just as were the formation of trade unions and factory committees and the development of other major components of the labor movement as a whole. Understandably, moderate socialist newspapers focused on workers' material difficulties and tended to report strikers' demands extensively. Both liberal and socialist strike reports emphasized the primacy of wage demands: these, as we have seen, constituted the great majority of specific claims. But as one might expect, the liberal and conservative press paid relatively more attention to demands about challenges to managerial authority, such as the eight-hour and six-hour workdays or changes in management personnel, while the socialist press was more likely to report demands about workers' rights: trade union and factory committee issues, rehiring fired workers, or specific questions of remuneration such as rate-setting and forms of payment. And whereas liberal writers gave attention to the government, socialist reporters concentrated on the activities of mediation commissions and the soviets.

Even more significant was the sheer abundance of strike reporting in the moderate socialist press, particularly in Menshevik newspapers and in the nonpartisan organs of the two soviets. Our best approximations are that the Menshevik press and the soviet organs each contributed over

---

[23] *Russkoe Slovo*, August 5, 1917; *Izvestiia* (Moscow), August 6, 1917.
[24] See *Novaia Zhizn'* May 13, 1917; *Delo Naroda*, May 13, 1917.

400 strike reports between March and October, Socialist Revolutionary newspapers at least 260, left-wing Menshevik papers another 150 at a minimum. The Bolshevik press also produced something over 260 reports, whereas the moderate liberal press accounted for at least 220. In the conservative press, we only find about 50, although again, we could not systematically canvass all papers, and these figures are only an approximation of the actual volume of strike reports, rather than an exact count. (Also, we did not record the length of these reports and hence do not distinguish the terse one-line reports of the telegraph agency from the lengthy, detailed accounts that sometimes appeared in the course of especially notable strikes.) Still, there is little doubt that the moderate socialist press dominated the field of strike reporting, and that the perspective generated by their reports reached a broad number of readers.

Moreover, both the moderate socialist press and the Bolshevik papers tended to play an important *functional* role in strikes, especially early in the year. Strike reports frequently carried appeals for funds or boycotts, and often gave information about where meetings would be held and under whose auspices. They served in particular as vehicles for trade unionists, emphasizing the need for organization, and at times even decrying the degree of "isolation" and "spontaneity" in strike actions. As trade unions became more organized, *Vlast' Naroda, Edinstvo, Delo Naroda, Rabochaia Gazeta,* and especially the soviet papers in Moscow and Petrograd emphasized efforts of trade unionists and soviet figures to settle strikes and return workers to their jobs. While *Rabochaia Gazeta* reported the appeal of striking Petrograd druggists for funds, and *Den'* emphasized ongoing mediation efforts in its accounts, *Edinstvo* reported that the union board and strike committee both were urging pharmacists to return to work, having received written confirmation of the owners' intention to accept the results of arbitration.[25]

There seems little question, in sum, that the moderate socialist press, deliberately or not, represented the interests of organized labor to its membership and to the public at large, just as the moderate liberal press both reflected and represented the interests of the state, and to some extent, of management as well. "Representation" here, moreover, is the proper word, since the views of liberal and socialist leaders alike about strikes were undoubtedly shaped by these reports, however they corresponded to actual events. Thus the relative indifference of the liberal press to workers' conditions and strike demands almost certainly reinforced tendencies to see strikes as essentially reckless and even conspiratorial in origin. Certainly without full reporting of each strike's characteristics, the logic and rationale of strike protests tended to be lost and worker unrea-

[25] *Edinstvo,* July 19, 1917.

sonableness exaggerated. At the same time, the better-informed readership of the socialist press undoubtedly understood much better the full
dimensions of social conflict unfolding in the factories, as well as its political implications. If strike reporting thus contributed to the increasingly
antilabor views of liberals and the right, it sharpened the awareness of
moderate socialists in the soviets about the difficulties of labor organization, and the dangers to moderate socialist ideals of increasing employer
intransigence in industrial relations.

The presence of violence in strikes also posed problems for those seeking to minimize political conflict between labor and management. As we
have indicated, violent behavior by strikers was not widespread. Virtually
all of the acts of violence receiving attention in the press were not directly
connected to strikes. But not all readers were exposed to the same representations of violence. Only the socialist press, for example, generally
mentioned repressive action against workers. To Mensheviks and other
moderate socialists, of course, violence on the part of workers was a sign
of the labor movement's immaturity. We would thus expect their newspapers to minimize the attention paid to it. Conversely, we would expect
the capitalist press to emphasize violence to prove the immaturity of the
labor movement and its unfitness to govern. Generally, the incidence of
reports of violence conforms to expectations: the Bolsheviks appear to
have mentioned violent actions least often, the right press the most frequently, with the moderate socialists and moderate liberals falling in the
middle.[26]

Reports in the moderate socialist press generally reflected as well a remarkably benign overall view of labor relations: on the whole, moderate
socialists tended to stress success as well as successful cooperation between labor and management. They also emphasized the organizational
characteristics of strikes and, more than other types of newspapers, described many subjective characteristics of the strike movement, like the
serious, peaceful, or spirited determination of strikers to do battle with
the bourgeoisie. The very dualism of the Menshevik position in 1917 is
reflected in its strike reporting; the proletariat was engaged in class struggle with the bourgeoisie and should hone all its weapons in this struggle,
but at the same time, the proletariat was also living in a society where its
class enemies were dominant. Strikes were thus represented as a major
element of class struggle in revolutionary Russia and a means by which
workers could improve their position collectively and individually. Yet
there is little in these reports to indicate that strikes could also topple the

---

[26] The frequencies are low but progress precisely according to expectations. Violence is
mentioned in 1.9 percent of Bolshevik reports (and 3 of 5 cite violence against workers), 2.7
percent of moderate socialist reports (2 of 36 cite violence against workers), 3.2 percent of
moderate liberal reports, and 4.1 percent of the right press reports.

bourgeois order itself. In fact, as largely presented in the moderate socialist press, strike activism in Russia—orderly, organized, widespread—indicated that a period of bourgeois economic and social relations could benefit workers and the nation alike, that strikes were very much an element of routine social relations.

Not so for the Bolsheviks. Unlike the liberal press, Bolshevik newspapers began to report on strikes as soon as the old regime fell. By May, the pages of *Pravda* were full of long and attentive reports of strikes among Petrograd woodworkers, salesclerks, dyers, and laundresses, as well, of course, as metalists. *Pravda* and *Sotsial Demokrat* devoted their attention largely to strikes in the two capitals.[27] They also tended to pay relatively little attention to outside intervention, in contrast to moderate socialist accounts.[28] Strikes may thus have appeared to their readers to be entirely the self-reliant activism of workers themselves, concentrated in the capitals. Reports of outcomes also diverged in interesting ways: the Bolshevik press was least likely to report success, most likely to report compromise and failure. Even if this was not an editorial effort to represent strikes as inexpedient, such a picture might well have heightened a sense of the urgency of class struggle among readers, rather than confidence in the ability of "bourgeois democracy" to meet labor needs.

We must be careful not to impute too much ideological motivation to overworked editors. What is so interesting about the reports in *Pravda* in particular, but also in *Sotsial Demokrat, Proletarii,* and *Rabochii Put'*, is not any particular degree of partisanship or distortion, but the very attentiveness of Bolshevik reporters to *all* strikes, especially those of clerks, salespeople, and other service-sector employees not usually identified as the party's constituents. *Pravda* covered the Petrograd laundry workers' strike in detail, for example, giving far more attention than any other paper to the efforts of women workers to organize and coordinate their efforts. *Pravda*'s reports paid particular attention to the activities of the "yellow" union organized by employers to thwart the strike and sounded frequent warnings about this and other "false inducements" to settle.[29]

---

[27] One obvious explanation for this, however, was the absence in the Bolshevik press of Russian Telegraph Agency reports, which added to the strike coverage of the moderate socialist newspapers. But whether the lack of provincial coverage was due to editorial preference, an inability to afford the RTA news service, or the RTA's unwillingness to provide such service, the result was that readers of the Bolshevik press drew their conclusions about strikes largely from the experience of workers in the capitals.

[28] Some 12 percent of all strike reports in the moderate socialist press, and 11 percent of liberal reports, included mention of the presence of government or conciliation board mediation; the Bolsheviks included such information less than half as frequently, in only 5 percent of their reports.

[29] *Pravda* had long accounts, for example, in its issues of May 20, 23, 25, 27, 29, 30, and June 1, 3, 8, and 13 (n.s.), as well as other, less lengthy reports.

The strike of sales clerks at Gostinnyi Dvor received similar treatment, as did that of the fishmongers and other food clerks at the Apraksin market complex.[30]

Finally, Bolshevik press reports often represented the mood of strikers as "firm" or "resolute," published appeals for solidarity and aid, and often represented owners as "yielding" or "about to yield."[31] Reports also tended to focus on the attacks of other papers against striking workers, frequently reported evidence of speculation among managers and shop owners, and decried rather consistently the ways in which industrialists and businessmen were organizing to resist worker demands. But it was not so much the obvious class biases of Bolshevik strike reports that distinguishes them as the apparent recognition that activist behavior by generally dormant workers like salesclerks and laundresses was itself a matter of real political import, reflecting class struggle in stark form, and worthy of extensive reporting in part as an example to others.

To some extent this was a characteristic of reporting in the moderate socialist press as well, which reported extensively, if not intensively, on strikes among nonindustrial workers, particularly in service, trade, communications, and transport. Socialist newspapers of all persuasions thus appeared to portray the elements of class struggle in strike activity in the broadest possible terms, appealing to diverse segments of the labor force, encouraging them to abandon their narrow interests and to identify with a proletariat that transcended the limits of manufacturing industries. Such a broad working class could more legitimately be entitled to share in determining Russia's political fate.

Strike Reporting: Two Case Studies

The interplay of strike reporting and its possible effect on the different readerships of the press can be seen from another perspective when reports of specific strikes are examined in detail. We have selected for elaboration two well-reported strikes for which accounts appeared in both the socialist and liberal press.

1. Petrograd Dyers and Drycleaners

Approximately 350 workers, mostly women, in Petrograd dye and dry cleaning works and some 150 sales people in affiliated retail shops began a strike on May 12 that would prove to be one of the longest of the revolutionary period. The strikers demanded a minimum wage of four rubles

[30] See, e.g., *Pravda*, June 1, 2, 7, and 8 through 13, 1917 (n.s.).
[31] See, for example, *Pravda*'s report on the Petrograd coopers' strike on July 11, 1917 (n.s.), among many others.

a day for women and five for men, goals which, if achieved, would also have involved the end of piece rates, an important gain in terms of extending workers' control over the pace of their work. According to one account, these wage levels were worked out in discussions between the Petrograd Soviet and the PSMFO.[32] Workers also demanded salaries of 150 and 175 rubles a month for those who worked in retail outlets.

The strike was coordinated by a newly organized union of chemical workers and led by a central strike committee, which appealed early to the Ministry of Labor for assistance. The latter attempted without success to persuade the owners' association to submit the case to arbitration. The firms of Danziger and Golaevskii agreed, as did a number of smaller establishments, and the strike here was settled quickly, raising hopes for a citywide agreement. But the largest plants, led by Peklie, held out. It was not until just before the October revolution that these enterprises finally announced their desire to settle and agreed to negotiate.

Three aspects of the way this long strike was reported are of interest. First, the strike caused a considerable inconvenience to many in Petrograd who had left their clothes and other goods for coloring, cleaning, and repair. *Rabochaia Gazeta*, *Izvestiia*, and other newspapers representing moderate socialist viewpoints indicated, however, that workers in some establishments, particularly the large Danziger works, were arranging to have goods returned. In contrast, as the strike dragged on, *Russkaia Volia* reported not the strike issues or the nature of the conflict itself, but the "significant number" of suits in local magistrate's courts for the return of (or compensation for) lost goods. In its account, all efforts of enterprise owners themselves to return goods to their owners had been blocked by workers, who remained adamant that "no work be allowed until the satisfaction of their demands."[33]

In fact, many firms had hired strikebreakers, an issue which very much concerned union leaders, especially as the strike continued. *Rabochaia Gazeta* even published a list of strikebreakers' names, while other socialist newspapers emphasized that no workers themselves were going back to work, despite various lures from management. (In the case of Peklie, this included an attempt to allow workers to buy stock in the firm, even offering to advance the fifty rubles each share would cost, if only they would call off the strike.)[34] Management also secured the cooperation of the militia, which protected the strikebreakers and reportedly arrested some strikers. At the same time, the moderate press repeatedly described the strike as peaceful, and workers as firm and unanimous in their commitment. There were no reports of violence.

[32] *Novaia Zhizn'*, July 20, 1917.
[33] *Russkaia Volia*, August 6, 1917.
[34] *Rabochaia Gazeta*, September 28, 1917.

At the outset of the strike, *Pravda* alone reported a major split in worker ranks between those who demanded the enterprises be seized and taken over by their employees, and those who thought this was a mistake because of the "danger of such an isolated action."[35] By contrast, the editors of *Rabochaia Gazeta* endeavored to emphasize the resistance of management, who sent deceitful representatives to bargain, falsely accused workers of stealing goods left for repair, and threatened strikers with weapons to force them to return to work.[36] Toward mid-July, rumors of shop seizures must have surfaced again, for the editors of *Rabochaia Gazeta* took pains to reassure readers that no such seizures had occurred or were planned. At the same time, the moderate socialist papers published appeals for contributions and listed the names of enterprises whose workers had sent funds.

Finally, the strike as a whole seemed very much to have mattered to the moderate socialist press as it dragged on, while it was virtually forgotten by left and right newspapers alike. Reports emphasized the hardships of striking workers as a result of weeks and months without wages and seemed to recognize the ways that this small group of underpaid women and men represented the hopes of many that revolution would finally bring some degree of material betterment and well-being. The final capitulation of the remaining holdouts was reported, without fanfare, only in the Mensheviks' *Rabochaia Gazeta* in the fall. For other papers, the strike lost both its news value and its relevance to the mounting political and economic crisis.

2. Petrograd Restaurant Workers

In several ways, the strike of some 10,000 waiters, waitresses, busboys and service people from Petrograd restaurants and tea shops was one of the most colorful of the entire revolutionary period. The walkout began with a massive march through the center of the city on June 30, after restaurant and tavern owners, organized by their Owners' Union,[37] refused to have the dispute arbitrated by the Labor section of the Petrograd Soviet. Strikers carried banners declaring "We Insist on Respect for Waiters As Human Beings," and "Down with Tips: Waiters are Citizens!" calling for "Protection for Women and Child Workers!" and "Full Satisfaction of Our Demands!" Workers from the Astoria Hotel, under military administration, also carried signs that said "We Demand the Removal of the Fourteen Generals Administering the Hotel!" The strike thus reflected both a newfound militance among Petrograd service people and

---

[35] *Pravda*, June 13, 1917.

[36] *Rabochaia Gazeta*, June 15, 1917.

[37] *Soiuz Vladel'tsev Traktirov, Chainykh, Stolovykh i Kukhmasterskikh g. Petrograda.*

a sharp consciousness about the social indignities of their work. It was hardly popular in Petrograd boulevard society.

Owners responded by raising their prices as much as 100 percent, partly in anticipation of meeting higher wage bills, partly, one suspects, to arouse public opinion against the strikers. Patrons responded angrily, and there was more than one incident of violence along the picket lines strikers had set up, especially in the aftermath of the July Days. The central issue of the dispute was whether waiters and waitresses would be put on salaries and treated in a dignified way as "workers." Some restaurant and tavern owners settled independently, but most resisted strongly what was, in effect, a strong attack on traditional social relations.

Full accounts of this strike were provided by both the liberal and moderate socialist press (especially *Birzhevyia Vedomosti* and *Novaia Zhizn'*). Other major newspapers also provided comprehensive coverage, especially on June 30 and July 1. Many reports were nearly identical. The major variant had to do with matters of organization, which were presented in great detail in the *Pravda-Edinstvo* account, and the responses of management, which *Birzhevyia Vedomosti* presented as "significant" and conciliatory. According to the latter on July 16, a subsection of the owners' association agreed to an eight-hour day, one month's vacation a year, 36 hours of monthly leave, and in addition to a salary, a stipend of 15 percent from the bill in large establishments, 10 percent in medium ones, and 5 percent in small tearooms and cafes off the main streets. *Birzhevyia Vedomosti* expressed some surprise over the strikers' rejection of these concessions.[38]

Although there are no apparent distortions of fact in these reports, they do reveal, again, a significant difference in comprehension, and hence presentation, of strike information. It is almost as if *Rech', Birzhevyia Vedomosti* and the nonsocialist press simply could not understand why tipping was an issue of such importance to Petrograd restaurant personnel, or why, particularly at the height of the military offensive, such issues mattered at all.

THE LEFT AND THE QUESTION OF BLAME:
PUBLIC RESPONSIBILITY AND
PUBLIC RELATIONS

The task of explaining such matters, and of responding to the increasing hostility toward strikes of any sort on the part of the business community in late June and early July, was also growing more difficult, especially for

[38] *Birzhevyia Vedomosti*, July 16, 1917.

trade union figures and moderate socialists. The special and complex way in which strikes syncretized Russian labor's revolutionary heritage and the routine practices of Western European "bourgeois democracy" complicated judgments about their value. Before 1917 the calculus was simple. The costs of striking were high, the real and intangible benefits relatively meager. At the risk of lost wages, repression, dismissal, and even arrest or conscription, strikers might secure minimal improvements, express their views, vent their anger, and possibly strengthen relations with their comrades. Strikes in moral terms were positive acts, even if sometimes tactically inexpedient. They were seen universally by socialists and labor activists of all persuasions as heroic salvos fired against the state-capitalist enemy—a vital part of Russia's revolutionary energies and traditions.

After February, the moral valuation of strikes was suddenly complicated by the contradictory premises of "revolutionary" and "bourgeois" democracy. On the one hand, the labor movement and its soviet leadership became overnight a central element of Russia's new sociopolitical order, especially in the cities. In state enterprises and on the railroads, workers themselves assumed substantial responsibilities for maintaining industrial production, and thus social order. They seemed to agree with their moderate soviet leaders that democratic rights entailed democratic responsibilities.

The cost of strikes consequently escalated, like that of everything else. Many began to view them as potentially harmful not simply to individual capitalist profiteers, but to a new economic and political order now under democratic control. Skobelev himself insisted that the government's most pressing responsibility was to implement social legislation in part as a means of heading off strikes, and suggested to a special council considering new strike legislation that strikes might even be prohibited if exceptional wartime circumstances seemed to demand it. Work on the new legislation stalled as council members became uncertain whether it would effectively contain strikes or simply encourage new ones.[39] On the other hand, as time went by, passivity in the work place increasingly implied both accommodation to an antagonistic managerial cohort, especially in Petrograd, and abandonment of the single most powerful weapon in the workers' arsenal, one that had brought the new regime to power. At Putilov, shop workers roughed up their own committee members for resisting demands to strike and accused them of supporting the "capitalists."[40] However sensible the arguments for labor peace in broad political and

[39] TsGAOR, f. 4100, op. 2, d. 25.
[40] I. I. Gaza, *Putilovets na putiakh k oktiabriu* (Moscow, 1933), pp. 108–12.

economic terms, many on the left found it impossible to dissuade their comrades from striking when the promises of February had yet to be fully realized, and when social conditions, in fact, appeared to be getting worse.

A dual valuation of strikes and their consequences thus emerged in the late spring of 1917. For many members of the democracy, workers and intellectual revolutionaries alike, strikes came to be seen as both harmful and necessary. They stopped production, and this weakened the ability of the revolution to defend itself, not to mention the safety of comrades at the front. Strikes also contributed to economic shortages, which rippled through the entire economy and ended ultimately by harming workers themselves. Yet strikes continued to symbolize vital political freedoms, won by just such actions. While harmful at one level, they were thus also justified on another simply because they demonstrated the autonomy, cohesion, and might of the working class, and reflected its heroic traditions.

Both positive and negative views of strikes were expressed throughout 1917, but the events of June and early July sharply reinforced critical outlooks. The rhetoric of many in the labor movement began to evidence an ethic that regarded the deliberate withdrawal of labor under present conditions as more harmful, improper, and inefficacious than good, a form of leverage and protest to be used as seldom as possible and only under the most pressing circumstances. This point of view was increasingly apparent in programmatic statements of trade union leaders. "Under the present critical conditions," argued Lozovskii, who would become leader of the trade union movement after October, "when the fate of the Russian revolution depends upon skillful, organized, unswerving and mobilized [*splochennye*] assaults by workers—at this time, for every strike, for every assault, we must be governed by the principle, 'measure thy cloth seven times, since thou canst cut it only once.' "[41]

Most trade union representatives at the Third All-Russian Conference in June agreed with these views. The strike remained a sacrosanct symbol of the labor movement, signifying its revolutionary heritage, its readiness to confront capital, and its commitment to the hopes of February. Strikes were also important agitational and organizational tools. Yet nearly every speaker also agreed that under present circumstances strikes had to be used carefully and selectively, as weapons of last resort, after other methods of conflict resolution had failed.[42]

[41] *Tret'ya vserossiiskaya konferentsiya professional'nykh soyuzov, 1917 goda. Stenograficheskii otchet*, ed. Diane Koenker (1927; reprint, Millwood, N.Y., 1982), p. 256.

[42] Ibid., especially pp. 255–56.

Given Lenin's own aspirations for power it is hardly surprising that a militant alternative was also expressed at the trade union conference, one that continued to insist on the primacy of strikes. A. M. Bakhutov, a Bolshevik representative of the Moscow central trade union bureau, vehemently challenged the prevailing mood. "On the basis of the experience which we have had in the course of three years of war—as the basis of all that we see, we have come to the conclusion, that the single serious revolutionary method is the strike."[43] For the time being, however, Bakhutov's militance was shared by only a small minority in high union circles. The majority attitude toward strikes reflected instead the prevailing Menshevik view, whose primary emphasis was on arbitration and other means of conciliation, particularly direct union-management negotiations. "In any case," the Menshevik Kol'tsov argued, for example, "any strike, any successful action, in the final analysis is settled by peaceful negotiation. In well-known cases trade unions have found it advantageous to conclude a peaceful agreement at the start, before a strike begins."[44] The greatest service union leaders could offer workers was a favorable contract, properly negotiated and legally binding. This was the essence of public responsibility.

Yet negotiation was obviously not quelling labor unrest, even if conciliation boards and other arbitration mechanisms were successful in numerous cases. Menshevik leaders in the soviets were consequently beginning to consider more carefully the idea of state intervention as a means of resolving conflict, as well as state regulation of the economy more generally. Socialist economists in the Economic Section of the Petrograd Soviet like Vladimir Groman also felt these measures were imperative in terms of Russia's overall economic well-being, and a necessary prelude to the gradual construction of a socialist order.

The problem with this regulatory view from a political standpoint, however, was twofold. On the one hand, it angered industrialists and manufacturers, especially those in the PSFMO and MSFMO, who continued to demand state intervention in *their* interests (as they had before 1917) and worried that the regime was moving rapidly to the left. On the other hand, it allied the Menshevik economists programatically with their increasingly hostile rivals on the left, the Bolsheviks, at least to some extent. The difficulty here was not so much ideological as practical. Sober economists like Groman, and even those in the cabinet who were responsive to the idea of intervention like Gvozdev and Skobelev, were indirectly strengthening the Bolsheviks' appeal.

[43] Ibid., p. 253.
[44] Ibid., p. 245.

Regulation (or *kontrol'*) as an alternative to isolated and individual work stoppages had emerged, in fact, as a central aspect of Lenin's own view of industrial relations in 1917, and by extension, of the perspective of the Bolshevik party leadership as a whole. At a minimum, workers' control gave supervisory power in the workplace to factory committees, and hence to autonomous workers' organizations. These were themselves instruments of solidarity and mobilization, whether or not they chose to struggle by means of strikes. The danger in strikes was largely one of tactics: scattered work stoppages fragmented energies and dissipated labor resources. They also engendered sharp reaction and potential repression, both potentially harmful to the party. The extension of workers' power *within* the workplace, however, was clearly a means of moving the revolution forward. Control of production was a fundamental source of power, after all, one which, if realized, would necessarily force a transformation of the state.

One consequently looks in vain in Lenin's writings in 1917 for any positive assessment of strikes as a revolutionary tool. Despite a great appreciation of the revolutionary significance of strikes in 1905, Lenin appears to have discounted the strike tactic in 1917, just as he seems to have discounted negotiations, arbitration boards, and other aspects of industrial relations that did not involve a direct extention of workers' power. Strikes against the government—railway and postal strikes in particular—interested Lenin, and he may have interpreted strikes overall as indicators of generalized worker despair, of which he wrote frequently. But in general, he and other Bolshevik leaders assigned little positive role to strikes as a means of resolving labor-management conflicts. These simply could not be settled except through further revolution, the creation of a proletarian regime willing to regulate the economy in the workers' interest.[45]

[45] This theme of proletarian control and regulation runs, of course, throughout Lenin's writings in 1917 and presages the economic policies the party would adopt during the civil war: not workers' control, but control by the workers' government. The view was codified in a resolution adopted at the Sixth Congress of the Bolshevik party. Workers were urged not to be provoked into strikes: "The proletariat should not succumb to the provocations of the bourgeoisie, who very much desire at the present time to incite workers to a premature fight." See *Protokoly shestogo s"ezda RSDRP(b). Avgust 1917 goda* (Moscow, 1934), p. 233. The alignment of opinion on the issue of strikes at the Sixth Congress, which Lenin did not attend, is extremely interesting. Miliutin, a trade unionist who would later resign from the Central Committee in protest of the party's refusal to share power after October, argued in favor of utilizing the strike wave to further politicize and radicalize workers (pp. 147–48). Osinskii, later to become a Workers' Oppositionist, countered that the current economic situation meant strikes could too easily lead to lockouts and that they should not be encouraged (p. 153). The Congress adopted a resolution based on Osinskii's position,

By the time the first coalition collapsed in early July, Bolsheviks and Mensheviks were thus both emphasizing the central value of production, of work itself. They differed not so much about the propriety of strikes in current circumstances as on the reasons *why* they were unsuitable, and on the alternatives to stopping work. And on these grounds, one can recognize why an essential element of strike reporting came to involve the justification to a broader public the necessity for, the unavoidability of, laying down tools.

In most cases, the explanation involved placing the blame for this antisocial act on the opposition. Striking pharmacy employees embarked on their walkout "not with easy hearts. . . . They applied all their strength to end the dispute by peaceful means. . . . It was not the employees, but the proprietors who refused to submit to the decisions of a [conciliation] chamber, when they saw it would go against them."[46] "Comrades and Citizens!" began the appeal of striking paper workers. "The irresponsibility of the capitalists, and our difficult hopeless conditions, the complete indifference of entrepreneurs to the ever-growing high cost of living, so difficult for workers, and the impossibility of obtaining an improvement in our economic situation by other more peaceful methods without the introduction of a strike—have forced us, workers in paper-manufacturing factories, to this ultimate method of struggle."[47] It was not the strikers who lacked public responsibility, but those who foreclosed improving conditions by other means.

Likewise, striking Petrograd printers instructed their union to make clear to the public that their strike could have been avoided were it not for the provocation of the owners' association, that the workers were not the guilty party.[48] Here and elsewhere strikers repeatedly stressed that the immediate causes of strikes were actions of management: refusing to meet demands, firing individual workers or their elected representatives, refusing to negotiate, reneging on previous agreements. In making such charges, whether from genuine conviction or in order to appeal for public understanding and support, workers were blaming the capitalists themselves for violating the conventions of bourgeois industrial relations; indeed, many felt this blame was entirely well placed.

The shifting of blame occurred not only in specific strike reports, usu-

---

but when someone suggested a change in the wording, from "premature fight" (*boi*) to "premature action" (*vystuplenie*), Stalin, as chairman, ruled that the latter wording would be too restrictive and could be interpreted as discouraging all demonstrations and strikes (pp. 233–34).

[46] *Rabochaia Gazeta*, April 25, 1917.

[47] Ibid., September 20, 1917.

[48] Ibid., August 15, 1917.

ally by local trade union organizers, but also in more general programmatic discussions of the strike movement and perilous economic situation. *Rabochaia Gazeta*, the Mensheviks' flagship paper, for example, editorialized in May about the impending economic catastrophe under the heading, "Who Is To Blame?" If workers' excessive demands were causing economic dislocation, as the industrialists argued, then the solution was government wage-and-price regulation, not the spiralling cycle of production-halting strikes. But if the government failed to impose such regulation, how could the workers be blamed for seeking to keep up with the cost of living? In a subsequent editorial the paper became even more pointed: industrialists, in effect, had declared war on workers. They were waging "Italian strikes" of their own by refusing to repair factories or renew fuel and materiel reserves, and otherwise slowing production. Workers were thus being forced to strike in order to exert any pressure at all, the paper implied, whereas industrialists cried "excessive wage demands!" shut down their plants, and blamed their employees for damaging the economy.[49]

Not all strike reports expressed regret, of course. Strikers were frequently described as "united," "firm," and "cheerful." In mid-June, for example, striking dye workers reported, "The strike continues in its second month with the same energy and hope in the support of our comrades which we encountered from the first day of the strike."[50] But the context of such reports, and the care with which organizers stressed the reasonableness of workers' grievances, reconfirms our belief that the mood was "cheerful" not so much because workers were increasingly optimistic in late June and early July, but because they believed in the righteousness of their cause.

Indeed, the tenor of these reports in sum by July—the public face of strikers—was one that emphasized the reasonableness of workers' behavior, their moderation, and their sense of public responsibility. Hence the appeals to comrades *and* citizens, the regretful tone in which many strike reports were couched. Strikers seemed determined to represent themselves as Russians, as citizens of the republic, not just as a special but distinct class. Yet the very shifting of blame, the assignment of guilt to specific parties—owners and industrialists—exemplified the underlying conflictual nature of industrial relations in 1917. The very rhetoric of guilt and innocence was reinforcing the sense of class polarization, of *kto kogo*, that would soon dominate society and politics everywhere.

[49] Ibid., May 19, 20, 1917.
[50] Ibid., June 15, 1917.

8

....

LABOR ACTIVISM

IN MIDSUMMER

The uprising in Petrograd and the simultaneous collapse of the first co-alition government cast a pall over political and economic activism every-where in the first weeks of July. The Bolshevik party suffered momentary disarray. The right-wing press launched a ferocious campaign charging that Lenin and his party were agents in the pay of Germany; Lenin fled to Finland to escape arrest; Trotsky, Kamenev, and Lunacharsky submitted to the Provisional Government's order for their arrest and found them-selves in the notorious Khresty prison. Rank-and-file Bolsheviks still at liberty bore the brunt of physical and verbal attacks on their party. Pop-ular support appeared to dwindle.[1]

For Bolsheviks, July was a month of retreat, of regrouping. For the right, their defeat gave new encouragement. The Provisional Committee of the Duma, which had yielded power to the Provisional Government in March, reassembled in July in order to revive the Duma as an alternative to the soviets and Provisional Government. "The State Duma is a trench defending the honor, the dignity, and the existence of Russia," pro-claimed the rightist deputy Maslennikov, "and in this trench we must either triumph or die."[2] Rightist political groups inside and outside the military stepped up their pressure for a military dictatorship, encouraged by Kerensky's pledge to bring discipline to the army by restoring the death penalty at the front.[3]

The Provisional Government, or what was left of it after the breakup of the coalition on July 2, occupied the middle. The moderate Soviet lead-

[1] See the discussion in Alexander Rabinowitch, *Prelude to Revolution: The Petrograd Bolsheviks and the July 1917 Uprising* (Bloomington, Ind., 1968).

[2] *Burzhuaziia i pomeshchiki v 1917 godu. Chastnye soveshchaniia chlenov gosudarstven-noi dumy*, ed. A. Drezin (Moscow and Leningrad, 1932), pp. 198–99.

[3] See, e.g., N. Bukhbinder, "Na fronte v predoktiabr'skie dni; po sekretnym materialam stavki," *Krasnaia Letopis'* 6 (1923), pp. 16–17. The decision to restore the death penalty was approved on July 12, in the midst of the cabinet crisis. See *Vestnik Vremennago Pravi-tel'stva*, July 13, 1917.

ership stood reluctantly behind the Provisional Government's repression of Bolshevik militants but at the same time formulated a list of "general principles" on which a new coalition must be based. These were published in the name of the rump cabinet, the "Government of the Salvation of Russia," on July 8, in its official journal *Vestnik Vremennago Pravitel'stva*. This July 8 program reflected the Soviet's agenda for the revolution: an international peace conference to end the war, elections for the Constituent Assembly to take place September 17, and the extension of local self-government. In the economic sphere, the program pledged the Provisional Government to regulate and control industry and to formulate new laws on trade union freedom, labor exchanges, conciliation boards, labor protection, and social insurance. The program also reaffirmed the Provisional Government's commitment to sweeping but orderly land reform, indicating its intention to abolish unilaterally social estates [*soslovie*] and liquidate civil ranks and orders. Most Kadet leaders thought the program a scandal. The Soviet itself seemed to be setting goals for the government that preempted the rights of the Constituent Assembly and flew in the face of liberal conceptions of constitutional legality and democratic practice. Prime Minister Lvov also found the program impossible to accept and followed the Kadet ministers into retirement. Kerensky was appointed by the remaining cabinet members as prime minister, with instructions to form a new cabinet, easier said than done.[4]

The program of July 8 also further alarmed Russia's leading industrialists. The Soviet's ability to restore order only reaffirmed the government's own dependence on socialist support. Many in the ranks of the PSFMO and MSFMO found themselves confronting the real possibility that the foundations of their own economic and political order might totally collapse.

In this situation, the changing lines of struggle were again redrawn. Concessions to workers, a willingness to grant most demands and to settle strikes quickly, a tolerance for conciliation mechanisms unsympathetic to their interests, even a willingness to accept an expanding role for factory committees, now legitimized by the government's legislation of April 23—such behavior had failed to guarantee labor peace. Concessions now seemed in commercial and industrial circles to have encouraged not stability or harmony in the workplace, nor a stronger political order, but increasingly unrealistic, self-interested worker demands, and new, massive, and unruly protests.

Signs of the change in managerial attitudes were apparent everywhere.

[4] See the discussion in William G. Rosenberg, *Liberals in the Russian Revolution* (Princeton, N.J., 1974), chap. 6.

On July 4 the metals branch of the PSFMO issued a sharply worded circular letter condemning "anarchy" and insisting that "all promises, written or oral, given to workers under threat or force, are not obligatory for the enterprise."[5] A few days later the PSFMO ordered its members not to pay workers for time lost during the July Days strike. Even the question of workers' paid vacations now emerged as a focus of managerial resistance. In Moscow, industrialists categorically forbade paid leaves for their employees. ("Paid leaves [otpusky] for workers should absolutely not be granted; if workers demand such leaves by threatening to strike, and if they actually begin such strikes, under no circumstance should agreements be reached which satisfy these demands or pay workers for their strike time.")[6] At the Trubochnyi plant, the Sestroretsk arms works, and elsewhere, workers were disarmed. At Sestroretsk, the factory committee was arrested. An urgent meeting of Vasil'evskii Island industrialists in Petrograd demanded the disarming of workers everywhere.[7] In Penza, wood-product manufacturers telegraphed the government that they no longer had any hope local officials could act effectively against "the growing anarchy" in their plants, and were asking local soviet leaders to intervene.[8]

Whether because of these attitudes, a broader sense of political or economic uncertainty, or perhaps even factors like summer agricultural work, the level of strikes dropped markedly in the aftermath of the July Days. Between July 7 and July 28, strikes in our file began at an average of only 2.4 per day, and on estimates of 80 percent of the strikes in these weeks, involved fewer than 450 new strikers daily, the lowest figure for the entire revolutionary period. A few strikes begun before the July Days continued. In Rostov-on-Don, a printers' strike begun in a small shop on June 26 spread throughout the city and concluded only on July 30, while retail clerks in a Kiev millinery shop stayed off the job from mid-May until well into July. But these were the exception. Most workers responded instead like those at Moscow's Khlebnikov jewelry factory (now engaged in defense work), who left their jobs on June 24 but returned to work on July 13 without a settlement in the interests of defense and "working class unity."[9] The strikes that began (or continued) during this

---

[5] *Ekonomicheskoe polozhenie Rossii nakanune velikoi oktiabr'skoi sotsialisticheskoi revoliutsii. Dokumenty i materialy*, 3 pts. (Moscow and Leningrad, 1957–67), pt. 1, p. 526.

[6] Ibid., p. 527.

[7] M. Bortnik, "Na Trubochnom zavode," in *Professional'noe dvizhenie v Petrograde v 1917 godu*, ed. A. Anskii (Leningrad, 1928), p. 273.

[8] *Postanovka i pobeda velikoi oktiabr'skoi sotsialisticheskoi revoliutsii v Penzenskoi gubernii. Sbornik dokumentov i materialov* (Penza, 1957), pp. 104–6.

[9] *Rabochaia Gazeta*, July 12, 1917; *Velikaia oktiabr'skaia sotsialisticheskaia revoliutsiia na Ukraine, fevral' 1917–aprel' 1918 godov*, 3 vols. (Kiev, 1957), vol. 1, p. 461; *Izvestiia*

July lull were also relatively small. Nor were they characterized by particularly militant tactics. As Kerensky struggled to construct a new coalition, he was spared for the moment the pressures generated by massive unrest in factories and work places.

At the same time, however, the government faced pressure of a different sort: the rapidly growing resistance among industrialists and manufacturers to reach local settlements with workers in their own enterprises. The PSFMO and MSFMO now strenuously advocated industrywide agreements, negotiated only with trade union leaders, in which they could hold a much more solid and forceful position. Managerial opposition to conciliation stiffened everywhere. In Petrograd, metalist union leaders and PSFMO representatives had begun contract negotiations on June 22, for example, and unionists at first strongly resisted management proposals to tie wages to guaranteed productivity norms. The talks stalled. Labor leaders struggled with their rank and file over this issue and finally secured acceptance of productivity clauses in principle on July 2 only by threatening to resign.[10] When the labor delegates returned to the bargaining table after the July Days, however, they found owners holding a much tougher line. Despite management's concern over Bolshevik agitation among unskilled metalists at the end of June, especially at Putilov, and despite angry resolutions by unskilled metalists demanding ten rubles a day and "a curb on the bloodsuckers and pirates," the metals section of the PSFMO now rejected a wage scale of eight to twelve rubles a day for unskilled males in their industry.[11] The matter went immediately to the Ministry of Labor, but despite several more weeks of negotiation, which saw new unrest in the shops at Putilov and elsewhere, PSFMO representatives refused to concede. On July 22 they rejected outright a proposal from the Ministry's arbitration commission recommending unskilled workers receive 20 percent less than their negotiators had proposed. Only when the Labor Ministry made the decision binding on employers was an agreement signed.[12]

A similar consolidation of industrialists' ranks took place elsewhere, in Moscow, South Russia, the Urals, and especially in the Ukraine, where metalworkers also met stiff resistance to wage and conditions demands. In Baku, oil industrialists participating in talks over a collective contract with union and soviet representatives closed ranks against concessions,

---

(Moscow), July 15, 1917; *Zemlia i Volia*, July 4, 1917; VOSR. *Khronika sobytii*, vol. 2, p. 418.

[10] *Metallist*, nos. 1–2, August 17, 1917. See the discussion in S. A. Smith, *Red Petrograd: Revolution in the Factories, 1917–1918* (Cambridge, 1983), pp. 121–29.

[11] I. I. Gaza, *Putilovets na putiakh k oktiabriu* (Moscow, 1933), p. 110.

[12] Smith, *Red Petrograd*, p. 126.

and when union leaders called for the transformation of oil production into a state monopoly, appealed to the Provisional Government for assistance. Labor Minister Skobelev announced he would come to Baku as soon as possible to prevent a strike which many thought would paralyze the country, and to attempt to reason with the now militant producers.[13]

Small tradesmen and shop owners evidenced similar resistance to concessions: the consolidation in employer ranks seemed now to transcend the rather sharp differences that had earlier characterized Russia's business community as a whole. In Petrograd, for example, the city's laundresses once again emerged as a symbol of workers' difficulties everywhere, just as their strike in May had signified a broad-based and enthusiastic renewal of activism under the first coalition. Already by the end of June it was clear that many laundry owners were reneging on the agreement reached to end the strike. A report to the first city district soviet indicated that the owners of many establishments were refusing to take back their former employees; others were shutting their doors entirely, "selling their machines and leaving for their dachas," according to one report.[14] A number of district soviets consequently began a new effort to help the laundresses, appealing to industrial workers for funds. On June 24, the Vyborg district soviet asked the central trade union bureau to support a renewal of the strike. Three days later, the Kolomenskii district committee asked factory committees throughout the city to give the laundresses support.[15] Shop owners, however, angered even more by the union's efforts to seize some of their shops, refused to yield. In the aftermath of the July Days, more establishments closed, but the minister of labor now felt compelled to "cancel" the union's "decree" on requisitioning them.[16] As the laundresses' hardship became an increasing concern of many in and outside the soviets, so, symbolically, did the intransigence of their employers, a clear indication of both consolidation and polarization between management and labor.

To some extent the response of employers reflected their own deteriorating economic circumstances in the summer, or at least the industrialists perceptions' of "impending catastrophe," as the journal of the PSFMO ed-

[13] A. N. Guliev, "Bor'ba Bakinskogo proletariata za kollektivnyi dogovor vesnoi i letom 1917 goda," in *Velikii oktiabr' i bor'ba za sovetskuiu vlast' v Azerbaidzhane* (Baku, 1958), pp. 91–92; A. Nikishin, *Ocherki Bakinskogo gorniatskogo profdvizheniia, 1917–1920 gody* (Baku, 1926), pp. 24–29. See also the discussion in Ronald Grigor Suny, *The Baku Commune* (Princeton, N.J., 1972), pp. 126–32.

[14] *Raionnye sovety Petrograda v 1917 godu*, 3 vols. (Moscow and Leningrad, 1964–66), vol. 1, p. 207.

[15] Ibid., pp. 208–9.

[16] *Edinstvo*, July 22, 1917.

itorialized on July 15.[17] Petrograd industrialists estimated, for example, that they needed 13,700,000 pounds of fuel oil for August. They threatened massive closings without it, even though their figure was almost 175 percent higher than what the rail lines were expected to deliver, and some 50 percent higher than what the government's Special Council for Fuel estimated they needed. But hardening attitudes also reflected renewed efforts on the part of the business community to unify its ranks politically and to take quick advantage of the momentary confusion and disorder that the July Days had sown in socialist ranks. The PSFMO's fuel estimate was almost certainly inflated to strengthen the industrialists' appeal for stronger government intervention against labor. The PSFMO now endorsed calls for the "mandatory fulfillment" of state orders, as well as the "mobilization" of skilled and unskilled workers both to repair locomotives and rolling stock, and to provide the city with firewood and other fuels.[18]

Industrialists also pressed hard to secure their positions in the government. When Kerensky asked S. N. Tret'iakov, the president of the Moscow Stock Exchange, to take the trade-industrial portfolio, Tret'iakov indicated he would accept only if there was a "radical break" with the past.[19] Partly because of this resistance, negotiations over a new coalition cabinet took more than three weeks and ended with the moderate Social Democrat S. N. Prokopovich taking the Ministry of Trade and Industry, rather than Tret'iakov.

This hardly pleased the industrialists or strengthened their confidence in the government. In Moscow, Iu. P. Guzhon of the Moscow Metal Works, now president of the MSFMO, gathered N. V. Nabgol'ts, Iu. I. Poplavskii, N. G. List, and others together to reinforce that group's efforts at holding the line against further economic and political deterioration.[20] To increase its ability to negotiate collectively, the PSFMO under A. A. Bachmanov, a leading figure in the G. A. Lessner complex and director of "Old Lessner," restructured itself along industrial branch lines. With more than 450 enterprises in its own ranks (employing some 270,000 workers) the PSFMO also prepared to host a national meeting of SFMO

[17] *Vestnik Petrogradskago Obshchestva Zavodchikov i Fabrikantov*, 20 (July 15, 1917), p. 1.

[18] Ibid.

[19] V. Ia. Laverychev, "Vserossiiskii soiuz torgovli i promyshlennosti," *Istoricheskie Zapiski* 70 (1961), pp. 46–48.

[20] *Promyshlennost' i Torgovlia*, 28–29 (August 5, 1917). The MSFMO executive committee now included V. I. Arandarenko, K. M. Zhemochkin, K. A. Malakhovskii, N. M. Mikhailov, V. V. Popov, and L. A. Rabenek, in addition to Guzhon, Poplavskii and Nabgol'ts.

representatives from around the country.[21] Its leaders also joined with the conservative Association of Trade and Industry, the Union of Donets Coal Producers, the Ural Metallurgical Industrialists' Association, the Baku Oil group, the All-Russian Sugar Manufacturers' Association, the Association of Private Petrograd Banks, and others to organize a Union of United Industrial Enterprises, designed "to coordinate actions against the interference of workers in industrial management" and to work for new state regulations and decrees.[22] And shortly afterwards, P. P. Riabushinskii, still widely regarded as one of Russia's more moderate and progressive industrial leaders, opened the second national Trade-Industrial Congress in Moscow with his famous attack on those who could not understand Russia's perilous condition and the need for firmness. Referring to "the bony hand of hunger and national destitution" grasping at the throats "of these false friends of the people, these members of various committees and soviets," Riabushinskii now demanded a government that could "think and act in a bourgeois manner."[23]

STRIKES IN MIDSUMMER

How all of this impacted on strikes, and how, in turn, strikes themselves further affected management-labor relations in this period, can readily be seen. The period of quiescence in strike activity barely lasted past the formation of the second coalition. On Saturday, July 29, the national press reported six new strikes involving at least 1,000 workers. On the following Monday, these strikers were joined by 4,500 Moscow tobacco workers and 3,800 factory workers in Revel', whose strike quickly spread to much of the city. Woodworkers walked off their jobs in Rostov, all the printers in the Lithuanian town of Iureev struck for higher wages, and metalworkers in provincial Orel left their jobs demanding wages and other concessions equivalent to those being offered elsewhere.[24] A strike by chernorabochie in the important Kharkov Locomotive works broadened into a massive lockout when the entire work force was officially

---

[21] See T. Shatilova, "Petrogradskoe obshchestvo zavodchikov i fabrikantov v bor'be s rabochim dvizheniem v 1917 godu," in Anskii, ed., *Professional'noe dvizhenie*, p. 103; D. M. Zol'nikov, "K voprosu o stachechnom dvizhenii proletariata osen'iu 1917 goda," *Uchenye Zapiski Tomskogo Gosudarstvennogo Universiteta*, 37, no. 1, (1959), pp. 47–70.

[22] *Promyshlennost' i Torgovlia*, 28–29 (August 5, 1917). Others included representatives from the metalworking, timber, paper, and private railroad associations, and a number of local SFMOs, including the PSFMO.

[23] *Ekonomicheskoe polozhenie*, pt. 1, pp. 200–1. See also Laverychev, "Vserossiiskii soiuz," p. 47.

[24] TSGIA, f. 23, op. 16, d. 245, l. 14; *Izvestiia* (Petrograd), August 1, 1917; *Rabochaia Gazeta*, August 1, 1917; VOSR. *Khronika sobytii*, vol. 3, p. 52.

dismissed in mid-August; workers themselves apparently prevented management from shutting down the furnaces, but the strike and lockout continued.[25] In Samara, only the urgent intervention by local soviet leaders ended a bakers' strike that threatened to cut off bread supplies to the garrison.[26] In all, between July 29 and August 26, when strike activism once again subsided, a minimum of 373,000 workers left their jobs to demonstrate their grievances.

If we look more closely at the composition of the strikers in this summer strike cluster, we also find that the geographic concentration of strikers had swung away from Petrograd and was now centered around Moscow. In contrast to nearly 350,000 strikers in Petrograd from the April crisis through the July Days, we estimate that only slightly more than 3,300 Petrograd workers now participated in strikes. Moscow, by contrast, accounted for only 11 of the 108 strikes in our file for the period, but these involved more than 227 industrial enterprises and over two-thirds of all reported strikers, a minimum of 260,000 workers off the job. Two mammoth strikes accounted for most of the Moscow strike force, but others were massive as well. In addition to the tobacco workers cited above, some 16,000 chemical workers struck on August 7, 14,000 construction workers on August 8, and 110,000 leather workers (in the city and surrounding region) on August 16. In the midst of these strikes called over factory issues, another 116,000 Moscow workers—at a minimum—walked off their jobs in a one-day political strike on August 12 to protest the assembled Moscow State Conference.

We will return to this important political strike, but for the moment it should not be allowed to obscure the broader contours of strike activism during these weeks. Although Moscow accounted for most of the strikers, other regions in the hinterland generated more strikes: 32 in the central Moscow region and 21 in the southeastern Kiev region. Over 22,000 workers participated in Moscow region strikes, 20,000 in the Petrograd region (excluding the city), and over 42,000 in the Volga region.

The pattern of geographic distribution in these midsummer weeks thus indicates a spread of strike activity away from its traditional center, Petrograd, and the involvement of large numbers of provincial workers in patterns of protest that had largely been characteristic of politically conscious workers in industrial centers like Petrograd's Vyborg district. A similar broadening of participation can be observed in the occupational composition of summer strikes. Metalworkers were less active in this pe-

[25] *Khar'kov i Khar'kovskaia guberniia v velikoi oktiabr'skoi sotsiatisticheskoi revoliutsii. Sbornik dokumentov, fevral' 1917–aprel' 1918 godov* (Kharkov, 1957), p. 158.

[26] *Revoliutsiia 1917–1918 godov v Samarskoi gubernii*, ed. I. I. Bliumental' (Samara, 1927), vol. 1, pp. 180–82.

riod than they had been earlier, chemical workers, leather workers, and construction workers far more so. In general, skilled workers were much less involved in strikes now than they had been before the July Days, possibly because they, too, shared concerns about deteriorating economic conditions.[27]

What this suggests about the relationship between political consciousness and strikes, however, is unclear. Employer associations like the Penza wood manufacturers clearly regarded the spread of strikes as evidence of growing anarchy, rather than a sign of increasing labor mobilization and organization; when leather workers at the large Alafuzov complex in Kazan ran out a foreman in a wheelbarrow in July, the company's directors refused to see this traditional form of protest as anything but a total breakdown of factory order.[28] Strikes now involved new groups of industrial workers, as table 8.1 indicates, but they also diminished among clerical and service-sector workers. We have been able to identify only 14

TABLE 8.1

Strikes and Strikers in Midsummer by Industry
(Single-Industry Strikes Only)

Industry	Number of Strikes	Minimum Number of Enterprises Involved[a]	Estimated Number of Strikers[b]	Strike Propensity
Animal products (leather)	5	71	116,710	19.56
Chemicals	2	6	16,520	2.09
Paper and printing	10	89	3,840	.56
Metals	19	42	18,020	.38
Textiles	18	32	13,940	.22
Food products	10	63	5,210	.18
Wood and wood products	3	6	760	.10
Minerals	1	1	450	.05

[a] Minimum estimates based on fragmentary factory inspector reports and accounts from other sources.
[b] Minimum estimates based on 74% of strikes in metals, 78% in textiles, 90% in food products, and all cases in remaining industries.

[27] See our discussion in "Skilled Workers and the Strike Movement in Revolutionary Russia," *Journal of Social History* 19, no. 4 (Summer 1986), pp. 611–13.
[28] *Kazanskii oktiabr'. Materialy i dokumentov*, ed. E. Grachev (Kazan, 1926), pp. 103–4.

service-sector strikes in these weeks, involving only a handful of strikers, in contrast to the spring, when something like 80,000 workers in the service sector were engaged in protests of this sort. If strike activism in midsummer thus shifted outwards from its traditional center, and from metalworkers to workers in other less-favored industries, strikes were also now more narrowly confined to workers within industrial production itself.

The content of strikes also changed in these weeks. Although the galloping inflation of the spring had slowed, the interest of workers in fighting for higher wages did not diminish: more than half of all strikers put forward wage demands between July 29 and August 28, a slightly higher percentage than in the spring cluster (tables 8.2 and 8.3). But other kinds of issues gained even more in importance: well over one-third of all strikers now made claims about better conditions, workplace control, and dignity. Workers striking over factory control issues did so at a rate triple that of the spring, and nearly half of all strikers now made demands that challenged managerial authority in some way, double the earlier rate

TABLE 8.2
Strikes and Strikers in Midsummer by Demand Group

Demand Group	Number of Strikes	%	Estimated Number of Strikers[a]	%	Estimated Number of Strikers per Strike[b]
Wages	72	66.6	204,970	54.9	3,153
Conditions	17	15.7	143,940	38.5	8,996
Dignity	8	7.4	129,100	34.6	18,443
Control	22	20.4	148,160	39.7	7,798
Politics	14	13.0	162,270	43.5	20,284
Challenge to managerial authority	36	33.3	175,030	46.9	5,646
All strikes	108		373,400		4,292

NOTE: Strikes and strikers are overlapped for strikes with principal demands in more than one category.
[a] Estimates based on 90% of wage strikes, 94% of conditions strikes; 88% of strikes over issues relating to workers' dignity; 86% of workers' control strikes; 57% of known political strikes; 86% of strikes challenging managerial authority; and 81% of all strikes.
[b] Calculated only for strikes with estimates of strikers.

TABLE 8.3
Strike Demands, Spring and Midsummer Clusters
(in Percent)

Demand Group	Strikes		Strikers[a]	
	Spring	Summer	Spring	Summer
Wages	71.5	66.6	48.9	54.9
Conditions	25.7	15.7	18.7	38.5
Dignity	7.8	7.4	9.2	34.6
Control	17.3	20.4	11.6	39.7
Politics	2.1	13.0	48.2	43.5
Challenge to managerial authority	37.8	33.3	23.8	46.9

[a] See tables 5.4 and 8.2 for percentages of strikes on which estimates for numbers of strikers were based.

(table 8.3). The number of political strikes also increased, as can be seen by comparing table 8.2 and table 5.4. In other words, while wage issues remained the dominant concern of strikers in this period, nonpecuniary matters seemed to assume a much more central place in strike demands.

A look at several individual strikes may help clarify these complex patterns. When Moscow leather workers brought that industry to a standstill on August 16, for example, 110,000 workers went on record demanding higher wage scales (wages), an eight-hour workday, paid vacations, and special clothing for certain workers (conditions), a grace period for tardiness and workers' participation in hiring and firing (control), and pay for the time spent on strike (dignity). Similar packages of demands characterized many other strikes, large and small, in these weeks. Four hundred tailors in Perm struck on August 23 with a list of 14 demands, including equalization of conditions for home workers and shop workers, hiring only through the union, and an end to gambling in shops. Petrograd printers struck en masse on August 12 in support of their proposed contract, which in addition to wage norms included provisions for an eight-hour workday, holidays (12 major religious holidays plus May 1 and the anniversary of the February revolution), and the rights of factory committees.[29]

[29] *Rabochii klass Urala v gody voiny i revoliutsii*, ed. A. Taniaev (Sverdlovsk, 1927), vol.

A critical point of contention in the Moscow leather workers' strike, however, had to do with workers participating in hiring and firing. Here Labor Minister Skobelev sided fully with the owners' position of total managerial control over all such employment decisions. But leather workers and others clearly thought otherwise. In the midsummer period this issue engaged the energies of at least 136,000 strikers, one-third of all the workers on strike between July 29 and August 28. Not content to press simply for wages, striking workers outside of Petrograd now demanded new concessions in all spheres of their factory lives, partly in emulation of their comrades in the capital, but partly in response themselves to conditions they perceived as increasingly threatening to their own well-being. If growing demands for workers' participation in hiring and firing seemed to owners to reflect a radical assault on well-established managerial prerogatives in a "bourgeois capitalist order," they were to many workers a logical and necessary device to ward off Riabushinskii's "bony hand of hunger." In any event, striking workers were extending this militant and assertive component of strikes much more than in the spring.

This assertiveness was paralleled by a growing change in the way many strikes were organized. Although the reported involvement of trade unions and factory committees in strikes actually declined a bit between spring and summer, the nature of strike organization itself seems to have been changing. Instead of factory committees and trade unions taking a prominent role in many strikes, as had been the case earlier, there was now a shift toward direction by strike committees, whose reported involvement more than doubled in comparison to the spring. Our data here may partly reflect changing patterns of reporting after the July Days, especially in the moderate socialist press, but many unions, like that of the Petrograd metalists and the railroad workers, hoped in these weeks to restrain their strike-inclined rank and file in favor of industrywide settlements, which they themselves negotiated. Strike committees consequently emerged in a growing number of cases as a means of circumventing the union.

Thus negotiations between Moscow leather workers and leather producers were begun in early June by the union's regularly constituted executive board (*pravlenie*). A new industrywide agreement was discussed broadly at a joint conference of Moscow and Petrograd regional workers and carefully crafted into a specific set of proposals by the union. On June 27, these were presented to the Moscow leather industry owners' association. A strike was to be the union's last resort, but leaders had great

2, pp. 265–66; A. Tikhanov, "Rabochie-pechatniki v 1917 godu," in *Materialy po istorii professional'nogo dvizheniia v Rossii* (Moscow, 1925), vol. 4, pp. 186–87.

difficulty restraining their rank and file after the July Days, when negotiations stalled. Four times the union leaders succeeded in postponing a strike in favor of continued negotiations, but when worker delegates voted to authorize a strike in early August and elected their own strike committee, the union agreed to a strike on August 14 if no settlement was reached. The strike committee itself prepared a long list of rules for the strike and directions for the collection and distribution of a strike fund; the strike began on August 16 essentially under its direction.[30]

There is some evidence as well that the character of strike leadership was changing partly in response to the growing extension of strikes beyond the gates of an individual enterprise, and often beyond a single industrial branch. The number of multiple-enterprise strikes increased by almost 15 percent between July 29 and August 26, in comparison to the spring; almost 44 percent of the strikes in this cluster involved more than one enterprise, with a total of more than 300 individual enterprises involved. Equally important, strikes in individual enterprises now engaged fewer than 12.5 percent of all strikers, according to our estimates. Strike committees were more likely to emerge in strikes uniting more than one enterprise, and particularly more than one industrial branch, which often brought unions themselves into conflict. Thus chemical workers in Moscow organized a central strike committee in August to coordinate strikes in the Treugol'nik, Kauchuk, Provodnik, and Bogatyr rubber plants, setting up subcommittees in each factory. Moscow leather workers did the same, empowering a central strike committee chosen at a large meeting on August 16 with the authority to approve or disapprove individual factory protests. So did striking Petrograd paper workers. In Baku, central and regional strike committees were organized by the oil workers union, again, to coordinate the strike activities of individual enterprises.

At the same time, since the size of strikes in individual enterprises was also expanding in the summer (from somewhere around 2,000 strikers per strike in the spring to more than 4,000 now), strike committees were clearly involved in more complex forms of mobilization and leadership. If the reported level of trade union and factory committee involvement in strikes remained relatively constant from spring to summer, there was nonetheless an important increase in the level of actual labor mobilization: these figures suggest the emergence of a new level of strike leadership among workers, quite possibly the result of accumulated strike experience, as well as a reflection of broader political changes.

The Petrograd printers' strike provides a good example of the "mush-

---

[30] See Diane Koenker, *Moscow Workers and the 1917 Revolution* (Princeton, N.J., 1981), pp. 320–22.

rooming" of small strikes into much larger work stoppages. On August 12, a number of Petrograd print shops shut down because negotiations with the owners' association had failed to produce an agreement on new wage scales. A strike and boycott of some 18 establishments followed, leaving a few shops open to meet the city's printing needs. When this partial strike failed to achieve quick results, the printers decided to escalate the protest; they hoped to increase economic pressure on the owners and political pressure on government and civic groups who had important interests at stake. By August 18, after some 25 shops had been closed, the minister of labor decided to take action, offering his own office for mediation. When the owners remained unmoved and announced on August 24 that they would refuse to submit to the minister's decision if they felt it was improper, the strike was extended to 32 enterprises, touching even the shops that printed official material for the army. Only the city's newspapers continued to publish freely.[31]

The trend toward larger-scale strikes over time appears to have occurred uniformly across Russia: in each city or locality, workers seemed to be developing similar uses of the strike weapon. To some extent, this process was encouraged by efforts to coordinate the labor movement itself on a national scale, particularly after the Third All-Russian Conference of Trade Unions in June. Delegates attended the conference from all over provincial Russia, and, as we have seen, the role of strikes was a major item on the agenda. Moreover, between the sessions of the All-Russian Conference, organizers of five specific industries also met to lay the foundations for their national consolidation.[32] Although the trade union movement produced no national publication until the first issue of *Professional'nyi Vestnik* (The Trade-Union Herald) appeared in the fall,[33] trade unions in Moscow, Petrograd, and elsewhere published local journals which served to inform workers everywhere of specific struggles and common organizational principles.[34] The socialist press also served, of course, as a similar conduit of strike experience.

In the summer of 1917, strikes were thus clearly educating working men and women on an increasingly national scale and in the process integrating workers into a class with important shared experiences. As

[31] See especially *Izvestiia* (Petrograd), August 8, 13, 16, 24, 1917; *Novaia Zhizn'*, August 15, 18, 1917; *Rech'*, August 15, 23, 1917; *Delo Naroda*, August 18, 24, 25, 1917.

[32] These were the metalworkers, tailors, textile workers, food products workers, and printers. See *Tret'ya vserossiiskaya konferentsiya professional'nykh soyuzov, 1917 goda. Stenograficheskii otchet*, ed. Diane Koenker (1927; reprint, Millwood, N.Y., 1982).

[33] *Professional'nyi Vestnik*, 1–2 (October 1, 1917).

[34] The leading journals in 1917 were *Ekho Derevoobdelochnika, Golos Kozhevnika, Pechatnik, Kharkovskii Pechatnik, Metallist,* and *Moskovskii Metallist.*

strikes spread, the patterns of protest they reflected also seemed to be shifting away from more routine elements of labor-management interaction to confrontation increasingly over broader matters of industrial organization and authority. Political conflicts were becoming more bitter, more intense, inside the workplace and out. Yet many workers and union organizers clearly continued to see strikes in traditional terms as well: as an appropriate and time-tested tactic to help secure new and favorable contracts with their employers and as the principal weapon in labor's arsenal everywhere in its struggle against employers for material gains. In these weeks as earlier, strikes did not reflect a single purpose, a single agenda, or a uniform march to October, and the nature and quality of management-labor interactions continued to structure activism as well as outlooks.

THE INTERACTIONS OF MANAGEMENT AND THE STATE IN MIDSUMMER

In the face of this growing mobilization of labor, the Provisional Government stepped up its efforts to forestall further disruption to Russia's fragile economy, while owners' associations like the PSFMO and MSFMO stepped up their campaigns against strikes. The two processes clearly overlapped. In early August the government issued new legislation on conciliation boards, urging their use "to prevent and settle disputes between workers and administrations of industrial enterprises."[35] Minister of Labor Skobelev and his assistant Gvozdev also pressed hard in individual cases for a peaceful settlement of conflicts. At the very end of July, Skobelev secured an agreement between the union of Volga shipping workers and the society of ship owners, averting a threatened transport strike; shortly afterward he travelled to Baku at the request of the oil workers' union to head off a major confrontation in the giant Caspian oil fields.[36] In a number of other cases, including major strikes by Petrograd and Kharkov metalworkers in August and an important strike of Kiev metalists in September, the Ministry worked closely with local soviet authorities to secure some form of agreement.

In the Kharkov case, however, and elsewhere as well, the settlement collapsed and enterprises closed. Such failures sent important signals to labor and management alike. Antilabor attitudes intensified sharply in a wide variety of industries and localities, along with lockouts and factory

---

[35] *Ekonomicheskoe polozhenie*, pt. 1, pp. 551–52; Robert P. Browder and Alexander F. Kerensky, eds., *The Russian Provisional Government, 1917: Documents*, 3 vols. (Stanford, Calif., 1961), vol. 2, pp. 742–43.

[36] *Rabochaia Gazeta*, August 4, 1917.

closings, and so did labor militance. Owners of restaurants and taverns in Petrograd began to renege on concessions that strikers had won in early July, refusing to include tip income in waiters' salaries; they ignored provisions establishing an eight-hour day and hired minors at extended hours to replace waiters who complained.[37] Leather manufacturers in Moscow refused to accept a compromise settlement proposed by Minister of Labor Skobelev after three weeks of negotiations had failed to avert a strike, despite terms that guaranteed plant administrators sole responsibility for hiring and firing. Workers were already at their benches expecting to resume work when the word came of the owners' refusal.[38]

The Likino textile manufacturing complex near Moscow also shut down in the beginning of August after owners refused, in the view of the Pokrovskii district zemstvo board, to take the necessary measures to assure continued production, including procuring needed supplies and repairing machinery.[39] And striking Singer sewing machine workers at plants and retail stores throughout Russia found themselves locked out after they agreed to a settlement proposed by the Ministry of Labor, which entered the dispute because of Russia's "critical political circumstances." Singer management insisted on the termination of interference by local committees of any sort in enterprise affairs, something neither workers nor the government itself could guarantee.[40] At the Kharkov locomotive works, one of the most important industrial complexes in the Kharkov-Ekaterinoslav region, management representatives held absolutely firm in their response to wage demands, evidently preferring to set a well-publicized example than to accept a settlement. When the dispute here escalated, and workers took over the plant to resume production, seizing some members of the factory administration in the process, the metals section of the Association of Trade and Industry telegraphed Kerensky to take "decisive measures" against the workers and restore industrial order.[41]

Lockouts continued to plague workers in many places. A conference of factory committees in Moscow in late July regarded them as a major political tactic of plant owners and warned about the danger of "hidden

[37] See e.g., *Rabochaia Gazeta*, August 1, 1917; *Zemlia i Volia*, July 9, 1917.

[38] *Golos Kozhevnika*, 4–5 (December 1, 1917).

[39] *Ekonomicheskoe polozhenie*, pt. 1, pp. 454–55.

[40] See especially *Russkaia Volia*, September 21, 1917, and *Ekonomicheskoe polozhenie*, pt. 1, pp. 214–16. There is also a good discussion of the Singer strike in A. M. Lisetskii, *Bol'sheviki vo glave massovykh stachek (mart–oktiabr' 1917 goda)* (Kishinev, 1974), pp. 214–16.

[41] *Ekonomicheskoe polozhenie*, pt. 1, pp. 490–91. See also L. S. Gaponenko, *Rabochii klass Rossii v 1917 godu* (Moscow, 1970), p. 387.

lockouts" because of inadequate government supervision over production.[42] In deteriorating economic conditions, a strike to force the end of a lockout was not expedient; strikes of this sort diminished after the July Days. (An important exception was a one-day strike by over 100,000 workers in the Perm province city of Ekaterinburg, where a general strike protesting the Moscow State Conference included in its demands a protest against the capitalists' *policy* of lockouts, as well as the growing threat of counterrevolution.)[43]

What seemed particularly galling to many workers was the disparity between the government's pressure for increased productivity and its condemnation of factory disorder, on the one hand, and the apparent growing indifference, even antipathy, of many plant owners towards issues of basic worker welfare, on the other. In Moscow, for example, metalworkers at the city-owned Moscow rolling mill went on strike when management refused to enroll the plant in an industrywide disability and illness fund. They planned to return to work after an arbitration court ruled in their favor in mid-July, but when management rejected the court's decision, the strike continued.[44]

This posture reflected managerial attitudes everywhere in late July and August. When Labor Minister Skobelev arrived in Baku in early August to mediate the oil fields dispute, his best efforts were beaten back by continued managerial recalcitrance, even though his journey had been made partly at the owners' behest. Sympathizing with the oil workers' situation, but alarmed at the likely implications of a strike, Skobelev wanted Nobel, Benkendorf, and the other firms of the Oil Producers' Council to pay out two months' advance wages as a form of bonus, charging it against a future settlement. At the same time, he insisted he was for "full and free exercise of the class struggle in principle, but in this particular branch of industry, which has such special importance to the state, the Ministry of Labor cannot help but intervene in order to decide the dispute as painlessly as possible."[45] Skobelev left Baku apparently thinking he had an agreement in hand, but the oil barons now responded to his intervention by demanding that the state itself pick up their new wage costs, and the conflict continued.

Similar patterns occurred with owners of woodworking plants in Petrograd, with Moscow coopers, and with owners of Petrograd printshops. In the case of the coopers, the owners offered a minimum wage scale running from eight to twelve rubles a day to the union's demand for thirteen,

[42] *Ekonomicheskoe polozhenie*, pt. 1, p. 410.

[43] *Rabochii klass Urala*, vol. 2, pp. 330–38.

[44] *Izvestiia* (Moscow), July 13, 1917; *Trud*, July 13, 14, 1917.

[45] *Bakinskii Rabochii*, August 6, 1917.

apparently telling workers in the process that their union was "pitiful" and hardly worth their time;[46] the association of printshop owners went so far as to issue a warning that if workers dared to strike in response to their own categorical refusal to make a new agreement effective as of August 1, they would immediately end all further negotiations.[47] An important conference of Petrograd metal union delegates deplored the "aggressive" posture of the employers' association and expressed its feeling that a peaceful agreement with the PSFMO was impossible.[48]

Yet the metalists' leaders also rejected calls for a strike, doubting its effectiveness and expediency. Angry common laborers from Putilov and elsewhere again demanded action, as they had in June, and castigated the union leadership for its timidity. Union spokesmen responded that the PSFMO was closing factories "simply to provoke workers," and militants were playing into its hands, especially the chernorabochie.[49] Bolshevik activists agreed and urged restraint, although the Petrograd party committee itself was divided on the question. Most metal-fabricating works and machine shops were now organized under factory committees in Petrograd and Moscow, and in places, substantial strike funds had already been secured. But many workers in both cities worried about plant shutdowns, and as many as 25,000 workers in July and early August faced unemployment, with few social services to fall back on. For the time being, the metalists' strategy was to pressure the Petrograd and Moscow Soviets to take a more active role, seek further intervention from the Ministries of Labor and Trade and Industry, and build strike funds for the future.[50]

Under these conditions, with the army struggling on the Austrian border and the new coalition preparing a national State Conference in Moscow to rally "all the organized forces of the country," workers everywhere found it increasingly difficult to achieve further gains. Despite their increase in size and scale, strikes became much harder to win outright, especially on wage issues. In aggregate terms, the percentage of outright successes dropped from a little more than 60 percent of strikes of known

[46] *Rabochaia Gazeta*, July 12, 1917.

[47] *Delo Naroda*, August 14, 1917.

[48] *Ekonomicheskoe polozhenie*, pt. 1, p. 528.

[49] See the discussion in Z. V. Stepanov, *Rabochie Petrograda v period podgotovki i provedeniia oktiabr'skogo vooruzhennogo vosstaniia* (Moscow and Leningrad, 1965), pp. 148ff.

[50] *Ekonomicheskoe polozhenie*, pt. 1, pp. 410, 529. For a discussion of Bolshevik restraint, see Lisetskii, *Bol'sheviki vo glave*, pp. 37–40; A. Ia. Grunt, *Moskva 1917–i: Revoliutsiia i kontrrevoliutsiia* (Moscow, 1976), pp. 109ff; and F. Bulkin, "Ekonomicheskoe polozhenie rabochikh Petrograda nakanune oktiabria 1917 goda," in Anskii, ed., *Professional'noe dvizhenie*, pp. 43ff.

outcome in May and June to 35 percent in late July and August. Sixteen percent were lost, compared to only 5 percent in the spring. In part, this may have been the result of the shift in strike goals away from wage issues alone toward issues touching managerial prerogatives much more directly, like participation in hiring and firing, but in part, it had to do simply with the increasing unwillingness of management to reach agreements that might have avoided strikes in any instance. At least insofar as their views were accurately represented in the labor press, Petrograd and Kharkov metalworkers, Moscow coopers and leather workers, Baku oil workers, and others now expected at least some satisfactory compromise in their disputes as a matter of course, having been persuaded to this view by their trade union leaders as well as past experience. In fact, our file includes no cases at all for these weeks in which workers themselves refused to enter into negotiations when they were requested to do so by management. Although our data on this question are not comprehensive, it does seem clear, as the labor press also began to argue, that management, not labor, was now primarily responsible for the decline in compromise settlements.

Other Forms of Protest in Midsummer: Petrograd and Moscow

In these circumstances one can readily understand why other forms of direct action against employers might have become increasingly attractive to many workers. Options were narrowing, particularly in the large industrial plants of the capitals. Shortly after Riabushinskii invoked "the bony hand of hunger" at the Trade-Industrial Congress in Moscow, an All-Russian Conference of Societies of Factory and Mill Owners convened in Petrograd, gathering together representatives from 16 such organizations.[51] The Congress represented around 2,000 enterprises, employing more than 1 million workers. On the very eve of the Moscow State Conference, it concentrated its energies on attacking the eight-hour day and the "chaotic demands of workers, which are devoid of reason and plan [*lishennyia razumnosti i plana*]." The tasks of both industrialists and the state were to "intensify" labor in the interests of increased productivity, on which Russia's future depended.[52] Meanwhile, in Moscow, other prominent members of the business community played an impor-

[51] *Vestnik Petrogradskago Obshchestva Zavodchikov i Fabrikantov*, 31 (August 10, 1917), p. 1. Some 40 delegates represented sFMOs in Kiev, Kharkov, Odessa, Riga, Kursk, Kazan, Revel', Iaroslavl', Rostov, Nizhnii Novgorod, Tiflis, Ivanovo-Voznesensk, Ekaterinoslav, and Orel, in addition to Moscow and Petrograd.

[52] Ibid. The words are A. A. Bachmanov's.

tant role in a closed conference of 400 "public figures," convened "to strengthen the statesmanlike and nationalist elements of the country."[53] Here Generals Alekseev, Brusilov, and the Cossack General Kaledin joined Miliukov, Riabushinskii, and others to try to "force a break," as Miliukov put it, with the "servants of utopia."[54] Even before the Moscow Conference revealed so clearly the growing cleavages in Russian society, voices of moderation in the business community were having a difficult time making themselves heard.

What our evidence suggests, however, is that along with strikes, other forms of factory action also declined in this period, most dramatically in August. Instead, collective actions *outside* strikes shifted to a significant degree from factories to the streets, and to apartment buildings, food stores, and various public places. Excluding incidents associated with the July Days, almost four times as many "street" actions as factory-based ones were reported in Moscow and Petrograd during the first three weeks of August.[55]

The reasons for this suggest themselves as we examine factory-based protests during these weeks more closely. Workers now seem to have been just as cautious about engaging in actions that could result in production cutbacks as they were about strikes, since "illegal" acts provided owners with an even better excuse for shutting their doors than did strikes. Such actions as were reported now seem to have been directed more toward maintaining production than settling grievances; indeed, the expansion of areas of worker control in production during these summer weeks was largely motivated by this same goal. In particular, workers now moved much more cautiously against plant foremen, supervisors, and salaried administrative personnel whose departure might threaten their own work. Expulsions of unpopular administrators practically ceased. We have found only one case of wheelbarrowing reported in the press for all of July and August, at the Sampsonievskaia textile mill in Petrograd on July 6. We find instead that an important shift occurred in the objects of factory-based protest during these weeks, a shift that may have been even more extensive than the data indicate. When workers engaged in direct action, they confronted plant owners, rather than foremen or lower-level managerial personnel, turning their attention in this way to the pinnacle

---

[53] *Otchet o Moskovskom soveshchanii obshchestvennykh deiatelei 8–10 avgusta 1917 goda* (Moscow, 1917), p. 3.

[54] Ibid., pp. 132–36.

[55] See the discussion in William G. Rosenberg and Diane P. Koenker, "The Limits of Formal Protest: Worker Activism and Social Polarization in Petrograd and Moscow, March to October, 1917," *American Historical Review* 92, no. 2 (April 1987) pp. 318–21.

of Russia's new socioeconomic order.[56] The majority of these and other protests occurred in those plants with the greatest management-labor friction in July and August: the metal-fabricating shops and machine works of Petrograd and Moscow.

Thus workers at the Brenner machine works seized the plant in late July to prevent owners from shutting it down and putting it up for sale, trade union activists took over the closed Ludwig Marx metals plant in Moscow, and factory committees at Shchetinin in Petrograd and the A. V. Bari boiler works in Moscow, among others, assumed *proprietary* as opposed to merely administrative responsibility for contracting the purchase of raw materials. Workers from the Moscow Automotive Works (AMO) even sued their owners in court in an effort to keep the plant open.

In contrast, collective actions outside the factories—on the streets, in apartment buildings, around food stores, in public places—increased during these weeks, at least in relative terms. And in these actions, too, one can perceive a shift in focus of some importance. During May and June, as we have seen, crowds commonly turned on thieves and burglars, often beating them unmercifully. Reports of attacks of this sort continued after the July Days but were far less frequent (although again, this decrease many have been caused by the process of reporting). But, at the same time, we find a substantial increase in reported food riots, attacks on hoarders, searches for food and other goods, and similar acts of protest, if that is the right word, against deteriorating material conditions, giving evidence that a significant shift in the arena of labor protest was indeed occurring. In Moscow, for example, a reduction in the daily bread ration to one-half pound (*funt*) per person appeared to touch off a series of street actions, some of which resembled in their orderliness and deference to institutions the *taxation populaire* of eighteenth-century France. On August 26, the newspaper *Russkoe Slovo* reported a crowd in the central Kitai-gorod district demanding that authorities search the house of a person suspected of hoarding; in another part of the city, a crowd examined loaded carts passing through the neighborhood, presumably for illicit transport of rationed goods. Still others searched a house for supplies of sugar and coffee; no sugar was found, but a large supply of coffee was seized and turned over to the neighborhood food supply committee. Elsewhere, sugar was found hidden in a warehouse; the 244 recovered bags

---

[56] Thus we catalog some 20 percent of factory-based protests in March and April as directed against plant owners or top management. In May and June this figure increases to 43 percent, in July and August, to almost 47 percent. Even allowing for reporting biases and other inaccuracies of the data, both the prevailing trend and the magnitude of the July–August increase seem clear.

were sealed and turned over to the authorities.[57] In other parts of the city, crowds were angrier. A riot in the suburban district of Alekseevskii ended with women threatening to beat officials from the local commissariat and its food supply section for failing to provide bread; on the same day came reports of the ransacking of a meat store.[58] The majority of riots focused on empty food shops, but militia and public officials who failed to provide for their constituents also incurred the crowd's wrath: when the Skorokhod outlet store in Moscow ran out of shoes, a crowd gathered to protest, and agitators were heard to denounce "the regime" [*vlast'*].[59]

It is impossible to determine whether (or how) these protests were related to the decreasing number of opportunities to secure gains in the workplace, or whether they were sparked solely by the absence of food. The inability of the regime to correct matters and the ineffective month-long debate in the Moscow Soviet over problems of food supply hardly raised hopes for improvements. In any case, the patterns of protest were the logical consequence of narrowing legal recourse, a sign of the rapidly diminishing appeal of "bourgeois-democratic" institutions and values. The weeks of August saw the expansion of the arena of protest from the factory to the community, from workers to entire families, and from primarily men to both men and women. During August, workers increasingly went into the streets to secure needs, rather than using "legitimate" means of protest, including strikes. This late summer period marked the emergence as targets of protest of state and soviet authorities, and the state itself, over managers and enterprises, even in incidents that were not overtly political. As conflict over issues like wages, rations, housing, and unemployment rights spilled into the streets, the extended forms of protest necessarily reflected not only the political mobilization of broader segments of the laboring population, but also the end of any shared assumptions there might have been about the authority and legitimacy of Russia's prevailing order.

Perhaps the most dramatic show of working-class protest occurred in mid-August in connection with the Moscow State Conference. As part of his effort to bolster the new coalition, Kerensky had invited representatives of "all the vital forces" of the country to discuss new programs and to consolidate national unity.[60] Leaders of the Bolshevik party in Petrograd, still wary from their July Days experience, chose not to mobilize workers in the capital against the conference, but in Moscow, working-

[57] *Russkoe Slovo*, August 26, 1917.

[58] *Russkoe Slovo*, September 2, 1917.

[59] *Trudovaia Kopeika*, September 6, 1917.

[60] Rosenberg, *Liberals*, pp. 214–18; Koenker, *Moscow Workers*, pp. 124–28; Lisetskii, *Bol'sheviki vo glave*, pp. 72–97.

class organizations narrowly approved a local Bolshevik initiative to hold a one-day political strike on the opening day of the conference. When delegates awoke on Saturday, August 12, they found the city at a standstill. Most factories and the municipal power station had ceased to operate. Waiters in luxury (but not ordinary) restaurants refused to work. Cab drivers, too, joined in the strike. From a careful sifting of the contemporary press, we have estimated that 116,000 workers and service people in Moscow participated in this strike; one socialist estimate put the figure at 400,000 in and around Moscow. Petrograd workers stayed quiet at this time, but echoes of the Moscow events reverberated throughout Russia. Around Kiev, in Moscow province, in Samara on the Volga, unspecified numbers of workers joined in the protest. An estimated 7,500 workers in volatile Kostroma province also put down their tools.[61] Five days later, 36,000 workers in Tsaritsyn also proclaimed a one-day general strike to show their opposition to the Moscow conference and the policies of its sponsors.[62]

THE KORNILOV EPISODE

The uncertainty created by these protests had a somewhat paradoxical effect on many industrialists. Increasingly, they expressed disdain for Kerensky and contempt for members of his cabinet, especially Nekrasov, the left Kadet minister of finance (and deputy minister-president), whose attitude of accommodation toward the left—"social romanticism," in the words of the PSFMO *Vestnik*—made "conciliation" an epithet in Petrograd industrialist circles.[63] Yet a sense of their own dependency on the state grew stronger. "Law and order" had to be brought forcefully to "bourgeois Russia," to use the phrase Riabushinskii himself had helped popularize at the Second Trade-Industrial Congress in early August, and a stronger regime had to be created by whatever means necessary "to enforce the law." At the same time, many industrialists demanded that Kerensky, Nekrasov, and the cabinet make every effort to provide them with additional subsidies and other support—to give aid, in effect, to the government's loudest critics.

It thus developed that at the very moment when members of the Con-

[61] Based on party archives, Lisetskii claims that the strike continued to spread in Kostroma during the next weeks, involving some 23,000 workers in all. See *Bol'sheviki vo glave*, p. 80.

[62] See Donald J. Raleigh, *Revolution on the Volga: 1917 in Saratov* (Ithaca, N.Y., 1986), p. 250.

[63] See, e.g., *Vestnik Petrogradskago Obshchestva Zavodchikov i Fabrikantov*, 27 (August 1, 1917), p. 1.

gress of Public Figures were exploring with General Kornilov and others the possibility of forcefully repressing the left, and perhaps placing Petrograd and Moscow under military rule, the directors of metal plants like the Bromley and Dinamo works in Moscow, Langenzippen and Lessner in Petrograd, and Donets Iron Fabricating in the Don region, were pressuring the Ministry of Trade and Industry for direct government assistance. At Bromley, where a long-smoldering conflict had followed workers' participation in the April demonstrations and the ouster of a number of unpopular administrators, the directors' decision to shut down outright in response to workers' wage demands in July was thwarted only by the government's granting a 2 million ruble subsidy, 1 million of which was transferred directly to management in mid-July.[64] Other loans were dispensed from the government's Special Council for Defense. Sormovo directors indicated they could not do with less than 10 million rubles.[65]

For its part, meantime, the struggling cabinet prepared to dispatch new special emissaries to South Russia and the Urals to explore the question of further assistance, and as Labor Minister Skobelev himself returned from his trip to Baku, it also determined to strengthen its own resistance to activist workers. One day after the Union of Industrial Congresses prominently denounced attempts by "ad hoc" organizations to represent workers' interests, insisting that even factory committees not elected strictly according to the government's April 23 legislation had no legal authority, Minister Skobelev himself issued a critical circular reaffirming the exclusive right of employers to hire and dismiss workers.[66] Thus the socialist minister of labor indicated that strike demands for shop-floor participation in this process were neither legitimate nor acceptable even to a socialist cabinet. Over angry protests, rejecting "with indigation the malicious slander of the Ministry of Labor," Skobelev went further, supporting owners' claims that workers should not be permitted to hold their meetings during working hours. Management in such cases had "the right to make deductions from pay for loss of working time."[67]

In fact, by demanding additional subsidies and a more active, interventionist state, leading trade-industrial figures like Bachmanov, the head of the PSFMO, were cultivating an approach to solving Russia's crisis that could (and soon would, of course) be used against their own interests.

---

[64] *Ekonomicheskoe polozhenie*, pt. 1, pp. 392, 597.

[65] Ibid., pp. 354, 361, 362, 399.

[66] V. L. Meller and A. M. Pankratova, eds. *Rabochee dvizhenie v 1917 godu* (Moscow and Leningrad, 1926), p. 112. Skobelev's circular is in *Vestnik Vremennago Pravitel'stva*, August 22, 1917, republished in Browder and Kerensky, eds., *The Russian Provisional Government*, vol. 2, p. 721–22.

[67] *Ekonomicheskoe polozhenie*, pt. 1, p. 558.

Lenin was thus not alone in reconsidering the relationship between state and revolution at this moment; the industrialists' own efforts at using the state may well have strengthened the Bolsheviks' appeal to do the same.

But if Bromley directors and others felt their choices were limited in August, so, of course, did Russia's workers. A deteriorating economy, rising prices, and threatening food shortages increased the necessity for higher wages and benefits just as they were becoming significantly more difficult to obtain. Faltering collective contract negotiations weakened hopes that even a strong trade union movement could adequately protect labor interests: the stronger the movement grew, the more management resisted. And the apparent identification of soviet leaders like Skobelev with the industrialists' own interests drastically undermined the prestige and authority of socialist moderates. Social polarization was intensifying in revolutionary Russia not simply as a result of politics or ideology, but as the logical outcome of increasingly intractable relations between management and labor.

In these circumstances, and in no small measure as a result of the encouragement given him implicitly and explicitly by the "public men," General Lavr Kornilov prepared to march on Petrograd. A. I. Putilov and other Petrograd bankers were ready with funds; Bachmanov and other industrialists stood by to applaud his suppression of "commissars and committees," and perhaps the government itself.[68] The mutiny began on August 26, seven days after Russian troops abandoned Riga to the Germans, six days after elections for a new city duma in Petrograd saw the Bolsheviks outpoll the Kadets by almost 70,000 votes. Although Kornilov's intentions were not clearly expressed ("the preservation of Great Russia!" and an end to the "betrayal of Russia into the hands of her ancient enemy, the German race"), there was little doubt in anyone's mind, including Kerensky's, about what military rule would mean.

At first, moreover, Kornilov's march on the capital seemed to meet little resistance. According to Kerensky himself on August 27, the outlook was "hopeless." Miliukov and the Kadets themselves became alarmed that the unexpected harshness of the rupture between Kerensky and his rebellious general would plunge Russia into civil war.[69] On August 28, they tried to mediate the conflict themselves, although it soon became clear that their efforts were not needed. It proved relatively simple for the Petrograd Soviet to mobilize armed workers in defense of the capital and to stop Kor-

[68] The literature on the Kornilov mutiny is vast, but see especially the memoirs of A. I. Putilov, and P. N. Finisov in *Posledniia Novosti* (Paris), January 20, 24, February 27, and March 6, 1937, excerpted in Browder and Kerensky, eds. *Russian Provisional Government*, vol. 3, pp. 1526–43.

[69] See the discussion in Rosenberg, *Liberals*, pp. 229–33.

nilov's troops along the rail lines; demoralized and confused, they readily gave up. Kornilov himself was arrested. A histrionic Kerensky, still Supreme Commander but virtually devoid of support among Petrograd workers and industrialists alike, announced the formation of a five-man Directory to attempt, again, to preserve Russian political democracy and bring the country to a Constituent Assembly. In the mutiny's aftermath, however, the battle lines of industrial conflict became those of the country at large.

9

. . . .

SOCIAL POLARIZATION

AND THE CHANGING CHARACTER OF

STRIKES IN THE FALL

The dramatic escalation of social conflict in the aftermath of the Kornilov mutiny is well known. If it was easy for Kerensky and the Soviet leadership to arm and mobilize Petrograd workers in defense of the revolution, it now proved nearly impossible to reverse the step and have workers turn in their arms. Kerensky's order to dissolve the various committees and organizations formed to fight counterrevolution was ignored. By September 3, the Central Council of Factory Committees reported there were as many as 25,000 armed factory militiamen in Petrograd.[1] Here and elsewhere, particularly in garrison towns of the northern military district, a number of suspected Kornilov supporters were lynched. *Rabochaia Gazeta*, in its words, "sounded the alarm":

> The Kornilov affair has revived once again the painful heritage of the tsarist regime . . . the undying echo of immemorial distrust toward the master now called "bourgeois." All the injustices of former years, a dark fear of return to the hated past, a panicky fear of treasonous and counterrevolutionary intrigues from everywhere, and especially from above—all of this has flared up in the aftermath of Kornilov with unprecedented force.[2]

Rabochaia Gazeta's Menshevik editors were writing about the army and the Baltic fleet, but their language suggested how far their concerns extended. Both Moscow and Petrograd Soviets were now in Bolshevik hands, the very premises of democratic governance under attack.

---

[1] The estimate was published in *Izvestiia* (Petrograd), September 5, 1917, Kerensky's order in *Vestnik Vremennago Pravitel'stva*, September 3, 1917. See the discussion in Rex A. Wade, *Red Guards and Workers' Militias in the Russian Revolution* (Stanford, Calif., 1984), pp. 157–64; V. I. Startsev, *Ocherki po istorii Petrogradskoi krasnoi gvardii i rabochei militsii (mart 1917–aprel' 1918 godov)* (Moscow and Leningrad, 1965), pp. 162–64.

[2] *Rabochaia Gazeta*, September 12, 1917.

Well-known, too, is the way the mutiny revealed the weaknesses of both army and state, the fundamental structures of bourgeois-democratic political control. For tens of thousands of industrial workers in Petrograd, Kornilov's attempted march on the capital was rightly understood as a frontal attack on their own opportunities for freedom and welfare, even if in the eyes of many labor leaders themselves the line between "freedom" and "industrial anarchy" was becoming increasingly blurred. Outlawing strikes was reported to be an essential part of Kornilov's program.[3] "Restoring order" in the capital surely meant repression. No episode of the entire revolutionary period, in fact, did more to cultivate political consciousness or turn rank-and-file workers in favor of a radical socialist state.

A new coalition was not organized until September 25, after the start of a nationwide rail strike. For most of September the country was under a "dictatorship of the democracy," as the Menshevik B. O. Bogdanov put it at a Soviet Executive Committee meeting on September 1. A temporary ruling directory emerged in the aftermath of the mutiny, led by Prime Minister Kerensky, Minister of Foreign Affairs M. I. Tereshchenko, the ministers of war and the navy, A. I. Verkhovskii and D. V. Verderevskii, and the Menshevik A. M. Nikitin, who held Tsereteli's former post of minister of post and telegraph, and who soon assumed control of the Interior Ministry, officially responsible for the police.[4] Few believed, however, that this Council of Five was capable of governing effectively. Even Tsereteli, while continuing to insist on the practical and moral necessity of a coalition, was ready to concede that "if it turns out there is not a single vital force in the country apart from ours, we will take full power into our hands."[5] Meantime, the Bolsheviks' growing strength was obvious. At the Democratic Conference, a national meeting of public organizations convened by the Soviet Central Executive Committee on September 14, a vote in favor of coalition passed by only the slimmest of margins.[6] One week later, district duma elections in Moscow produced a substantial Bolshevik majority citywide.[7]

[3] A. Il'in-Zhenevskii, "Neudavshiisia Bonapart," in *Miatezh Kornilova. Iz belykh memuarov* (Leningrad, 1928), p. 11; P. N. Miliukov, *Istoriia vtoroi Russkoi revoliutsii* (Sofia, 1921), vol. 1, vyp. 2, p. 120; A. M. Lisetskii, "Ob otnoshenii bloka kontrrevoliutsionnykh sil k zabastovochnomu dvizheniiu proletariata Rossii (mart–oktiabr' 1917 goda)," *Uchenye Zapiski Kishinevskogo Gosudarstvennogo Universiteta* 95 (1968), p. 7.

[4] See *Izvestiia* (Petrograd), September 2, 3, 1917.

[5] Ibid.

[6] *Izvestiia* (Petrograd), September 20, 1917. The vote was 766 in favor of coalition, 688 against, with 38 abstentions.

[7] See the discussions in Diane Koenker, *Moscow Workers and the 1917 Revolution* (Princeton, N.J., 1981), especially pp. 133–42, 208–27; William G. Rosenberg, *Liberals in the Russian Revolution* (Princeton, N.J., 1974), chap. 7.

General Kornilov's ignominious and humiliating failure also left his supporters in the Petrograd and Moscow industrial communities anxious and exposed. It was now most unlikely that real benefits could come from the efforts of Riabushinskii and others to defend bourgeois interests by strengthening their political ties with the Kadets or other nonsocialist parties. Many suspected the worst: that *any* efforts in this direction would only increase conflict and prove utterly futile. "Life presses us closer to politics," A. A. Bachmanov, the president of the PSFMO council, told his colleagues on September 5, but there were no longer any means to realize effectively "the wishes and needs of the industrial class."[8] With the Germans' offensive against Riga, Russia's rapidly deteriorating economy, the initiation of contingency plans to evacuate major Petrograd plants, and the collapse once again of the governing coalition, tensions increased everywhere: between peasants and landlords in the countryside, between radicals and moderates in the meeting chambers of local dumas and soviets, and particularly between rulers and ruled in the factories. Literally and figuratively, the building of barricades had begun.

Behind them was a pervasive uncertainty, as much a concern to men and women worried that their factory gates would be locked as it was to industrialists, merchants, and bankers anxious to salvage their investments and their way of life. By the end of the summer, production even in favored defense industries had fallen dramatically, in some cases to as little as 60 percent of February levels. Supply shortages in textiles were relieved only by the annual industry holiday, which came in August, but reserves of fuel and other essential goods remained precarious, and no one thought the situation would soon improve. The supply of foodstuffs was no more plentiful. According to a report sent to the Special Council on Transport early in August, freight shipments on the railroads were off more than 244,000 cars in July, compared to 1916; more than 25 percent of the country's locomotives were out of service, some 5,180 "undergoing repair," 1,705 more than in 1916. In Moscow, somewhat better supplied than Petrograd, food prices increased on the average more than 20 percent between August and September, and were up 62 percent from May. The jump in Petrograd was even steeper.[9]

Among ordinary workers the conviction was also growing that deprivation was not equitably shared. In many places one could hear along

---

[8] *Ekonomicheskoe polozhenie Rossii nakanune velikoi oktiabr'skoi sotsialisticheskoi revoliutsii. Dokumenty i materialy*, 3 pts. (Moscow and Leningrad, 1957–67), vol. 1, p. 205.

[9] *Ekonomicheskoe polozhenie*, pt. 2, pp. 74–79, 90, 163, 244–46; *Statistika Truda*, 1 (1918), pp. 10–11. See also the discussion in Z. V. Stepanov, *Rabochie Petrograda v period podgotovki i provedeniia oktiabr'skogo vooruzhennogo vosstaniia* (Moscow and Leningrad, 1965), pp. 142–44, 182–206; S. A. Smith, *Red Petrograd: Revolution in the Factories, 1917–1918* (Cambridge, 1983), pp. 168–71; and Koenker, *Moscow Workers*, pp. 251–52.

with complaints about inadequate food and provisions the demand that luxury restaurants and cinemas be closed, and as Kornilov had insisted on the death penalty for deserters, some called angrily for equally harsh punishments for speculators and hoarders.[10] Popular rage over the gap between privilege and need was growing even faster than the widening gulf itself.

THE CHANGING CHARACTER OF STRIKES

In these circumstances, the character of labor protests changed. Relatively few work stoppages occurred in the immediate aftermath of the Kornilov mutiny, but in mid-September a new wave of strikes broke out across Russia, more intense and more powerful than any the country had seen since before the war, and lasting until the Bolshevik takeover on October 25. What was most significant about this third cluster of strikes, however, was not so much the frequencies involved, which were roughly comparable to those in the spring and summer clusters, but its context and scope. The extremely difficult circumstances in which most workers now found themselves should ordinarily have discouraged strikes, since any halt in production jeopardized jobs and livelihoods.[11] Instead, industrial and nonindustrial workers alike struck in record numbers between the middle of September and October 25. By our estimates, which are based on only 68 percent of the strikes in our file, more than 1,200,000 workers began strikes in this period, and 200,000 to 300,000 workers remained off the job in strikes begun in August and earlier. From an average size of

[10] See, for example, *Izvestiia* (Moscow), supplement to no. 181 (Stenogram of the Soviet plenum, August 26, 1917); and *Sotsial Demokrat*, October 6, 1917.

[11] A consistent relationship between economic circumstances and strikes has not, however, been demonstrated in the literature. The point has been made with respect to the American context by Albert Rees, "Industrial Conflict and Business Fluctuations," *Journal of Political Economy* 60 (1952), pp. 371–82, and Andrew R. Weintraub, "Prosperity versus Strikes: An Empirical Approach," *Industrial and Labor Relations Review* 19 (1965–66), pp. 231–38, which challenges Theodore Levitt, "Prosperity versus Strikes," *Industrial and Labor Relations Review* 6 (1952–53), pp. 220–26. Dale Yoder, "Economic Change and Industrial Unrest in the United States," *Journal of Political Economy* 48 (1940), pp. 222–37, finds correlations, but no simple "parallelism." See also the discussion by Michael Shalev, "Trade Unionism and Economic Analysis: The Case of Industrial Conflict," *Journal of Labor Research* 1, no. 1 (1980), pp. 133–73. Orley Ashenfelter and George E. Johnson, "Bargaining Theory, Trade Unions, and Industrial Strike Activity," *American Economic Review* 59 (1969), pp. 35–49, argue that workers' expectations about improvements in their welfare are more important determinants of strikes than material conditions themselves. But see James E. Cronin, "Theories of Strikes: Why Can't They Explain the British Experience?" *Journal of Social History* 12, no. 2 (1978–79), pp. 194–218, for a thorough critique of this and other theories of strikes.

300 strikers in April and 640 in May, strikes rose to an average of almost 9,800 for all of September and 5,100 for October.[12] The sheer magnitude of the fall strike cluster measured in numbers of strikers suggests the determination of workers throughout Russia to effect a radical change in workplace relations, however this affected the economy and the regime.

Strikes also spread geographically during these weeks, but what was even more important in political terms was the renewal of activity among industrial workers in and around Petrograd, particularly in contrast to the summer. Strikes became more frequent in Petrograd, Moscow, and South Russia, especially in the Donets basin and Baku, where the hopes of oil and mine workers for negotiated settlements were clearly exhausted. Petrograd's share of all strikes grew from less than 6 percent in the summer to 14 percent; Moscow's, from 10 percent to 13 percent. In terms of numbers of strikers, the change in Petrograd was even more significant: a 14-fold increase, from little more than 3,300 workers on strike between the end of July and the Kornilov mutiny, to at least 46,000 strikers between and the October revolution. This estimate is based, moreover, on only 61 percent of the strikes we know occurred in the capital during these last weeks of the Provisional regime; the actual number of strikers was even larger. These Petrograd numbers were dwarfed by the 300,000 strikers in Ivanovo-Kineshma (Moscow Industrial Region) and by 700,000 railway strikers in this period, but the increase in strikes and strikers in the capital reflected nonetheless a significant renewal of energy in the historic center of strike activism.

At the same time, the evidence also indicates that new strikes in the fall came increasingly from groups of industrial workers that had been relatively less active in the spring and summer, measured by our index of strike propensity. As tables 9.1 and 9.2 show, wood and textile workers were much more inclined to initiate new strikes in September and October than earlier. If one recognizes that metalworkers dominated spring strikes (in relative terms), and leather workers (animal products) dominated in the summer, the pattern indicated in table 9.2 is largely one of hitherto less strike-prone industries joining their more active comrades.

Consistent with this, the evidence also suggests that fewer skilled workers were now initiating strikes, in contrast to the spring and summer, and that higher numbers of less-skilled workers were participating in strikes for the first time. This shift in the composition of strikers reflected the involvement of large numbers of Ivanovo and Kineshma textile workers

---

[12] The average size of strikes was of course swollen by the single large railway strike in September, with 700,000 workers out, and the October textile strike in Ivanovo-Voznesensk, with 300,000 workers involved. But the median size of strikes, a measure that better adjusts for these outliers, also doubled from 100 strikers in July to 200 strikers in October.

TABLE 9.1
Strikes and Strikers in the Fall by Industry
(Single-Industry Strikes Only)

Industry	Number of Strikes	Minimum Number of Enterprises Involved[a]	Estimated Number of Strikers[b]	Strike Propensity
Textiles	13	170	309,370	2.00
Wood and wood products	10	85	33,052	1.77
Metals	43	143	80,074	.68
Paper and printing	16	249	9,772	.56
Animal products (leather)	6	7	1,335	.09
Food products	17	45	2,841	.04
Chemicals	4	5	640	.02
Minerals	2	2	215	.01

[a] Minimum estimates based on 69% of strikes in textiles, 90% in wood, 81% in metals, 88% in paper and printing, 67% in animal products, 76% in food products, 75% in chemicals, and 50% in minerals.

[b] Minimum estimates based on fragmentary factory inspector reports and accounts from other sources.

as first-time strikers in October, but strikes among such groups as sawmill workers, tobacco workers, and miners increased as well. In contrast, strikes among electrical machine apparatus employees, whose skill levels were very high, decreased somewhat, as they did among shoemakers, jewelry makers, and more skilled branches of the clothing industry, such as tailoring.

At the same time, the scale of strikes continued to increase, as smaller work stoppages gave way to larger actions. Some 25 percent of all strikes we have recorded for October took place in plants or production units with more than 1,000 employees. Strikes involving more than one enterprise became even more frequent in the fall than in the summer: while a little more than half of all strikes (56 percent) continued in the fall to take place in individual enterprises, a minimum of 728 enterprises were involved in the 207 strikes in this period. Strikes involving more than one enterprise now encompassed more than 90 percent of all industrial work-

TABLE 9.2
Industrial Strike Propensities by Cluster
(Single-Industry Strikes Only)

Industry	Spring Propensity	Summer Propensity	Fall Propensity
Minerals	.04	.05	.01
Metals	3.20	.38	.68
Wood and wood products	.30	.10	1.77
Chemicals	.09	2.09	.02
Food products	.04	.18	.04
Animal products (leather)	.76	19.56	.09
Textiles	.22	.22	2.00
Paper and printing	.26	.56	.56

ers on strike and almost 95 percent of strikers from all sectors! From September 16 until October 25, some 27 percent of all strikes were reported as citywide, in contrast to 20 percent in the summer cluster and 17 percent in the spring. Strikes embracing entire provinces or regions, like the October textile strike, along with national strikes on the railways and against the Singer sewing machine company, accounted for only 1.4 percent of all strikes in the fall, but involved as many as a million workers.

STRIKE DEMANDS AND SOCIAL POLARIZATION

As we have indicated in chapter 2, the most common group of demands throughout the revolutionary period as a whole was for some form of wage relief: in every month between February and October, wage demands were the most frequently declared objective of strikes and strikers (even if accompanied, of course, by others). In the aggregate, the intensity of wage demands over time was remarkably constant. As figure 9.1 shows, nearly the same number of wage strikes occurred before July as after. Demands for higher wage levels emanated from the largest group of strikers in every month of the revolutionary period except August, according to the data in our file.

The fall strike cluster, however, saw a dramatic escalation of the total number of strikers seeking wage relief, a tendency which reached a climax in October. During the fall cluster of strikes, 1.2 million workers included wage demands as part of their package of grievances: these economic de-

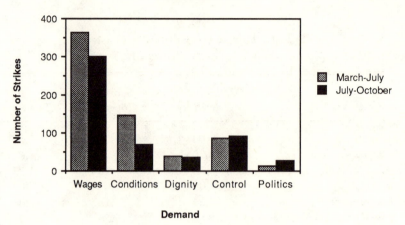

Figure 9.1 Strikes by Demands, March–July, July–October, 1917

mands figured in two-thirds of all strikes and involved 99 percent of all known strikers. Although the number of strikes for which we know the size of the strike force declined in September and October, this indication of near-unanimity represents a doubling of the share of wage demands in economic strikes from the first period of activism in the spring.

The sharp increase in the number of wage strikers can be explained in part by its close correlation with rising prices. As Table 9.3 shows, the price index for Russia as a whole continued to rise in August, September, and October, as it had earlier (see chapter 5), but the month with the sharpest increase in this period, October, saw the greatest share by far of wage strikers.

TABLE 9.3
Economic Demands and Inflation, July–October, 1917

	Minimum Estimated Number of Strikers[a]	Percent of Strikers Making Economic Demands	Percent Change in Price Index
July	384,560	26	16
August	379,480	57	2
September	965,000	83	9
October	441,450	97	38

SOURCE: See table 5.5.

[a] Minimum estimates based on reports as follows: July, 75% of strikes; August, 76%; September, 72%; October, 63%.

The jump in prices during October must have particularly angered textile workers, who had not struck in significant numbers since just after the fall of the tsar, but whose wages remained quite depressed, as they had been throughout the war. The jump followed a short period of relatively stable wartime inflation and marked a sharp change from 1916, when the traditionally low price levels of August and September (depressed by the annual harvest) had been generally maintained through the fall. As table 9.3 indicates, the rate of increase leaped in 1917 from 2 percent in August to 9 percent in September, and 38 percent in October, the largest increment of the entire revolutionary period.[13]

This return to the springtime pattern of rapid inflation adds a critical political dimension to the predominance of wage strikes in the fall. To many, the resumption of the inflationary spiral seemed directly related to the inability, or in the view of some, the unwillingness of Kerensky and his colleagues to hold down prices. The Provisional Government itself may thus have assumed as much culpability for deteriorating economic circumstances as plant owners in many workers' eyes, even if explicit political demands were largely absent from the strikers' bills of particulars. It is not surprising, then, that strikes in the fall were directed far more than in the spring or summer against state and municipal enterprises. Our data suggest a more than threefold increase in strikes in state-owned plants in comparison with the spring, and a doubling of strikes against municipal authorities.

The growth in the share of strikers making wage demands cannot therefore be seen as a purely economic phenomenon, as a manifestation of the paradigm of routine labor-management relations. And yet, even by October, such routine elements remained; not all of the predominance of economic strikes need or should be explained in terms of the concurrent political crisis, overwhelming though it was. Wage strikes may have increased in frequency toward the end of the summer in part because workers believed they might be more effective than strikes over other issues. Strikes with wage components were shorter, on average, than strikes including other kinds of demands, suggesting that employers dealt more readily on wage demands than on other issues, something workers undoubtedly knew from past experience.[14]

[13] Price indices are from M. P. Kokhn, *Russkie indektsy tsen* (Moscow, 1926), p. 10. The index is constructed from the market basket of goods consumed by an average unskilled worker as of 1918 (ibid., pp. 23–26). These figures are for all industrial workers in Russia, but the rate of change follows closely the prices reported for Moscow alone. (See, however, Koenker, *Moscow Workers*, p. 130n, for a discussion of discrepancies.)

[14] The differences are small but consistent: the median length of strikes including wage demands was six days, and four days when wage demands were the only issue involved; the median length of strikes about work conditions was seven days, strikes about control eight days, and strikes about dignity ten days.

The question is complicated, however. Politics and economics were by now inextricably intertwined for workers on all levels, even if strikes reflected one or another goal or interest. Although the turn toward wage strikes may thus have reflected a growing maturity on the workers' part about strikes, indicating that they now recognized that the system responded more quickly to wage demands than to other kinds of challenge, their very participation in strikes on any issue in the late summer and fall of 1917 contributed simultaneously to escalating political conflict. A great proportion of striking workers in October, for example, came from the textile plants in Vladimir, Kostroma, and other towns of the Central Industrial Region. Since only some 55,000 textilists struck before October by our estimates, almost all strikers in October had to be participating in the movement for the first time, at least for the revolutionary period. Entering the strike arena some seven months after overthrow of the tsar, these textilists undoubtedly demanded higher wages in part because their incomes were miserably low, in part because prices were rising sharply, and in part because wage demands were likely to be more acceptable to their adversaries in the corridors of the Moscow stock exchange. But while textile workers struck over economic conditions and met daily at their factories to hear about the progress of the strike, they also heard speaker after speaker lecture them about the mounting political crisis. Indeed, the parallel economic and political crises were constantly linked in the official proclamations and appeals of their own union.[15]

It is therefore essential to look at the rest of the picture drawn by the scope of strike demands. In the entire period from July 7 to October 25, as figure 9.2 indicates, the number of workers making all types of demands except political ones increased substantially in comparison to the first half of the year. In the fall cluster of activity, all types of demands increased, even in comparison with midsummer. The share of strikers demanding better conditions more than doubled from the summer, as did the share of strikers making demands specifically related to job control. Over 90 percent of all strikers addressed such issues in the fall cluster.[16] Demands challenging managerial authority also followed this pattern, as table 9.4 makes clear. In both September and October, nine out of every

[15] S. K. Klimokhin, ed., *Kratkaia istoriia stachki tekstil'shchikov Ivanovo-Kineshemskoi promyshlennoi oblasti* (Kineshma, 1918).

[16] The number of strikes involving each issue increased more modestly. Strikes over factory conditions actually declined from 26 percent of all strikes in the spring to 16 percent in the fall. Strikes over job control rose slightly from 17 percent of all strikes in the spring cluster to 25 percent in the fall. But given the tremendous growth in the size of strikes in the fall, it makes more sense to rely on the share of strikers than of strikes in order to understand the changing complexion of workers' demands.

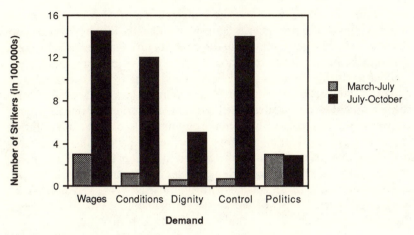

Figure 9.2 Strikers by Demands, March–July, July–October, 1917

ten strikers not only demanded higher wages, but also sought to shift the balance of power within the enterprise.

The demand that workers make decisions about hiring and firing, which engaged one-third of all strikers in the midsummer cluster, continued to figure prominently in strike protests. Over 350,000 striking workers in the fall, just about 30 percent of all strikers, included this single demand in their strikes. Adding this number to the 110,000 striking Mos-

TABLE 9.4

Strike Demands Challenging Managerial Authority by Month

	Number of Strikes	Number of Strikers[a]	Percent of Month's Strikers
March	27	8,530	20
April	35	5,840	33
May	81	67,680	74
June	51	61,970	54
July	32	12,870	3
August	35	170,570	45
September	47	940,830	97
October	36	401,870	91

[a] Minimum estimates based on reports as follows: March, 80% of strikes; April, 77%; May, 75%; June, 72%; July, 75%; August, 76%; September, 72%; October, 63%.

cow leather workers, whose strike remained unsettled precisely on account of this issue, produces a figure that indicates just how bitter and
contentious strike activism was in the weeks before October 25. Workers
demanded not just what they hoped they could win. Impossibly, they
wanted it all: higher wages and better conditions from an economy in
collapse, and workplace control from a managerial class that now refused
to yield any of its perquisites. The logic that led workers to this maximalist position followed directly from the cumulative economic and political
experience of the preceding months. Nonetheless, for socialist moderates
reading about strike demands, the cumulative effect may well have created the impression that workers themselves had become too maximalist
and too irrational to be trusted with political power. Even Bolsheviks
feared that some groups of workers were demanding more in October
than any regime, their own included, could possibly provide.

Management Reactions and the Role of the State

As one might expect in these circumstances, industrialists, manufacturers,
even restaurant owners and other service sector employers dug in their
heels even further after the Kornilov fiasco and resisted new concessions,
especially in Moscow and Petrograd. Although the number of strikes for
which we have definite information is small, our data suggest that the
number of outright victories for workers in the two capitals was lower in
October than in any other month of the year, and may have fallen from
approximately 69 percent of all strikes in the spring to fewer than 25
percent between mid-September and October 25.[17] (For strikes settled at
least partially in the workers' favor, however, the rate increased from 37
percent in the spring to almost 69 percent, although again, frequencies
are small.) The decline in successful wage strikes was especially sharp,
from 55 percent in May to 30 percent in October. For the country at
large, the rate for strikes at least partially won by workers also plum-
meted in the fall, from approximately 40 percent in the summer to around
24 percent, substantially lower than in the spring, when more than one-
third of all strikes were reported as workers' victories.

Negotiations over collective wage agreements, some of which had been
going on for a number of weeks, also fell victim to the post-Kornilov
reaction. One of the most important of these, between metalists and the
PSFMO, had been signed in Petrograd on August 7 after the Ministry of
Labor made the agreement binding on employers. Many assumed this

---

[17] We have definite information on outcomes for only 25 strikes that began in Moscow
and Petrograd in September and October, in contrast to data on 59 strikes in May and June.

accord would become the model for comparable agreements elsewhere, despite its generally unfavorable terms for unskilled workers. For a time, it had brought a modicum of peace between employers and most metalists in Petrograd, at least on the wage issue. In other localities, however, where wage scales were lower than the capital, what occurred was just the opposite: the agreement led to new pressure for higher wages, and consequently, to stout resistance from employers. Metalists in the Kiev and Kharkov regions in particular demanded comparable terms. The result was a broad-based rejection among industrialists of the very notion of collective wage accords.

Thus Kiev metalists left their jobs in September when management negotiators refused to accept Petrograd standards, breaking off two months of discussions. The metalworking section of the MSFMO not only also resisted a collective contract, but warned members not to enter into any individual settlements until the matter was settled by the courts.[18] In the Donbass, mine owners informed the Provisional regime that they would close down entirely if workers would not agree on "reasonable," *regional* wage rates, and demanded state subsidies to support any increases. Calls were also heard from these and other quarters for government aid in suppressing worker protests. The Main Economic Committee appointed a special commissar, Vice-Minister of Trade and Industry A. S. Orlov, to negotiate in the Don, and although he apparently agreed to subsidize wage increases, no collective settlement was reached and strikes continued.[19]

The MSFMO had enormous difficulty as well persuading its members to accept a collective wage agreement worked out with the union of woodworkers, so much so, in fact, that a woodworkers' strike there extended past the Bolsheviks' coming to power. In this case, representatives of heavy industrial enterprises with large numbers of employed woodworkers accepted the agreement, but representatives from the small and medium-size plants refused, insisting they had no "authority" to do so.[20] In Petrograd, meantime, PSFMO leaders refused to accept a collective agreement reached between printers and representatives of the typographical section of the society, insisting that those who had signed the accord "exceeded their powers."[21] And in Baku, the oil companies refused after the Kornilov uprising to sign any collective agreement at all, despite the pressure exerted earlier in August by Skobelev on his special mission to the

[18] *Ekonomicheskoe polozhenie*, pt. 1, p. 535.

[19] S. Strel'bitskii, "Na zare profdvizheniia gorniakov," *Letopis' Revoliutsii* 5–6 (1927), pp. 340–51.

[20] *Rabochaia Gazeta*, October 24, 1917.

[21] Stepanov, *Rabochie Petrograda*, p. 87.

region. Only after some 55,000 oil workers went on strike on September 27 did Baku industrialists agree reluctantly to a contract.[22]

The reasons for these hardening attitudes in the business community are hardly difficult to discern. Industrialists and businessmen understood very well that the current of events in September threatened the basic principles on which industry and commerce were structured under the Provisional regime, and as they had often done in the past, they now turned increasingly for help to the state. September and October consequently witnessed increasing government involvement in management-labor relations and, with important consequences for workers, a growing interdependence between the state's needs and those of major industrial enterprises, particularly those involved in military production.

This interdependence found expression, as we know, even before the Kornilov revolt. It was particularly well evidenced in the efforts of Labor Minister Skobelev to shore up managerial authority in August with his notorious circular, "Concerning Worker Interference in Hiring and Firing," which reflected precisely management's position.[23] In early September, however, an increasing number of industrialists' groups sought more active state intervention, both to settle conflicts with workers and to provide other forms of direct support. Cotton cloth manufacturers circularized their colleagues in the Moscow Stock Exchange Committee on September 15 on the urgent need to transfer all matters concerning raw materials and food supplies to the hands of government specialists. They also called on the state to take "the most energetic measures" to restore transport, and to reconstruct immediately the state's tax and financial system, castigating past policies of labor and government leaders both as "disastrous": if the government "was genuinely imbued with a wish for the nation's welfare, victory over the enemy, and the establishment, even minimally, of normal order in the country," it had to take forceful action.[24] Similar appeals came from Kievan industrialists, who demanded help from Petrograd to end the metalists' strike there by means of guaranteed advances on present and future orders, as well as additional state purchases. Workers in any event had to be forced back to their jobs.[25]

In September, spokesmen for the business community also demanded a

[22] A. N. Guliev, "Bor'ba Bakinskogo proletariata za kollektivnyi dogovor vesnoi i letom 1917 goda," in *Velikii oktiabr' i bor'ba za sovetskuiu vlast' v Azerbaidzhane* (Baku, 1958), p. 132; *Rabochii Put'*, October 11, 1917.

[23] *Vestnik Vremennago Pravitel'stva*, August 22, 1917.

[24] *Ekonomicheskoe polozhenie*, pt. 1, pp. 209–11.

[25] The strike ended quickly only when the Labor Ministry in effect used the Petrograd model to impose a settlement. See *Materialy po izucheniiu istorii professional'nogo dvizheniia na Ukraine* (Kharkov, n.d.), p. 158.

lengthened workday in all industrial branches and called for new laws to restore factory discipline. The cotton cloth manufacturers even urged the immediate establishment in all localities of "authoritative administration and judicial organs" legally empowered to put an end to the "anarchistic interference of all sorts of private, class-oriented, and political organizations in the economic life of the country."[26] Yet as many on the shop floor recognized, it made little sense to abolish the eight-hour working day when shortages of raw materials made increased production unlikely, and when employers claimed they lacked the means to pay a higher wage bill. Also, barring foreign assistance, state finances could only be improved with higher taxes on industry and commerce, which almost all industrialists also deemed impossible. And "victory over the enemy," as virtually every thinking person in Moscow and Petrograd came to realize in September, was probably the *least* likely means to a rapid peace, even if an independent settlement with Germany was "unthinkable." Such contradictions, however, only bespoke the enormous degree of urgency in the industrialists' position in September and October, and the reasons why, paradoxically, they now turned increasingly toward the state as the last best means of defending private enterprise.

Views similar to those of the Moscow cotton cloth manufacturers were heard everywhere in the fall, especially in the government's own Main Economic Committee, now headed by the prominent Moscow textile magnate and president of the Moscow Stock Exchange Committee, S. N. Tret'iakov. In September, the Main Committee called for new legislation to control factory closings, even to *prohibit* employers in defense-related industries from shutting their doors or discharging their workers. In the Committee's view, an "extreme tension" now affected management-labor relations: workers' excesses against factory administrators, which lay "at the heart of economic destruction and which prolonged the catastrophic fall in the productivity of labor," were "taking on an especially ominous [*zloveshchii*] character and threatening to eliminate the last hope of saving the country from anarchy and economic bankruptcy." This, in turn, was forcing "terrorized employers," who were quite inclined earlier to concessions, "[to swing] to the opposite extreme: the massive closing of enterprises without regard for how harmful this [was] for the needs of the nation's defense."[27] Similar views were expressed in September by the Special Council for Defense.[28]

It is thus hardly surprising that state agencies attempted to play a more

[26] *Ekonomicheskoe polozhenie*, pt. 1, pp. 209–11.
[27] Ibid., pp. 420–21.
[28] Ibid., p. 563.

active role in settling labor disputes in September and October, especially in plants involved in military production, although the material has not been available to us to determine to what extent. The Special Council for Defense itself intervened at the Sormovo works, Dinamo, the Moscow Metal Works (Guzhon), and elsewhere, heading off strikes and arranging in some cases for state loans or advances on purchases sufficiently large to ward off further wage demands. In return for wage concessions, settlements in these cases often secured a formal reaffirmation of managerial rights for factory administrators and prohibited workers from interfering in plant administration. Symbolically, they also frequently restricted the role of conciliation boards to hear conflicts over hiring and firing, which were similarly reaffirmed as managerial prerogatives.[29] While relieving some immediate financial pressures, settlements of this sort also thus defined even more sharply the lines of struggle over factory control, allowing managers and plant owners to withdraw from earlier, more accommodating positions behind a new, tougher resistance, even to established conciliation mechanisms. By the end of September, in fact, factory conciliation boards everywhere had lost virtually all of their earlier authority. The employers' associations in Petrograd had become "completely indifferent" to their operations; even the Central Conciliation Board in Petrograd, whose decisions had earlier set industry standards, virtually ceased functioning in mid-September because employers refused to send their representatives.[30]

The growing estrangement between capital and labor also showed itself clearly in increasing management refusal to honor past agreements. The issue was of some concern earlier, particularly in May, but during all other months from March through September, demands that prior agreements be honored—secondary demands—were made by fewer than one percent of all strikers. By the fall, many workers clearly thought that their employers were no longer bargaining in good faith, that they would not abide by agreements already made, and that negotiations were no longer taking place within a system of industrial relations that assumed equality on both sides. This was a major issue in the massive textile strike in October, but it emerged in virtually every other industrial branch as well. Strikes initiated to force management to carry out previous agreements may have occurred as much as three times more frequently in the fall than the spring. The very fact of these demands, and just as important if not more so, their reports in the press, certainly contributed to a growing

[29] Ibid., pp. 562–63.

[30] N. Dmitriev, "Primiritel'nye kamery v 1917 godu," in *Professional'noe dvizhenie v Petrograde v 1917 godu*, ed. A. Anskii (Leningrad, 1928), pp. 907–97. See also *Ekonomicheskoe polozhenie*, pt. 1, p. 532.

notion in the factories that the gulf between workers and owners could not be bridged.

Some employers obviously saw the issues in terms of inability to honor contracts rather than refusal to do so. But throughout 1917, Don industrialists, the PSFMO, and others blamed workers sharply for Russia's deteriorating economic circumstances. Many genuinely believed workers' demands were excessive, making production unprofitable. To some, this justified nullifying or ignoring existing contracts. In turn, when workers went on strike in response to management abrogation of agreements—as over 300,000 textile workers did in October—this may have only reinforced management's sense that those on the shop floor could not be equal partners in the defense of Russia's best interests, or even, for that matter, of their own. The system of cooperative bourgeois industrial relations that had existed so briefly in Russia in 1917 had, in many places, almost completely broken down.

PERCEPTIONS AND SOCIAL REALITIES ON THE EVE OF OCTOBER

In these circumstances, the state and the business community became increasingly identified with each other, despite Kerensky's and others' commitment to a socialist program. It also became extremely difficult for factory committee members or trade union activists to defend the existing order, whatever their personal politics. To resist rank-and-file pressure was to invite recall and replacement; to yield was to lend credibility to the Bolsheviks. As we have seen, trade unions and factory committees did not support strike actions in every instance throughout 1917. Just as with lockouts, there was a tendency in the spring for these organizations to try to contain spontaneous strikes in order, as the metalist union leadership in Kharkov expressed it, "to protect the image of the Soviet" and otherwise demonstrate proletarian responsibility.[31] Railroad union leaders in Kiev, for example, had wired their Moscow comrades in June to "show an example of sacrifice of personal interests for the sake of the general good;"[32] the food workers' union had put tremendous pressure on striking flour mill workers in early July to continue to work even though their strike would "officially" continue.[33] This was true elsewhere as well, and in different industries and circumstances.[34] By mid-September, published

[31] *Velikaia oktiabr'skaia sotsialisticheskaia revoliutsiia na Ukraine, fevral' 1917–aprel' 1918 godov*, 3 vols. (Kiev, 1957), vol. 1, p. 514.

[32] *Volia i Dumy Zheleznodorozhnika*, June 1, 1917.

[33] *Delo Naroda*, July 3, 1917; *Rabochaia Gazeta*, July 12, 1917.

[34] *Vpered*, June 6, 1917; *Zemlia i Volia*, June 9, 1917.

reports of active trade union support for strikes were relatively scarce, occurring only in a little more than 13 percent of the cases in our file (although this undoubtedly underrepresents the true state of affairs). In October the entire Petrograd Trade Union Council intervened to forestall the carpenters' and woodworkers' strike mentioned above, even though its members felt the PSFMO was unconscionably irresponsible in failing to settle a dispute that touched so many enterprises in different industries. Instead, the union promised woodworkers moral and material support and urged negotiations.[35]

The union leaders' conflicts in this regard were exemplified by the national railroad strike, which was called on the night of September 23–24 by Vikzhel, the railroad union's national executive committee. Although it was not understood at the time, Vikzhel's members acted with varying degrees of reluctance and regret, quite concerned about the potential economic and political implications of bringing Russia's vast rail network to a halt. One of the principal reasons the strike occurred, however, was that union leaders themselves were under pressure from radical rank-and-file workers to produce the long-awaited wage improvements promised by a series of commissions and committees throughout 1917.[36] Although alarmed about the consequences of a shutdown, many in Vikzhel feared even more that alienated workers might strike on their own, strengthening Bolshevik influence. Kerensky's government itself dithered excessively on the question of wage rates and bonuses, and in some places, line officials withheld raises and bonuses already committed. Meantime, material conditions worsened along the lines, particularly for those responsible for line repairs (many of whom were women and among Russia's lowest paid laborers).

Until the last moment, government and union leaders expected a settlement. A commission under Labor Minister Gvozdev worked out a new system of wage rates and bonuses, higher than those proposed earlier by a comparable commission under Georgii Plekhanov, the venerable founder of Russian Social Democracy, now a conservative socialist. These concessions were rejected by Kerensky and his Council of Five as too costly. As it was, the lower wage rates and bonuses proposed by the Plekhanov commission would still cost the government 250 million rubles before January 1, 1918, and as much as 700 million in 1918. It was de-

---

[35] *Rabochaia Gazeta*, October 4, 1917.

[36] See O. Piatnitskii, "Vikzhel do, vo vremia i posle oktiabr'skikh dnei," in *Put' k oktiabriu* (Moscow, 1923), pp. 175–79. See also I. M. Pushkareva, "Vseobshchaia sentiabr'skaia stachka zheleznodorozhnikov v 1917 godu," in *Rabochii klass i rabochee dvizhenie v Rossii v 1917 godu* (Moscow, 1964), pp. 180–202; P. F. Metel'kov, *Zheleznodorozhniki v revoliutsii* (Leningrad, 1970), pp. 201–14.

cided instead that the issue would have to be brought before the Constituent Assembly. Vikzhel then felt it had no choice but to allow the strike to begin.

The walkout lasted a little more than two days in most places. The vast majority of strikers went back to work on September 26 after a number of parties joined the negotiations, and Vikzhel's representatives yielded to pressure from the Ministries of Labor and Transport and the Moscow and Petrograd Soviets. The government promised to make food and clothing available immediately to railroaders from commissary stores at fixed prices and agreed to other similar concessions. Those issues still in dispute were to be mediated rather than left to the Constituent Assembly. Union leaders felt they had won a substantial victory, strengthening their position among the railroad rank and file.[37] The importance of this strike, however, was not so much in the benefits it brought railroaders or even its impact on Russia's faltering economy, both of which were negligible, but in the way it demonstrated clearly the power of organized workers and the lethal potential of strikes. It hardly went unnoticed that the railroaders struck practically on the anniversary of their 1905 general strike, a massive and determined action, which, like the metalists' strikes in February, had precipitated fundamental changes in Russia's state structure. Yet memories of the horrendous repression against railroaders and others following the revolution in 1905 were also very much alive, reinforcing workers' convictions twelve years later that whatever Russia's future, state power should never again be concentrated in the hands of those overtly hostile to workers' interests.

In the crisis weeks of late September and October, consequently, as the scale of strikes continued to expand, the struggle to *define* workers' interests and to relate them specifically to strikes also assumed a new intensity, particularly in the councils of state and party, and in the press. The liberal editors of *Rech'* and *Russkiia Vedomosti* represented the railroad strike as immoral, irresponsible, and potentially suicidal for workers themselves. Strikes in general made no economic sense to most Kadet leaders in current circumstances; insofar as they raised class interests above the nation's, at least as liberals defined them, strikes now violated basic premises of democratic political morality.[38] Kadets also thought the railroad

---

[37] *Delo Naroda*, September 26, 1917; *Novaia Zhizn'*, September 18, 1917; *Rabochaia Gazeta*, September 27, 1917. See also P. Vompe, *Dni oktiabr'skoi revoliutsii i zheleznodorozhniki v revoliutsii 1917 goda* (Moscow, 1924); A. Taniaev, *Ocherki po istorii dvizhenii zheleznodorozhnikov v revoliutsii 1917 goda* (Moscow and Leningrad, 1925); and D. M. Zol'nikov, "Stachechnoe dvizhenie zheleznodorozhnikov v 1917 godu," *Uchenye Zapiski Tomskogo Gosudarstvennogo Universiteta* 38 (1961), pp. 34–41.

[38] See especially *Russkiia Vedomosti*, September 26, 27, 1917; *Rech'*, September 26, 1917.

strike and others patently illegal, since state employees were involved. Alone of the national newspapers, the liberal press emphasized that the Ministry of Justice would open an investigation into the strike and "take all necessary measures" to bring those responsible to justice. Strike leaders would be tried by jury. Their sentences, convictions assumed, would have both "repressive and moral import."[39]

The moderate socialist press, while extensively reporting the renewal of strike activity in the fall, did so in discernably defensive tones, emphasizing the degree to which the government's own ineptitude was contributing to the crisis but castigating "irresponsible" labor leaders as well. An editorial in *Rabochaia Gazeta* on September 26 went so far as to level blame for the railroad strike equally on both parties. "We must ask what conditions created the soil for such a scandalous occurrence," the paper noted, but whatever the answer, "the democracy will not forgive the railroad workers' general staff. Special interests need to be subordinated to the interests of the working class as a whole."[40] The Socialist Revolutionary (SR) press was somewhat less accusatory, undoubtedly because the complexion of the union leadership was so heavily SR. *Delo Naroda* opened its pages to Vikzhel's statements and declarations and printed announcements of the strike committee, several of which emphasized that railroaders had been struggling for more than six months, and that they went on strike as a last resort, their patience exhausted. For its part, the Bolshevik press gave rather little attention to the railroad strike, although the fact that as many as three-quarters of a million workers may have been striking against the state hardly went unnoticed by party leaders.

In the aftermath of the railroad strike, consequently, the whole question of worker activism became a matter of most intense concern to everyone involved in the exercise of state power. On September 25, the last coalition cabinet was finally organized, disputes among principals softened by the railroaders' action.[41] "Profound discord has come once more

---

[39] *Russkiia Vedomosti*, September 26, 1917. The liberal press also insisted that many local lines and stations had opposed the strike and supported the regime. (See *Rech'*, September 26, 1917.) How extensive this schism in railroader ranks actually was is impossible to determine. So too, in fact, is the number of railroad workers who actually went on strike. The strike began and ended too quickly for any accurate evidence of size to be gathered.

[40] *Rabochaia Gazeta*, September 26, 1917.

[41] The new government consisted of A. F. Kerensky, minister-president; A. I. Verkhovskii, minister of war; D. V. Verderevskii, minister of the navy; A. M. Nikitin, minister of the interior and post and telegraph; M. I. Tereshchenko, minister of foreign affairs; S. N. Prokopovich, minister of food; M. V. Bernatskii, minister of finance; S. S. Salazkin', minister of education; A. V. Liverovskii, minister of transport; A. I. Konovalov, minister of trade and industry; N. M. Kishkin, minister of welfare; P. N. Maliantovich, minister of justice; K. A. Gvozdev, minister of labor; S. L. Maslov, minister of agriculture; A. V. Kartashev, ober-

into our national life," Kerensky intoned in announcing its formation. "Waves of anarchy are sweeping the land, pressure from the foreign enemy is increasing, counterrevolution is raising its head." The government's tasks first and foremost were "to raise the fighting efficiency of the army," in order to "keep indissoluble the bond between the rear and the front, to guard the economy from further disintegration, decreasing the suffering which lies so heavily on the shoulders of the laboring masses." This meant setting fixed prices on basic commodities and "regulating the mutual relations of capital and labor." To this end, legislation was promised relating to state control over industry, "with the participation of the laboring and industrial classes and the active intervention in the management of enterprises, with the object of increasing their productivity."[42]

SR and Menshevik leaders remained pessimistic. *Delo Naroda* doubted that the members of the new cabinet had sufficient "energy and loyalty" to realize their goals.[43] *Izvestiia* hoped the Council of the Republic, a new national body that the government convened to shore up its support and prepare the groundwork for the Constituent Assembly, would allow the government's program to be realized.[44] *Novaia Zhizn'* was scornful.[45] But among the parties it was the right-wing liberals, under former Foreign Minister Miliukov, who most clearly rejected the government's approach and castigated even their own party colleagues for conciliatory attitudes. The four Kadets joining the coalition again included the prominent Muscovite industrialist A. I. Konovalov, who resumed the trade-industrial post he had left in May, but to Miliukov and others on the liberal right, it was precisely such accommodating attitudes that were a major cause of the crisis.

At the Kadets' tenth party congress, which convened in early October, a majority agreed that only a consolidation of right-wing forces could save Russia and defend the party's interests. The government's program was "illegitimate." It favored workers and usurped the rights of the Constituent Assembly. Whatever the public's reaction, the party's task was to "bring into the liberal orbit" all those who continued to believe in "law and order," particularly industrialists and others associated with Riabushinskii and the so-called Union of Public Figures. The party would support the government "only insofar as [*postol'ku poskol'ku*] it moves without hesitation on the path towards reestablishing lawful conditions

---

procurator of the Holy Synod; S. A. Smirnov, state controller; and S. N. Tret'iakov, chairman of the Economic Council. (*Vestnik Vremennago Pravitel'stva*, September 28, 1917.)

[42] Ibid.

[43] *Delo Naroda*, September 28, 1917.

[44] *Izvestiia* (Petrograd), September 26, 1917.

[45] *Novaia Zhizn'*, September 27, 1917.

in the country."[46] With conscious irony, the Kadet majority was now adopting the very posture the Petrograd Soviet had assumed when liberals themselves had held power in March.

The political polarization reflected in this approach was in no small measure the result of the ways Kadets and others now perceived strikes. By early October, the boundaries of legitimate labor protest were as insecure as the legal barriers around gentry property or the no-man's-land at the front. According to the available evidence, workers were becoming increasingly violent toward factory owners and managerial personnel alike. In contrast to the spring and summer, clashes unrelated to strikes shifted back into the factories, at least in Moscow and Petrograd. At the Okhtenskii powder works, for example, workers arrested the head of the factory; at the Peter the Great Arsenal, they forcefully blocked the evacuation of equipment and temporarily took over the armaments plant. In Petrograd, some 60 armed Skorokhod leather plant workers took the firm's board of directors hostage to secure wage increases. At the Vtorov chemical factory outside Moscow, women workers attempted to expel the director in a wheelbarrow; Putilov, the Nevskii shoe works, and a number of other plants in the capitals witnessed similar episodes of coercion.[47] Workers' committees seized factory supplies, demanded access to accounts, and expanded factory militias.

In many instances, such actions also led to strikes. When the management of the Nevskii shoe factory attempted to evacuate equipment in early September, angry workers placed a guard at the factory gates to block the move and ordered that nothing be taken from the plant without a pass from the factory committee. Management responded by attempting to withhold committee members' wages on grounds that they were not engaged in productive work, which led to a strike involving violence and threats of violence against administrative personnel. In response, the plant was formally closed, leading workers on October 4 to plan to seize it by force in an effort to restart production, and provoking an appeal for troops from S. N. Tret'iakov, chairman of the Main Economic Committee, to the commander of the Petrograd military district.[48] Striking work-

[46] *Russkiia Vedomosti*, October 17, 1917.

[47] VOSR. *Khronika sobytii*, vol. 3, pp. 486, 532, vol. 4, p. 255. *Revoliutsionnoe dvizhenie v Rossii v sentiabre 1917 goda: Obshchenatsional'nyi krizis* (Moscow, 1961), pp. 302, 380–81; *Sotsial Demokrat*, September 28, 1917; *Revoliutsionnoe dvizhenie v Rossii nakanune oktiabr'skogo vooruzhennogo vosstaniia (1–24 oktiabria 1917 goda)* (Moscow, 1962), p. 276.

[48] See *Rabochii Put'*, September 10, 1917; VOSR. *Khronika sobytii*, vol. 4, p. 255; *Torgovo-Promyshlennaia Gazeta*, October 3, 1917; *Revoliutsionnoe dvizhenie v Rossii nakanune oktiabr'skogo*, p. 251.

ers at the Kibbel' printing works, the Krel paper works, and the Benno-Rontaller button factory only returned to work in late September and early October after their factory committees had seized the plants. At Benno-Rontaller, workers seized the factory when management refused to implement a collective wage agreement that had been negotiated for nine similar factories; management demanded the matter go once more to a conciliation commission, but workers refused and simply took over.[49] Even Moscow woodworkers and Petrograd pharmacy clerks, neither of whom had shown especial militance in 1917, seized some of their enterprises and forcefully expelled owners and administrators in October when strike settlements could not be reached. Like the Benno-Rontaller workers, Moscow woodworkers seized as many as six plants themselves rather than agree to send their prolonged wage dispute back to arbitration. In the eyes of the business community, strikes of this nature had nothing whatsoever in common with a established traditions of Western bourgeois democracies or a capitalist order.

Further, available reports indicate that factory-based actions in September and October continued to be concentrated overwhelmingly in the metal plants, despite the existence of a collective wage agreement for both Moscow and Petrograd.[50] Of the remainder, the largest number occurred in the strife-torn leather trade, caught in the midst of one of the period's longest and most contentious strikes. Even labor peace secured through collective wage agreements was no longer a substantial basis for social order in enterprises of the capitals; the revival of strike activity among metalists was perceived from above as especially dangerous for the nation's defense, as much or more so now, in fact, as in the spring, because of the army's virtual collapse.

At the same time, an increase in the number of reported factory-based actions in these weeks was accompanied by a decline in reports of street actions. Again, this may reflect a bias in reporting more than social reality, but the changing nature of samosudy suggests otherwise. Reports of crowd attacks on burglars and thieves by angered crowds in Petrograd and Moscow are almost entirely gone. Certainly there was no *prevalent* wave of anger or intolerance reported for this form of lawbreaker after

[49] Reports are in *Russkiia Vedomosti*, October 15, 1917; *Izvestiia* (Petrograd), October 15, 1917. See also VOSR. *Khronika sobytii*, vol. 4, p. 62; *Revoliutsionnoe dvizhenie v Rossii v sentiabre*, p. 326.

[50] Some 60 percent of all reported factory-based actions in our file were linked to metal plants in September and October, compared to approximately 45 percent in July and August. Because of the army's collapse, however, workers in defense-related production may have received disproportionate attention from newspapers and others providing evidence of direct action in these factories.

the Kornilov affair, in sharp contrast to the spring. Instead, reports of street actions in the capitals have much more to do with food shortages and intolerance for officialdom: threats to lynch city officials responsible for food distribution, looting of food stores, seizing food stores, or searching and looting shops or buildings where food caches were suspected—as if the crowd had abandoned any attempt to forge a civil society in common with other social elements.

Finally, as this suggests, a much larger number of the type of worker actions that previously occurred without the cessation of work seem to have been directly connected to strikes themselves in these last weeks before October. Strike tactics were changing because the old calculus of strikes—weighing potential benefits against risks—no longer operated. Withdrawal of labor alone was clearly no longer sufficient for strikers to achieve their goals. Indeed, strikes that involved simple work stoppages readily played into the hands of plant owners seeking acceptable grounds to halt production. Workers now had little economic leverage and hence appeared also to reject economically benign acts of protest, such as evicting a rate setter while maintaining production. In other words, by September and October, previously separate forms of protest appear to have merged: workers used the traditional strike form, a passive work stoppage, but they also utilized coercive, active measures to force concessions. The increasing use of force was a sign of the narrowing options for workers in their efforts to define the extent of their new freedoms. We must emphasize again that our data on such nonstrike activism are not quantitatively systematic or complete, and that perceptions of changes in this regard may most of all reflect biases in reporting. Nonetheless, the magnitude of the change is startling. Fully 75 percent of the reports we have been able to assemble on worker violence, attacks on managerial personnel, the seizure of factories, the blockage of goods shipments, and other similar actions that took place in connection with strikes during 1917 occurred between September 1 and October 25. With a greater or lesser degree of political consciousness, such actions implicitly strengthened the social bases on which the Bolsheviks would soon take power.

Petrograd Pharmacists and the Nobel Oil Depot Workers: Strike Activism and Social Tensions in October

Two strikes in Petrograd on the eve of the Bolshevik takeover brought these broader issues into sharp relief. The first was by Petrograd pharmacy workers, who left their jobs on October 3 at all but a handful of pharmacies in hospitals and clinics. As a result, supplies of medicine quickly disappeared, causing serious hardships. As the strike dragged on, feelings became so intense that it was not settled until several weeks after the Bolsheviks came to power. "Who is to blame" became a central point of conflict, not only for the strike itself, but for Russia's circumstances as a whole.

The central issue was wages, although an important subsidiary question was the role of the union in hiring. Earlier, in April, conflict between pharmacy owners and their employees had led to a brief strike when owners refused to abide by the decision of a conciliation chamber on hours, wages, and procedures for terminating employment. At that time the pharmacy clerks, many of whom were Jewish, struck quite reluctantly, "not with easy hearts." While *Petrogradskii Listok* attacked them roundly, barely concealing its antisemitic proclivities, the Petrograd Soviet explicitly blamed the owners' side, and insisted the resulting hardships were their responsibility.[51] The April strike produced a settlement favorable to the clerks, but the agreement failed to protect them from the ravages of inflation and the enmity of their employers.

By the fall, the union of pharmacy workers, led by moderate socialists, was quite active. Just before the railroad strike, a union conference approved a new salary schedule, worked out by its contract commission. The new rates ranged from 100 rubles a month for minors under age 16 to 300–350 rubles for assistant pharmacists and 425 rubles for highly skilled senior specialists (*provizory*). The delegates were reluctant to approve the new scale since it still left them behind other professional groups, but they did so avowing they were making a substantial personal sacrifice for the city's (and nation's) benefit. On September 18, they submitted their proposal to the Society of Pharmacy Owners.

The Society, however, rejected it outright, claiming the new rates would cause "financial ruin." They remained obdurate even after both sides were brought together by Assistant Minister for Internal Affairs Bogutskii. Soviet spokesmen and city duma representatives quickly pressed for additional mediation through the offices of the Ministry of Labor and the Petrograd Soviet. When these, too, proved unsuccessful, the strike began.

At first the Union agreed to staff some 40 pharmacies to permit the dispensing of medicine on an emergency basis. Pharmacy owners also tried to staff their shops with strikebreakers or family members. An anxious public, at first inconvenienced, was soon enraged at the resulting shortage of available medicine. The issue was taken up at various levels

[51] *Rabochaia Gazeta*, April 25, 1917; *Pravda*, May 9, 1917 (n.s.); *Novaia Zhizn'*, April 25, 26, 1917.

of municipal and national government, and in both the district and city soviets.

Pharmacists blamed the Society of Owners for both the strike and the shortages, reporting that the society threatened to withhold supplies from any pharmacy yielding to strikers' demands.[52] Society spokesmen accused pickets of preventing customers from entering the open shops.[53] The most serious conflict developed over who was responsible for sabotaging emergency procedures: the owners, for deliberately swamping the few pharmacies that remained open with union sanction, or the clerks, for refusing to fill urgent prescriptions.

Violence soon erupted, largely, according to press reports, on the part of armed owners who assaulted the clerks. The union announced that it would not staff even emergency pharmacies if its members could not be protected. By mid-October, government and soviet figures both were discussing municipalizing or nationalizing the pharmacies, placing a cloud of "socialization" over the whole dispute. For pharmacy owners, refusing to yield now symbolized the entire struggle to hold back the socialist tide. For the clerks, who tried to absolve themselves from the blame for widespread hardship, the owners' tactics reflected the most unacceptable callousness of bourgeois society toward the needs of ordinary people.

These positions, in turn, were variously represented to the country at large by the Petrograd press. The liberal papers, predictably, emphasized the fiscal problems of management, repeating that pharmacy owners faced "financial ruin," the same term used by the Society of Owners itself. *Rech'* took pains to point out in October that municipalization of the shops would place them under military administration (the city duma's plan), making pharmacy workers "military personnel." The Kadet organ also indicated, with no mention of shop owners, that excesses by strikers were being reported to city authorities. In contrast, *Vpered* and especially *Novaia Zhizn'* emphasized the owners' hostility. Here their actions were given critical prominence, along with reports about shop owners ignoring essential prescriptions as a way of aggravating tension.

A similar picture of tension emerges from a strike that began at the Nobel Brothers oil storage depots in Petrograd on October 9, threatening the capital with a near total cutoff of oil and kerosene. The depots supplied a number of industrial enterprises and almost all city institutions, including the tramways and electrical stations, in addition to providing retail stores with fuel for heating and cooking. The strike thus caused tremendous concern. When the city's SR Mayor G. I. Shreider failed to

[52] *Delo Naroda*, October 10, 1917.
[53] *Rabochaia Gazeta*, October 7, 1917.

bring the sides together, the Ministry of Labor called representatives from the Central Trade Union Council, the military, the city administration, and the parties to the dispute to a meeting in the Marble Palace, but this also failed to produce a settlement. By October 20, a number of enterprises in the city had been forced to close.

This strike, too, brought deep antagonisms into the open, and is particularly interesting because of the sharply different pictures drawn in the socialist and nonsocialist press. From the start, the question again of which side was "to blame" was a matter of great contention. As *Delo Naroda* reported, both white-and blue-collar workers had presented the Nobel administration with a proposal for wage increases as early as July, indicating their willingness to abide by norms worked out between management and labor in other oil supply firms in the capital. The Nobel administration had refused, however, caught up with others in the intransigent mood of the post-July Days period, and the conflict had remained unresolved through the beginning of October. When the strike began, workers insisted not only that rates in use elsewhere be applied to them, but that management pay them for time lost through the strike.

According to *Rabochaia Gazeta* and the socialist press, the strikers were willing to have the matter arbitrated, but management categorically refused. Wages for time lost by strikers was a matter of principle which could not be compromised. Because the fuel situation was urgent, workers pledged to honor special military needs and agreed on October 21 to a three-day reprieve. *Rech'* and *Birzhevyia Vedomosti*, however, presented the matter quite differently. Here it was management that was proposing to have the wage issue submitted to mediation, and workers and employees who refused. And here readers learned that work was being resumed by part of the administrative staff, who "did not consider it possible to leave the city in such a perilous situation at the present time," while strikers continued adamantly to refuse to release fuel. Omitted from *Rech'* were any indication of the long history of the dispute and the point that management's suggestion for arbitration excluded the contentious issue of strike time and was bound to fail. According to *Birzhevyia Vedomosti*, workers were raising "new economic demands," and it was therefore impossible to say when the dispute could be settled.

This was hyperbole. When other Petrograd industrialists brought pressure to bear on Nobel management on October 24, the strike ended immediately. Management agreed to submit the question of wages lost during the strike to arbitration, a major concession. Even more, they agreed to give workers an immediate advance amounting to one-half the average wages lost during the strike, pending the outcome of the arbitration commission. The strike ended the moment an agreement on this question was signed.

It is therefore difficult to escape the conclusion that the Nobel strike was unnecessary, a symptom instead of broader social antagonism. The matter of wage increases had been before management for three months. Comparable workers elsewhere were paid more, and the virtual monopoly Nobel had in supplying city tram and electrical stations should have made management more responsive to the city's own efforts to secure an agreement.

THE IVANOVO TEXTILE STRIKE

By mid-October, the public was acutely aware of the barriers now erected between labor and management. The Petrograd pharmacists' strike, the Nobel strike, the continuing Moscow leather and woodworkers' strikes, and a threatened strike of all Moscow municipal employees, from fire-fighters to hospital attendants, all reinforced the sense of opposition, of polarization. But the largest strike of the period, that of 300,000 textile workers in central Vladimir and Kostroma provinces, was yet to begin. This was a major event in terms of its size and its organization. It is also a critical strike historically, both because it reveals the extent of polarization in October, and because it shows how the logic of labor protest continued to develop along lines extrinsic or parallel to the gathering political crisis. In short, the Ivanovo strike brings together many strands of the complex strike process that contributed to the development of the revolution. Our final case for analysis, it also vividly illustrates the role of the public and public perceptions in labor conflict in 1917.

Conflict had been simmering in the textile-manufacturing region of Ivanovo-Kineshma since the spring of 1917, and in May, the workers' union invited factory owners to meet to discuss the issues of contention: factory committee rights, conciliation chambers, the eight-hour workday, pay raises, work norms, medical funds, and workplace safety.[54] The owners offered pay raises ranging from 100 percent to 120 percent over existing levels, but a general agreement failed to materialize, and the workers' representatives walked out of the conference. The textile union appealed to Labor Minister Skobelev but resisted rank-and-file pressure to call a strike; instead, they continued to organize workers in the textile districts.

By August, the union had enrolled 100,000 members out of 300,000

---

[54] G. Korolev, *Ivanovo-Kineshemskie tekstil'shchiki v 1917 godu (Iz vospominanii tekstil'shchika)* (Moscow, 1927), p. 26. See also the full account of the strike in William B. Husband, "Local Industry in Upheaval: The Ivanovo-Kineshma Textile Strike of 1917," *Slavic Review* 47, no. 3 (1988), pp. 448–63.

employed in the region, and a delegates' meeting in mid-August agreed that workers must now consider a unified strike against all the region's proprietors. But despite the example of the Moscow leather workers' strike and others that erupted in the month of August, the delegates resisted a call to action. First they would collect information about workers' conditions in order to formulate a list of demands. This project, carried out democratically by production workers and not by union officials, took another month. The final proposals were presented to workers in all factories, who then made additional suggestions, all of which were apparently incorporated into the final document of grievances. Consequently, when union delegates assembled on October 11, they could be confident that they represented a consensus of rank-and-file textile workers' grievances and that their constituents had been widely informed about the issues separating labor and management.

The October 11 delegates' meeting set the strike mechanism in motion. The group resolved that the workers' demands would be presented to the Union of United Industrialists, with an October 18 deadline for a reply. The delegates elected an 18-member negotiating commission to carry out discussions, and at the same time, anticipating the failure of these talks, elected a nine-person central strike committee (*Tsentrostachka*). The strike, if called by Tsentrostachka, would begin "everywhere and at once" and would "proceed peacefully without any force permitted." Workers would leave work quietly and without commotion. This meeting, which not only authorized the strike but laid down an elaborate schedule of strike procedures, lasted through the night, adjourning only at 6:30 in the morning.[55]

On October 13, the union dispatched a letter to the owners, stressing the deterioration of workers' living conditions and the harmfulness for both labor and capital of individual strikes to secure improvements.

> Now relations [between labor and capital] have reached such a state, that only a decisive review of all conditions of labor in all factory enterprises of our region can guarantee the peaceful resumption of work, only collective agreements through the introduction of a tariff and collective agreements on hiring can guarantee the end of separate actions by this or the other side; actions which you recognize as utterly undesirable and harmful.[56]

The tone of the letter was at once conciliatory and defiant. The union stressed its willingness to negotiate and to reach a settlement without the

[55] Ibid., p. 38.
[56] Klimokhin, ed., *Kratkaia istoriia stachki*, p. 8.

cessation of production; it stressed the community of interests between labor and capital. But the letter also firmly insisted on the virtue of the workers' claims, on their right to put forward these demands under the threat of the withdrawal of labor. And of course, the letter gave the manufacturers only a four-day term in which to respond.

On the same day that this letter was received in the Moscow offices of the industrialists' union, October 14, the textile workers' union also issued a florid manifesto "To All Comrade Workers of the Region," explaining the history of the conflict. This public appeal was directed primarily at textile workers, but its function was to justify in the eyes of a broad public the claims that strikers were about to insist upon. The language here was militant, in the literal sense of the word. After the inconclusive May conference, "workers declared to their opponents that they were leaving the meeting and henceforth considered themselves to be in the position of combattants"; now the strike committee was "commissioned in the event of necessity to lead into battle the workers' batallions in defense of their demands."[57]

The union and its strike committee then sat to await the industrialists' reply. "On the streets, in the squares, in the bazaars," recalled a union leader, "the only conversation was about the coming action. Tension was near the limit."[58] Local committees appointed pickets, chosen from the most "reliable and experienced comrades."[59] They organized meetings and rallies. When the October 18 deadline brought no reply from the industrialists, Tsentrostachka made preparations for the strike, now set to begin on October 21. On October 19, with still no reply, Tsentrostachka issued a manifesto labeled "Order Number One" (an allusion to the Petrograd Soviet's famous order to the garrison on March 1), instructing local committees to deploy their pickets and to block the removal of any goods from factories, lest the manufacturers try to salvage what they could and then abandon their enterprises.

The strike began on the morning of October 21, but only after a confusing exchange of telegrams. The industrialists cabled a follow-up query to the letter offering negotiations that they claimed to have sent. The union cabled back that no such letter had arrived, and workers enthusiastically marched out of their factories, to the relief of union leaders, who had had last-minute doubts about rank-and-file commitment. Only at the end of the first day of the strike did union leaders receive the owners' lost reply. The industrialists' union invited workers to send their negotiators

[57] Ibid., pp. 10–11.
[58] Korolev, *Ivanovo-Kineshemskie tektil'shchiki*, p. 41.
[59] Klimokhin, ed., *Kratkaia istoriia stachki*, p. 16.

to Moscow for talks which would be coordinated by the Soviet's labor section.[60]

This delayed token of conciliation was heatedly discussed by the central strike committee, but in the end, its members decided not to call off a strike "so unanimously begun," and they wired new conditions to the owners. The union would agree to negotiate in Ivanovo, not Moscow, and only if the owners first agreed to a minimum daily wage of 7.50 rubles. The owners refused; and the strike continued past the October seizure of power. Negotiations finally commenced on November 11. A settlement was worked out on November 14, and work resumed November 17.[61]

Inevitably the transfer of power to the Bolsheviks complicated the significance of the strike, and to consider fully its relationship to the October revolution itself would take us beyond our present task. Yet the public face presented by the strike and its different participants is worth attention, particularly in the period between October 11 and October 25, when the political terrain so suddenly shifted.

The focus of public debate in this period was the "missing letter." The union had made the strike conditional on a reply; its Order Number Two to the "Worker Army," explaining the strike, began with the statement: "The hour of decisive and relentless struggle has begun. The capitalists have not even answered our demands."[62]

An article in Moscow's *Izvestiia* also began, "On October 21, at 10 o'clock in the morning, the central strike committee, having received no answer of any kind [*nikakogo*] from the union of united industrialists, summoned three hundred thousand workers to begin a strike."[63] It was obviously important for the union to argue that they had been willing to negotiate, that they were moderate, that they were forced to cease work by the behavior of the capitalists. The stream of proclamations that issued forth from Tsentrostachka made clear that the target of their explanations included the entire population of the region, but especially the workers themselves. At the decisive hour, the leaders had worried that no one would follow them into the strike. So the rhetoric of self-defense and moral superiority was clearly intended to mobilize rank-and-file workers.

Strikers also appealed for the moral support of soldiers in the region. Describing the pitiful conditions created by the imperialist war, a union manifesto of October 21 maintained,

[60] Ibid., p. 26.
[61] Korolev, *Ivanovo-Kineshemskie tekstil'shchiki*, pp. 59–70.
[62] Klimokhin, ed., *Kratkaia istoriia stachki*, p. 17.
[63] *Izvestiia* (Moscow), October 24, 1917.

We do not demand anything excessive, we do not wish to destroy industry. We want only to be paid enough so we can afford to put clothes on our backs, to not have to go barefoot. To our demands, to the demands of your fathers, brothers, wives, and sisters, exhausted by want, the capitalists do not wish even to answer.[64]

An appeal to "citizens of the region" explained the dire conditions of factory workers during the war. "It is no wonder that for these reasons a worker, driven on by the 'bony hand of hunger,' would go to a capitalist and demand from him a raise. But his demands remained 'the voice of one crying in the wilderness.' "[65] The proclamation pleaded with the population not to believe falsehoods about their cause.

In order to disclose the truth, in order to show society the complete soundness of our demands, we decided to turn to you. Let no slanderer dare to falsely accuse workers. We want to live like human beings, we can no longer live without enough to eat or drink, dressed in rags, going without shoes so that the capitalists can dress in silk and velvet, adorn themselves with gold, dine on sweets, sleep as long as they like, and endlessly amuse themselves.[66]

This was a powerful message. Workers insisted on their reasonableness and on their good faith, but they also claimed basic human rights. And their accusation of those who refused to be reasonable, the capitalists, was laced with images of inequality and injustice.

In response, the industrialists launched a public relations counteroffensive on October 22. They too were reasonable people, as they claimed in a leaflet distributed in thousands of copies throughout the region. "Recognizing the correctness of raising present wages, the union of united industrialists of the central region hastened to answer, having informed the trade union's leadership on the same October 14 by registered letter sent to its address in the city of Ivanovo-Voznesensk, that it was prepared to enter into negotiations on the proposed demands."[67]

The manufacturers also took their case to the public press, something the workers by and large did not do. On October 21, *Russkoe Slovo* reported on the union's Order Number One, which deployed pickets to guard factory premises. In the newspaper's view, this order clearly instructed workers to seize their factories. Further, to prevent the good sense of local workers from interfering with the strike, the order forbade

---

[64] Klimokhin, ed., *Kratkaia istoriia stachki*, p. 19.
[65] Ibid., p. 20.
[66] Ibid., p. 21.
[67] Ibid., pp. 27–28.

workers from talking to any commissars, representatives of public organizations, or ministers, and told them to subordinate themselves to the orders of the central strike committee. "Yesterday from the morning on, according to information received in Moscow, on the basis of this 'manifesto' in Ivanovo-Voznesensk, Shuia, and Vichuga, armed groups of workers began to occupy the telephone exchanges in factories and to seize their offices. In the majority of factories there prevails total anarchy."[68] Such a picture contrasts sharply with the union's presentation of these instructions as insuring an orderly, peaceful, restrained, and disciplined labor conflict.

Two days later, *Russkoe Slovo* charged that union speakers in the region deliberately avoided the "misunderstanding" issue, that workers actually had never authorized a strike and had been essentially duped by the trade union. On October 24, this time responding to the union's Order Number Two, the paper again reminded the public that the industrialists had agreed to enter negotiations before the strike began. At the same time, to add pressure to their protestations of innocence, two owners nailed up their own proclamations on their factory gates, threatening to dismiss any striking worker who did not return to work in three days' time.[69] Like the workers' organizations, industrialists also presented two faces, reasonableness to the broad public, and militance toward their class opponent. The public representation of the strike clearly indicates that both parties to the dispute saw it necessary, even on the eve of October, to demonstrate their desire to compromise, to negotiate, to avoid the ultimate and devastating course of closing down factories, of halting production.

At the same time that Ivanovo workers and industrialists carried out their battle in the public press, of course, the Bolshevik party was preparing its seizure of power to accompany the coming Second All-Russian Congress of Soviets. Dissident Bolsheviks hinted at these plans in the Petrograd press, and in that city and elsewhere, privileged Russians and workers alike awaited the congress with a sense of foreboding, but also with hopes that the political impasse would finally be resolved. Workers, however, did not wait. Twenty-two new strikes began in the last week before the congress, including not only the massive Ivanovo strike on October 21, but also walkouts by Petrograd cabdrivers on October 22, by 3,000 dockworkers in Rostov, by savings association clerks in Tiflis on October 23, and by 1,000 shipbuilders in Petrograd on October 24.[70]

[68] Ibid., p. 47.
[69] Ibid., p. 30.
[70] *Volia Naroda*, October 20, 1917; *Rech'*, October 24, 25, 1917; *Narodnoe Slovo*, October 25, 1917; *Russkiia Vedomosti*, October 25, 1917; *Novaia Zhizn'*, October 26, 1917.

Other strikes begun earlier remained unresolved. The bitter Moscow leather workers' strike, begun in mid-August, ended only on October 22, with a settlement still to be worked out: politics played a direct role there, as the Moscow Soviet voted to impose unilaterally a strike settlement. Six thousand woodworkers in Moscow continued their strike begun October 9, and ongoing strikes in other cities remained in the public eye.[71] The picture of widespread labor conflict and increasing violence in struck plants, and the language emanating from strikes like those in Moscow and Ivanovo, indicated the way in which strikes as a form of protest had come to challenge Russia's social order itself.

[71] I. S. Iuzefovich, *Iz klassovykh boev 1917 goda (stachka Moskovskikh kozhevnikov)* (Moscow, 1928); *Izvestiia* (Moscow), October 10, 1917; *Trud*, October 10, 1917, and throughout the month; *Russkiia Vedomosti*, October 21, 1917.

10

. . . .

STRIKES AND

THE REVOLUTIONARY PROCESS

Revolutions are rare and infinitely complex events. To explain them, to understand the forces that propel revolutionary processes toward one outcome or another, constitutes one of the historian's greatest challenges. What forces drove the 1917 revolution toward the Bolshevik triumph in October? Traditional explanations have focused on personalities, on ideas and the clash of ideas, on the contradictions between ideology and reality, on the irreconcilability of broad social and economic interests, and on the politics of international conflict. More recently, social historians have added to these interpretations an examination of the way groups of individuals combined to influence events and to assert their interests in the workplace, in political institutions, and in the streets. For social historians, the dissection of what has been called the "elemental" social forces or Trotsky's "molecular mass" into smaller, identifiable aggregates, has permitted new and deeper understanding of the revolutionary process.

When we ask, "What forces drove the revolution?" we are thus also asking, "Who drove the revolution, and how?" As social phenomena, strikes emerged as a key element in the "particle physics" of Russia's broad revolutionary process, but their importance in this respect was only partly related to the ways in which strike activism mobilized workers, articulated their goals, and structured socially cohering perceptions and identities. It related as well to the kinds of workers involved, and to the ways this particular form of activism directly involved virtually all hired labor in changing the frontiers of political struggle through action, inside the workplace and out.

By way of concluding our study, let us therefore consider more closely this important aspect of the sociology of revolutionary protest in 1917 and explore in some detail the question of strike leadership and the related issues of skill, gender, industrial concentration, and geography. As in chapter 2, we shall again treat these issues in overview, summarizing now, however, on the basis of what we have learned about the changing contours of strike activism over time, and emphasizing the important shifts we believe occurred between March and October.

THE "VANGUARD" HYPOTHESIS

Let us take up first the question of strike leadership and explore the factors that might explain the prominence of certain types of workers in strike activity. We must confront first the concept of a workers' "vanguard," which plays such an important role in explaining the Bolsheviks' coming to power whether one investigates Russia's revolutionary history in Soviet or Western studies. In its most common form, this view holds that particularly militant and conscious sectors of Russia's urban proletariat formed an early and solid alliance with the Bolshevik party's political leadership, joining the party as an activist cadre on the one hand, and mobilizing broader strata of Russia's workforce behind party objectives and outlooks on the other. Views about the extent and precise nature of this organic relationship vary considerably from historian to historian, but agreement has emerged on at least four matters: that vanguard workers were generally skilled; that they were concentrated heavily in large plants, especially Petrograd metal plants involved in war production; that they consistently led the way during 1917 in mounting strikes, demonstrations, and other forms of political protest; and that the goals of these actions were directed in one way or another toward replacing the institutions and values of a liberal (and capitalist) democracy with those of a socialist order of some kind. In John Keep's view, "workers in metallurgical plants fulfilling defense contracts, who were one of the best-paid groups in industry, assumed a vanguard role."[1] In the view of the prominent Soviet historian, P. V. Volobuev, it was Russia's working class "in the narrow sense of the term," industrial workers, workers in the mining and metallurgical industry, and workers in state enterprises who "ideologically and politically dominated the broader proletarian milieu and fulfilled for it a vanguard role."[2] According to Lenin, "it is well known that the metalists were the most developed and leading workers not only in Petrograd, but throughout Russia. . . . The metalists were the *vanguard* (leading stratum) of the entire proletariat of Russia."[3]

Studies of strikes in Western Europe and North America, on the other

[1] John L. H. Keep, *The Russian Revolution: A Study in Mass Mobilization* (New York, 1976), p. 69.

[2] P. V. Volobuev, *Proletariat i burzhuaziia Rossii v 1917 godu* (Moscow, 1964), p. 17.

[3] V. I. Lenin, *Polnoe sobranie sochineniia*, 5th ed., 55 vols. (Moscow, 1958–65), vol. 24, pp. 100–1. The italics are his. Lenin was writing in 1913.

hand, have generally ignored the vanguard notion. In modernization-based strike theory, strike activists are depicted not as an advance guard, but as a rear guard, the necessary victims of temporary social dislocation. The structuralist analysis of Clark Kerr and Abraham Siegel likewise relegates strike activism to factors independent of and unrelated to political mobilization. Economic theories of strike behavior tend to focus only on immediate material causation and allow no room for the idea that strikes have a political content. Only Shorter and Tilly, and more generally the adherents of what Cronin calls the "political-organizational" approach, leave room for the idea that political activism in general terms might logically be related to strike activism. In other words, their conclusion that strike activism corresponds to political mobilization suggests that we might expect to find a congruence between the revolutionary vanguard, whose general parameters are outlined above, and those most active in strikes.[4]

Let us test as carefully as our data allow the belief that strikes were led in any meaningful way by vanguard workers, particularly skilled metalworkers in large Petrograd defense plants. We readily accept the logic of this hypothesis. Some excellent scholarship has shown that skill goes far in explaining propensities of workers everywhere to engage in a wide sphere of activity, including organized protest. The importance of skilled workers to production and the fact that they are almost always men makes them less vulnerable to repression. Relatively favorable working hours facilitate organization. A special pride of craftsmanship leads to a strong defense of relative independence and autonomy. Literacy, access to the press, and a rich associational tradition often provide an organizational base from which to mobilize.[5] In prerevolutionary Russia, particularly in the war years, Petrograd metalists dominated strike activity generally, as we have indicated, and played an extraordinary role in the political strikes that rocked the capital in 1916. Their role in the February events needs no further rehearsal. Can we now say this was the case for the months between March and October, and if it was, can we sensibly identify a workers' vanguard in this way?

As we take up this question, however, we must emphasize that explor-

---

[4] Edward Shorter and Charles Tilly, *Strikes in France, 1830–1968* (Cambridge, 1974); James E. Cronin, "Theories of Strikes: Why Can't They Explain the British Experience?" *Journal of Social History* 12, no. 2 (1978–1979), pp. 194–220.

[5] See, e.g., Dick Geary, *European Labour Protest, 1848–1939* (London, 1981); Bryan D. Palmer, *A Culture in Conflict: Skilled Workers and Industrial Capitalism in Hamilton, Ontario, 1860–1914* (Montreal, 1979); Michael P. Hanagan, *The Logic of Solidarity: Artisans and Industrial Workers in Three French Towns* (Urbana, Ill., 1980); Robert Gray, *The Aristocracy of Labor in Nineteenth-Century Britain, c. 1850–1914* (London, 1981); P. K. Edwards, *Strikes in the United States, 1881–1974* (Oxford, 1981).

ing strikes obviously addresses only part of the problem of identifying and analyzing the nature of Russia's "leading proletarian elements" in 1917. What might be described as an advanced guard of politically conscious, experienced, militant worker activists clearly existed in 1917 quite apart from strike activity, working in trade unions, factory committees, or local soviets, and expressing their militance in party work and political demonstrations. The Bolsheviks' role here has also been amply demonstrated. In conceptual terms, it may therefore make sense to distinguish a revolutionary vanguard of this sort from those workers most actively involved in strikes. If we can determine that a discrete and clearly discernible sector of Russia's workforce led or dominated this particular aspect of labor protest, however, we should, at the very least, understand more fully the social dynamics of Russian labor protest in 1917, and the role of strikes themselves as an aspect of the broader revolutionary process.

THE SOCIAL COMPOSITION OF
RUSSIA'S STRIKE FORCE, MARCH TO OCTOBER

We must approach the question of social composition from several different angles. Strike reports are most complete and precise when identifying economic sector, industrial branch, and geographic location, but these categories are so broad that they may hide substantial social and economic variation in the composition of the workers they include. Strike reports are less informative (and often silent) about other factors that might be useful in identifying those most active in strikes: plant size, strikers' skill levels, gender, age, wage levels, productivity, level of urbanization, and experience on the job. We will begin by reviewing the broad categories of economic and industrial sectors in order to uncover general patterns of strike leadership; we can then turn to more indirect evidence of other characteristics of the strike force in 1917.

Let us recapitulate. We have seen in chapter 2 how Russia's overall strike force between March and October 1917 was dominated by industrial workers, but with a significant role played by nonindustrial workers in the service and transport sectors (tables 2.6 and 2.7). Among industrial workers subject to the Factory Inspectorate, four groups dominated strike activism relative to the numbers of workers employed: leather workers, metalists, textile workers, and woodworkers (table 2.8). Metalworkers and textilists together accounted for over 58 percent of all industrial strikers.

In terms of numbers alone, one might thus maintain that metalists and textile workers, despite enormous differences between the two groups in skill level, geographic location, sex ratios, and the nature and quality of both work processes and social relations, constituted the vanguard of

1917 strike activists. On the other hand, since the textile and metal industries employed the largest number of workers in industry, their large number of strikers might merely correspond to the large pool of potential strikers from which to draw. We compensate for this problem by measuring strike propensity, the ratio of an industry's share of strikers and workers. As we saw in chapter 2, adjusting for the different sizes of the industrial labor force sectors reveals that metal and textile workers were absolutely dominant in terms of raw numbers (table 2.6), as well as relatively active in strikes in 1917 (table 2.8). Neither group, however, was as proportionally active as workers in the animal products industry, primarily leather workers, whose high level of strike participation came largely (but not exclusively) from the protracted industrywide strike in Moscow from August to October.

What implications do these figures have for our understanding of the social bases of strikes, the vanguard issue? In order to understand their meaning in these terms, it is necessary to probe beyond the broad industrial categories employed so far. Clearly, a worker employed in a metal plant or a leather factory was far more likely to strike during 1917 than a worker in a food-processing plant or a munitions factory, but why? What distinguishes workers in the four most strike-prone industries from those in the four least?

The organization of the work process is one feature specific to industrial divisions. Metalworking (particularly machine-building), leather production, and woodworking were typically carried out in small workshops within larger plants, a work structure that could facilitate organization. But the textile industry was highly mechanized and organized for mass production, and workers here were also very strike prone. Printers, on the other hand, with a small-scale organization of work, were not especially active in strikes.

The specific economic position of each industry also fails to explain the differences in strike propensity. There is no overall statistical correlation between industrial strike propensities and any industry-level indices for workers' wages, output, or change in the value of production. There is some evidence that industries with a high rate of productivity in 1917, measured in terms of output per worker, had the highest strike propensities, but when the wage factor is introduced, this correlation disappears. One might conclude from this that workers may have struck in part because their wages did not correspond to the value they added to the capitalist enterprise (i.e. their productivity), but this is clearly not the whole story.[6]

[6] The statistical analysis by industry is described in Appendix 1. The productivity variable is the value of production per worker per year, reported for 1917 in TSSU, *Trudy*, vol. 26,

In fact, one of the important components of a categorization along industrial lines is the element of skill. Some industries—wood, printing, and metal—employed a large proportion of skilled workers, while others hired unskilled, untrained labor. It may well be that the most important quality defining strike leadership in 1917 was the level of skill, and that metalworkers and leather workers were especially active in strikes for this reason.

THE ROLE OF SKILL

Skill is an elusive quality. It is not readily measured, nor is it an attribute one can reduce to precise objective indices such as age, gender, years on the job, wages, plant size, or geographical location. Such statistical relationships as can be drawn represent, at best, only suggestions based on a somewhat arbitrary taxonomy of work.[7] Yet skill was clearly perceived as an important characteristic in defining vanguard workers in 1917, as well as in structuring labor activism as a whole. For one thing, the relative importance of skilled workers in maintaining production (and hence the livelihoods of their comrades) increased greatly during the war in some industries, especially metals, as we observed in chapter 1. And as the value of skill itself increased, so did the power associated with its attributes, and reciprocally, the potential antagonism toward skilled workers both from administrators above and fellow workers below, whose dependency increased with increasing deprivation. For another, it was the skilled workers in the metal-processing plants and machine-construction plants in particular, especially those in Petrograd's Vyborg district, whom many rightly regarded before 1917 as Russia's most politically conscious workers, and hence, by extension, most active in labor protest.

Workers customarily defined as skilled carried with them an ability to perform special tasks which normally took years to acquire, but which were also vulnerable to new technology. In Russia, the metals industry demanded legions of skilled machinists and fitters in machine-building, tool-making, and instrument manufacture, but skilled workers could also be found elsewhere: in the textile industry as engravers, and in woodworking, chemical, and printing plants. In defining skilled workers, we rely heavily on traditional Russian usage. We have included in the category both traditional craftsmen and artisans and skilled workers in factory industry.[8] Artisans and craftsmen tended to work in small shops

---

vyp. 1, "Fabrichno-zavodskaia promyshlennost' v period 1913–1918 godov," table 19, pp. 174–83. For a discussion of the problems with this source, see Diane Koenker, *Moscow Workers and the 1917 Revolution* (Princeton, N.J., 1981), pp. 372–73.

[7] See Appendix 1.

[8] As elsewhere, skilled workers in Russia gained their abilities largely through apprentice-

(even if they were employed by large factories), where they exercised a great deal of day-to-day control over their working lives. Russian industrialization by 1917 had supplemented their work but had not replaced them, and they could be found everywhere, especially in the urban economy.[9]

Skilled workers of all sorts were easily distinguished in revolutionary Russia from the other broad category of worker, the unskilled chernorabochie, literally "black workers," who labored in foundries and elsewhere, carrying iron, loading wagons, and lifting huge weights in dangerous and stifling "hot shops." Little was required of these ordinary workers besides muscle power, and they had little say in what occurred on the shop floor.[10] Many were also recently arrived from the countryside—*prishlie*—and were relatively easy to replace. Between 1914 and 1917, they also provided the overwhelming mass of urban recruits for the army, a circumstance which obviously made them even more vulnerable to factory autocrats.

Between the ranks of the skilled and unskilled was a third group we think it important to identify, although it was at best heterogeneous and at worst only slightly different in some industries from chernorabochie. These were what might best be called "semiskilled" workers, generally identified in Russia and elsewhere with the introduction of new technology. Workers in this category staffed assembly lines, worked with interchangeable parts, or labored as machine operators in mechanized industries such as textiles, tobacco, or shoe production. They performed simple jobs that required some training but little of the discretion and personal talent characteristic of their skilled comrades. The most important group of workers in this category, clearly, were the legions of textilists, men and especially women who often came straight to the factory from the village, and within a few months were able to perform the routine tasks necessary to operate the complex mechanical looms and other similar equipment.

In this and other cases, "semiskilled" may seem to designate little in the way of special craft or artisanal abilities. Some historians, in fact, regard

---

ship and practical experience, but also as a result of factors outside the work process, such as access to education or the ability of a group of workers to combine and artificially restrict entry into their trade. S. A. Smith calls this latter process "skill via class struggle" (*Red Petrograd: Revolution in the Factories, 1917–1918* (Cambridge, 1983), p. 27); Charles More, *Skill and the English Working Class, 1870–1914* (New York, 1980), pp. 9, 16, calls it "socially constructed skill" as opposed to "genuine skill" learned through training and practice.

[9] See the further discussion in Diane Koenker and William G. Rosenberg, "Skilled Workers and Strike Movement in Revolutionary Russia," *Journal of Social History* 19, no. 4 (Summer 1986), especially pp. 607–8.

[10] See the memoirs of P. Timofeev in Victoria E. Bonnell, ed., *The Russian Worker: Life and Labor under the Tsarist Regime* (Berkeley, 1983), especially pp. 77–81.

it as of little conceptual value.[11] But such workers were generally distinguishable from unskilled laborers in both tasks performed and social culture, often working long and boring hours, in some cases with none of the job variety that even chernorabochie enjoyed. And insofar as semiskilled workers behaved differently as a group from their (more clearly defined) skilled and unskilled comrades, the category is important analytically, even if imprecise.

As we know, the evidence indicates that skilled workers constituted the core of labor protesters in January and February 1917 and carried Russia into the revolution. Some 676,000 workers reportedly left their benches in these two months, according to available estimates, from some 1,330 striking enterprises, 1,140 of which protests were labeled "political" by the Factory Inspectorate.[12] In Petrograd, police records indicate that some 320,000 workers participated in over 280 strikes. Most active here was a core of skilled metalworkers in the Vyborg district.[13] In Moscow, just about 100,000 workers and some 300 enterprises struck during these two months (20 percent on February 28, the first day of the revolution in Moscow, but these strikers tended to come from the same factories as those before that date). Of these strikers, some 60 percent were metalists, which suggests that almost 130 percent of the labor force in metals saw strike action in early 1917. Others especially active (in proportion to their numbers) included tram workers (including skilled metalists in repair depots), printers, and woodworkers. Chemical workers also played a role.[14]

[11] See, e.g., the comments by David Montgomery in I. Wallerstein, ed., *Labor in the World Social Structure* (Beverly Hills, Calif., 1983), pp. 14–15. Certainly there are many grades of skill, and semiskilled workers are often difficult to identify. Whereas semiskilled workers in the textile industry worked in dead-end jobs without much room for advancement from, say, operating a power loom, in the metal industry the machines to be operated were much more complex. A moderately assiduous boy who began work on a simple cartridge-pressing machine might expect to move up gradually by mastering increasingly complicated machines. In his working life he might work through all the categories of skill defined by the Petrograd metalworkers' union, in a series of small progressions: unskilled, semiskilled, skilled, and highly skilled. Yet we believe the distinction between "skilled" and "semiskilled" is analytically important in understanding strikes in 1917, since we think these categories of workers may have been subject to different kinds of pressures and consequently tended to play somewhat different roles, as we shall indicate.

[12] K. N. Iakovleva, "Zabastovochnoe dvizhenie v Rossii za 1895–1917 gody," in *Materialy po statistike truda*, vyp. 8 (Moscow, 1920), pp. 5–6.

[13] See Leopold Haimson and Eric Brian, "Labor Unrest in Imperial Russia during the First World War: A Quantitative Analysis and Interpretation," in *War, Strikes, and Revolution: The Impact of the War Experience on Italy, Germany, France, England, and Russia*, ed. Giulio Sapelli and Leopold H. Haimson (Milan, forthcoming). See also Tsuyoshi Hasegawa, *The February Revolution: Petrograd, 1917* (Seattle, 1981), p. 101 and Appendix 2; Smith, *Red Petrograd*, p. 52.

[14] TSGAOR, ff. 63 and 102 (police reports from January and February, 1917.)

Prerevolutionary perceptions of a skilled workers' vanguard were thus strongly reinforced by the events of February and naturally carried forward into 1917. To what extent, then, can we say that skilled workers continued in this way to dominate Russian strikers from March to October? If we look first at strikes in the aggregate, an approximate division by skill level appears as shown in table 10.1, which indicates that approximately 41 percent of all strikes among production workers, but only about 9 percent of strikers, came from plants employing predominantly skilled workers. At first glance, skilled workers thus seem to fade from the leading ranks of strike activists, replaced by semiskilled workers. Even if we allow a leadership role for skilled workers in those 43 strikes involving both types of workers, it would still appear that the pattern of skilled worker activism from the prerevolutionary period had radically changed after February.

This is a critical issue in understanding labor activism, and in order to sort it out we must ask first how these proportions compare to the relative weight of skilled and semiskilled workers in the labor force as a whole, a task handicapped by the fact that figures characterizing Russia's labor force overall in terms of skill in this period do not exist. We can, however, extrapolate rather roughly from more limited data. Information for Petrograd for 1918 indicates, for example, that some 34 percent of the workforce here consisted of skilled workers, 24 percent of semiskilled, and some 37 percent unskilled (with 5 percent unknown), figures which undoubtedly overstate the proportion of skilled workers in the 1917 work-

TABLE 10.1
Strike Participants by Skill Level
(Individual Industrial Strikes Only)

Skill Level	Strikes		Estimated Strikers[a]	
	Number	Percent	Number	Percent
Skilled	299	41	117,870	9
Semiskilled	330	46	799,420	63
Unskilled	52	7	26,710	2
Skilled and semiskilled	43	6	334,060	26
Total	724	100	1,278,060	100

[a] Minimum estimates based on 76% of strikes by skilled workers, 78% of strikes by semiskilled, 71% by unskilled, and 72% of skilled and semiskilled striking together.

force, since they come from a time when chernorabochie and semiskilled workers were being drastically affected by industrial and military demobilization.[15] If we apply these rough divisions to 1917 (dividing the 334,000 strikers in the plants combining skilled and semiskilled workers according to the 1918 ratio of skilled to semiskilled), we can estimate some 315,000 skilled workers and some 936,000 semiskilled workers in the strike force overall, an approximation which suggests at the very least that *un*skilled workers were relatively insignificant in 1917 strikes.[16] In other words, even if we estimate that a minimum 37 percent of the industrial labor force was unskilled (based on the 1918 figures, which generously estimate the size of this group), fewer than 2 percent of industrial workers striking alone in 1917 appear to have been unskilled.[17] At the same time, these figures suggest that skilled workers themselves did not participate in strikes in 1917 at the same rate as their less-skilled comrades.

The relative representation of skilled workers in strikes and the strike force can also be assessed by examining strike propensities of different industries. When we do so, we find that two of the three most strike-prone industries (leather, with a propensity of 3.38 and metals, with 1.68) were characterized by the predominance of skilled workers in their labor force, but that the workers of the printing industry, also largely skilled, struck relatively little in 1917 (with a strike propensity of .46) (table 2.8). Moreover, both leather workers and printers shared traits of small-scale production and a history of trade union organization, factors which would predispose them to collective action, yet leather workers seem to have struck at a rate almost four times higher than their share of the labor force, while printers struck much less. It would thus seem the attributes

---

[15] V. Z. Drobizhev, A. K. Sokolov, and V. A. Ustinov, eds., *Rabochii klass sovetskoi Rossii v pervyi god proletarskoi diktatury* (Moscow, 1975), p. 84.

[16] This estimate is based on the following calculation. The ratio of skilled to semiskilled workers (extrapolating from their relative weight in the 1918 Petrograd work force) is 59:41. We can thus divide the skilled-and-semiskilled category (334,060 workers) proportionally, in order to compare the distribution of strikers with that of the work force at large.

117,870 skilled + 59% of 334,060 = 314,965 skilled
799,420 semiskilled + 41% of 334,060 = 936,385 semiskilled

[17] This comparison can be summarized as follows:

DISTRIBUTION OF SKILL LEVELS IN
THE LABOR FORCE AND STRIKE FORCE

	Labor Force % 1918	Strike Force % 1917
Skilled	34	25
Semiskilled	24	73
Unskilled	37	2

of skill alone, particularly artisanal craft skill, did not necessarily predispose workers to strike in 1917.

Our calculations here may understimate the number of unskilled workers initiating strikes within industrial enterprises in 1917, and many of those we call semiskilled may have been seen during the revolutionary period (and classified in 1918) as unskilled. Nonetheless, our evidence clearly suggests that the bulk of Russia's strikers from March to October came from near the center of the skilled to unskilled spectrum, and that these semiskilled workers dominated strikes numerically and proportionally when we consider 1917 as a whole. In this we see a phenomenon parallel to the masses of clerical workers, shop clerks, and other service-sector employees who also entered the strike force in such large numbers in 1917. Workers historically less favored in Russia's economy were now able to use this powerful weapon routinely against their employers, a weapon placed at their disposal by new conditions of political freedom. Their participation thus extended strikes sociologically, even as the political significance of the act of striking itself intensified. We can still say with some confidence, despite the roughness of our data, that skilled workers continued to be quite active in strikes after February 1917, as they were before, but their role in this form of activism, at least, was no longer paramount.

THE ROLE OF PLANT SIZE AND URBAN CONCENTRATION

If the prerevolutionary vanguard of skilled workers seems to yield precedence to less-skilled comrades after February, what of other features associated with labor activism: the mobilizing role of large factories and urban concentration? One of the most interesting issues of strike mobilization in 1917 has to do with plant size. Simply stated, the question is whether Russian workers employed in large plants were more prone to strike than others, as they had been in 1905, and as they have proved to be in other labor movements.[18] In terms of understanding a workers' vanguard, the question is whether industrial workers in large enterprises took a leading role in labor activism during 1917, dominating strikes both in the sense of shaping their overall contours and in stimulating complementary activism in other types of enterprises.

One should assume from what we already know that large enterprises provided the overwhelming number of strikers. By 1915, more than 45

---

[18] Over a seventy-year period in France, from 1900 to 1968, workers in larger plants also tended to strike more frequently than those in smaller ones. See Shorter and Tilly, *Strikes in France*, pp. 61–64.

percent of all Russian industrial workers in nine major branches were employed in plants with more than 1,000 workers, more than 80 percent in plants with more than 100.[19] Also, approximately 65 percent of Russia's textile workers and almost 60 percent of all metalworkers were employed in plants with more than 1,000 workers.[20] Indeed, our aggregate data hold no surprises. For those strikes for which we have reasonably good information about both the size of the enterprise and the number of striking workers in 1917, the dominance of Russia's largest enterprises is quite considerable. As much as 60 percent of the strike force between March and October may have come from plants employing more than 1,000 workers. These large plants also show the greatest evidence of having been organized in some way by trade unions, factory committees, or other workers associations; as we know, they were also the principal targets of Bolshevik party organizers.

This dominance is affirmed by our relative indices. Although almost one quarter of all workers were employed in plants with between 101 and 500 workers, they furnished only 18.0 percent of the strikers from individual plants; 63.8 percent of these strikers came from a pool of just 45.5 percent of the labor force. Moreover, the relationship between strike pro-

TABLE 10.2
Distribution of Workers, Strikers,
and Strike Propensities by Size of Plant

Factory Size	Percent of All Workers[a]	Percent of All Strikers[b]	Strike Propensities[c]				
			All	Metals	Textiles	Leather	Wood
1–50	9.2	0.9	.098	.15	.10	.12	.04
51–100	6.8	3.8	.559	.39	.13	.36	.25
101–500	23.8	18.0	.756	.96	.64	.67	.95
501–1000	14.7	13.6	.925	1.21	.75	1.73	5.65
Over 1000	45.5	63.8	1.400	1.13	1.19	1.67	11.30

SOURCE: 1915 data from TSSU, *Trudy*, vol. 7, vyp. 1, table 2, pp. 36–37.
[a] Single industry strikes only.
[b] Percentages of workers by plant size are for 1915. $N = 12,649$ plants.
[c] Percentages of strikers by plant size are for 1917. $N = 398$ plants.

[19] TSSU, *Trudy*, vol. 7, vyp. 1, "Statisticheskii sbornik za 1913–1917 gody" (Moscow, 1921), table 2, pp. 36–37.
[20] Ibid.

pensity and plant size is remarkably linear, as table 10.2 indicates, not only for all workers, but also for each of the four most strike-prone industries in 1917.

At the same time, the possibilities of efficient mobilization even in smaller plants are apparent in data for the paper and printing industry. Although 20 percent of this industrial group's labor force was employed in plants with more than 500 workers, relatively few of these plants engaged in strikes in 1917. Instead, printing plants employing between 51 and 100 workers had the highest propensity to strike (2.56) and produced 45 percent of the strikers in the industry against only 18 percent of the workers.

Several factors might account for the disproportionate strike activity among smaller printing plants. One is the effect of reporting: printers, with their generally high rates of literacy and access to the world of newspapers, might be more successful than workers in other industries in attracting attention to their strikes. Second, printing establishments tended to be smaller than their partners in the industry, paper and cardboard manufacturing enterprises. Printers traditionally were better organized than paper workers and struck in their smaller plants more actively. Finally, small size in industries such as printing, organized on an artisanal basis, may have facilitated organization, whereas the size of large plants, with many independent sections, may have discouraged combined action. However, the wood and leather industries shared some of the industrial organizational characteristics of printing, yet their strikes still tended to be concentrated in larger plants.

These figures relate only to strikes that took place in individual enterprises, but based on this limited sample, we can conclude that the larger the plant, the more likely its workers to strike. However, in most cases, combinations of more than one plant served as a substitute for the cohesion provided by large individual plant size. In the printing industry, for example, smaller plants were more strike-prone than large plants, but in total, only 7 percent of all the industry's strikers were involved in these single-plant walkouts: 93 percent of striking printers participated in strikes that united two or more enterprises. By contrast, the metal industry, with 66 percent of its strikers coming from plants larger than 1,000, also tended to produce more single-plant strikes: approximately 22 percent of its strikers were involved in strikes limited to one enterprise. The textile industry stands out as an exception again; although coming predominantly from large plants, only 15 percent of its strikers struck independently of other plants.

The relationship between factory size and strike behavior is obviously a complex one: from all this it is still not certain that the size of an enterprise alone was more significant in fostering strikes than other factors, such as geographic location, skill, or economic factors. Let us turn now to the question of whether geography, and particularly urban concentration, contributed to the formation of a strike vanguard.

URBAN CONCENTRATION:
THE ROLE OF PETROGRAD AND MOSCOW

The political volatility of Petrograd and the critical role played by its workers in 1905 and in the years before 1917 have rightly earned for that city pride of place in the revolutionary movement. Did workers in Petrograd then play a leading role in the 1917 in the strikes as well, giving credence to Lenin's dictum that "any step of Petersburg is a leading example for all Russia"?[21] And what about the role of urban concentration in general, and the opportunities city and town environments offered for coordinating and mobilizing strike actions?

Our data suggest that as far as strikes were concerned, notions about the primacy of Petrograd need some correction. Peter the Great's handsome city on the Neva was larger than Moscow in 1917, and certainly the center of revolutionary politics, but all indices suggest that Moscow was the more strike-prone. In aggregate figures, nearly one-quarter of all the strikes we have recorded took place in Moscow, compared to 12 percent in Petrograd. In relative terms, Moscow registered 12.0 strikes per 10,000 workers, while Petrograd had only 3.3 strikes per 10,000 workers. Nor did Petrograd compensate for its relatively few strikes by the number of workers involved. In terms of estimated strikers, Moscow's industrial strike force (its intensity) was 184.1 percent of its factory labor force—almost double—while Petrograd's industrial strikers amounted to 95.4 percent of its factory labor force (table 10.3).[22]

If we look at strike-prone provinces in addition to the larger regions depicted in table 10.3, the absence of a strictly defined geographic vanguard can be seen even more clearly (table 10.4). The Volga province of Kazan, for example, dominates the city of Moscow as a leader in strike intensity. Saratov on the Volga, the combined provinces of Vladimir and Kostroma in the Central Industrial Region, and Baku on the Caspian also

---

[21] V. I. Lenin, *Polnoe sobranie sochineniia*, vol. 32, p. 225.

[22] These calculations necessarily exclude nonindustrial workers. There are no reliable estimates of the number that serves as the denominator for these measures of intensity and propensity: the regional labor forces in services and other sectors. We must therefore use the pattern of industrial strikers as a proxy for broader patterns.

TABLE 10.3
Strike Intensities by Region
(Industrial Strikes Only)

Region	Number of Strikes	Number of Strikers	Number of Workers	Strike Intensity[a]
Urals region	20	122,000	45,050	270.8
Moscow city	211	379,130	205,900	184.1
Petrograd city	65	366,800	384,600	95.4
Volga region	28	99,450	114,250	87.0
Caspian region	7	55,310	63,650	86.9
Moscow region[b]	152	432,210	794,210	53.3
Petrograd region[c]	53	26,550	67,560	39.3
Kiev region	77	67,720	195,100	34.7
Rostov region	34	16,965	65,100	26.1
Kharkov-Ekaterinoslav region	44	30,855	171,630	18.0
Transcaucasus region	10	1,965	18,620	10.6
Odessa region	15	1,720	74,900	2.3

[a] The strike intensity is defined as the percentage of the region's industrial labor force on strike.
[b] Excluding city of Moscow.
[c] Excluding city of Petrograd.

rival Moscow. All of these provinces reported nearly as many or more strikers than the number of workers employed in industry.

Thus, although Moscow and Petrograd were important, they did not monopolize strike activity as one might have predicted given their predominant political and economic roles. Quite obviously, biases in strike reporting would favor the central cities; missing strikes and concentrations of strikers in our data are more likely to be from outlying provinces than from the center. In any event, it is essential to acknowledge the extent to which strikes spread across the width and breadth of Russia in 1917, to appreciate the degree to which this form of labor mobilization and activism encompassed workers everywhere.

All of this does not mean, however, that Petrograd strikes were less important to the course of events than those in Moscow and elsewhere. Clearly, strike activism in Petrograd most directly influenced Soviet leaders and the Provisional Government; in terms of strikes, the perception political activists in the center developed was one, as we have seen, in

TABLE 10.4
Strike Intensities in Provinces with
Intensities Greater than 50 Percent
(Industrial Strikes Only)

Province	Strike Intensity for 1917
Kazan	259.1
Petrograd (including city)	132.0
Kostroma-Vladimir	119.0
Saratov	110.9
Baku	96.8
Moscow (including city)	94.4
Kuban	75.4
Kiev	69.6
Estland	67.6
Nizhnii Novgorod	53.7

which economic rationality was being overwhelmed by large political strike-demonstrations, especially in the aftermath of the July Days. In fact, as our data suggest, the strike process across Russia, frequently provoked by challenges from management, was far more rational, orderly, and a part of more routine aspects of labor-management relations than a function of maximalist greed, although such attributes were often obscured.

A Look at Gender

The dominant role of textile workers in strikes suggests that women might have been disproportionately active in strikes. This highly strike-prone industry was one in which well over half of the labor force was female. Direct information on strike participation by gender, however, is extremely hard to come by. Gender was not a category of particular interest to labor activists in the early twentieth century, in Russia as elsewhere; reports of strikes rarely even mention the presence of women, let alone focus on their role, even in enterprises in which we know from other sources that women constituted a large part of the labor force. In the Ivanovo textile strike, which must have involved nearly 200,000 women workers, the role of these women went unreported. And none of the local union officials or central strike committee members was a woman, despite women's two-to-one predominance in the labor force.[23]

Nonetheless, indirect evidence suggests that women were becoming mobilized for activism in 1917 to a far greater extent than ever before in Russia, despite the obstacles of their own traditional deference to authority and the lack of attention paid them by male organizers. Women played an important role in food disorders and other urban episodes of protest, beginning with the February strikes and continuing in the street disorders in Moscow in late summer and early fall. And if our statistical indices pay scant attention to the involvement of women in most strikes, we can isolate some 50 strikes in which women participated for which we have reasonably good data, most in the city of Moscow. What is particularly interesting about these strikes is not, in fact, their concentration in textiles, but their distribution over a range of industrial branches, including metals, paper, and leather, and the fact that they largely occurred in small workshops, rather than large plants. Only two strikes for which we have good information, in fact, occurred in major textile plants: the Girault (Zhiro) silk manufacturing complex, employing some 3,500, and the Mussi silk works, with 2,400 workers. Both these strikes occurred in Moscow in June, both were largely over wages, and both involved men as well as women. And both were characterized more by a reluctance to strike than by an obvious desire to do so.

At the Girault works, where most women were earning less than 30 rubles a month, workers were clearly hesitant at factory meetings early in June to go on strike for fear that the plant would simply be shut down. Although a strike threat was raised on June 5, no decision was made for at least five days, as workers waited for management's response. When the Girault owners refused to raise wages without other plants also doing so, a brief work stoppage occurred, but ended quickly when the Moscow textile union leadership insisted that such walkouts could seriously damage the union movement. Shortly afterwards, the management at Girault agreed to give bonuses, a compromise allowing them to preserve their own solidarity with other manufacturers.[24] At Mussi, a similar conflict unfolded somewhat differently. Workers struggled here for most of May and June over a new minimum wage, but again, without success. By several accounts, workers attempted in vain to have the matter settled by arbitration, by court decision, and by direct negotiation. When manage-

[23] G. Korolev, *Ivanovo-Kineshemskie tekstil'shchiki v 1917 godu* (Moscow, 1927); S. K. Klimokhin, ed., *Kratkaia istoriia stachki tekstil'shchikov Ivanovo-Kineshemnskoi promyshlennoi oblasti* (Kineshma, 1918).

[24] *Vpered*, June 6, 15, 1917; *Zemlia i Volia*, June 15, 1917.

ment refused these demands, and refused as well to recognize the workers' committee or the union as legitimate workers' organizations, a strike began on June 23, lasting until early September. Throughout, however, workers insisted they would return to work as soon as serious negotiations began.[25]

Far from advocating militant goals, women workers in both these cases appear to have been almost plaintively defensive, as were women in strikes in other industrial sectors, both in Moscow and elsewhere. When owners of the Shabat envelope company in Moscow fired five female workers in mid-April because of production cutbacks, workers attempted to have the overall number of workdays for all workers reduced as an alternative to the dismissals, acknowledging, in effect, the owners' right to reduce the workforce.[26] When waiters, cooks, and other employees struck Moscow restaurants in mid-May, a number of women returned to work after one or two days, insisting their interests were not the same as those of the men.[27] And perfume workers in Moscow, rather than quitting their stations, slowed down production in June as a way of gaining wage increases. Such evidence reinforces the impression that women did not appear in the forefront of strikes, and that when they struck, they did so reluctantly. One important and by now familiar exception to this pattern, however, was the Petrograd laundry workers, whose strike militancy captured the attention of the country.

UNDERSTANDING CHANGES IN THE STRIKE FORCE

So far we can describe strikers in 1917 as predominantly male, concentrated in large plants, and involving a disproportionate number of metalists, all features traditionally associated with a revolutionary vanguard in Russia. But we also know in addition that skilled workers, even in the metal industry, were less likely to strike in 1917 than workers in less skilled industrial occupations, that Petrograd occupied a proportionately less prominent role in strike activity than Moscow and even locations farther afield, and that industrial workers less known for their political activism, especially leather workers and woodworkers, were just as strike-prone or more so than the proud metalists, bearers of the revolutionary tradition.

In these respects, similarities between the strike force and Russia's revolutionary "vanguard" in 1917 become increasingly less pronounced.

---

[25] *Vpered*, June 29, July 13, 28, 1917; *Sotsial Demokrat*, July 5, 14, 1917; *Trud*, June 29, July 4, 9, September 14, 1917.

[26] *Vpered*, April 26, 1917; *Zemlia i Volia*, April 27, 1917; *Trud*, April 29, 1917.

[27] *Novaia Zhizn'*, May 14, 23, 1917.

Clearly the metalists' role in other forms of political activism must partly account for this change, especially after the July Days; so, too, must the relatively favorable contractual agreements worked out even with resistant employers by forceful leaders of the metalworkers' union. Let us look, however, at less apparent possible factors such as changing wages, levels of productivity, age, literacy, gender, ties to the countryside, and urban concentration. Data on these matters are not available for each set of strikers, but do exist in more aggregate form, for each of the 50-odd Russian provinces during the time of the revolution. Using multivariate regression analysis, we can try to sort out which factors appear to be most clearly related to strike intensity.[28]

These statistical techniques yield a more vivid, and in some ways rather surprising, overall portrait of strike activists. The most important explanatory factors concern wages. Strike intensities were highest in 1917 in provinces where the average nominal wage for 1916 was high but also where the real wage had fallen relative to 1913. Insofar as wages measure skill and experience, this result tends to contradict our finding that skilled workers were relatively inactive in strikes. We find also that, controlling for wages, strike intensities were highest in provinces where the average factory size was large. This, by contrast, confirms our analysis discussed above. Strike intensities were also high in provinces with high concentrations of industrial workers, but not in highly urbanized provinces.[29] We also find simple correlations between the percentage of female workers in a province and strike intensities, and also between the percentage of textile workers and strike intensities. The gender factor becomes insignificant when wages are accounted for, but textile workers remain a positive factor in strike intensities.

Other factors that we might expect to relate to strike intensities—age structure, literacy, ties to the land, and previous strike history—do not. The relationship between wages and strike intensities dominates almost everything else. Moscow and Petrograd were clearly important centers of strikes, but once we control for the higher wages of these two cities, urban concentration per se has no significant impact.

We might generalize our statistical results into a model striker, one whose properties turn out to be somewhat inconsistent. He, or she, would be reasonably well-paid (a skilled worker, perhaps, with a considerable degree of work experience, and therefore likely to be male), but one whose real wages had fallen considerably since the start of the war, espe-

---

[28] For a discussion of this technique, see Appendix 1.

[29] We find a simple positive correlation between strike intensities and urban population, but once the wage effect is taken into consideration, this correlation becomes insignificant.

cially in comparison with other well-paid workers. This striker would most likely work in a area of high industrial concentration, where the scale of factories was large, but not necessarily in a city: this sounds remarkably like the textile-manufacturing provinces of the Central Industrial Region. Since most large-scale enterprises employed large numbers of semiskilled and unskilled workers, the model striker seems just as likely to have been a semiskilled female as a skilled male.

In contrast to the notion of a revolutionary vanguard leading strikers toward October, the picture we now can draw of the social composition of the strike force in 1917 is thus quite complex. Metalworkers and skilled workers (as indicated by the wage factor) were important components, but so were textile workers, semiskilled workers, and workers in mass production enterprises. Urban centers were important, but so were provincial industrial centers like Kazan, Saratov, and Baku. In sum, we cannot speak of a strike vanguard at all in terms of social indices, since there are no really consistent patterns. Strikes in 1917 were a mass phenomenon, not the provenance of a vanguard. All kinds of wage earners participated—young, old, highly skilled, not so skilled, urban and provincial, industrial workers, sales clerks, and laundresses alike. And although strikes in many instances were also prompted, at least in part, by militant Bolshevik workers or others closely affiliated with radical parties, as the Soviet historian A. M. Lisetskii argues in particular,[30] the more important fact about strike activism in 1917 is that it was such a highly generalized, social phenomenon, not in any evident way the consequence of specific political agitation. In Russia's democratic revolution, labor protest, like so much else, had become fully democratized.

This is certainly true if we look at the period from March to October as a whole. But obviously one cannot ignore the dynamic element of strikes in revolutionary Russia. Workers did not strike just because they were prompted to do so by changing real wages, skill level, or the number of workers in their plants. As we have tried to emphasize, the strike process was a highly interactive one; the revolution created new opportunities for bargaining and redressing old wrongs, which expressed themselves in strikes. Strikes created pressures on management and on the economy, and they provoked responses that led to new pressures and new protests. Timing, then, or rather Russia's specific historical conjuncture, obviously remained a critical element in changing contours of strike activism after February.

This can be measured statistically as well. As we have detailed in the

---

[30] A. M. Lisetskii, *Bol'sheviki vo glave massovykh stachek (mart–oktiabr' 1917 goda* (Kishinev, 1974).

preceding chapters, strike activism in 1917 clustered in three distinct periods; May to early July, late July through much of August, and mid-September to October 25, when the Bolsheviks came to power. This periodization emerges directly from our data on strike frequencies. When we compare summer and fall strikes, however, and then contrast these two clusters of activity together with strikes in the spring, we find that the most significant turning point in the character of strike activism for all of 1917 was the first week of July, a familiar and even conventional breakpoint in the revolutionary process as a whole.

Provinces with the highest strike intensities before July 6 were those with the highest nominal wages, but a decline in real wages. These wage effects appear to dominate all other characteristics. Once these are controlled for statistically, we find that factory size and urban concentration do not affect strike intensities in the first half of the year. Past strike experience, however, measured by participation in strikes from 1913 to 1916, does turn out to be significantly correlated with strike intensities between March 3 and July 6. We can therefore say with a high degree of certainty that strike-prone provinces before July 6 were those that had struck most before the February revolution and had high wages but a falling real wage. As we suggested in chapter 7, we can glimpse here for the first time the idealized revolutionary vanguard: skilled workers (largely metalists), experienced in labor activism and suffering in 1917 relative economic deprivation.

After the important divide of July 6, however, this sharp picture dissolves. At first strike activity declined precipitously, as we have documented in chapter 8, only to reemerge at the end of the month at a much higher level of intensity than before. Yet in sharp contrast to strikes in the spring, we now find *no* significant statistical correlations after July 6 between strike intensities and wages or strike history. Instead, strong bivariate correlations emerge between strike intensity, on the one hand, and factory size, industrial concentration, and share of provincial workers employed in the textile industry, on the other. Here, then, are the striking semiskilled workers and workers in mass industry. We cannot say that "leadership" in strike activism has passed to these groups, or we would find a negative correlation between wages and strike intensities instead of no correlation at all. What we see instead is that these workers have, in effect, joined those of their comrades who struck in the spring to create a genuinely mass movement.

The hypothesis of two different sets of strike activists before and after July 6 can be tested by returning to our other indices of the social composition of strikers. In terms of the broad categories of industry, table 10.5 shows how the propensity to strike of the eight major industries

TABLE 10.5
Strike Propensities by Industry before and after July 6
(Single-Industry Strikes Only)

Industry	Strike Propensity March 3–July 6	Strike Propensity July 7–October 25
Minerals	.04	.06
Metal	2.98	.67
Wood and wood products	.33	1.35
Chemicals	.09	.60
Food products	.04	.08
Animal products (leather)	.88	5.38
Textiles	.38	1.44
Paper and printing	.23	.64

NOTE: Calculations show relative propensities among these industrial branches only. Mining, mixed products, and other industrial sectors are excluded.

changed between the first and second halves of the year. Figures in the first column recapitulate our argument in chapter 7: clearly, the metal industry dominated Russia's industrial strike force in the early half of the year, continuing its central position in the labor movement as a whole. No other industrial group's share of strikers approached its share of the labor force: all propensities were below 1 except that of the metalists. But strike activism in this group faded after July 6, both relatively and absolutely, while that of all other groups increased.

It is pertinent that clerical workers and other service sector employees also struck most extensively before rather than after July 6. Our minimum estimates suggest that the number of striking service workers fell from approximately 60,000 before July 6 to less than 16,000 after; striking retail employees from approximately 11,500 to a little more than 4,000. Also, the absolute participation of skilled workers in strikes did not seem to vary from the first half of the year to the second. The number of strikers in plants employing predominantly skilled workers remained constant; the number of semiskilled and skilled workers striking together rose, and the number of unskilled workers fell. The big change occurred in the massive numbers of semiskilled workers striking after July 6.

The shift in strikes away from the old revolutionary vanguard can be seen as well by considering the change in the rates of strikers across regions (table 10.6). In the period before July 6, the two cities of Petrograd

TABLE 10.6
Strikes and Strike Intensities by Region before and after July 6
(Industrial Strikes Only)

Region	March 3–July 6		July 7–October 25	
	Strikes	Strike Intensity	Strikes	Strike Intensity
Petrograd region[a]	27	4.9	25	34.4
Petrograd city	35	81.9	26	12.7
Moscow region[b]	79	10.0	67	42.6
Moscow city	142	49.3	58	132.8
Kiev region	37	3.2	37	31.3
Odessa region	9	1.2	6	1.1
Kharkov- Ekaterinoslav region	12	2.7	29	14.2
Rostov region	9	1.3	22	23.1
Transcaucasus region	4	1.4	5	9.1
Caspian region	3	0.4	4	86.5
Volga region	9	13.0	16	74.0
Urals region	4	3.4	16	267.4

[a] Excluding city of Petrograd.
[b] Excluding city of Moscow.

and Moscow stood far above the other regions in the activism of their workers. In none of the other regions did the level of strikers exceed 13 percent of the respective labor forces. In the second half of the year, however, when strike activity incorporated over a million industrial workers across the country (and more than 1,800,000 overall, including service-sector employees and transport workers), Petrograd's activism is remarkably low. Now, when workers of the Urals struck at a rate equal to two-and-a-half times the size of their industrial labor force, when Moscow put more workers in the streets than were employed in industry, when one-third or more of the workers almost everywhere went on strike, only 12.7 percent of Petrograd workers joined them. In every region except Petrograd and Odessa, the rate of strike participation at least doubled between the two periods.

To summarize: the strongest conclusion from this additional evidence is that those commonly recognized as the labor vanguard—skilled workers, Petrograd metalists—remained in the forefront of strike activism only until approximately the first week of July. Afterwards, their participation in strikes declined, or at the very least was overshadowed by the participation of hundreds of thousands of workers whose revolutionary credentials were not so well recognized. Thus, through early July, strikes were dominated by workers who bore a strong resemblance to contemporary (and subsequent) conceptions of Russia's revolutionary vanguard, and who resembled the picture of 1912–1914 and 1915–1917.

Does it then follow that the strikes these workers engaged in were simply an extension of the revolutionary strikes that toppled the tsar? We think not. Although they involved an often intense struggle for power within the workplace, as we have emphasized, they were overwhelmingly economic in their essential character, focusing on labor-management issues owners and workers themselves could try to resolve. If we think in terms of "routine" or "bourgeois-democratic" labor relations, the changing pattern of the social composition of the strike force follows a clear mobilizational-economic logic. The old revolutionary vanguard dominated strikes before July because these workers were the most capable of mobilizing resources and energy to take advantage of the new open climate in labor relations. Their past strike experience furnished workers in Petrograd and Moscow with valuable lessons in organization. They also had the benefit of contacts with trade union organizations before the revolution and were likely to have developed networks that would facilitate strike organization. Although well-paid, our statistical analysis suggests they did not strike because of their high wages but because of their declining real wages: higher wages provided the economic resources to carry out further struggle.

Continuing with this logic, workers in "rearguard" industries and outside Petrograd struck more intensively in the second half of the year in part because they simply were not able to mobilize resources without a lengthy period of planning and organization. Each of the four massive strikes of the late summer and fall, for example, had been long in preparation. Moscow leather workers began to organize their assault on management on June 5, although the strike began only on August 16.[31] While workers in better-paid industries already possessed the resources they needed to strike, Ivanovo textile workers, who had no trade union before the February revolution, spent the early months of the revolution organizing a union to unite the region's workers and began negotiations in early May that culminated in their huge strike in October. The same was true with railroaders and with oil industry workers around Baku. In each instance unions continued to build their organizations, collected eco-

---

[31] I. S. Iuzefovich, *Iz klassovykh boev 1917 goda (Stachka Moskovskikh kozhevnikov)* (Moscow, 1928), p. 4.

nomic data to make their case more strongly, and entered into negotiations. Workers in each case also accumulated strike funds to support themselves, even though pay for strike time was invariably included in their list of demands. The kind of organization demonstrated in the September oil strike or the strike of textile workers in October simply could not have developed without long and arduous organizing activity.[32]

Economics and the logic of mobilization, however, are only two of the links between strikes and the revolutionary process in 1917, and they suffer in explanatory power because they do not account for the change in the political context within which strikers had to make their decisions between February and October. We have argued that labor relations were often conducted early in the year as more-or-less routine adjuncts of bargaining in a democratic capitalist system, that they could also be expected to follow rules of behavior such a system might regard as sensible and rational. According to this paradigm, strikers were essentially exercising their economic power within the system of private property and capitalist relations, even if all strike activism also involved a struggle for power within the workplace and hence had significant political implications more generally. In other words, the fact that many strike activists between March and July had also participated in earlier revolutionary activity does not necessarily mean that all post-February strikes also carried radical political implications. The overwhelming number of strikes in the first half of the year sought to achieve gains within the established (if also evolving) system, or at most to extend the limits of workers' power within it. They were not necessarily aimed at overturning the prevailing pattern of property and ownership relations.

But as we have seen, "routine" labor-management relations were fragile at best in Russian political culture and began to unravel very early. As the stability of Russia's particular form of capitalism progressively weakened, strikes became a dubious method of extracting real concessions from management. In these circumstances the need for state intervention and the more radical alternative of industrial nationalization—of state ownership of the means of production—understandably became more attractive even to those mobilized workers who were not otherwise persuaded by Bolsheviks or other radicals. Thus we see strikes after July becoming increasingly contentious over issues of control, of power, rather than of economic leverage. One might say that more routine patterns of strike activism gave way, or were joined by, strikes that were essentially revolutionary in character, in the sense that hundreds of thousands of workers downed their tools in August, September, and October, even though a purely economic calculus indicated that their chances for lasting

[32] Korolev, *Ivanovo-Kineshemskie tekstil'shchiki*, pp. 20, 26.

gains were virtually nil. Were they striking irrationally, elementally destroying the sources of their livelihood, as contemporary commentators and some historians have alleged? We would argue their behavior was only irrational under the old, "bourgeois" rules of labor relations. Never firmly established in any case, these rules were now changing as workers from every economic sector sought to mobilize a democratic polity in support of their own rights and privileges.

Hence it is no surprise that our statistical techniques cannot explain the post-July strike force in terms of wage differentials or social background. Strikes having become a mass phenomenon, it is not possible to identify a vanguard or a leadership role for particular groups. Politicized by the development of events, strikes became events that were themselves shaped by the diverse and contending perceptions of consolidating social classes and the contradictory goals they sought. In the process, economic, organizational, and political attributes of strikes merged together to transform their character. Largely outmoded, as weapons of struggle in the course of labor-management conflict, strikes by October symbolized the *rejection* of bourgeois values (and the processes for resolving labor-management conflicts in Western bourgeois societies). For both management and labor, they had largely come instead to reflect the developing tensions, mentalities, and violence of civil war.

We think it no paradox that the revolutionary pioneers, the vanguard of 1912–1914 and February 1917, did not dominate this latter wave of mass strikes. In the aftermath of July, as strikes spread away from Moscow and Petrograd and into other industrial sectors, the militance of Petrograd and Moscow metalists was itself channeled in different directions. One might say that the "revolutionary vanguard" disassociated itself from the strike tactic after the July Days, at least to some extent, moving through Bolshevik party committees and workers' militias into other forms of direct action. Conscious metalists and others, particularly in workers' committees and the trade union movement, appreciated the need to defend against further economic collapse but did so by seeking relief through revolutionary politics. As the factory committee of the Petrograd Cable plant argued in attempting to quell a strike among workers of the India-rubber section on October 24, "Their demands are completely correct, but in view of the political situation—the necessity of the transfer of power to the Soviets—we advise not only our comrades in the India-rubber section, but all workers in the plant to refrain from individual actions."[33] Identical sentiments were expressed by workers elsewhere.[34]

[33] Z. V. Stepanov, *Rabochie Petrograda v period podgotovki i provedeniia oktiabr'skogo vooruzhennogo vosstaniia* (Moscow and Leningrad, 1965), p. 83.

[34] *Izvestiia* (Moscow), October 24, 1917.

Many union leaders also clearly discouraged strikes at this point. As the Moscow metal union's journal declared, for example,

Now when the revolution places on the agenda the basic question of regulating all productive activities—even such new and important questions as the promulgation of collective tariff agreements are pushed aside by life as if part of a secondary plan. Now more than ever it is clear that *the economic struggle has turned into a political one.* . . .

Every superfluous day on strike, every superfluous stoppage of production, under conditions of both naturally developing and artificially induced catastrophe, threaten the existence of the class organizations of the proletariat. . . . Every organized worker ought to understand that outside this [political] struggle every economic strike will be fruitless. Our thrust should be a classwide lightning attack along the entire front in the form of a general organized political strike.[35]

The Moscow central bureau of trade unions on October 13 echoed these sentiments, discussing how to defend workers' interests by other means than strikes. Representatives of the leather workers, tailors, metalists, and confectioners all agreed that strikes were no longer effective; they considered instead how to use public opinion to force the Moscow Soviet to take power by unilaterally declaring all strikes settled in the workers' favor.[36] If skilled metalists (and others) recognized with these union activists the decreasing usefulness of strikes as either economic or political weapons by the fall of 1917, they may have felt industrial relations at this point could only be handled effectively, if at all, through the formation of a radical socialist regime. If this is true, as our evidence suggests, then we have on the eve of October a revolutionary workers' vanguard somewhat at odds with more strike-prone comrades, but still central to the process of revolution in 1917, and moving with varying degrees of commitment and enthusiasm toward the Bolsheviks' coming to power.

In interesting ways, strikes in revolutionary Russia thus confound theory, which largely treats them as phenomena exogenous to a world it tries to explain: as indicators of the dislocations of modernization, of structural characteristics (and especially deformations) of particular societies, of economic cycles, or of political processes. There is much that one must accept in this analysis. But the experience of strikes in the Russian revolution, as we have presented it here, shows that strikes are also much more than mere indicators: they are also endogenous to their historical

[35] *Moskovskii Metallist*, 4 (October 16, 1917), p. 1–2.
[36] *Moskovskii sovet professional'nykh soiuzov v 1917 godu (Protokoly)* (Moscow, 1927), pp. 100–11.

contexts, and they take on a life of their own. Strike events—and, of course, perceptions of strikes—influence the structure of the society in which they occur; they influence perceptions about rules and appropriate behaviors quite apart from their considerable economic impact. In revolutionary Russia, strikes and other forms of activism did not just reflect the way workers, managers, and political figures thought about social and economic relationships. Much more powerfully, they changed the way these participants perceived the *political* process, demonstrating to managers that they could not exercise hegemony over the labor process once the tsarist apparatus was removed. They also were a means by which workers came to realize, after attempts at various forms of mediation and conciliation, that management would not willingly yield its power in the workplace. Thus each strike, each confrontation, added to the climate of polarization, of mutual distrust and hostility, that became so pervasive by October.

STRIKES AND REVOLUTION IN RUSSIA

Throughout this discussion, we have avoided the term "strike movement" in describing strike activity in 1917.[37] The word "movement" implies a linearity, a uniformity, a teleology of events moving toward an October climax that obscures the complex and multivalent nature of strikes in the revolution of 1917. We have stressed rather two parallel conceptualizations of these strikes: they must be seen both as routine tools of labor-management relations in a system with mutually acceptable rules, and as instruments for revolutionary change outside established social and political boundaries. Strikes functioned in both ways and further contributed to the very definition of these boundaries. The malleability of the rules of the game was of course a characteristic feature of the revolutionary situation.

The term "movement" is also inappropriate to describe the process of mobilization and strike participation. There were many paths to a strike, many different histories that formed the critical background to a particular conflict, many ways of mobilizing fellow workers around a cause. Factory workers in large plants with a single entrance through a courtyard mobilized differently from sales clerks in sprawling covered markets or waiters, waitresses, and cooks in resort hotels. Metalworkers, with their history of political activism, also possessed prior networks and resources with which to mobilize more readily than workers with less past experience in protest. Mobilization brought conflict, too, between impa-

---

[37] In this we were much encouraged by Lewis Siegelbaum.

tient rank-and-file strikers and their leaders who worked to mobilize for the longer haul, or between fearful laundresses and their aroused leaders who put out the stoves so the workers would have to quit work. Mobilization took different forms, as well; the strike was not the only outcome of labor mobilization. And as we have stressed, workers were not always the masters and mistresses of their own fates: their decision when, how, and whether to strike was often forced or influenced by the actions of management and the intervention of state or other superordinate mediating agencies.

Finally, the term "movement" obscures the richness of the workers' goals as well as their experience. The agenda of strikers in 1917 appeared to be predominantly economic, certainly predominantly directed toward the workplace. Higher pay was a central issue of most strikes, regardless of the specific economic or political context. But money was not the only issue at stake: workers' demands reflected longstanding and deep-seated grievances about factory order and human dignity. The explosion of labor protest ignited by the fall of the old regime in 1917 must be seen in part as the product of many years of pent-up labor-management conflict. The extent and spread of demands about job control and about defining the boundaries of managerial authority signified an effort to establish new patterns of routine workplace relations, patterns that would parallel the democratization occurring in political life outside the factories. And still, although workers' demands focused on relations within the workplace, a number of Russian workers continued to use strikes—withdrawal of labor—to signify grievances against the state and the political order. Such political strikes erupted sporadically, if in great force, and between March and October they did not have the same instrumental effect on state power that strikes had in the February revolution. If the massive strikes in September and October helped to undermine the Provisional regime, they were still, in the main, directed against the entrepreneurial class rather than the regime itself.

These diverse patterns of strike experience make it difficult and perhaps pointless to create a single set of postulates about strike behavior, about revolutionary strikes, or about a single strike movement. At the same time, we can argue for the formation in the course of 1917 of a working class largely conscious of its identity, a class formed in the process of these struggles in the workplace. We reject the notion of a teleological and mass movement, in other words, but we embrace the notion of class and the role of strikes in class formation. We have argued that all social actors in 1917 possessed multiple social identities and allegiances. Workers possessed regional, shop, and trade loyalties that often produced stronger ties than classwide identities; economic divisions between workers in favored, well-paying industries and workers in unfavored sectors of the economy also loomed large during the war. But in the economic conditions of 1917, with a massive decline in productivity and utter uncertainty about Russia's economic future, distinctions between favored and unfavored sectors tended to disappear. All workers, however privileged or unprivileged, began to see themselves as common partners in the struggle against this collapse.

Added to this material component of a developing class identity for workers was the subjective experience of strikes and labor relations in 1917. We have shown how the process of conflict encouraged both sides to coalesce around common positions identified early in the spring as *class* positions. The very patterns of mobilization—appeals for and pledges of outside support, press reports of the justice of the workers' cause, and, of course, the principled resistance of management—contributed to the formation of a cohesive working class in Russia, conscious of its collective position in the social order. Each strike, whether directly experienced or only shared through the press, contributed to this sense of cohesion.

We have shown also how the language of the press reports and the various representations of strike activism in the socialist and bourgeois press shaped perceptions of class identity and class struggle. And we have argued that class identities took firm shape on both sides of the labor-management divide. The threat of socialization that seemed to underlie the claims of workers and their leaders surely helped to undermine deep-seated differences among entrepreneurs, the divisions between Petrograd and Moscow industrialists, between small owners and industrial giants. The language of class was increasingly the language of both management and workers in 1917.

Bolshevik programs and politics have been largely absent from this discussion, but this is certainly not to minimize that party's role in the unfolding revolutionary process as a whole in 1917. The Bolshevik press, like that of other socialist parties, was active in promoting news of strikes and labor organizations, and Bolsheviks were influential in mobilizing some of the largest political strikes in the March–October period, the July Days and the Moscow Conference protests. And although many party leaders rejected the utility of strikes, especially after July, individual Bolsheviks, as well as Mensheviks and SRs, dominated many factory committees, strike committees, and trade union organizations. But in relation to strikes, they served largely as workers and as socialists rather than as party agitators. Party labels were significantly absent from strike activity. They also cannot be found to any extent in strike reporting, where this form of protest was collectively represented as a symbol of class solidarity rather than partisan policy.

Strikes were consequently central to the course of Russia's revolution. Their changing contours did not merely track its path or illustrate processes of revolutionary conflict. Strikes were the central experience of more workers than any other form of participatory politics. They thus served as the central conduit of labor mobilization and, to a large extent, of management mobilization as well. The strike was also the flash point of labor-management relations, and these relations constituted the core of the process of struggle for power in the revolutionary arena. Above all, this process of struggle itself conditioned relations in other arenas, in the Provisional Government, in municipal dumas and soviets, and in the streets. To understand fully Russia's revolutionary process, one cannot, therefore, simply recognize the importance of Lenin's leadership qualities, Kerensky's failure to strengthen the army, the power of socialist ideology, or the very real social pressures in the countryside that propelled peasants to appropriate private property for themselves. One must also recognize the powerful forces emanating from the rank and file of the Russian labor force, the depth of their grievances, and the logic of their participation in the revolutionary struggle.

APPENDIX 1

. . . .

METHODOLOGY AND SOURCES

Strikes in 1917: The Dataset

Strikes

The basic source for our quantitative discussion of strikes in 1917 is a set of data describing 1,019 strikes reported to have begun in the Russian Empire between March 3 and October 25, 1917 (old style). Territories under foreign occupation were not included. We use these dates to exclude strikes occurring in connection with the February revolution and the October revolution. Our focus is labor relations in revolutionary Russia, not the transfer of power in either February or October.

We define a strike as a work stoppage with common goals or organization, whether the unit is a single enterprise, a series of enterprises, or a group of individuals acting in concert. This was the common usage in 1917. It permits us to distinguish between strikes in individual locations and large-scale organizational efforts, and it is sometimes the only way to characterize strikes in nonindustrial sectors, in which the unit on strike could be as small as a single cabdriver with his horse. Our definition differs from other usages, in which a strike is counted as a single enterprise that stops work. This is the definition employed by prewar Russian factory inspectors, by Soviet historians (although not explicitly), and by some Western analysts of strikes. For reasons outlined in our introduction, we think our definition is a useful and appropriate one. For problems of comparability between our set of strikes and those reported by Soviet sources, see below, under "Enterprises on Strike."

Sources

The sources for our dataset are of three types. Closest to the contemporary events are daily newspapers published in Russia in 1917. We used exclusively the papers of Petrograd and Moscow, which are listed in the bibliography. Regional newspapers were not available to us in a systematic way, and this naturally gives our dataset a bias toward strikes in the capitals. We have tried to compensate by employing the large number of documentary collections on revolutionary activity in 1917 published since then by Soviet historical institutions, many issued to commemorate the anniversaries of 1957 and 1967. We were able to consult volumes compiled for Russia as a whole and for a substantial number of regions and localities. The sources for these collections were national, regional, and local newspapers and both national and local archives. In the course of our work, we discovered a substantial overlap between the information reported here and that collected from our sample of newspapers, indicating that Soviet-period documentary collections are reasonably accurate. We cannot, of course, account for any omissions in these collections, but our comparisons do not suggest any systematic omission or distortion of the strike information they include.

Our third type of source is the body of archival reports of the tsarist Factory Inspectorate, furnished to us from the Central State Historical Archive (TSGIA) in Leningrad. We have had access to 41 documentary *dela* (sets), with material on strikes in the provinces of Arkhangel, Astrakhan, Baku, Enisei, Estland, Kazan, Kaluga, Kharkov, Kherson, Kiev, Kostroma, Lifland, Minsk, Moscow, Nizhegorod, Orel, Penza, Perm, Petrograd, Podolsk, Poltava, Riazan, Saratov, Smolensk, Stavropol', Taurida, Tambov, Tver, Tiflis, Tula, Vitebsk, Vladimir, Vologda, and Voronezh, as well as the Baikal, Don, Kuban, and Primorskaia (Vladivostok) regions. These files also included reports covering the country at large. Although the Factory Inspectorate produced complete records of all strikes in enterprises under its jurisdiction before 1917, this was not the case between March and October 1917. The accounts available to us are therefore fragmentary. The basic form of these reports are ledgers for each province, compiled on a monthly basis, describing the work stoppages that took place.[1] We do not have reports for every province for every month; we also have reports that state, "No strikes occurred," for a given province and month, although we have other positive evidence of strikes in that location and period. The Factory Inspectorate material is thus not complete but adds an important further dimension to our dataset.

Data Management

As historians who use quantitative techniques know, transforming masses of qualitative and quantitative information into manageable form is a laborious and daunting task. The generation and analysis of statistical de-

---

[1] The reports were transcribed to a personal computer dataset using the Notebook II program; elsewhere in this appendix we refer to it as the factory inspector dataset.

scriptions—tables and other demonstrations of relationships—is a small part of the huge task of preparing such information for utilization. We began our research by developing a questionnaire that would systematize the recording of strike reports. There was to be one strike recording sheet for each report. These were compiled by a group of able research assistants, graduate students at the University of Michigan, and were augmented by records we gathered ourselves from materials in the Lenin Library. This process generated over 3,000 separate records. The next step was to group the records for each discrete strike; the strike was then given an identification number. A single strike could be represented by one strike recording sheet or by as many as 50. Duplicate sets of the original strike recording sheets are filed in strike order in multiple loose-leaf binders in each of our offices, along with xerox copies in many cases of the source account itself.

The information on the strike recording sheet was next coded according to our codesheet. We used the Midas statistical and data-processing package developed at the University of Michigan for its MTS operating system. Qualitative information, such as province, town, or industry of the striking workers, was recorded as a series of categorical variables and given a numerical code and a brief descriptive tag. Quantitative data, such as numbers of workers on strike, were coded as analytical (numerical) variables. In this first stage of coding, we created two datasets. The first, labeled the objective data file, included information about strikes unlikely to be biased by the nature of the source of the report and included such items as the date the strike began, its location, its economic sector, and whether it occurred in a single plant or in multiple plants. In the objective data file there was one case, or record, for each strike. The second file, labeled the subjective data file, included information more likely to be biased according to the affiliation of the source, such as who provoked the strike, the demands made, and assessment of success or failure. In the subjective data file, there could be multiple cases, or records, for a single strike, one for each strike report. The two files could be linked through the use of the strike's identification number, one unique number for each strike.

We then expanded each file with information from the other. We added the strike's objective data to each record in the subjective data file, a simple mechanical task. More challenging was to add the sometimes contradictory subjective data to the single record for each strike in the objective data file. In the case of conflicting reports about strike size, we entered into the objective data file the minimum, maximum, and average of the size estimates for each strike. In the case of demands, we included all of the reported demands, up to 14 for a single strike. In the case of conflicting reports about outcome, violence, or the mood of the strikers, we carefully evaluated the evidence and included the information most likely to be accurate. The result was an expanded dataset, with one case for each strike and more than 100 variables, or discrete pieces of coded information. This dataset became our primary source of information for aggregate analysis of strikes in 1917. The subjective data file was used primarily for consideration of reporting biases, discussed extensively in chapter 7, and for comparison of the reliability of Soviet-period collections against our newspaper reports. (Duplicate sets of each file are installed on the disks of two University of Michigan mainframe computers, which we each access over telephone lines using personal computers as terminals.)

Once we began to examine the aggregate data, we made further decisions about collapsing categories. We made an early decision to preserve in the initial coding as much diversity of information as possible, so that demands, for example, were first coded under more than 200 separate categories, possible outcomes under 21, sources of outside support under 12. For purposes of generalization, however, we had to reduce these categories to more manageable proportions, and so we created new variables which represented a grouping of some initial categories. This was done in some cases mechanically, recoding whole families of codes, and at other times on a case-by-case basis. Throughout this process, we generated one-way and two-way tables, histograms, and other measures of frequency distribution, and we checked and rechecked the data.

Given the nature of our information, we were confronted, as are all historians, with the problem of missing data. Not one strike report furnished information on all categories. The Midas program is particularly helpful in dealing with missing data, allowing us to distinguish, for example, between a strike for which a strike committee is known not to exist as opposed to one for which this information was just not available. It allows us easily to consider only the set of cases for which information is known. We try to make clear in the text when problems created by missing data may affect our analysis.

A list of the major variables in the main strike file is included at the end of this section of the appendix, but the construction and definition of certain of these require some explanation here.

PLANT SIZE AND THE NUMBER OF STRIKERS

We sought to determine as precisely as possible the number of workers employed in a striking unit and the number of strikers involved in a strike, both for cumulative purposes and to explore patterns of participation rates. Information on plant size was available for those industrial enterprises monitored by the factory inspectors and industrial associations, but seldom for other types of enterprises or service agencies.[2] The number of strikers was taken from the strike reports themselves. These sometimes varied widely, and in two-thirds (720) of our strikes, there was no information at all on the number of strikers. We believed it was important to supplement this information since the number of workers on strike was such a crucial index of strike activity, and so we proceeded to construct a new variable, labeled estimated number of strikers. We observed that most strikes in 1917 for which we had information on participation were unanimous or nearly so. We felt it reasonable to assume that in cases where we knew plant size but not strike size, the number of workers was a plausible estimate of the number of strikers. In other cases, such as city-wide bakers' or printers' strike, we sought aggregate information on the size of the industry's labor force in the given locality, and used these data for our estimates of strike size. In all such cases, we took care to err on the side of underestimates. In this way, we were able to estimate the size of strikes in a total of 738 strikes, or 72 percent of the total. Those strikes for which we do not know the size tend to be small, and the missing information seems to be distributed more or less evenly across industries and geographic regions, so we are confident that the numbers we have calculated reasonably portray relative magnitudes. Nonetheless, our data on strike size can ultimately be only an estimate, and an underestimate at that, and we have tried to make this clear in the text and the tables.

Enterprises on Strike

Although we count our strikes differently from the Factory Inspectorate, it is useful at some points to make approximate comparisons between our universe and the magnitude of the Factory Inspectorate strike universe. Hence we have created a variable that estimates the number of enterprises on strike. These data are always provided by our archival sources, and sometimes by other accounts as well, although here, too, reports sometimes conflict or are lacking. When we know a citywide strike occurred, for example, of printshops in a given locality, we count as striking all the enterprises registered for that locality in the listing of the Association of Industry and Trade.[3] When all else fails, and we know a strike involved more than one unit, we give it a value of two. Thus, when we write about

---

[2] The most complete sources of plant size were Sovet S"ezdov predstavitelei promyshlennosti i torgovli, *Fabrichno-zavodskiia predpriiatiia Rossiiskoi Imperii* (Petrograd, 1914); *Spisok fabrik i zavodov Moskvy i Moskovskoi gubernii* (Moscow, 1916).

[3] Sovet S"ezdov, *Fabrichno-zavodskaia predpriiatiia*.

the number of enterprises involved in strikes, our estimates, again, are on the conservative side.

Geographic Region

We recorded information on geographic location by town (and districts within Petrograd and Moscow cities), province, and industrial region. We have found the region the most appropriate way to present geographic diversity, and we have followed the regional definitions established by the State Economic Council on January 1, 1917.

Petrograd region includes the provinces of Arkhangel', Olonetsk, Petrograd (excluding the city), Novgorod, Pskov, Vitebsk, Finland, Estland, Lifland, and Kurland.

Petrograd city includes the city and suburbs of Petrograd.

Moscow region includes the provinces of Moscow (excluding the city), Smolensk, Tver, Vladimir, Kostroma, Iaroslav, Nizhegorod, Riazan, Tambov, Tula, Orel, Kaluga, Penza, and Vologda.

Moscow city includes the city and suburbs of Moscow.

Kiev region includes the provinces of Kiev (including the city), Chernigov, Mogilev, Minsk, Podol'sk, Volynsk, and Poltava.

Odessa region includes the provinces of Bessarabia and Kherson.

Kharkov-Ekaterinoslav region includes the provinces of Kharkov, Kursk, Voronezh, and Ekaterinoslav.

Rostov region includes the provinces of Donets, Kuban, Tauride (Chernomorsk), and Stavropol'.

Transcaucasus region includes the provinces of Tiflis, Kutais, Elisavetpol'sk, Erivan, Karsk, Batumi, Sukhumi, Zakatal'sk, and Vladikavkaz.

Caspian region includes the provinces of Baku, Tersk, Dagestan, and Ostrov Chiliken.

Volga region includes the provinces of Astrakhan, Kazan, Samara, Saratov, Simbirsk, Orenburg, Ural'sk, and Turgai.

Ural region includes the provinces of Viatka, Perm, Ufa, and Tobol'sk.

Western Siberia region includes the provinces of Tomsk, Enisei, Akmolinsk, and Semipalatinsk.

Eastern Siberia region includes the provinces of Irkutsk, Iakutsk, Zabaikal, Amur, and Primorsk.

Turkestan region includes the provinces of Syr-Dar'insk, Zakaspiia, Fergan, Samarkand, Semirech'e, Khiva, and Bukhara.

Note that the Petrograd and Moscow regions exclude the cities of Petrograd and Moscow, while provincial distinctions include their capitals.

Industry and Strike Propensity

We employed three separate variables to identify the economic activity of units of strike: production sector by industry or service, which uses the major industrial categories of the tsarist and Soviet statistical administrations but adds nonindustrial categories such as retail, transport, and education; branch of industry or service; and major product of the enterprise. For the most part, we rely on 26 production and service categories, but we have also grouped strike units more broadly under industrial enterprises, transport, and services. The main problem here is labeling strikes involving more than one type of industry or more than one type of economic activity. Where we are confident that the overwhelming number of strikers were from a single industrial group, such as the July Days strike in Petrograd, which was largely, although not entirely, metalists, we have classified strikes according to the dominant economic group. In other cases we have used the designation "industrial-varied" and included these strikes and strikers in aggregated industrial totals, but not in arguments or calculations about individual industries.

A group of eight industries under Factory Inspectorate supervision provides us with the material to assess relative *strike propensities*: metals, minerals, chemicals, food and food processing, animal byproducts (leather), wood, paper and printing, and textiles. (Because workers in the mining industry were inconsistently included in aggregate statistics, we have excluded them from these calculations.) Strike propensity is a measure of the involvement of a group of workers in strikes relative to its size in the labor force. The strike propensity of a particular industrial group, such as woodworkers, is figured as the ratio of its share of all strikers to its share of all workers. This statistic requires complete information on the size of the labor force, which is possible only for these eight Factory Inspectorate industries. Therefore, when we figure industrial strike propensities, we use for the figure "total workers," all workers in those eight industries, and for "total strikers," strikers only in those eight industries. The nature of statistical information on nonindustrial workers prevents us from using this comparative measure for workers outside the factories monitored by the Factory Inspectorate.

Dates and Lengths of Strikes

We have recorded wherever possible the month and day a strike began and the month and day it concluded. When the precise date is not given, we can sometimes date a strike by the date of the newspaper account reporting it, but when this is not possible, we list the month the strike began and record the date as missing. Our information on the dates strikes began is more complete than on the dates they ended; where both are known, we can calculate the length of the strike, but we have been able to do this for only 403 of our 1,019 strikes. Hence a measure commonly used in strike statistics of "worker-days lost," which requires complete information for length and size of strike, is not feasible in this study.

We regularly use three aggregates of strike timing: the month a strike began; whether it began before or after July 6, which we have concluded is a logical dividing point in the year; and strike clusters, the three periods of intense strike activity. The first cluster includes strikes beginning between April 19 and July 6, the second, strikes beginning between July 29 and August 26, and the third, strikes beginning between September 16 and the Bolshevik seizure of power on October 25. Strikes that began in April, July, August, and September for which we do not know the precise starting date were not assigned to a cluster category.

DEMANDS

Although some strike studies (and the Factory Inspectorate) assign a primary cause to strikes, we wanted to account for all the demands presented by workers in their disputes. Accordingly, in the initial coding, we allowed for a listing of up to eight separate demands for each strike report. When we collapsed the report records into strike records, we allowed room for up to 14 specific demands. At this point, we also regrouped the initial 259 categories into a more manageable 40: these are listed in appendix 2, table A.3. We further grouped these into five categories: wages, conditions, dignity, control, and politics. For each strike we recorded these as five different variables: *e.g.*, wage demands, yes or no. This allowed us to preserve the diversity of demands but also to aggregate them more usefully. Finally, we returned to the initial 259 categories and recoded a new set of demand variables: challenges to authority, demands having to do with nonfulfillment of earlier promises (secondary demands), and demands relating to other workers rather than or as well as employers.

SKILL LEVEL

The category of skill level derives initially from the three variables on industry, industrial branch, and product of the enterprise. We constructed the categories of skilled, semiskilled, and unskilled, following classifications suggested by Perrot,[4] the U. S. Department of Commerce,[5] and the

---

[4] Michelle Perrot, *Les Ouvriers en grève: France, 1871–1890*, vol. 1, pp. 334–95; see also

International Labour Office.[6] The distinction between skilled and un-skilled service is our own, and the category of combined skilled and semi-skilled strikes was dictated by the nature of specific plants, like Putilov, which could not fit into a specific category. Although we are aware that wage levels do not always move uniformly with skill levels, we also judi-ciously consulted the listings of wage levels for hundreds of Russian oc-cupations, compiled for the period 1913–1918 by the Central Statistical Administration, in order to seek further guidance on assigning skill lev-els.[7] In some cases, where the industry branch product codes were insuf-ficiently informative, we returned to the original strike report sheets, identified the factory involved, and were able to classify the skill level using available descriptive material about these plants.

VARIABLES IN THE STRIKE DATA SET

1. Strike identification number
2. Strike force: workers, employees, artisans
3. Management affiliation
4. Women striking, yes or no
5. Trade union role
6. Factory committee role
7. Strike committee role
8. Strike fund
9. Past strikes
10. Political affiliation of workers
11. Presence of outside agitation
12. Strikers' mood
13. Nature of provocation, if any
14. Defensive or offensive
15. Lockout or Italian strike
16. Type of negotiations
17. Presence of meetings or picketing
18. Presence of outside support
19. Boycotts
20. Correlation with political events

Michael B. Katz, "Occupational Classification in History," *Journal of Interdisciplinary History* 3 (1972), pp. 63–88.

[5] U.S. Department of Commerce, Bureau of the Census, *1970 Census of Population: Classified Index of Industries and Occupations* (Washington, 1971).

[6] International Labour Office, *International Standard Classifications of Occupation* (Geneva, 1969).

[7] TSSU, *Trudy*, vol. 26, vyp. 1, table 13, pp. 126–52.

21. Violence
22. Retaliation against strikers
23. Outcome
24–38. Demands (set of 40)
39. Economic demands, yes or no
40. Wage demands, yes or no
41. Conditions demands, yes or no
42. Job control demands, yes or no
43. Dignity demands, yes or no
44. Political demands, yes or no
45. Demands challenging managerial authority, yes or no
46. Demands challenging civil authority, yes or no
47. Secondary demands, yes or no
48. Demands about other workers, yes or no
49. Kind of other workers
50. Nonpolitical demands, yes or no (sum of categories 40–44 above)
51. Number of employees
52. Number of workers (average of reports)
53. Reported strike size (average of reports)
54. Percent of workers in the plant on strike
55. Number of women strikers
56. Percent of strikers who are women
57. Length of strike
58. Identification number from factory inspector data set, if reported there
59. Number of plants involved in the strike
60. Factory-Inspectorate supervised industry, yes or no
61. Size information available, yes or no
62. Role of employees (aggregate of variable 2)
63. Presence of any organization: trade union, factory committee, strike committee (aggregate of variables 5–7)
64. Mood (aggregate of variable 12)
65. Provocation (aggregate of variable 13)
66. Outcome (aggregate of variable 23)
67. Plant size group (aggregate of variable 52)
68. Economic sector: industry, service, transport
69. Geographic region
70. City district, for Petrograd and Moscow
71. Industry
72. Branch of industry
73. Product
74. Technology of plant

75. Type of ownership
76. Type of management
77. Month strike began
78. Day of month strike began
79. Month strike ended
80. Day of month strike ended
81. Nature: single, multiplant, citywide
82. Town
83. Province
84. Strike period: beginning before July 6 or after
85. Skill level
86. Cluster: spring, summer, or fall

GEOGRAPHIC DATA SET

The information in our strike data set describes strike characteristics only. We wanted also to be able to explain these characteristics in terms of other social, economic, and political factors, but lack of data precluded this on a strike-by-strike basis. We sought, then, to conduct this analysis on an aggregate level, that of the province. Social, economic, and political data were compiled for the eight basic industries in each province during this period. We aggregated strike information about industrial strikes by province, and linked this in a data set with relevant aggregate descriptive data. There are 88 cases in this geographic data set, one for each of the 88 provinces for which data are available. This data set is also stored on disk on the Michigan mainframe computers.

The following is a list of the variables in this data set. Not all variables were used in the analyses described in the text. Not all provinces generated information on all variables. In particular, the information from TSSU, *Trudy*, vol. 26, vyp. 2, pertains only to some 25 central provinces under Soviet jurisdiction in August 1918. Sources for the nonstrike data are given; when no source is given, the data are from the strike file described above.

1. Province
2. Largest industry in the province (number of workers)
3. Percent of labor force in mining
4. Percent of labor force in metals
5. Percent of labor force in minerals
6. Percent of labor force in chemicals
7. Percent of labor force in food
8. Percent of labor force in animal byproducts

9. Percent of labor force in wood
10. Percent of labor force in paper and printing
11. Percent of labor force in textiles
12. Percent of labor force in utilities
     Source for 2–12: TSSU, *Trudy*, vol. 7, vyp. 1, pt. 1, table 1, pp. 4–36.
13. Percent of all Russian industrial workers
14. Percent of provincial population in industry
     Source for 13–14: *Statisticheskii ezhegodnik Rossii* (St. Petersburg, 1913), vol. 10; (St. Petersburg, 1915), vol. 12.
15. Average plant size
     Source: same as for 2–12.
16. Percent of national industrial output
     Source: TSSU, *Trudy*, vol. 26, vyp. 1, table 33, pp. 374–413.
17. Percent of males in work force
18. Percent of adults in work force
19. Percent of males ages 15 to 17 in work force
     Source for 17–19: TSSU, *Trudy*, vol. 7, vyp. 1, pt. 1, table 3, pp. 38–39.
20. Median age of work force (August 1918)
21. Percent of workers who are literate (August 1918)
     Source for 20–21: TSSU, *Trudy*, vol. 26, vyp. 2, table 5, pp. 18–23.
22. Average 1913 nominal wage
23. Change in wage 1913–1916
     Source for 22–23: TSSU, *Trudy*, vol. 26, vyp. 1, table 15, pp. 156–61.
24. Percent of workers engaged in defense production
     Source: *Rossiia v mirovoi voine, 1914–1918 goda (v tsifrakh)* (Moscow, 1925).
25. Percent of workers holding land in 1917
     Source: TSSU, *Trudy*, vol. 26, vyp. 2, table 25, pp. 118–19.
26. Percent of workers habitually leaving for summer fieldwork
     Source: TSSU, *Trudy*, vol. 26, vyp. 2, table 31, pp. 134–37.
27. Percent of workers in factory housing
     Source: TSSU, *Trudy*, vol. 26, vyp. 2, table 37, pp. 150–53.
28. Percent of workers on paid vacation in 1917
29. Percent of workers in public organizations in 1918
30. Percent of workers belonging to trade unions in 1918
     Source for 28–30: TSSU, *Trudy*, vol. 26, vyp. 2, table 41, pp. 166–67.
31. Percent of workforce on strike in 1913
32. Percent of workforce on strike in 1914
33. Percent of workforce on strike in 1915
34. Percent of workforce on strike in 1916

35. Percent of all strikers between 1913–1916
36. Total strikers, 1913–1916
37. Total strikes, 1913–1916
38. Average size of strike, 1913–16
    Source for 31–38: TSSU, *Trudy*, vol. 7, vyp. 1, pt. 2, tables 5, 8, 11, 14.
39. Party receiving the most votes in the Constituent Assembly elections November 1917
40. Percent of Bolshevik vote in Constituent Assembly elections
41. Percent of Kadet vote in Constituent Assembly elections
    Source for 39–41: L. M. Spirin, *Klassy i partii v grazhdanskoi voine v Rossii* (Moscow, 1968), pp. 420–22.
42. Distance to Petrograd in kilometers
    Calculated from a map of the Soviet Union.
43. Percent of population in cities
    Source: *Statisticheskii ezhegodnik Rossii* (St. Petersburg, 1915), vol. 12.
44. Change in size of labor force 1913–1916
    Source: TSSU, *Trudy*, vol. 7, vyp. 1, pt. 1, table 1, pp. 4–36.
45. Number of strikes, March–October 1917
46. Number of strikers, 1917
47. Strike propensity, 1917
48. Share of all strikes in 1917
49–56. Number of strikes each month, March to October
57–64. Share of that province's strikes beginning in each of the months from March to October
65. Median length of strike
66. Share of strikes in one factory only
67. Share of province's strikes with trade union support
68. Share of strikes with factory committee support
69. Share of strikes with strike committee support
70. Share of strikes with strike committee presence
71. Share of strikes with any organizations present
72. Share of strikes concluding in worker success
73. Share of province's strikes for wages
74. Share of strikes for conditions
75. Share of strikes for control
76. Share of strikes for dignity
77. Share of strikes for political demands
78. Median size of strike
79. Average size of strike
80. Strike intensity (percent of all industrial workers involved in strikes)

APPENDIX ONE

INDUSTRY DATA SET

Aggregate information for industries was also collected in a fashion analogous to the geographic data set, but here the number of cases is much smaller: essentially the data set consists of social, economic, physical, and strike characteristics (before and during 1917) for nine major industries: mining, metals, minerals, chemicals, food, animal products, wood, paper and printing, and textiles. Statistical analyses using so few cases are not very useful, but we did use this data set in one instance. This information is also stored on the University of Michigan mainframe computer. The variables and their sources follow; where no source is given, the data are from our strike file.

1. Industry
2. Number of workers in the industry in 1917
3. Industry's share of total industrial workers, 1917
   Source for 2–3: TSSU, *Trudy*, vol. 26, vyp. 1, table 11, pp. 64–119.
4. Change in size of work force, 1914–1917
   Source: A. G. Rashin, *Formirovanie rabochego klassa Rossii*, 2d. ed. (Moscow, 1958), p. 75.
5. Average factory size
   Source: same as variable 3–4.
6. Nominal average wage, 1916
7. Nominal average wage, 1917
8. Change in real wage, 1913–1916 (using 1913 ruble as base)
9. Change in real wage, 1913–1917
   Source for 6–9: TSSU, *Trudy*, vol. 26, vyp. 1, table 14, pp. 153–55.
10. Productivity: 1917 value of production per worker per year
11. Share in rubles of industrial output
12. Change in value of production, 1913–1917
    Source for 10–12: TSSU, *Trudy*, vol. 26, vyp. 1, table 19, pp. 174–83.
13. Percent of workers in defense production
    Source: *Rossiia v mirovoi voine, 1914–1918 gody (v tsifrakh)* (Moscow, 1925), pp. 71–73.
14. Percent of male workers, 1917
15. Percent change in women, 1913–1917
16. Percent of male youths, 1917
    Source for 14–16: TSSU, *Trudy*, vol. 26, vyp. 1, table 11, pp. 64–119.
17. Median age of workers, 1918
18. Percent of literate workers, 1918
    Source for 17–18: TSSU, *Trudy*, vol. 26, vyp. 2, table 8, pp. 40–47.
19. Percent of unmarried workers, 1918

20. Percent of married workers with complete families, 1918
    Source for 19–20: TSSU, *Trudy*, vol. 26, vyp. 2, table 21, pp. 110–11.
21. Percent of workers with land before the revolution
    Source: TSSU, *Trudy*, vol. 26, vyp. 2, table 26, pp. 120–21.
22. Percent of workers leaving regularly for fieldwork
    Source: TSSU, *Trudy*, vol. 26, vyp. 2, table 30, pp. 130–33.
23. Percent of workers in factory housing
    Source: TSSU, *Trudy*, vol. 26, vyp. 2, table 38, pp. 154–57.
24. Percent of workers with paid leave in 1917
    Source: TSSU, *Trudy*, vol. 26, vyp. 2, table 34, pp. 144–45.
25. Percent of labor force striking in 1913
    Source: TSSU, *Trudy*, vol. 7, vyp. 1, pt. 1, table 2, pp. 36–37; pt. 2, table 7, pp. 136–39.
26. Percent of labor force striking in 1914
    Source: TSSU, *Trudy*, vol. 7, vyp. 1, pt. 1, table 2, pp. 36–37; pt. 2, table 10, pp. 146–49.
27. Percent of labor force striking in 1915
    Source: TSSU, *Trudy*, vol. 7, vyp. 1, pt. 1, table 2, pp. 36–37; pt. 2, table 13, pp. 156–59.
28. Percent of strikers 1913–1915 for wages
29. Percent of strikers 1913–1915 for other plant-related reasons
30. Percent of strikers 1913–1915 for political reasons
    Source for 28–30: TSSU, *Trudy*, vol. 7, vyp. 1, pt. 2, tables 7, 10, 13, pp. 136–39, 146–49, 156–59.
31. Total strikes
32. Total strikers
33. Percent of all strikes
34. Strike propensity
35. Median length of strike
36. Percent of single-plant strikes
37. Percent of strikes won (of known outcome)
38. Percent of strikes won (of all strikes)
39. Percent of strikes with wage demands
40. Percent of strikes with conditions demands
41. Percent of strikes with control demands
42. Percent of strikes with dignity demands
43. Percent of strikes with political demands
44. Percent of strikes with any form of organization
45. Strike intensity (percent of labor force on strike)
46. March–June strike propensity
47. July–October strike propensity

APPENDIX ONE

Nonstrike Protest

In order to compare the extent of nonstrike and extrastrike collective action with the extent of strikes, we compiled an additional data set, starting with a questionnaire asking for information on such episodes of collective action. Our research assistants then read through the major newspapers for Moscow and Petrograd, as well as other major documentary collections, and identified all such actions reported to have taken place in the two cities. These included plant-related actions—expulsion of foremen, seizure of property, and physical violence—and actions that may have involved workers outside the factory setting—food disorders, mob justice, protest demonstrations, product boycotts, and political arrests. In all, 340 separate incidents were recorded. Data sheets (and xeroxes of original source reports in many instances) were arranged according to assigned identification numbers in looseleaf notebooks in the same fashion as our strike data. Individual protests were then categorized according to ten topics: date, city, group or enterprise involved, industry, if any, description of action, type and target of the action, whether violence was involved, and whether a political affiliation was reported. These records were listed on IBM-compatible personal computers and sorted alphanumerically according to the various categories using the DOS Sort program.

APPENDIX 2

· · · · · · · · · · · · · · · · · · · ·

SUPPLEMENTARY

STATISTICAL INFORMATION

TABLE A.1
Industrial Workers by Region, January 1917

Region	Workers in Industry
Petrograd region[a]	67,562
Petrograd city	392,828
Moscow region[b]	794,214
Moscow city	205,919
Kiev region	195,096
Odessa region	74,903
Kharkov-Ekaterinoslav region	171,632
Rostov region	65,101
Transcaucasus region	18,620
Caspian region	63,655
Volga region	114,250
Urals region	45,053

SOURCE: TSSU, *Trudy*, vol. 7, vyp. 1, pt. 1, table 3, p. 38, except Moscow and Petrograd cities, for which see *Fabrichno-zavodskaia promyshlennost' goroda Moskvy i Moskovskoi gubernii, 1917–1927 gody*, p. 1; Stepanov, *Rabochie Petrograda*, p. 29. Cf. Rashin, *Formirovanie*, pp. 83–85.
[a] Excluding city of Petrograd.
[b] Excluding city of Moscow.

TABLE A.2
Strikes and Strikers, 1895–1916
(Enterprises Subject to Factory Inspection Only)

	Strikes			Strikers		
	Economic	Political Demonstrative	Total	Economic	Political Demonstrative	Total
1895	68	—	68	31,195	—	31,195
1896	113	5	118	29,288	239	29,527
1897	143	2	145	59,353	517	59,870
1898	209	6	215	41,590	1,560	43,150
1899	178	11	189	54,375	3,123	57,498
1900	115	10	125	25,210	4,179	29,389
1901	159	5	164	31,698	520	32,218
1902	112	11	123	31,629	5,042	36,671
1903	424	126	550	67,810	19,022	86,832
1904	66	2	68	24,403	501	24,904
1905	4,190	9,085	13,995	1,020,511	1,842,622	2,863,173
1906	2,545	3,569	6,114	457,721	650,685	1,108,405
1907	973	2,600	3,573	200,004	540,070	740,074
1908	428	464	892	83,407	92,094	176,101
1909	290	50	340	55,803	8,363	64,166
1910	214	8	222	42,846	3,777	46,623
1911	442	24	466	96,730	8,380	105,110
1912	732	1,300	2,032	175,678	549,813	725,491
1913	1,379	1,025	2,404	390,605	496,457	887,062
1914						
Jan.–Jul.	1,205	2,288	3,493	345,087	982,810	1,327,897
Aug.–Dec.	34	7	41	6,716	2,845	9,561
1915	726	202	928	385,265	154,263	539,528
1916	1,046	242	1,288	646,785	310,290	957,075

SOURCES:
1895–1912: K. N. Iakovleva, "Zabastovochnoe dvizhenie v Rossii za 1895–1917 gody," in *Materialy po statistike truda*, vyp. 8 (Moscow, 1920), p. 61.
1913–1916: TSSU, *Trudy*, vol. 7, vyp. 1, 2, tables 6, 9, 12, 15, pp. 132–35, 142–45, 152–55, 162–63. Iakovleva's total figure for 1913 is 887,096, and because she considers the category "other causes" as non-economic, her divisions between economic and political strikers for the 1913–1915 period vary slightly. There are also slight discrepancies in both the published and archival records for 1916 strikes. Compare ibid., tables 15 and 16, pp. 162–63, 164, and see the discussion in Leopold H. Haimson and Eric Brian, "Labor Unrest in Imperial Russia during the First World War: A Quantitative Analysis and Interpretation," in *War, Strikes, and Revolution: The Impact of the War Experience on Italy, Germany, France, England, and Russia*, ed. Giulio Sapelli and Leopold H. Haimson (Milan, forthcoming), appendix 4a.

TABLE A.3
Categories and Frequencies of Strike Demands
(March 3–October 25)

Aggregated Demand Category	Groups Included in Aggregated Categories	Frequency of Cases in Our File	
		March 3–July 6	July 7–October 25
1. WAGES			
	Wages	273	218
	Pay other than wages	84	58
	Changes in rate system	74	45
	Economic, unspecified	68	84
	Bonuses	29	9
	Overdue pay	3	6
2. WORK CONDITIONS			
	Eight-hour workday	81	19
	Vacation and leave	38	20
	Working conditions	35	31
	Hours (other than 8 or 6)	10	7
	Medical care	9	6
	Change in work schedules	7	5
	Change in food supply system	7	2
	Six-hour workday	5	5
	Special clothing	5	2
	Tools provided	1	1
	Child labor	1	1
3. JOB CONTROL AND ORGANIZATION			
	Rehiring fired workers	27	11
	Hiring and firing by workers	25	39
	Trade unions	17	7
	Change in work rules	15	12
	Change in management personnel	15	11
	Factory committees	13	13
	Workplace rights (unspecified)	11	25
	Opening of closed factories	3	3
	Limit on profits	0	1

Aggregated Demand Category	Groups Included in Aggregated Categories	Frequency of Cases in Our File	
		March 3– July 6	July 7– October 25
4. DIGNITY			
	Personal dignity	13	2
	Arbitration	10	13
	Equal pay for men and women	8	2
	No retribution for striking	4	4
	Solidarity with other strikers	4	8
	Negotiation	3	11
	Honor of prior agreements	0	3
5. POLITICS			
	Politics	6	29
	Education reform	2	4
	Local tax protests	2	0
	Insurance issues	1	0
	Electoral reform	1	0
	Religious freedom	0	2
	War	0	2
Total number of strikes		511	461

SELECTED BIBLIOGRAPHY

. . . .

ARCHIVAL MATERIALS

(TSGAOR). Tsentral'nyi Gosudarstvennyi Arkhiv Oktiabr'skoi Revoliutsii
SSSR
  fond 63: Moscow Security Department (Okhrana), 1916–17.
  fond 102: Department of Police, 1916–17.
  fond 4100: Ministry of Labor, 1917.
(TSGIA). Tsentral'nyi Gosudarstvennyi Istoricheskii Arkhiv SSSR
  fond 23: Ministry of Trade and Industry, 1917. Factory inspector
  reports.

CONTEMPORARY NEWSPAPERS AND JOURNALS

Bakinskii Rabochii. Baku, 1917.
Birzhevyia Vedomosti. Petrograd, 1916–17.
Delo Naroda. Petrograd, 1917.
Den'. Petrograd, 1917.
Edinstvo. Moscow, 1917.
Ekho Derevoobdelochnika. Petrograd, 1917–19.
Gazeta Kopeika. Moscow, 1917.
Golos Kozhevnikov. Moscow, 1917.
Golos Zheleznodorozhnika. Moscow, 1917.
Gorno-zavodskoe Delo. Kharkov, 1917.
*Izvestiia Ispolnitel'nogo Komiteta Moskovskogo Uzla, Moskovsko-Ka-
zanskoi Zheleznoi Dorogi.* Moscow, 1917.
Izvestiia Moskovskogo Soveta Rabochikh Deputatov. Moscow, 1917.
Izvestiia Petrogradskogo Soveta Rabochikh Deputatov. Petrograd, 1917.
Metallist. Petrograd, 1917.
Moskovskii Metallist. Moscow, 1917.
Narodnoe Slovo. Petrograd, 1917.
Novaia Zhizn'. Petrograd, 1917.
Novoe Vremia. Petrograd, 1917.
Pechatnik. Moscow, 1917.
Pravda. Petrograd, 1917.
Professional'nyi Vestnik. Petrograd, 1917.

Proletarii. Moscow, 1917.
Proletarii. Petrograd, 1917.
Promyshlennost' i Torgovlia. Petrograd, 1917.
Rabochaia Gazeta. Petrograd, 1917.
Rabochii Khimik. Petrograd, 1918.
Rabochii Put'. Petrograd, 1917.
Rech'. Petrograd, 1917.
Russkaia Volia. Petrograd, 1917.
Russkiia Vedomosti. Moscow, 1917.
Russkoe Slovo. Moscow, 1917.
Sotsial Demokrat. Moscow, 1917.
Statistika Truda. Moscow, 1918.
Torgovo-Promyshlennaia Gazeta. Petrograd, 1917.
Trud. Moscow, 1917.
Trudovaia Kopeika. Moscow, 1917.
Utro Rossii. Moscow, 1916–17.
Vestnik Ekaterininskoi Zheleznoi Dorogi. Ekaterinoslav, 1917.
Vestnik Iuzhnykh Zheleznykh Dorog. Kharkov, 1917.
Vestnik Omskoi Zheleznoi Dorogi. Omsk, 1917.
Vestnik Petrogradskogo Obshchestva Zavodchikov i Fabrikantov. Petrograd, 1917.
Vestnik Vremennago Pravitel'stva. Petrograd, 1917.
Vlast' Naroda. Moscow, 1917.
Volia i Dumy Zheleznodorozhnika. Moscow, 1917.
Volia Naroda. Petrograd, 1917.
Vpered. Moscow, 1917.
Zemlia i Volia. Moscow, 1917.
Zhurnal Zasedanii Vremennago Pravitel'stva. Petrograd, 1917.

MEMOIRS, DOCUMENTS COLLECTIONS, AND STATISTICAL MATERIALS

Avdeev, N., ed. *Revoliutsiia 1917 goda (Khronika sobytii).* 6 vols. Moscow, 1923.
Bonnell, Victoria E., ed. *The Russian Worker: Life and Labor under the Tsarist Regime.* Berkeley: University of California Press, 1983.
Bor'ba rabochikh i krest'iane pod rukovodstva bolshevistskoi partii za ustanovlenie i uprochenie sovetskoi vlasti v Tambovskoi gubernii (1917–18 gody). Sbornik dokumentov. Edited by I. Z. Komissarov. Tambov, 1957.
Bor'ba trudiashchikhsia Chernigovshchiny za vlast' sovetov (1917–18 gody). Chernigov, 1957.

Bor'ba trudiashchikhsia mass za ustanovlenie i uprochenie sovetskoi vlasti na Stavropol'e. Edited by A. P. Chevelev. Stavropol', 1957.

Bor'ba trudiashchikhsia Orlovskoi gubernii za ustanovlenie sovetskoi vlasti v 1917–18 godakh. Orel, 1957.

Bor'ba trudiashchikhsia Volynii za vlast' sovetov. Zhitomir, 1957.

Bor'ba za oktiabr'skuiu revoliutsiiu vo Vladimirskoi gubernii (1917–1918 gody). Vladimir, 1957.

Bor'ba za pobedu sovetskoi vlasti v Gruzii. Tbilisi, 1958.

Bor'ba za sovetskuiu vlast' na iuzhnom Urale (1917–1918 gody). Cheliabinsk, 1957.

Bor'ba za sovetskuiu vlast' na Kubane v 1917–1920 godakh. Krasnodar, 1957.

Bor'ba za sovetskuiu vlast' v Voronezhskoi gubernii, 1917–18 gody. Sbornik dokumentov i materialov. Voronezh, 1957.

Bor'ba za ustanovlenie i ukreplenie sovetskoi vlasti v Riazanskoi gubernii. Riazan', 1957.

Bor'ba za ustanovlenie i uprochenie sovetskoi vlasti. Khronika sobytii. Moscow, 1962.

Bor'ba za ustanovlenie i uprochenie sovetskoi vlasti na Severe. Arkhangel, 1959.

Bor'ba za ustanovlenie i uprochenie sovetskoi vlasti v Karelii (sbornik dokumentov). Petrozavodsk, 1957.

Bor'ba za ustanovlenie i uprochenie sovetskoi vlasti v Kurskoi gubernii. Sbornik dokumentov i materialov. Kursk, 1957.

Bor'ba za ustanovlenie i uprochenie sovetskoi vlasti v Simbirskoi gubernii, mart 1917–iiun' 1918 godov. Ulianovsk, 1957.

Bor'ba za velikii oktiabr' na Nikolaevshchine. Nikolaev, 1957.

Bor'ba za vlast' sovetov na Donu, 1917–1920 gody. Rostov-na-Donu, 1957.

Bor'ba za vlast' sovetov v Donbasse. Stalinskoe oblastnoe izdatel'stvo, 1957.

Bor'ba za vlast' sovetov v Irkutskoi gubernii, oktiabr' 1917–iiulia 1918 godov. Irkutsk, 1957.

Bor'ba za vlast' sovetov v Moldavii (mart 1917–mart 1918 godov.) Sbornik dokumentov. Kishinev, 1957.

Bor'ba za vlast' sovetov v Tomskoi gubernii (1917–1919 gody). Tomsk, 1957.

Bor'ba za vlast' sovetov v Vologodskoi gubernii, 1917–1919 gody. Edited by P. K. Perepelnenko. Vologda, 1957.

Browder, Robert P., and Alexander F. Kerensky, eds. *The Russian Provisional Government, 1917: Documents.* 3 vols. Stanford, Calif.: Stanford University Press, 1961.

Bukhbinder, N. "Na fronte v predoktiabr'skie dni; po sekretnym materi-alam stavki." *Krasnaia Letopis'* 6 (1923), pp. 9–63.

Buryshkin, P. A. *Moskva kupecheskaia.* New York: Chekhov, 1954.

Burzhuaziia i pomeshchiki v 1917 godu. Chastnye soveshchaniia chlenov gosudarstvennoi dumy. Edited by A. Drezin. Moscow and Leningrad, 1932.

Dinamika rossiiskoi i sovetskoi promyshlennosti v sviazi s razvitiem na-rodnogo khoziaistva za sorok let, 1887–1926 gody Vol. 1, *Svod statis-ticheskikh dannykh po fabrichno-zavodskoi promyshlennosti s 1887 po 1926 gody* Edited by V. E. Varzar and L. B. Kafenguaz. Moscow, 1930.

Dokumenty velikoi oktiabr'skoi sotsialisticheskoi revoliutsii v Nizhego-rodskoi gubernii. Gorki, 1945.

Dune, Eduard. "Zapiski krasnogvardeitsa." Nicolaevsky Collection, Hoover Institution on War, Revolution, and Peace. Manuscript.

Dzhaparidze, P. A. *Izbrannye stat'i, rechi, i pis'mi 1905–1918 godov.* Moscow, 1958.

Ekonomicheskoe polozhenie Rossii nakanune velikoi oktiabr'skoi sotsi-alisticheskoi revoliutsii. Dokumenty i materialy. 3 parts. Moscow and Leningrad, 1957–67.

Fabrichno-zavodskaia promyshlennost' goroda Moskvy i Moskovskoi gubernii, 1917–1927 gody. Moscow, 1928.

Fabrichno-zavodskie kometety Petrograd v 1917 godu. Protokoly. 2 vols. Moscow, 1979–82.

Fleer, M. G., ed. *Rabochee dvizhenie v gody voiny.* Moscow, 1925.

Furmanov, D. A. *Sobranie sochineniia.* 5 vols. Moscow, 1928.

Goncharskaia, S. S. "Profsoiuz prachek v 1917 g." In *V ogne revoliut-sionnykh boev (Raiony Petrograda v dvukh revoliutsiiakh 1917 goda),* vol. 1, pp. 477–86. Moscow, 1967.

Gordienko, I. *Iz boevogo proshlogo.* Moscow, 1957.

Grave, B. B., ed. *Burzhuaziia nakanune fevral'skoi revoliutsii.* Moscow and Leningrad, 1927.

————. *K istorii klassovoi bor'by v Rossii v gody imperialisticheskoi voiny.* Moscow, 1926.

Iakovleva, K. N. "Zabastovochnoe dvizhenie v Rossii za 1895–1917 gody." In *Materialy po statistike truda,* vyp. 8. Moscow, 1920.

Il'in-Zhenevskii, A. "Neudavshiisia Bonapart." In *Miatezh Kornilova. Iz belykh memuarov.* Leningrad, 1928.

Kazanskii oktiabr'. Materialy i dokumenty. Edited by E. Grachev. Kazan, 1926.

Kerensky, Alexander. *Russia and History's Turning Point.* New York: Duell, Sloan, and Pearce, 1965.

Khar'kov i Khar'kovskaia guberniia v velikoi oktiabr'skoi sotsialisticheskoi revoliutsii: Sbornik dokumentov, fevral' 1917–aprel' 1918 godov. Kharkov, 1957.

Khronika revoliutsionnykh sobytii Tambovskoi gubernii. Edited by P. Kroshitskii and S. Sokolov. Tambov, 1927.

Klimokhin, S. K., ed. *Kratkaia istoriia stachki tekstil'shchikov Ivanovo-Kineshemskoi promyshlennoi oblasti.* Kineshma, 1918.

Korablev, Iu. I., ed. *Rabochee dvizhenie v Petrograda v 1912–1917 godakh. Dokumenty i materialy.* Leningrad, 1958.

Korolev, G. *Ivanovo-Kineshemskie tekstil'shchiki v 1917 godu (Iz vospominanii tekstil'shchika).* Moscow, 1927.

Kursk v revoliutsii (Sobranie materialov 1917–18 godov). Kursk, 1927.

Lenin, V. I. *Polnoe sobranie sochineniia.* 5th ed. 55 vols. Moscow, 1958–65.

Letopis' revoliutsionnykh sobytii v Samarskoi gubernii, 1902–1917 gody. Edited by F. G. Popov. Kuibyshev, 1969.

Lockhart, R. H. Bruce. *The Two Revolutions: An Eye-Witness Account of Russia, 1917.* Chester Springs, Pa.: Dufour Editions, 1967.

Luxemburg, Rosa. *The Mass Strike.* Translated by Patrick Lavin. Detroit: Marxian Educational Society, 1925.

Marx, Karl, and Friedrich Engels. *Selected Works of Marx and Engels.* New York: International Publishers, 1968.

Materialy po izucheniiu istorii professional'nogo dvizheniia na Ukraine. Kharkov, n.d.

Meller, V. L., and A. M. Pankratova, eds. *Rabochii dvizhenie v 1917 godu.* Moscow and Leningrad, 1926.

Miliukov, Paul. *Political Memoirs, 1905–1917.* Edited by Arthur P. Mendel. Ann Arbor, Mich.: University of Michigan Press, 1967.

Moskovskii soiuz rabochikh-portnykh v 1917 godu. Edited by Sh. P. Muranovskii. Moscow, 1927.

Moskovskii sovet professional'nykh soiuzov v 1917 godu (Protokoly). Moscow, 1927.

Nabokov, V. D. *V. D. Nabokov and the Russian Provisional Government, 1917.* Edited by Virgil D. Medlin and Steven L. Parsons. New Haven, Conn.: Yale University Press, 1976.

Nikishin, A. *Ocherki Bakinskogo gorniatskogo profdvizheniia, 1917–1920 gody.* Baku, 1926.

Oktiabr' na Brianshchine. Briansk, 1957.

Oktiabr' v Ekaterinoslave: Dokumenty i materialy. Dnepropetrovsk, 1957.

Oktiabr' v Tule: Sbornik dokumentov i materialov. Tula, 1957.

Oktiabr'skaia revoliutsiia i fabzavkomy. 2 parts. Moscow, 1927.

Oktiabr'skoe vooruzhennoe vosstanie: Semnadtsatyi god v Petrograde. 2 vols. Leningrad, 1967.

Organizatsiia i stroitel'stvo sovetov rabochikh deputatov v 1917 godu. Sbornik dokumentov. Edited by P. O. Gorin. Moscow, 1928.

Otchet o Moskovskom soveshchanii obshchestvennykh deiatelei 8–10 avgusta 1917 goda. Moscow, 1917.

Paleologue, George Maurice. *An Ambassador's Memoirs, 1914–1917.* 3 vols. Translated by F. A. Holt. London: Hutchinson and Co., 1923–25.

Pankratova, A. M., ed. *1905 god. Stachechnoe dvizhenie.* Moscow and Leningrad, 1925.

Pazhitnov, K. A. *Primiritel'nyia kamery i treteiskii sud v promyshlennosti.* Petrograd, 1917.

Pervaia rabochaia konferentsia fabrichno-zavodskikh komitetov. Petrograd, 1917.

Petrogradskii sovet rabochikh i soldatskikh deputatov. *Protokoly zasedanii ispolnitel'nogo komiteta i biuro.* Moscow and Leningrad, 1925.

Piat' let raboty. Moscow, 1922.

Piatnitskii, O. "Vikzhel do, vo vremia i posle oktiabr'skikh dnei." In *Put' k oktiabriu.* Moscow, 1923.

"Piterskie rabochie ob iiul'skikh dniakh." *Krasnaia Letopis'* 9 (1924), pp. 19–41.

Pobeda oktiabr'skoi sotsialisticheskoi revoliutsii v Nizhegorodskoi gubernii. Gorki, 1957.

Pobeda sovetskoi vlasti na Khersonshchine, 1917–1920 gody. Kherson, 1957.

Pobeda sovetskoi vlasti v Zakavkaz'e. Tbilisi, 1971.

Pobeda velikoi oktiabr'skoi sotsialisticheskoi revoliutsii i ustanovlenie sovetskoi vlasti na Ukraine. Kiev, 1957.

Pobeda velikoi oktiabr'skoi sotsialisticheskoi revoliutsii v Kazakhstane, 1917–1918 gody. Alma-Ata, 1957.

Pobeda velikoi oktiabr'skoi sotsialisticheskoi revoliutsii v Samarskoi gubernii. Kuibyshev, 1957.

Podgotovka i pobeda oktiabr'skoi revoliutsii v Moskve. Moscow, 1957.

Podgotovka i provedenie velikoi oktiabr'skoi sotsialisticheskoi revoliutsii v Tverskoi gubernii. Kalinin, 1960.

Polnoe sobranie zakonov Rossiiskoi imperii, Sobranie 3. St. Petersburg, 1905.

Postanovka i pobeda velikoi oktiabr'skoi sotsialisticheskoi revoliutsii v Penzenskoi gubernii. Sbornik dokumentov i materialov. Penza, 1957.

Protokoly shestogo s"ezda RSDRP(b). *Avgust 1917 goda.* Moscow, 1934.

Rabochii klass Urala v gody voiny i revoliutsii. 3 vols. Edited by A. Taniaev. Sverdlovsk, 1927.

Rabochii kontrol' i natsionalizatsiia promyshlennosti v Kostromskoi gubernii. Sbornik dokumentov 1917–1919 godov. Kostroma, 1960.

Raionnye sovety Petrograda v 1917 godu. 3 vols. Moscow and Leningrad, 1964–66.

Rasskazy o velikikh dniakh. Vospominanii starykh bol'shevikov Donbassa. Donetskoe oblastnoe izdatel'stvo, 1957.

Revoliutsiia 1917 goda v Azerbaidzhane. Khronika sobytii. Edited by S. Belen'kii and A. Shanvelov. Baku, 1927.

Revoliutsiia 1917–1918 godov v Samarskoi gubernii. Edited by I. I. Bliumental'. 2 vols. Samara, 1927.

Revoliutsionnoe dvizhenie v Rossii nakanune oktiabr'skogo vooruzhennogo vosstaniia (1–24 oktiabria 1917 goda). Moscow, 1962.

Revoliutsionnoe dvizhenie v Rossii posle sverzheniia samoderzhaviia. Moscow, 1957.

Revoliutsionnoe dvizhenie v Rossii v aprele 1917 goda. Aprel'skii krizis. Moscow, 1958.

Revoliutsionnoe dvizhenie v Rossii v avguste 1917 goda. Razgrom kornilovskogo miatezha. Moscow, 1959.

Revoliutsionnoe dvizhenie v Rossii v mae–iiune 1917 goda. Iiun'skaia demonstratsiia. Moscow, 1959.

Revoliutsionnoe dvizhenie v Rossii v sentiabre 1917 goda. Obshchenatsional'nyi krizis. Moscow, 1961.

Rossiia v mirovoi voine, 1914–1918 goda (v tsifrakh). Moscow, 1925.

Rubin, I. *Primiritel'naia kamera i treteiskii sud.* Moscow, 1917.

Schwarz, S. *Fabrichno-zavodskie komitety i profsoiuzy v pervye gody revoliutsii.* Hoover Institution on War, Revolution, and Peace. Manuscript. 1935.

Shestnadtsat' zavodov. Edited by L. Averbakh. Moscow, 1933.

Shipulinskii, F. *Trud i otdykh (Vos'michasovoi rabochii den').* Moscow, 1917.

Sobolev, P. N., ed. "Zabastovka rabochikh-kozhevnikov Moskvy v avguste–oktiabre 1917 goda." *Istoricheskii Arkhiv* 6 (1957), pp. 61–81.

Sovet s"ezdov predstavitelei promyshlennosti i torgovli. *Fabrichno-zavodskaia predpriiatiia Rossiiskoi imperii.* Petrograd, 1914.

Spisok fabrik i zavodov goroda Moskvy i Moskovskoi gubernii. Moscow, 1916.

Statisticheskii sbornik po Petrogradu i Petrogradskoi gubernii. Petrograd, 1922.

Strel'bitskii, S. "Na zare profdvizheniia gorniakov." *Letopis' Revoliutsii* 5–6 (1927), pp. 340–51.

Sukhanov, N. N. *The Russian Revolution*. Edited by Joel Carmichael. Princeton, N.J.: Princeton University Press, 1985.

———. *Zapiski o revoliutsii*. 7 vols. Berlin: Z. I. Grzhebin, 1922–23.

Tret'ya vserossiiskaya konferentsiya professional'nykh soyuzov, 1917 goda. Stenograficheskii otchet. 1927. Reprint, edited by Diane Koenker. Millwood, N.Y.: Kraus International, 1982.

Tsentral'noe Statisticheskoe Upravlenie. *Trudy*. Vol. 7, vyp. 1–2. Moscow, 1921.

Tsentral'noe Statisticheskoe Upravlenie. *Trudy*. Vol. 26, vyp. 1. Moscow, 1926.

Tsentral'nyi Statisticheskii Komitet. *Statisticheskii ezhegodnik Rossii, 1913*. St. Petersburg, 1914.

Tsereteli, I. G. *Vospominaniia o fevral'skoi revoliutsii*. 2 vols. Paris: Mouton, 1963.

Tysiacha deviatsot semnadtsatyi god vo Vladimirskoi gubernii. Edited by N. Shakhanov. Vladimir, 1927.

Tysiacha deviatsot semnadtsatyi god v Ivanovo-Voznesenskom raione. Khronika. Edited by M. K. Dianov and P. M. Ekzempliarskii. Ivanovo-Voznesensk, 1927.

Tysiacha deviatsot semnadtsatyi god v Saratovskoi gubernii. Saratov, 1957.

Tysiacha deviatsot semnadtsatyi god v Stalingradskoi gubernii. Edited by G. T. Gavrilov. Stalingrad, 1927.

Tysiacha deviatsot semnadtsatyi god v Tsaritsyne. Edited by M. Ia. Kleinman. Stalingrad, 1957.

Tysiacha deviatsot semnadtsatyi god v Voronezhskom gubernii (Khronika). Edited by B. M. Livygin. Voronezh, 1928.

Uprochenie sovetskoi vlasti v Moskve i Moskovskoi gubernii. Moscow, 1958.

Ustanovlenie i uprochenie sovetskoi vlasti v Kazakhstane (mart 1917–iiun' 1918 godov). Edited by T. E. Eleuov. Alma-Ata, 1961.

Ustanovlenie i uprochenie sovetskoi vlasti v Pskovskoi gubernii, 1917–1918 gody. Pskov, 1957.

Ustanovlenie i uprochenie sovetskoi vlasti v Smolenskoi gubernii. Smolensk, 1957.

Ustanovlenie sovetskoi vlasti v Iaroslavskoi gubernii. Iaroslavl', 1957.

Ustanovlenie sovetskoi vlasti v Kaluzhskoi gubernii. Kaluga, 1957.

Ustanovlenie sovetskoi vlasti v Kostrome i Kostromskoi gubernii. Kostroma, 1957.

V bor'be za oktiabr' (mart 1917–ianvar' 1918 godov.) Odessa, 1957.

Velikaia oktiabr'skaia sotsialisticheskaia revoliutsii v Kazakhstane. Alma-Ata, 1967.

Velikaia oktiabr'skaia sotsialisticheskaia revoliutsiia i pobeda sovetskoi vlasti v Armenii. Erevan, 1957.

Velikaia oktiabr'skaia sotsialisticheskaia revoliutsiia. Khronika sobytii. 4 vols. Moscow, 1957–61.

Velikaia oktiabr'skaia sotsialisticheskaia revoliutsiia na Ukraine, fevral' 1917–aprel' 1918 godov. 3 vols. Kiev, 1957.

Velikaia oktiabr'skaia sotsialisticheskaia revoliutsiia v Belorussii. 2 vols. Minsk, 1957.

Velikaia oktiabr'skaia sotsialisticheskaia revoliutsiia v Estonii. Tallin, 1958.

Vompe, P. *Dni oktiabr'skoi revoliutsii i zheleznodorozhniki v revoliutsii 1917 goda.* Moscow, 1924.

Woytinsky, W. S. *Stormy Passage: A Personal History through Two Russian Revolutions to Democracy and Freedom, 1905–1960.* New York: Vanguard Press, 1961.

Za vlast' sovetov. Sbornik dokumentov o bor'be trudiashchikhsia Zabaikalia v 1917–1920 godakh. Chita, 1957.

Za vlast' sovetov. Sbornik dokumentov o bor'be za vlast' sovetov v Eniseiskoi gubernii (1917–1918 gody). Krasnoiarsk, 1957.

SECONDARY AND OTHER WORKS

Alekseev, V. V. *Velikii oktiabr' i sotsialisticheskoe preobrazovaniie v Sibiri.* Novosibirsk, 1980.

Amman, Peter. "Revolution: A Redefinition." *Political Science Quarterly* 77 (1962), pp. 36–53.

Amsden, John, and Stephen Brier. "Coal Miners on Strike: Transformation of Strike Demands and the Formation of a National Union." In *Industrialization and Urbanization,* edited by Theodore K. Rabb and Robert I. Rotberg, pp. 137–70. Princeton, N.J.: Princeton University Press, 1981.

Andreev, A. M. *Mestnye sovety i organy burzhuaznoi vlasti (1917 god).* Moscow, 1983.

Andreyev, A. (Andreev). *The Soviets of Workers' and Soldiers' Deputies on the Eve of the October Revolution.* Moscow, 1971.

Anskii, A., ed. *Professional'noe dvizhenie v Petrograde v 1917 godu.* Leningrad, 1928.

Antoshkin, D. V. *Professional'noe dvizhenie sluzhashchikh, 1917–1924 gody.* Moscow, 1927.

Arskii, R. "Rabochii klass vo vremia voiny." *Trud v Rossii* 1 (1925), pp. 18–32.

Ashenfelter, Orley, and George E. Johnson. "Bargaining Theory, Trade

Unions, and Industrial Strike Activity." *American Economic Review* 59 (1969), pp. 35–49.

Askwith, George Ranken. *Industrial Problems and Disputes.* 1920. Reprint. Freeport, N.Y.: Books for Libraries Press, 1971.

Astrakhan, Kh. M. "Partiinost' naseleniia Rossii nakanune oktiabria (po materialam vyborov v gorodskie dumy v mae–oktiabre 1917 goda)." *Istoriia sssr* 6 (1987), pp. 134–55.

Balabanov, M. "Rabochii klass nakanune revoliutsii." In *Professional'noe dvizhenie v Petrograde v 1917 godu*, edited by A. Anskii, pp. 5–27. Leningrad, 1928.

Basin, S. G. "Professional'nye soiuzy i fabrichno-zavodskie komitety srednego povolzh'ia vo glave ekonomicheskoi bor'by rabochego klassa nakanune oktiabria." In *Iz istorii srednego Povolzh'ia i Priural'ia*, vyp. 2, pp. 55–74. Kuibyshev, 1972.

Bater, James H. *St. Petersburg: Industrialization and Change.* London: Edward Arnold, 1976.

Batstone, Eric, Ian Boraston, and Stephen Frenkel. *The Social Organization of Strikes.* Oxford: Basil Blackwell, 1978.

Bazilevich, K. V. *Professional'noe dvizhenie rabotnikov sviazi (1917–1918 gody).* Moscow, 1927.

Blau, Peter M., and Otis Dudley Duncan. *The American Occupational Structure.* New York: John Wiley and Sons, 1967.

Bonnell, Victoria E. *Roots of Rebellion: Workers' Politics and Organizations in St. Petersburg and Moscow, 1900–1914.* Berkeley: University of California Press, 1983.

Bordogna, Lorenzo, and Giancarlo Provasi. "Il movimento degli scioperi in Italia (1881–1973)." In *Il movimento degli scioperi nel XX secolo*, edited by G. P. Cella. Bologna: Il Mulino, 1979.

Borshchevskii, V. Ia. "Stachechnoe dvizhenie v Donbasse v period podgotovki oktiabria." In *Rabochii klass i rabochee dvizhenie v Rossii v 1917 godu*, pp. 136–44. Moscow, 1964.

Bortnik, M. "Na Trubochnom zavode." In *Professional'noe dvizhenie v Petrograde v 1917 godu*, edited by A. Anskii, pp. 268–78. Leningrad, 1928.

Bradley, Joseph. *Muzhik and Muscovite: Urbanization in Late Imperial Russia.* Berkeley: University of California Press, 1985.

Brinton, Crane. *The Anatomy of Revolution.* 1938. Reprint. New York: Vintage, 1965.

Brinton, M. *The Bolsheviks and Workers' Control.* London: Solidarity, 1970.

Brooks, Jeffrey. "The Breakdown in the Production and Distribution of Printed Material, 1917–1927." In *Bolshevik Culture*, edited by Abbott

Gleason, Peter Kenez, and Richard Stites, pp. 151–74. Bloomington, Ind.: Indiana University Press, 1985.

———. *When Russia Learned to Read: Literacy and Popular Literature, 1861–1917*. Princeton, N.J.: Princeton University Press, 1985.

Brown, Geoff. *Sabotage: A Study in Industrial Conflict*. London: Spokesman Books, 1977.

Bulkin, F. "Ekonomicheskoe polozhenie rabochikh Petrograda nakanune oktiabria 1917 godu." In *Professional'noe dvizhenie v Petrograde v 1917 godu*, edited by A. Anskii, pp. 28–44. Leningrad, 1928.

Burdzhalov, E. N. *Vtoraia russkaia revoliutsiia*. Vol. 2, *Moskva, front, periferiia*. Moscow, 1971.

Bystrykh, F. P. "Rabochee stachechnoe dvizhenie na Urale v period podgotovki velikoi oktiabr'skoi sotsialisticheskoi revoliutsii." In *Rabochii klass i rabochee dvizhenie v Rossii v 1917 godu*, pp. 117–35. Moscow, 1964.

Cass, Millard. "The Relationship of Size of Firm and Strike Activity." *Monthly Labor Review* 80 (1957), pp. 1330–34.

Chamberlin, William H. *The Russian Revolution*. 2 vols. New York: Macmillan, 1935.

Chermenskii, V. *Stachka*. Moscow, 1928.

Chernomaz, I. Sh. "Bor'ba rabochikh Ukrainy za povyshenie zarabotnoi platy v marte–oktiabre 1917 goda." In *Nekotorye problemy sotsial'no-ekonomicheskogo i politicheskogo razvitiia Ukrainskoi SSR*, pp. 103–13. Dnepropetrovsk, 1972.

Chevalier, Louis. *Classes laborieuses et classes dangereuses*. Paris: Plon, 1958.

Costas, Ilse. "Management and Labor in the Siemens Plant in Berlin, 1906–1920." In *War, Strikes, and Revolution: The Impact of the War Experience on Italy, Germany, France, England, and Russia*, edited by Giulio Sapelli and Leopold H. Haimson. Milan: Feltrinelli Foundation, forthcoming.

Crew, David F. "Steel, Sabotage and Socialism: The Strike at the Dortmund 'Union' Steel Works in 1911." In *The German Working Class, 1888–1933*, edited by Richard J. Evans, pp. 108–41. Totowa, N.J.: Barnes and Noble, 1982.

Crisp, Olga. *Studies in the Russian Economy before 1914*. London: Macmillan, 1976.

Cronin, James E. *Industrial Conflict in Modern Britain*. Totowa, N.J.: Rowman and Littlefield, 1979.

———. "Industry, Locality, and the State: Patterns of Mobilization in the Postwar Strike Wave in Britain." In *War, Strikes, and Revolution: The Impact of the War Experience on Italy, Germany, France, England,*

and Russia, edited by Giulio Sapelli and Leopold H. Haimson. Milan: Feltrinelli Foundation, forthcoming.

————. "Labor Insurgency and Class Formation: Comparative Perspectives on the Crisis of 1917–1920 in Europe." In *Work, Community, and Power: The Experience of Labor in Europe and America, 1900–1925*, edited by James E. Cronin and Carmen Sirianni, pp. 20–48. Philadelphia: Temple University Press, 1983.

————. "Theories of Strikes: Why Can't They Explain the British Experience?" *Journal of Social History* 12, no. 2 (1978–79), pp. 194–220.

Cronin, James E., and Carmen Sirianni, eds. *Work, Community, and Power: The Experience of Labor in Europe and America, 1900–1925*. Philadelphia: Temple University Press, 1983.

Cross, Gary. "Redefining Workers' Control: Rationalization, Labor Time, and Union Politics in France, 1900–1928." In *Work, Community, and Power: The Experience of Labor in Europe and America, 1900–1925*, edited by James E. Cronin and Carmen Sirianni, pp. 143–72. Philadelphia: Temple University Press, 1983.

Diakin, V. S. *Russkaia burzhuaziia i tsarizm v gody pervoi mirovoi voiny, (1914–1917)*. Leningrad, 1967.

Dmitriev, N. "Primiritel'nye kamery v 1917 godu." In *Professional'noe dvizhenie v Petrograde v 1917 godu*, edited by A. Anskii, pp. 78–100. Leningrad, 1928.

Drobizhev, V. Z., A. K. Sokolov, and V. A. Ustinov, eds. *Rabochii klass sovetskoi Rossii v pervyi god proletarskoi diktatury*. Moscow, 1975.

Dubofsky, Melvyn. "Abortive Reform: The Wilson Administration and Organized Labor, 1913–1920." In *Work, Community, and Power: The Experience of Labor in Europe and America, 1900–1925*, edited by James E. Cronin and Carmen Sirianni, pp. 197–220. Philadelphia: Temple University Press, 1983.

Edelman, Robert. *Proletarian Peasants: The Revolution of 1905 in Russia's Southwest*. Ithaca, N.Y.: Cornell University Press, 1987.

Edwards, P. K. *Conflict at Work: A Materialist Analysis of Workplace Relations*. Oxford: Basil Blackwell, 1986.

————. *Strikes in the United States, 1881–1974*. Oxford: Basil Blackwell, 1981.

Edwards, P. K., and H. Scullion. *The Social Organization of Industrial Conflict*. Oxford: Basil Blackwell, 1982.

Edwards, Richard. *Contested Terrain: The Transformation of the Workplace in the Twentieth Century*. New York: Basic Books, 1979.

Eldridge, J.E.T. *Industrial Disputes: Essays in the Sociology of Industrial Relations*. London: Routledge and Kegan Paul, 1968.

Engelstein, Laura. *Moscow, 1905: Working-Class Organization and Political Conflict*. Stanford, Calif.: Stanford University Press, 1982.

Feldman, Gerald D. *Army, Industry, and Labor in Germany, 1914–1918*. Princeton, N.J.: Princeton University Press, 1966.

———. "Labor Unrest and Strikes in Saxony, 1916–1923." In *War, Strikes, and Revolution: The Impact of the War Experience on Italy, Germany, France, England, and Russia*, edited by Giulio Sapelli and Leopold H. Haimson. Milan: Feltrinelli Foundation, forthcoming.

Ferro, Marc. *La Révolution de 1917: La chute du tsarisme et les origines d'octobre*. Paris: Aubier, 1967.

Fleer, M. "K istorii rabochego dvizheniia 1917 goda." *Krasnaia Letopis'* no. 2 (13) (1925), pp. 239–43.

Freidlin, B. M. *Ocherki istorii rabochego dvizheniia v Rossii v 1917 godu*. Moscow, 1967.

Galili y Garcia, Ziva. "Commercial-Industrial Circles in War and Revolution: The Failure of 'Industrial Progressivism'." Unpublished paper presented at Hebrew University, Jerusalem. 1988.

———. *The Menshevik Leaders of the Petrograd Soviet, 1917: Social Realities and Political Strategies in the Russian Revolution*. Princeton, N.J.: Princeton University Press, 1989.

Gamson, William. *The Strategy of Social Protest*. Homewood, Ill.: Dorsey Press, 1975.

Gaponenko, L. S. *Rabochii klass Rossii v 1917 godu*. Moscow, 1970.

———. "Rossiiskii proletariat, ego chislennost' i territorial'noe razmeshchenie po osnovnym promyshlennym raionam nakanune sotsialisticheskoi revoliutsii." In *Rabochii klass i rabochee dvizhenie Rossii v 1917 godu*, pp. 14–48. Moscow, 1964.

Gaponenko, L. S., and V. E. Poletaev. "K istorii rabochego dvizheniia v Rossii v period mirnogo razvitiia revoliutsii (mart–iiun' 1917 goda)." *Voprosy Istorii* 2 (1959), pp. 21–44.

Gatrell, Peter. *The Tsarist Economy, 1850–1917*. New York: St. Martin's Press, 1986.

Gaza, I. I. *Putilovets na putiakh k oktiabriu*. Moscow, 1933.

Geary, Dick. *European Labour Protest, 1848–1939*. London: Croom Helm, 1981.

———. "Radicalism and the German Worker: Metalworkers and Revolution, 1914–1923." In *Society and Politics in Wilhelmine Germany*, edited by Richard J. Evans, pp. 267–86. London: Croom Helm, 1978.

Gerschenkron, Alexander. "The Rate of Growth of Industrial Production in Russia since 1885." *Journal of Economic History* 7, supplement (1947), pp. 144–74.

Gitelman, H. M. "Perspectives on American Industrial Violence." *Business History Review* 47 (1973), pp. 1–23.

Glickman, Rose L. *Russian Factory Women: Workplace and Society, 1880–1914*. Berkeley: University of California Press, 1984.

Goetz-Girey, Robert. *Les Mouvements des grèves en France, 1919–1962*. Vol. 3 of *L'Économique*, edited by Henri Guitton and Alain Barrère. Paris: Éditions Sirey, 1965.

Goodrich, Carter L. *The Frontier of Control: A Study in British Workshop Politics*. New York: Harcourt, Brace and Howe, 1920.

Gordon, M. Ia. *Ocherk ekonomicheskoi bor'by rabochikh v Rossii*. Leningrad, 1924.

Gordon, Michael A. "The Labor Boycott in New York City, 1880–1886." *Labor History* 16, no. 2 (Spring 1975), pp. 184–229.

Gray, Robert. *The Aristocracy of Labour in Nineteenth-Century Britain, c. 1850–1914*. London: Macmillan, 1981.

Graziosi, Andrea. "Common Laborers, Unskilled Workers, 1890–1915." *Labor History* 22 (1981), pp. 512–44.

Griffen, Clyde. "Occupational Mobility in Nineteenth-Century America: Problems and Possibilities." *Journal of Social History* 5 (1972), pp. 310–30.

Grunt, A. Ia. *Moskva 1917–i: Revoliutsiia i kontrrevoliutsiia*. Moscow, 1976.

Guliev, A. N. "Bor'ba Bakinskogo proletariata za kollektivnyi dogovor vesnoi i letom 1917 goda." In *Velikii oktiabr' i bor'ba za sovetskuiu vlast' v Azerbaidzhane*, pp. 70–145. Baku, 1958.

Haimson, Leopold H. "The Problem of Social Identities in Early Twentieth Century Russia." *Slavic Review* 47, no. 1 (1988), pp. 1–20.

———. "The Problem of Social Stability in Urban Russia, 1905–1914." Parts 1, 2. *Slavic Review* 23, no. 4 (1964), pp. 619–42; 24, no. 1 (1965), pp. 1–22.

Haimson, Leopold H., and Eric Brian. "Labor Unrest in Imperial Russia during the First World War: A Quantitative Analysis and Interpretation." In *War, Strikes, and Revolution: The Impact of the War Experience on Italy, Germany, France, England, and Russia*, edited by Giulio Sapelli and Leopold H. Haimson. Milan: Feltrinelli Foundation, forthcoming.

Haimson, Leopold H., with Eric Brian. "Changements démographiques et grèves ouvrières à St. Pétersbourg, 1905–1914." *Annales: Économies, Sociétés, Civilisations* 4 (July–August 1985), pp. 781–803.

Haimson, Leopold H., and Ronald Petrusha. "Two Strike Waves in Imperial Russia (1905–07, 1912–14): A Quantitative Analysis." In *Strikes, Wars, and Revolutions in an International Perspective: Strike*

Waves in the Late Nineteeth and Early Twentieth Centuries, edited by Leopold H. Haimson and Charles Tilly. New York: Cambridge University Press, 1989.

Haimson, Leopold H., and Charles Tilly, eds. *Strikes, Wars, and Revolutions: in an International Perspective: Strike Waves in the Late Nineteenth and Early Twentieth Centuries*. New York: Cambridge University Press, 1989.

Hammett, Richard S., Joel Seidman, and Jack London. "The Slow-Down as a Union Tactic." *Journal of Political Economy* 65 (1957), pp. 126–34.

Hammond, Thomas T. *Lenin on Trade Unions and Revolution, 1895–1917*. New York: Columbia University Press, 1957.

Hanagan, Michael P. *The Logic of Solidarity: Artisans and Skilled Workers in Three French Towns*. Urbana, Ill.: University of Illinois Press, 1980.

Hasegawa, Tsuyoshi. "Crime and Revolution in Petrograd, 1917." Unpublished, 1981.

———. *The February Revolution: Petrograd, 1917*. Seattle, Wash.: University of Washington Press, 1981.

Heron, Craig, and Bryan D. Palmer. "Through the Prism of the Strike." *Canadian Historical Review* 58, no. 4 (1977), pp. 423–58.

Hibbs, Douglas A., Jr. *Long-Run Trends in Strike Activity in Comparative Perspective*. Cambridge, Mass.: MIT Press, 1976.

———. *The Political Economy of Industrial Democracies*. Cambridge, Mass.: Harvard University Press, 1987.

Hicks, J. R. *The Theory of Wages*. New York: Peter Smith, 1948.

Hiller, E. T. *The Strike: A Study in Collective Action*. Chicago: University of Chicago Press, 1928.

Hinton, James. *The First Shop Stewards' Movement*. London: George Allen and Unwin, 1973.

Hogan, Heather. "Conciliation Boards in Revolutionary Petrograd: Aspects of the Crisis of Labor-Management Relations in 1917." *Russian History* 9, no. 1 (1982), pp. 49–66.

———. "Industrial Rationalization and the Roots of Labor Militance in the St. Petersburg Metalworking Industry, 1901–1914." *Russian Review* 42 (1983), pp. 163–90.

———. "The Origins of the Scientific Management Movement in Russia." In *Technological Change and Workers' Movements*, edited by Melvyn Dubofsky, pp. 77–99. Beverly Hills, Calif.: Sage Publications, 1985.

Holton, Robert. *British Syndicalism, 1900–1914*. London: Pluto Press, 1975.

Horowitz, Daniel L. *The Italian Labor Movement*. Cambridge, Mass.: Harvard University Press, 1963.

Husband, William B. "Local Industry in Upheaval: The Ivanovo-Kineshma Textile Strike of 1917." *Slavic Review* 47, no. 3 (1988), pp. 448–63.

Hyman, Richard. *Strikes*. London: Fontana, 1972.

Ingham, Geoffrey. *Strikes and Industrial Conflict, Britain and Scandinavia*. London: Macmillan, 1974.

International Labour Office. *International Standard Classifications of Occupation*. Geneva, 1969.

Iuzefovich, I. S. *Iz klassovykh boev 1917 goda (Stachka Moskovskikh kozhevnikov)*. Moscow, 1928.

Ivanov, L. M., ed. *Rabochii klass i rabochee dvizhenie v Rossii (1861–1917)*. Moscow, 1966.

Ivanova, N. A. "Voprosy stachechnoi bor'by proletariata Rossii v sovetskoi istoriografii." *Istoricheskie Zapiski* 85 (1970), pp. 307–67.

Johnson, Robert Eugene. *Peasant and Proletarian: The Working Class of Moscow in the Late Nineteenth Century*. New Brunswick, N.J.: Rutgers University Press, 1979.

Kasarov, G. G. "Stachechnoe dvizhenie v Moskve v gody pervoi mirovoi voiny." *Vestnik Moskovskogo Gosudarstvennogo Universiteta* (seriia istorii) 6 (1970), pp. 28–42.

Kats, A. "K istorii primiritel'nykh kamer v Rossii." *Vestnik Truda* 10 (1923), pp. 185–97.

Katz, Michael B. "Occupational Classification in History." *Journal of Interdisciplinary History* 3 (1972), pp. 63–88.

Keep, John L. H. *The Russian Revolution: A Study in Mass Mobilization*. New York: Norton, 1976.

Kennan, John. "The Economics of Strikes." In *Handbook of Labor Economics*, edited by Orley Ashenfelter and Richard Layard, vol. 1, pp. 1091–134. Amsterdam: North-Holland, 1986.

Kerr, Clark, and Abraham Siegel. "The Inter-Industry Propensity to Strike." In *Industrial Conflict*, edited by Arthur Kornhauser, Robert Dubin, and Arthur M. Ross, pp. 189–212. New York: McGraw-Hill, 1954.

Kerr, Clark, Frederick H. Harbison, John T. Dunlop, and Charles A. Myers. "The Labour Problem in Economic Development." *International Labour Review* 71 (1955), pp. 223–35.

Khromov, P. A. *Ekonomicheskoe razvitie Rossii v XIX–XX vekakh*. Moscow, 1950.

Kir'ianov, Iu. I. *Rabochie iuga Rossii, 1914–fevral' 1917 goda*. Moscow, 1971.

————. *Zhiznennyi uroven' rabochikh Rossii*. Moscow, 1979.

Kleinbort, L. M. *Istoriia bezrabotitsy v Rossii, 1857–1919 gody*. Moscow, 1925.

Knowles, K.G.J.C. *Strikes*. Oxford: Basil Blackwell, 1952.

Koenker, Diane. *Moscow Workers and the 1917 Revolution*. Princeton, N.J.: Princeton University Press, 1981.

Koenker, Diane, and William G. Rosenberg. "Skilled Workers and the Strike Movement in Revolutionary Russia." *Journal of Social History* 19, no. 4 (Summer 1986), pp. 605–29.

Kogan, I. *Rostovskaia stachka*. Moscow, 1928.

Kokhn, M. P. *Russkie indektsy tsen*. Moscow, 1926.

Kolychevskii, I. "Zabastovochnoe dvizhenie v Moskve s fevralia po oktiabre 1917 goda." *Proletarskaia Revoliutsiia* 8, no. 55 (1926), pp. 55–117.

Korbut, M. "Kazanskie rabochie pered oktiabr'skoi revoliutsii." *Uchenye Zapiski Kazanskogo Gosudarstvennogo Universiteta* 88, no. 1 (1928), pp. 112–35.

Korpi, Walter. "Conflict, Power, and Relative Deprivation." *American Political Science Review* 68 (1974), pp. 1569–78.

Korpi, Walter, and Michael Shalev. "Strikes, Power, and Politics in Western Nations, 1900–1976." In *Political Power and Social Theory*, edited by Maurice Zeitlin, pp. 299–332. Greenwich, Conn.: JAI Press, 1980.

Kovalenko, D. A. "Bor'ba fabrichno-zavodskikh komitetov Petrograda za rabochii kontrol' nad proizvodstvom (mart–oktiabr' 1917 goda)." *Istoricheskie Zapiski* 61 (1957), pp. 66–111.

Kovalevskii, V. I., ed. *La Russie á la fin du 19e siècle*. Paris: Dupont, 1900.

Koz'minykh-Lanin, I. M. *Semeinyi sostav rabochikh*. Moscow, 1912.

Kreizel', Iu. *Iz istorii profdvizheniia goroda Khar'kova v 1917 godu*. Kharkov, 1921.

Kruze, E. E. *Polozhenie rabochego klassa Rossii v 1900–1914 godakh*. Leningrad, 1976.

————. *Usloviia truda i byta rabochego klassa Rossii v 1900–1914 godakh*. Leningrad, 1981.

Laverychev, V. Ia. *Po tu storonu barrikad (Iz istorii bor'by Moskovskoi burzhuazii s revoliutsiei)*. Moscow, 1967.

————. "Vserossiiskii soiuz torgovli i promyshlennosti." *Istoricheskie Zapiski* 70 (1961), pp. 35–60.

————., ed. *Rabochii klass Rossii, 1907–fevral' 1917 godov*. Moscow, 1982.

Leiberov, I. P. *Na shturm samoderzhaviia. Petrogradskii proletariat v gody pervoi mirovoi voiny in fevral'skoi revoliutsii*. Moscow, 1978.

Leiberov, I. P. "O revoliutsionnykh vystuplenii Petrogradskogo proletariata v gody pervoi mirovoi voiny i fevral'skoi revoliutsii." *Voprosy Istorii* 2 (1964), pp. 63–77.

———. "Petrogradskii proletariat v bor'be za pobedu fevral'skoi burzhuazno-demokraticheskoi revoliutsii v Rossii." *Istoriia sssr* 1 (1957), pp. 41–73.

———. "Stachechnaia bor'ba Petrogradskogo proletariata v period pervoi mirovoi voiny (19 iiulia 1914–16 fevralia 1917 godov)." In *Istoriia rabochego klassa Leningrada*, vol. 2, pp. 156–86. Leningrad, 1963.

Levitt, Theodore. "Prosperity versus Strikes." *Industrial and Labor Relations Review* 6 (1952–53), pp. 220–26.

Lisetskii, A. M. *Bol'sheviki vo glave massovykh stachek (mart–oktiabr' 1917 goda)*. Kishinev, 1974.

———. "Iz istorii stachechnoi bor'by proletariata Moskvy nakanune i v khode vooruzhennogo vosstaniia (oktiabr'–noiabr' 1917 goda)." *Uchenye Zapiski Kishinevskogo Gosudarstvennogo Universiteta* 72 (1964), pp. 3–19.

———. "K voprosu o mezhdunarodnom znachenii opyta stachechnoi bor'by proletariata Rossii v period podgotovki velikoi oktiabr'skoi sotsialisticheskoi revoliutsii." *Uchenye Zapiski Kishinevskogo Gosudarstvennogo Universiteta* 104 (1968), pp. 299–309.

———. "K voprosu o statistike zabastovok v Rossii v period podgotovki velikoi oktiabr'skoi sotsialisticheskoi revoliutsii." *Trudy Kafedry Istorii kpss, Khar'kovskogo Gosudarstvennogo Universiteta imeni Gor'kogo* 7 (1959), pp. 271–83.

———. "O kharaktere stachechnoi bor'by proletariata Rossii v period podgotovki oktiabr'skoi revoliutsii (mart–oktiabr' 1917 goda)." In *Tezisy dokladov ob"edinennoi nauchnoi sessii instituta istorii AN MSSR*, pp. 7–13. Kishinev, 1961.

———. "O nekotorykh osobennostiakh zabastovochnoi taktiki bol'shevikov v period podgotovki oktiabr'skoi sotsialisticheskoi revoliutsii." *Uchenye Zapiski Khar'kovskogo Gosudarstvennogo Universiteta imeni Gor'kogo* 103 (1959), pp. 93–106.

———. "O nekotorykh voprosakh kolichestvennoi kharakteristiki zabastovochnogo dvizheniia v Rossii v period podgotovki oktiabria." *Uchenye Zapiski Kishinevskogo Gosudarstvennogo Universiteta* 65 (1963), pp. 3–15.

———. "Ob otnoshenii bloka kontrrevoliutsionnykh sil k zabastovochnomu dvizheniiu proletariata Rossii (mart–oktiabr' 1917 goda)." *Uchenye Zapiski Kishinevskogo Gosudarstvennogo Universiteta* 95 (1968), pp. 3–23.

———. "'Pravda' i stachechnaia bor'ba proletariata Rossii v period podgotovki velikoi oktiabr'skoi sotsialisticheskoi revoliutsii." *Uchenye Zapiski Khar'kovskogo Gosudarstvennogo Universiteta* 123 (1962), pp. 43–65.

———. "Predvaritel'nye itogi geograficheskogo i otraslennogo raspredeleniia stachek." *Uchenye Zapiski Kishinevskogo Gosusdarstvennogo Universiteta* 112 (1969), pp. 365–85.

Lockwood, David. "Sources of Variation in Working-Class Images of Society." *Sociological Review* 14 (1966), pp. 249–67.

Lyashchenko, Peter I. *History of the National Economy of Russia to the 1917 Revolution*. Translated by L. M. Herman. New York: Macmillan, 1949.

Maevskii, I. V. *Polozhenie Russkogo proletariata i ego stachechnaia bor'ba nakanune oktiabria 1917 goda*. Moscow, 1957.

Mandel, M. David. *The Petrograd Workers and the Fall of the Old Regime*. London: Macmillan, 1983.

———. *The Petrograd Workers and the Soviet Seizure of Power*. London: Macmillan, 1984.

McCarthy, William. "The Reasons Given for Striking." *Bulletin of the Oxford University Institute of Statistics* 21 (1959), pp. 17–29.

McKay, John P. *Pioneers for Profit: Foreign Entrepreneurship and Russian Industrialization, 1885–1913*. Chicago: University of Chicago Press, 1970.

Metel'kov, P. F. *Zheleznodorozhniki v revoliutsii*. Leningrad, 1970.

Miliukov, P. N. *Istoriia vtoroi Russkoi revoliutsii*. 2 vols. Sofia: Rossiisko–Bolgarskoe Izdatel'stvo, 1921.

Mills, Charles M. *Vacations for Industrial Workers*. New York: Ronald Press, 1927.

Mints, I. I. *Istoriia velikogo oktiabria*. 3 vols. Moscow, 1967–72.

Montgomery, David. "New Tendencies in Union Struggles and Strategies in Europe and the United States, 1916–1922." In *Work, Community, and Power: The Experience of Labor in Europe and America, 1900–1925*, edited by James E. Cronin and Carmen Sirianni, pp. 86–116. Philadelphia: Temple University Press, 1983.

More, Charles. *Skill and the English Working Class, 1870–1914*. New York: St. Martin's Press, 1980.

Musso, Stefano. "Scioperi e conflitto sociale durante la prima guerra mondiale a Torino." In *War, Strikes, and Revolution: The Impact of the War Experience on Italy, Germany, France, England, and Russia*, edited by Giulio Sapelli and Leopold H. Haimson. Milan: Feltrinelli Foundation, forthcoming.

Ocherki istorii rabochego klassa Azerbaidzhanskoi SSR. Edited by V. E. Poletaev. 2 vols. Baku, 1974.

Owen, Thomas C. *Capitalism and Politics in Russia: A Social History of the Moscow Merchants, 1855–1905.* Cambridge: Cambridge University Press, 1981.

Paialin, N. "Putilovskii zavod v 1917 godu." Parts 1–4. *Krasnaia Letopis'* 3 (1932), pp. 165–88; 4 (1932), pp. 113–36; 5–6 (1932), pp. 135–73; 2 (1933), pp. 146–62.

Palmer, Bryan D. *A Culture in Conflict: Skilled Workers and Industrial Capitalism in Hamilton, Ontario, 1860–1914.* Montreal: McGill-Queen's University Press, 1979.

Pankratova, A. M. *Politicheskaia bor'ba v Rossiiskom profdvizhenii. 1917–1918 gody.* Leningrad, 1927.

Perrot, Michelle. *Les Ouvriers en grève: France, 1871–1890.* 2 vols. Paris: Mouton, 1974.

Polianskii, N. N. *"Russkoe ugolovnoe zakonodatel'stvo o stachkakh" i drugiia stat'i po ugolovnomu pravu.* Moscow, 1912.

Portal, Roger. *La Russie industrielle de 1881 à 1927.* Paris: Centre de documentation universitaire, 1976.

Potthoff, Heinrich. *Gewerkschaften und Politik zwischen Revolution und Inflation.* Düsseldorf: Droste, 1979.

Procacci, Giovanna. "The Changing Nature of Popular Protest and Labour Unrest in Italy, 1917–1918: the Political Content." In *War, Strikes, and Revolution: The Impact of the War Experience on Italy, Germany, France, England, and Russia,* edited by Giulio Sapelli and Leopold H. Haimson. Milan: Feltrinelli Foundation, forthcoming.

Pushkareva, I. M. "Vseobshchaia sentiabr'skaia stachka zheleznodorozhnikov v 1917 godu." In *Rabochii klass i rabochee dvizhenie v Rossii v 1917 godu,* pp. 180–202. Moscow, 1964.

Rabinowitch, Alexander. *Prelude to Revolution: The Petrograd Bolsheviks and the July 1917 Uprising.* Bloomington, Ind.: Indiana University Press, 1968.

Rabochii klass i rabochee dvizhenie v Rossii v 1917 godu. Moscow, 1964.

Raleigh, Donald J. *Revolution on the Volga: 1917 in Saratov.* Ithaca, N.Y.: Cornell University Press, 1986.

Rashin, A. G. "Dinamika rabochego sostava promyshlennosti za 1913–1922 gody." *Voprosy zarabotnoi platy. Sbornik statei.* Moscow, 1923.
———. *Formirovanie rabochego klassa Rossii.* Moscow, 1958.

Rees, Albert. "Industrial Conflict and Business Fluctuations." *Journal of Political Economy* 60 (1952), pp. 371–82.

Rieber, Alfred J. *Merchants and Entrepreneurs in Imperial Russia.* Chapel Hill, N.C.: University of North Carolina Press, 1982.

Robert, Jean-Louis. "Les Grèves parisiennes (août 1914–juillet 1919)." In *War, Strikes, and Revolution: The Impact of the War Experience on*

Italy, Germany, France, England, and Russia, edited by Giulio Sapelli and Leopold H. Haimson. Milan: Feltrinelli Foundation, forthcoming.

Roosa, Ruth A. "Russian Industrialists and State Socialism." *Soviet Studies* 23, no. 3 (July 1972), pp. 395–417.

Rosenberg, William G. "The Democratization of Russia's Railroads in 1917." *American Historical Review* 5, no. 88 (December 1981), pp. 983–1008.

———. *Liberals in the Russian Revolution*. Princeton, N.J.: Princeton University Press, 1974.

———. "Les Libéraux Russes et le changement de pouvoir en Mars 1917." *Cahiers du Monde Russe et Soviétique* 9, no. 1 (1968), pp. 46–57.

———. "The Russian Municipal Duma Elections of 1917." *Soviet Studies* 21, no. 2 (1969), pp. 131–63.

Rosenberg, William G., and Diane P. Koenker. "The Limits of Formal Protest: Worker Activism and Social Polarization in Petrograd and Moscow, March to October, 1917." *American Historical Review* 92, no. 2 (April 1987), pp. 296–326.

Rosenzweig, Roy. *Eight Hours For What We Will: Workers and Leisure in an Industrial City, 1870–1920*. Cambridge: Cambridge University Press, 1983.

Ross, Arthur M., and Paul T. Hartman. *Changing Patterns of Industrial Conflict*. New York: John Wiley and Sons, 1960.

Rozenblium, D. "Revoliutsiia i rabochee dvizhenie." In *God Russkoi revoliutsii, 1917–1918 gody*, edited by A. N. Bakh. Moscow, 1918.

Sapelli, Giulio, and Leopold H. Haimson, eds. *War, Strikes, and Revolution: The Impact of the War Experience on Italy, Germany, France, England, and Russia*. Milan: Feltrinelli Foundation, forthcoming.

Sentsov, A. A. *Rozhdenie Kubano-Chernomorskoi Respubliki, 1917–1918 gody*. Krasnoiarsk, 1984.

Shalev, Michael. "Trade Unionism and Economic Analysis: The Case of Industrial Conflict." *Journal of Labor Research* 1, no. 1 (1980), pp. 133–73.

Shatilova, T. "Petrogradskoe obshchestvo zavodchikov i fabrikantov v bor'be s rabochim dvizheniem v 1917 godu." In *Professional'noe dvizhenie v Petrograde v 1917 godu*, edited by A. Anskii, pp. 175–90. Leningrad, 1928.

Shepelev, L. E. *Aktsionernye kompanii v Rossii*. Leningrad, 1973.

Shkaratan, O. I. *Problemy sotsial'noi struktury rabochego klassa SSSR*. Moscow, 1970.

Shlosberg, D. "Iz istorii ekonomicheskoi bor'by rabochikh v Donbasse, fevral'–oktiabr' 1917 goda." *Letopis' Revoliutsii* 2 (1927), pp. 189–98.

Shmukker, M. M. *Ocherki finansov i ekonomiki zhelezno-dorozhnogo transporta Rossii za 1913–1922 gody.* Moscow, 1923.

Shorter, Edward, and Charles Tilly. *Strikes in France, 1830–1968.* Cambridge: Cambridge University Press, 1974.

Shteinbakh, E. M. *Professional'noe dvizhenie v Krymu, 1917–1927 gody.* Simferopol', 1927.

Sidorov, A. L. *Ekonomicheskoe polozhenie Rossii v gody pervoi mirovoi voiny.* Moscow, 1973.

Sidorov, K. F. "Rabochee dvizhenie v Rossii v gody imperialisticheskoi voiny." In *Ocherki po istorii oktiabr'skoi revoliutsii,* edited by M. N. Pokrovskii, vol. 1, pp. 179–331. Moscow and Leningrad, 1927.

———. *Zabastovochnoe dvizhenie v Rossii (v diagrammakh).* Moscow, 1923.

Siegelbaum, Lewis H. *The Politics of Industrial Mobilization in Russia, 1914–1917: A Study of the War-Industries Committees.* New York: St. Martin's Press, 1983.

Sindeev, I. *Professional'noe dvizhenie rabochikh stroitelei v 1917 godu.* Moscow, 1927.

Smith, S. A. *Red Petrograd: Revolution in the Factories, 1917–1918.* Cambridge: Cambridge University Press, 1983.

Snyder, David. "Institutional Setting and Industrial Conflict: Comparative Analyses of France, Italy, and the United States." *American Sociological Review* 40 (1975), pp. 259–78.

Snyder, David, and William R. Kelly. "Industrial Violence in Italy, 1878–1903." *American Journal of Sociology* 82 (1976), pp. 131–62.

Sorenson, Jay B. *The Life and Death of Soviet Trade Unions, 1917–1928.* New York: Atherton Press, 1969.

Spriano, Paolo. *The Occupation of the Factories.* Translated by Gwyn Williams. London: Pluto Press, 1975.

Stachechnaia bor'ba rabochikh Sibiri v period imperializma: (khronika, statistika, istoriografiia). Edited by N. V. Blinov. Tomsk, 1978.

Stachki. Istorii i sovremennost'. Edited by K. M. Kuntor, A. A. Gulkin, and R. Ia. Evzerov. Moscow, 1978.

Startsev, V. I. *Ocherki po istorii Petrogradskoi krasnoi gvardii i rabochei militsii (mart 1917–aprel' 1918 godov).* Moscow and Leningrad, 1965.

Stearns, Peter N. "Against the Strike Threat: Employer Policy toward Labor Agitation in France, 1900–1914." *Journal of Modern History* 40 (1968), pp. 474–500.

———. "Measuring the Evolution of Strike Movements." *International Review of Social History* 19 (1974), pp. 1–27.

———. *Revolutionary Syndicalism and French Labor.* New Brunswick, N.J.: Rutgers University Press, 1971.

———. "The Unskilled and Industrialization: A Transformation of Consciousness." *Archiv für Sozialgeschichte* 16 (1976), pp. 249–82.

Steinberg, Mark David. "Consciousness and Conflict in a Russian Industry: The Printers of St. Petersburg and Moscow, 1855–1905." Ph.D. dissertation, University of California, Berkeley, 1987.

Stepanov, Z. V. *Rabochie Petrograda v period podgotovki i provedeniia oktiabr'skogo vooruzhennogo vosstaniia.* Moscow and Leningrad, 1965.

Stern, Robert N. "Methodological Issues in Quantitative Strike Analysis." *Industrial Relations* 17, no. 1 (1978), pp. 32–42.

Stone, Lawrence. "Theories of Revolution." *World Politics* 18 (1966), pp. 159–76.

Strumilin, S. G. "Dinamika tsen za 1918–1922." In *Izbrannye proizvedeniia,* vol. 1, pp. 197–213. Moscow, 1963.

———. *Na khoziaistvennom fronte. Sbornik statei (1921–25).* Moscow and Leningrad, 1925.

———. "Sostav proletariata sovetskoi Rossii v 1917–1919 godakh" In *Dva goda diktatury proletariata 1917–1919 godov,* pp. 13–24. Moscow, 1920.

———. "Zabastovki i revoliutsii." In *Materialy po statistike truda,* vyp. 8, pp. i–vi. 1920.

———. *Zarabotnaia plata i proizvoditel'nost' truda v Russkoi promyshlennosti za 1913–1922 gody.* Moscow, 1923.

Suhr, Gerald. "Petersburg Workers in 1905: Strikes, Workplace Democracy, and the Revolution." Ph.D. dissertation, University of California, Berkeley, 1979.

Suny, Ronald Grigor. *The Baku Commune, 1917–1918: Class and Nationality in the Russian Revolution.* Princeton, N.J.: Princeton University Press, 1972.

Taniaev, A. *Ocherki po istorii dvizhenii zheleznodorozhnikov v revoliutsii 1917 goda.* Moscow and Leningrad, 1925.

Tenfelde, Klaus, and Heinrich Volkmann, eds. *Streik: Zur Geschichte des Arbeitskampfes in Deutschland wahrend der Industrialisierung.* Munich: Beck, 1981.

Thompson, John M. *Revolutionary Russia, 1917.* New York: Charles Scribner's Sons, 1981.

Thurston, Robert W. *Liberal City, Conservative State: Moscow and Russia's Urban Crisis, 1906–1914.* New York: Oxford University Press, 1987.

Tikhanov, A. "Rabochie-pechatniki v 1917 godu." In *Materialy po istorii professional'nogo dvizheniia v Rossii*, vol. 4, pp. 157–99. Moscow, 1925.

Tilly, Charles. *From Mobilization to Revolution*. Reading, Mass.: Addison-Wesley, 1978.

Tilly, Charles, and Lynn Lees. "Le Peuple de juin 1848." *Annales: Économies, Sociétés, Civilisations* 29 (1974), pp. 1061–91.

Tilly, Charles, Louise Tilly, and Richard Tilly. *The Rebellious Century, 1830–1930*. Cambridge, Mass.: Harvard University Press, 1975.

Tomassini, Luigi. "Industrial Mobilization and State Intervention in Italy during World War I: Effects on Labor Unrest." In *War, Strikes, and Revolution: The Impact of the War Experience on Italy, Germany, France, England, and Russia*, edited by Giulio Sapelli and Leopold H. Haimson. Milan: Feltrinelli Foundation, forthcoming.

Trempé, Rolande. *Les Mineurs de Carmaux, 1848–1914*. Paris: Éditions ouvrières, 1971.

Trotsky, Leon. *The History of the Russian Revolution*. Translated by Max Eastman. 3 vols. New York: Monad Press, 1980.

Trukan, G. A. "O nekotorykh voprosakh rabochego dvizheniia v tsentral'nom promyshlennom raione." In *Rabochii klass i rabochee dvizhenie v Rossii v 1917 godu*, pp. 103–16. Moscow, 1964.

———. *Rabochii klass v bor'be za pobedu i uprochenie sovetskoi vlasti*. Moscow, 1975.

Tseitlin, D. A. "Fabrichno-zavodskie komitety Petrograda v fevrale–oktiabre 1917 goda." *Voprosy Istorii* 11 (1956), pp. 86–97.

Tugan-Baranovsky, M. I. *The Russian Factory in the Nineteenth Century*. Translated by Arthur and Claora S. Levin. Homewood, Ill.: Dorsey Press, 1970.

U.S. Department of Commerce. Bureau of the Census. *1970 Census of Population: Classified Index of Industries and Occupations*. Washington: Government Printing Office, 1971.

Usloviia byta rabochikh v dorevoliutsionnoi Rossii (po dannym biudzhetnykh obsledovanii). Moscow, 1958.

Varzar, V. E. *Ocherki osnov promyshlennoi statistiki*. Moscow, 1925.

Volkmann, Heinrich. "Modernisierung des Arbeitskampfs zum Formwandel von Streik und Aussperrung in Deutschland, 1864–1975." In *Probleme der Modernisierung in Deutschland: Sozialhistorische Studien zum 19. und 20. Jahrhundert*, edited by Hartmut Kaelble, Horst Matzerath, Hermann-Josef Rupieper, Peter Steinbach, and Heinrich Volkmann, pp. 110–70. Opladen: Westdeutscher Verlag, 1978.

Volobuev, P. V. *Proletariat i burzhuaziia Rossii v 1917 godu*. Moscow, 1964.

Von Laue, Theodore. "Russian Labor between Field and Factory, 1892–1903." *California Slavic Studies* 3 (1964), pp. 33–65.

Vorob'ev, N. Ia. "Izmeneniia v Russkoi promyshlennosti v period voiny i revoliutsii." *Vestnik Statistiki* 14 (1923), pp. 115–54.

Wade, Rex A. *Red Guards and Workers' Militias in the Russian Revolution.* Stanford, Calif.: Stanford University Press, 1984.

Wallerstein, I., ed. *Labor in the World Social Structure.* Beverly Hills, Calif.: Sage Publications, 1983.

Ward, Benjamin. "Wild Socialism in Russia." *California Slavic Studies* 3 (1964), pp. 127–48.

Webb, Sidney, and Harold Cox. *The Eight Hour Day.* London: Walter Scott, n.d.

Weintraub, Andrew R. "Prosperity versus Strikes: An Empirical Approach." *Industrial and Labor Relations Review* 19 (1965–66), pp. 231–38.

Wildman, Allan K. *The End of the Russian Imperial Army: The Old Army and the Soldiers' Revolt (March–April 1917).* Princeton, N.J.: Princeton University Press, 1980.

Yoder, Dale. "Economic Change and Industrial Unrest in the United States." *Journal of Political Economy* 48 (1940), pp. 222–37.

Zagorsky, S. O. *State Control of Industry in Russia during the War.* New Haven, Conn.: Yale University Press, 1928.

Zlokazov, G. I. "K istorii ustanovleniia vosmichasogo rabochego dnia na Petrograde (mart 1917 goda)." *Uchenye Zapiski Gor'kovskogo Pedagogicheskogo Instituta* 49 (1965) (seriia istorii, sb. 7).

———. *Petrogradskii sovet rabochikh i soldatskikh deputatov v period mirnogo razvitiia revoliutsii.* Moscow, 1969.

Zol'nikov, D. M. "K voprosu o stachechnom dvizhenii proletariata osen-'iu 1917 goda." *Uchenye Zapiski Tomskogo Gosudarstvennogo Universiteta* 37, no. 1 (1959), pp. 47–70.

———. "Stachechnoe dvizhenie zheleznodorozhnikov v 1917 godu." *Uchenye Zapiski Tomskogo Gosudarstvennogo Universiteta* 38 (1961), pp. 28–41.

INDEX

. . . .